The Early Roman Empire in the East

edited by

Susan E. Alcock

Oxbow Monograph 95
1997

Published by
Oxbow Books, Park End Place, Oxford OX1 1HN

© Oxbow Books, 1997

ISBN 1 900188 52 X

This book is available direct from
Oxbow Books, Park End Place, Oxford OX1 1HN
(Phone: 01865–241249; Fax: 01865–794449)

and

The David Brown Book Company
PO Box 511, Oakville, CT 06779
(Phone: 860–945–9329; Fax: 860–945–9468)

Printed in Great Britain by
The Short Run Press, Exeter

Contents

List of Contributors

SUSAN E. ALCOCK
Department of Classical Studies,
University of Michigan

DAVID BRAUND
Department of Classics and Ancient History,
University of Exeter

SARAH CORMACK
Department of Art and Art History,
Duke University

JAS' ELSNER
Courtauld Institute of Art,
University of London

MICHAŁ GAWLIKOWSKI
Polish Centre of Mediterranean Archaeology,
University of Warsaw

YIZHAR HIRSCHFELD
Institute of Archaeology,
The Hebrew University of Jerusalem

MARTIN MILLETT
Department of Archaeology,
University of Durham

D.T. POTTS
The School of Archaeology,
University of Sydney

A.D. RIZAKIS
Research Centre for Greek and Roman
  Antiquity,
The National Hellenic Research Foundation

CHARLES BRIAN ROSE
Department of Classics,
University of Cincinnati

ANDREAS SCHMIDT-COLINET
Institut für Klassische Archäologie,
Universität Wien

GEORGE TATE
Université de Versailles Saint-Quentin-en-
  Yvelines

GREG WOOLF
Brasenose College,
Oxford University

Preface: East is East?

Susan E. Alcock

Book prefaces have come under increasing scrutiny in recent years. Together with other supporting elements, such as titles, dedications and jacket-cover blurbs, prefaces play a role as 'paratext', recently defined as:

> ...the means by which a text makes a book of itself and proposes itself as such to its readers, and more generally to the public. Rather than with a limit or a sealed frontier, we are dealing in this case with a threshold, or – the term Borges used about a preface – with a 'vestibule' which offers to anyone and everyone the possibility either of entering or of turning back (Genette 1991: 261).

The title of this book is straightforward enough. *The Early Roman Empire in the East* was designed and commissioned as a companion volume to Blagg and Millett's *The Early Roman Empire in the West* (1990). That the western volume should have appeared first will surprise no one: it has long been acknowledged that there exists something of a leaning to the west in the study (particularly the *archaeological* study) of the Roman empire, a bias which has emerged from a complex blend of historical, intellectual and geopolitical factors. It is a sign of the times, however, that an eastern version should now follow. Just since 1990, a wide range of books on the archaeology, history, literature, rhetoric, and artistic production of the Roman east has appeared. Even if we restrict the list largely to publications in English, and exclude individual fieldwork reports or journal articles, it would include: Alcock 1993; Anderson 1993; Arafat 1996; Dodgeon and Lieu 1991; Edwards 1996; Gleason 1995; Humphrey 1995; Isaac 1990; Kallet-Marx 1995; Kennedy 1996; Kennedy and Riley 1990; Millar 1993; Mitchell 1993; Rogers 1991; Rose 1997; Safrai 1994; Sartre 1991; Stoneman 1992; Sullivan 1990; Swain 1996.

In the prefaces and introductions to several of these volumes, a wake-up call is sounded: the world of the eastern empire is no longer to be patronized, marginalized or ignored. This announcement takes various forms, from the confessional style of Maud Gleason:

> 'As a student in Athens, I ridiculed the crudity of Roman walls and affected regret that the barbarian hordes had not wrecked every brick...' (1995: xvii)

to my own pragmatic version:

...the study of post-Classical Greece has long held the status of a clear also-ran in terms of popularity and prestige when compared with that of the Classical epoch, or indeed even of the preceding Archaic age. But times are changing: the Roman and Byzantine periods are increasingly finding favor, especially among younger scholars eager to explore new problems and fresh territory of their own... (1993: xvii)

to the disciplinary exhortation of Millar:

If the book serves, by its manifest imperfections, to goad some Semitists into acquiring a wider historical training, or some Graeco-Roman historians into gaining a wider linguistic base, so much the better (1993: xvi)

and to the valedictory remarks of Maurice Sartre:

Si du moins cet essai donne à quelques-uns l'envie d'aller aux sources et leur suggère quelques pistes de recherche, je m'estimerais bienheureux d'avoir fait partager un enthousiasme qui ne m'a jamais abandonné pendant ces années de travail (1991: 12).

It is in the spirit of these various prefatory remarks that the organization of the present book has proceeded.

'A paratextual element... may impart an authorial and/or editorial *intention* or *interpretation*; this is the cardinal function of most prefaces...' (Genette 1991: 268). Some sense of 'editorial intention' is especially necessary here, for with a topic as mammoth as 'the early Roman empire in the east', an embarrassment of riches obviously abounds – both of themes to explore and of papers that might have been commissioned. In choosing which way to go in such a toy shop of possibilities, I have followed several basic guiding principles. First, the intention was to have a variety of approaches, especially archaeological approaches, represented in the volume, with papers incorporating excavation data, survey evidence, visual imagery, mortuary studies, epigraphic data, literary texts and documentary evidence. Second was the desire to gather an international set of papers, bringing together the work of distinguished scholars which otherwise might not easily be found in the same volume in the same language. In the end, institutional affiliations in eight different countries are represented by the thirteen contributors to the volume.

When contributions were invited, the authors were encouraged to write for an intelligent, but non-specialist audience, in hopes that the book might prove useful to a range of people, including students still finding their way about the Roman empire. And, finally, the collection was intended to touch on some themes and some regions that have perhaps been under-represented thus far in the study of the eastern empire – hence the presence of the Black Sea and the Persian Gulf; hence a more limited emphasis than might have been expected on the army in the east, on the Roman *limes* and road systems, or on the major cities and civic monuments. As in any short collection of this sort, there are inevitable and unfortunate gaps in coverage; the scope of topics touched upon, however, does begin to give some sense of the variety of this huge and multiple world.

The volume is divided into three main sections: 'Urban Structures', 'Regional Studies', and 'Images and Identities', although the reader will discover significant overlap between different papers and across sections. 'Urban Structures' starts off with an overview by Greg Woolf, offering suggestions for the differential development of cities, both between the eastern and western empire, and among the urban units of the east itself. Athanasios Rizakis in turn provides a detailed study of the impact – on population, land holdings and social structure – of imperial foundations in one area, Roman Greece.

'Regional Studies' begins with two papers on the Syrian countryside. The first is a wide-ranging review of the area, its physical topography, political and ethnic geography, and artistic characteristics, by Michał Gawlikowski; the second, by Georges Tate, explores the processes of change in this area, identifying key factors in the region's development. A very clear shift in rural settlement, revealed through excavation and survey, in what is today Israel is analyzed by Yizhar Hirschfeld, who links the abandonment of dispersed settlement by Jews to changing religious and social practices after the first century AD revolt against Rome. Finally, the volume advances beyond the bounds of the empire proper, with D.T. Potts' examination of the impact of Rome and Roman material culture in the Persian Gulf, an area Rome did not control, but nonetheless affected.

'Images and Identities' moves into the world of symbolic expression and the negotiation of social roles within the eastern empire. Brian Rose discusses imperial portraits in the east, considering mechanisms of commissioning and display. The struggle for recognition by Black Sea communities, an area usually viewed as marginal to the 'genuine' Hellenic world and thus left vulnerable in the cultural climate of the Second Sophistic, is next analyzed by David Braund. Two analyses employing mortuary evidence – an underutilized source of data in the eastern empire – follow next. The first, by Sarah Cormack, pulls together the evidence for Roman Asia Minor, debating the issue of 'romanization' here through the lens of tomb and sarcophagus design. Andreas Schmidt-Colinet works with the more well-known Palmyrene tomb data, arguing that simultaneous processes of 'Romanization' and 're-orientalization' must be appreciated in the evolution of these monuments. Finally in this section, Jas' Elsner offers an overarching paper dealing with how the east 'struck back' at the west, through the affirmation and diffusion of eastern cults and deities – ultimately to triumph with the acceptance of Christianity.

As a bow to the origin of this volume as a companion to Blagg and Millett's *The Early Roman Empire in the West*, Martin Millett provides one man's reaction to these papers, as seen from a western Roman perspective, and ending the volume – ironically – by arguing against any sharp 'east versus west' characterizations. Millett points out that our increasing appreciation of regional variability across the empire (a variability underlined by the papers in this volume) is working to make such simplistic bipolar divisions sound very old-fashioned indeed. Paradoxically, the end-result of volumes such as *The Early Roman Empire in the West* and *The Early Roman Empire in the East* may well be to make books with such titles obsolete. But that will only happen, of course, if the same people read both books and note the many points of contact between them; this bridging of the east/west divide in audience, of course, remains the battle yet to be won.

As Genette remarks 'no one is bound to read a preface' (1991: 263), but a note about practicalities might be helpful and acknowledgments must certainly be made. All journal abbreviations follow the conventions set out in the *American Journal of Archaeology* 95 (1991) 1–16; ancient works are abbreviated following the conventions employed by the *Oxford Classical Dictionary*. As for acknowledgments, Liza Hall translated from the French the papers by Rizakis and Tate; Geoffrey Compton (of the Interdepartmental Program in Classical Art and Archaeology at the University of Michigan) admirably organized several of the illustrations; and the Office of the Vice President of Research (OVPR) at the University of Michigan generously supported these necessary endeavors.

Above all, I thank David Brown of Oxbow Books for asking me to undertake this project in the first place; all the contributors for their kind cooperation and patience; and John Cherry for his continual assurances that editing is indeed worth the effort.

Bibliography

Alcock, S.E. (1993) *Graecia Capta: The Landscapes of Roman Greece*, Cambridge.

Anderson, G. (1993) *The Second Sophistic: A Cultural Phenomenon in the Roman Empire*, London.

Arafat, K. (1996) *Pausanias' Greece: Ancient Artists and Roman Rulers*, Cambridge.

Blagg, T.F.C. and M.J. Millett, eds. (1990) *The Early Roman Empire in the West*, Oxford.

Dodgeon, M.H. and S.N.C. Lieu, eds. (1991) *The Roman Eastern Frontier and the Persian Wars, AD 226–363*, London.

Edwards, D.R. (1996) *Religion and Power: Pagans, Jews and Christians in the Greek East*, New York.

Genette, G. (1991) "Introduction to the Paratext," *New Literary History* 22: 261–72.

Gleason, M. (1995) *Making Men: Sophists and Self-Presentation in Ancient Rome*, Princeton.

Humphrey, J.H. ed. (1995) *The Roman and Byzantine Near East: Some Recent Archaeological Research*, Ann Arbor.

Isaac, B. (1990) *The Limits of Empire: The Roman Army in the East*, Oxford.

Kallet-Marx, R. (1995) *Hegemony to Empire: The Development of the Roman Imperium in the East from 148 to 62 BC*, Berkeley.

Kennedy, D.L., ed. (1996) *The Roman Army in the East* (*JRA* Suppl. 18), Ann Arbor.

Kennedy, D.L. and D. Riley (1990) *Rome's Desert Frontier from the Air*, Austin.

Millar, F. (1993) *The Roman Near East, 31 BC–AD 337*, Cambridge, Mass.

Mitchell, S. (1993) *Anatolia. Land, Men and Gods in Asia Minor* (two volumes), Oxford.

Rogers, G. (1990) *The Sacred Identity of Ephesus: Foundation Myths of a Roman City*, London.

Rose, C.B. (1997) *Dynastic Commemoration and Imperial Portraiture in the Julio-Claudian Period*, Cambridge.

Safrai, Z. (1994) *The Economy of Roman Palestine*, London.

Sartre, M. (1991) *L'Orient romain. Provinces et sociétés provinciales en Méditerranée orientale d'Auguste aux Sévères (31 avant J.-C. – 235 après J.-C.)*, Paris.

Stoneman, R. (1992) *Palmyra and its Empire: Zenobia's Revolt against Rome*, Ann Arbor.

Sullivan, R. (1990) *Near Eastern Royalty and Rome, 100–30 BC*, Toronto.

Swain, S. (1996) *Hellenism and Empire: Language, Classicism and Power in the Greek World AD 50–250*, Oxford.

Will, E. (1992) *Les Palmyréniens. La Venise des sables*, Paris.

List of Abbreviations

BMC	*Coins of the Roman Empire in the British Museum* (H. Mattingly *et al.*)
BullEpigr	*Bulletin épigraphique, Revue des études grecques* (J. Robert and L. Robert, eds.)
CIG	*Corpus Inscriptionum Graecarum* (A. Boeckh, J. Franz, E. Curtius and A. Kirchhoff)
CIL	*Corpus Inscriptionum Latinarum*
CIS	*Corpus Inscriptionum Semiticarum*
FD	*Fouilles de Delphes*
GIBM	*Ancient Greek Inscriptions in the British Museum* (C.T. Newton, ed.)
I.Delos	*Inscriptions de Délos* (F. Durrbach)
IG	*Inscriptiones Graecae*
IGR	*Inscriptiones Graecae ad Res Romanas Pertinentes* (R. Cagnat)
IGSK	*Inschriften Griechischer Städte aus Kleinasien*
IGLS	*Inscriptions grecques et latines de la Syrie* (L. Jalabert, R. Mouterde, *et al.*)
I.Ephesos	*Die Inschriften von Ephesos* VII.2 (IGSK 17.2; R. Meric, R. Merkelbach, J. Nollé and S. Sahin, eds.)
I.Kyme	*Die Inschriften von Kyme* (IGSK 5; H. Engelmann, ed.)
ILS	*Inscriptiones Latinae Selectae* (H. Dessau, ed.)
Inv.	*Inventaire des inscriptions de Palmyre*
IO	*Inscriptiones Olbiae* (T.N. Knipovich and E.N. Levi, eds.)
IOSPE	*Inscriptiones Orae Septentrionalis Ponti Euxini*
I.Priene	*Inschriften von Priene* (F. Hiller von Gaertringen, ed.)
I.Sardis	*Sardis VII.1: Greek and Latin Inscriptions* (W.H. Buckler and D.M. Robinson)
LIMC	*Lexicon Iconographicum Mythologiae Classicae*
MAMA	*Monumenta Asiae Minoris Antiquae* (W.M. Calder and J.M.R. Cormack, eds.)
OGIS	*Orientis Graecae Inscriptiones Selectae* (W. Dittenberger)
P. Lond	*Greek Papyri in the British Museum* (F.G. Kenyon et al., eds.)
PLRE	*The Prosopography of the Later Roman Empire I, AD 260–395* (A.H.M. Jones, J.R. Martindale, and J. Morris, eds.)
RE	Pauly-Wissowa, *Real-Encyclopädie der klassischen Altertumswissenschaft*
SEG	*Supplementum Epigraphicum Graecum*
SIG	*Sylloge Inscriptionum Graecarum*
TAM	*Tituli Asiae Minoris*

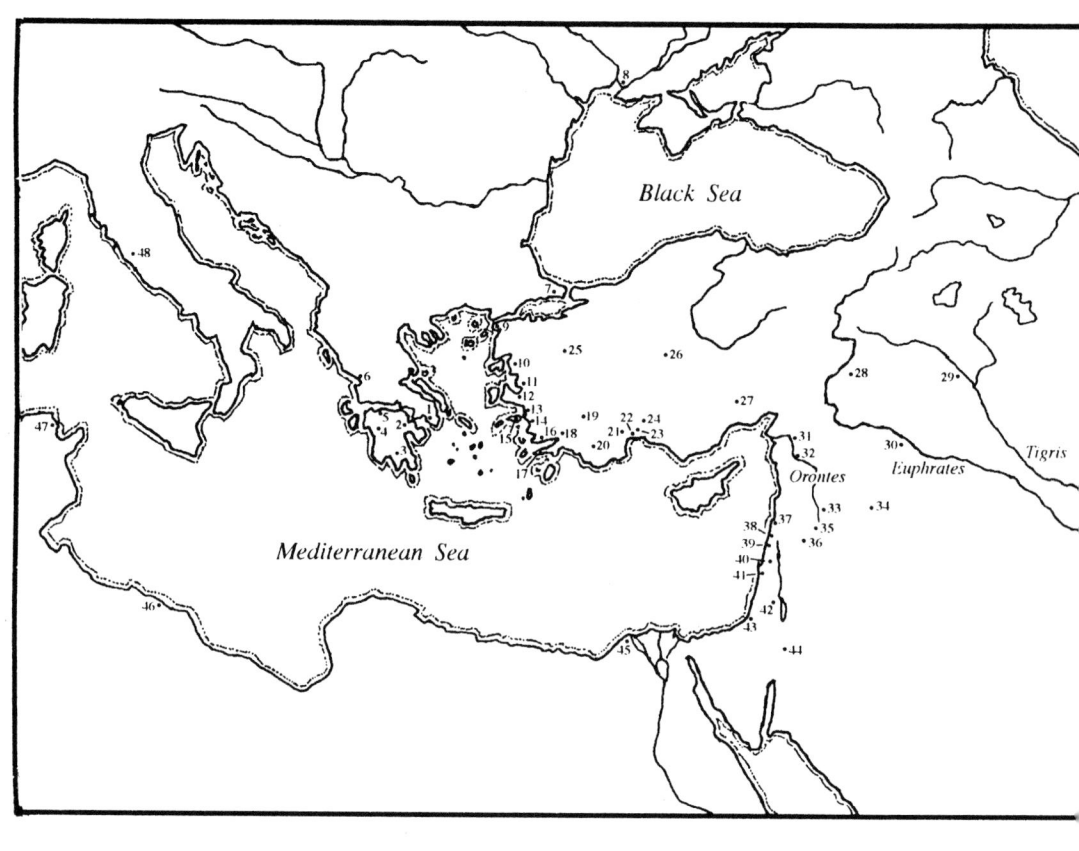

1	Athens	17	Knidos	33	Emesa
2	Corinth	18	Mylasa	34	Palmyra
3	Sparta	19	Aphrodisias	35	Baalbek
4	Olympia	20	Oinoanda	36	Damascus
5	Patras	21	Termessos	37	Berytus
6	Nikopolis	22	Antalya	38	Side
7	Byzantium	23	Perge	39	Tyre
8	Olbia	24	Cremna	40	Sepphoris
9	Troy	25	Aezanoi	41	Caesarea Maritima
10	Pergamon	26	Gordion	42	Jerusalem
11	Sardis	27	Tyana	43	Gaza
12	Klazomene	28	Edessa	44	Petra
13	Ephesos	29	Hatra	45	Alexandria
14	Miletos	30	Dura-Europos	46	Leptis Magna
15	Samos	31	Antioch	47	Carthage
16	Halikarnassos	32	Apamea	48	Rome

1. The Roman Urbanization of the East

Greg Woolf

It is commonly known that an urban network was established in western Europe for the first time under the Roman Empire in the early part of the first millennium AD. It represented the expression of ideas from the centre of the Empire through to its periphery (Jones 1987: 47).

From the last decades of the last millennium BC, Roman rule over parts of western and central Europe was indeed marked by the appearance of an urban network. By most criteria, ancient as well as modern, this urbanization was extremely meagre. Between 5 and 10% of the population of non-Mediterranean Gaul and Britain lived in cities, and many of that number were probably peasants. Most cities were tiny, urban populations being typically in the low thousands, and they were far apart, with up to 100 km between cities in some parts of Gaul (Fig. 1). The monumental equipment of these cities was also unimpressive. Nonetheless they shared features that clearly distinguish them from their prehistoric predecessors, features alluded to by Rick Jones in focusing on the notion of an urban network. Many prehistoric settlements have been claimed as urban on the basis of their architecture, population, internal organization or the services they may have provided for their immediate hinterlands. But no one has ever seriously argued that there existed, before Rome, an interconnected *network* of cities articulated by frequent communications and exchanges of all kinds, through which services were provided and functions distributed throughout an extensive system. Assessed in functional terms, urban settlements are the links between local societies and settlement patterns and regional systems of power and exchange (cf. Hohenberg and Lees 1985: 47–73). Rome's temperate, western European cities may have been small and unimpressive but they nevertheless performed these functions.

The point of these observations is not simply to emphasise the greater level of urbanization in the Roman east. It is true that – in terms of mean and peak size, of individual and total urban populations, of scale, elaboration and cost of monumental architecture and of density of urban settlement – the eastern provinces far outdo the west. But the crucial impact of Rome on iron age settlement patterns in the west was to create that network of cities which was one aspect of a global reorganization of the landscape, creating villages and 'countryside' for the first time as well as cities. Urbanization in these terms – as social and cultural differentiation – is rarely examined in the east

1

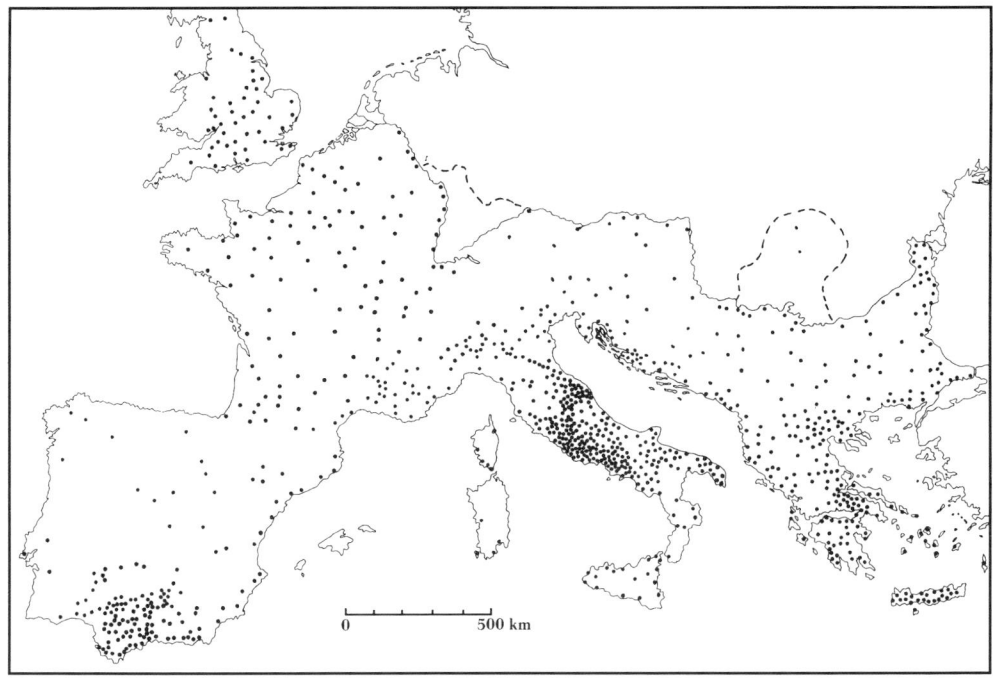

Fig. 1. Distribution of cities within the Roman empire (after Pounds 1973)

where classical archaeology and ancient history have concentrated on individual cities and have, perhaps unreflectively, adopted antique formulations of the problem.

Two such formulations in particular are worth signalling. The first is a concentration on the monumental, usually prefaced with a reference to Pausanias' (10.4.1) comment that Panopeus barely qualified for urban status because it lacked public buildings, a gymnasium, a theatre or fountains. Monumental architecture may have been central to Greek and Roman idealisations of civic life, and has been prominent in archaeological studies for obvious reasons (cf. Macready and Thompson 1987), but in practice settlements might function as cities without monuments (as Pausanias tacitly acknowledges) and monumental architecture was also a feature of sanctuaries, villages and indeed some private houses. The second formulation is a focus on the spread of the *polis*, from its Aegean origins throughout the east, under first Hellenistic royal and then Roman imperial patronage. Yet here we have to do with the extension of a particular socio-political form that included within itself rural as well as urban spheres, and the instititutions and ideologies by means of which the two were articulated. These two approaches do not reveal precisely the same image of urbanization. Villages, the importance of which has only recently been realised (cf. Lloyd 1991), illustrate the problems inherent in both approaches. Architecturally and in terms of size and probable economic function the line is difficult to draw between larger villages and smaller cities; indeed many villages had magistrates and officials of the same kind as cities did. Only in terms of the ideology of the *polis* is the distinction clear between the settlement regarded as the centre or focal point of the political and religious life of a given people – the *asty* – and other nucleated settlements within its *chora*. Those *komai* might, by all other criteria, appear more urban than smaller *poleis* and *civitas* capitals elsewhere, while the largest *poleis* like Athens in fact contained within them small urban networks.

One way of cutting the Gordian knot is to reject the monumental and political definitions of the ancient city altogether. There are some general advantages to this approach, which reveals the *polis* as an ideological construct and political formation quite distinct from what geographers would recognise by the term 'city', and with a different history to that of urbanism in antiquity (cf. Morris 1991). *Poleis*, cities and monumental architecture all predated Roman intervention in much of the east, of course, and their close interconnections mean that no one component can be discussed in complete isolation from the others. The focus of this discussion, however, will be firmly on the impact of Rome on the urban networks of her eastern provinces; indeed significant changes in the nature of the *polis* during the Roman period are only explicable in relation to the development of these urban networks.

The Spread of Urban Forms

A.H.M. Jones's view, in his magisterial study *The Greek City from Alexander to Justinian* (1940), was that Rome presided over the extension of processes already begun in the Hellenistic period or even earlier. That remark is truest of the extension of the *polis* (cf. Sartre 1991: 121–26). Hellenistic kings had followed Alexander in founding *poleis*, often with dynastic names, throughout their territory, even if these foundations were often on the site of pre-existing settlements. Roman generals and emperors adopted and adapted this practice like so many others, partly as a means of communication with their subjects. The Augustan Nicopoleis, like Pompey's Magnopolis on the site of Mithridates' Eupatoria, represent clearly intelligible statements within a pre-existing symbolic system (Purcell 1987), actions that may be compared to the removals and restorations of cult images (cf. Alcock 1993: 175–80). New foundations with names like Germanicopolis, Tiberias and the numerous Sebasteiae, Caesareiae, Sebastopoleis and the like continued to be founded either by imperial princes or through the agency of others, especially client kings, on the models of the Alexandriae, Antiochs, Laodicaeae and Arsinoae of the Hellenistic period. More significant was the parallel expansion of *polis* institutions. The model here was Pompey's settlement of Bithynia, by which the defeated kingdom was divided up into territories, each attributed to an urban centre, and the resulting units treated as analogous to city-states and required to run their affairs, subject to Roman rule, as *poleis* (Mitchell 1984). Galatia was a case in point: divided up into three territories each notionally equivalent to that of a pre-existing tribe and each with a new capital city named for the emperor (Mitchell 1993: 86–89). Egypt offers another variant. While *nomes* remained the basis of administration and differed from *poleis* in that they did not collect taxes, had no councils and remained subject to *strategoi*, nevertheless each *metropolis* came to resemble the chief urban settlement (the *asty*) at the centre of a *polis*, both architecturally and in their social and political structure (Bowman 1992; Bowman and Rathbone 1992). No uniform model was ever imposed on the east, but Rome did promote *polis*-type institutions at the expense of kingdoms, temple-states, tribes, villages and all other administrative systems with the sole exception of leagues, with which *polis* organization was largely compatible. Finally, a few colonies were founded in the east, each constituted effectively as a miniature Rome (Levick 1967; Millar 1990). Some foundations served largely symbolic ends, as in the case of Corinth;

others had more mundane military aims, as in Pisidia; yet others, like Nikopolis, were aimed at restoring prosperity to an area (Purcell 1987). These motives were not mutually exclusive, of course, and each foundation also responded, like all Roman colonization, to domestic pressures. Dynastic (re-)foundations, the division of the provinces into mosaics of *poleis* and the foundation of *coloniae* were used in west and east alike, albeit with local variations everywhere. Each might, but need not, be accompanied by monumental building, mostly funded by local élites – whether aristocrats or kings – with encouragement from governors and emperors and very occasionally more tangible support from the centre (MacMullen 1959; Mitchell 1987; Isaac 1990: 333–71).

Yet this story of municipalization followed by monumentalization captures only part of the urbanization of the east under Roman rule. To begin with, the view that sees Rome as simply filling in the gaps in the map of *poleis* or redistributing statuses and revenues from her enemies to her friends, has nothing to say about the centres of the Roman urban system in the east, cities like Ephesos and Smyrna, Pergamon and Cyrene, Athens and Sparta, the Syrian Tetrapolis and Alexandria. True, many were already major centres in the Hellenistic period, yet the new cultural forms that developed within them during the second sophistic are inexplicable without Rome (Swain 1996), while the scale (and styles) of their extant remains make clear how far they were physically transformed in the Roman period (Macready and Thompson 1987; Millar 1993a). In economic terms we might well ask what services those cities offered that paid for their ornamentation and provisioning. At the other extreme, the spread of the *polis* provides no explanation for the rise of villages in this period, especially in Anatolia, Syria and Egypt. The ideology of the *polis* might have been expected to lead to an erosion of village life, as lesser settlements were subordinated to the central *asty* of the *polis*, yet the reverse seems to have been the case, with the physical and institutional development of villages and the occasional promotions of large *komai* to *polis* status (Harper 1928; Frézouls 1987). Clearly the urban system was undergoing transformations in the period that cannot be accounted for simply in terms of the spread of *polis* institutions and of monumental architecture.

Roman Urban Networks

Students of ancient urbanism are hampered in their investigation of urban networks by the paucity of empirical data. By contrast Jan de Vries, in his study *European Urbanization 1500–1800* (1984) was able to gather material sufficient to establish a data base of 379 European cities, each of which had had 10,000 or more inhabitants at some point within the three centuries considered, and to assess each of their populations over time. On the basis of these figures he was able to draw successive rank-size distributions and to separate out demographic trends from changes in the level of settlement hierarchization, phenomena which proved explicable in historical terms (Fig. 2). Such an analysis of the Roman urban system is impossible, but nevertheless some general features of the urban networks of the Roman East may be hypothesized.

Most obviously, it is apparent that these networks were very hierarchical indeed. As yet this is most evident at the level of individual provinces. Rathbone's (1990) study of population and settlement in Egypt, based largely on papyrological evidence, produced the following population estimates. Alexandria had between half and three-quarters of a million inhabitants; Arsinoe had perhaps 46,000; more certainly Hermoupolis Magna had about 42,000 in the late third century; second century Thmouis had perhaps 21,500; Oxyrhynchus had a similar figure; and Apollonopolis Heptacomias

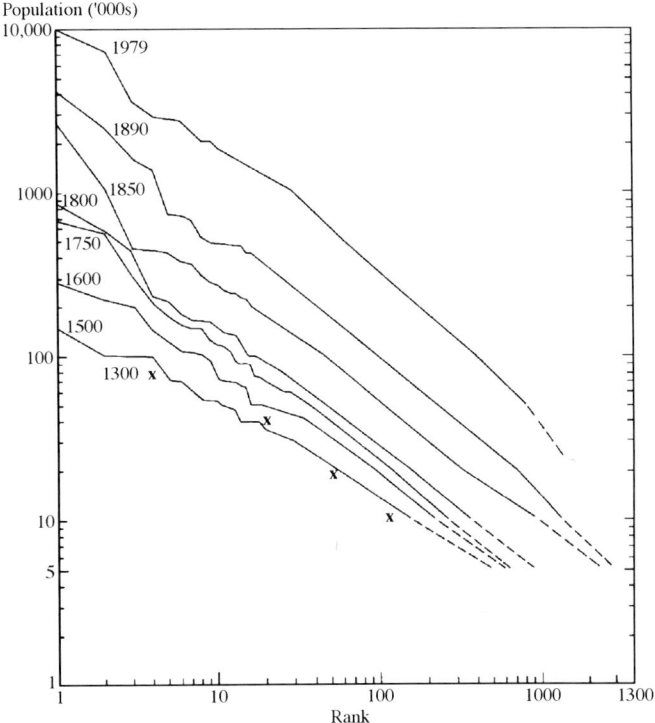

Fig. 2. Rank-size distributions: Europe, 1300–1979 (after de Vries 1984: 94)

about 7000. Recorded and estimated village sizes ranged in the Fayum from Narmouthis with maybe 6,500 inhabitants to tiny settlements like Soknopaiou Nesos with only 420. Naturally the precise figures might be challenged, but they allow some general conclusions to be drawn. The first point to emerge is that settlement size varied widely and that the hierarchy ranged from 500,000 to 500 inhabitants. The smallest metropolis population is 7000, while that of the largest village recorded is just 500 people smaller. Romano-British cities display a similar hierarchy (albeit at a smaller level) with the smallest civitas capital only a little larger in area than the largest small town (Fig. 3; Millett 1990: 144). Beyond such evidence, our range of figures for Egypt is incomplete so a complete rank-size hierachy cannot be constructed: the most important omissions are population estimates for the second order cities of Roman Egypt, Coptos, Memphis and Ptolemais. But it remains likely that the complete rank-size distribution would be strongly primate in form, that is to say marked by a few very large centres, very many small ones and little in between. Alcock's (1993: 160–71) research on the province of Achaia demonstrates, on the basis of the surface area of a number of cities, a similar hierarchy among the cities of Roman Greece (Fig. 4). Again no complete series of figures can be gathered but the difference between Corinth, covering well over 600 ha and smaller cities in the province, uniformly under 100 ha in size, is striking. Even Sparta probably had fewer

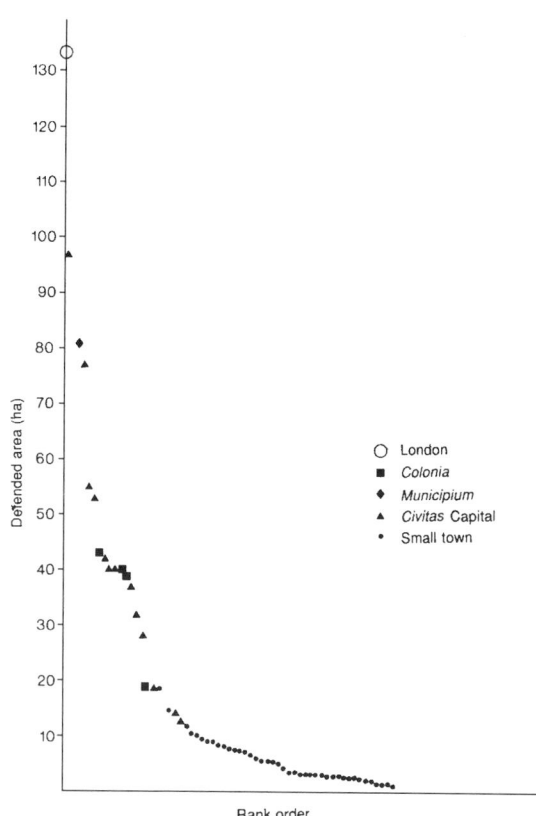

Fig. 3. Rank-size distribution of the defended areas of urban sites in Roman Britain (after Millett 1990: 144)

than 12,000 permanent residents (Cartledge and Spawforth 1989: 133). These examples are naturally only suggestive, but are unlikely to mislead in terms of the broad pattern, that may be summarized as follows. First, the cities of eastern provinces were more differentiated than ever before in terms of size and presumably population. Second, no province so far examined has shown a preponderance of middle ranking cities. Finally, a few very large cities did develop in the period.

Those large cities offer the best approach to the shape of the urban network in the Roman East as a whole. Population estimates even for the largest cities of the empire vary wildly, yet it is clear that a number of cities had populations in excess of 100,000 inhabitants. Rome, Alexandria and Antioch certainly fall into this category. Of western cities only Carthage (certainly) and Gades (possibly) are contenders, but in the east Corinth, Athens, Pergamon, Ephesos, Smyrna, Apamea and Cyrene all seem possible candidates. Precision is impossible, but assuming it is correct that between six and twelve cities did cross the 100,000 inhabitants threshold at some point in the early imperial period, we have the basis for a contrast with early modern Europe.

Four European cities had exceeded 100,000 inhabitants by 1500 AD (de Vries 1984). The total rises to eight by 1600, eleven by 1700 and sixteen by 1800. By that estimate the largest cities of the Roman world were comparable in number to the largest in Europe before the industrial revolution. But even in 1800 no city population could compare to the 1,000,000 odd inhabitants of imperial Rome, and only two (Paris and London) had more than half a million – the likely size of Alexandria and perhaps Carthage and Antioch – while only three others had more than 200,000 inhabitants. Europe in 1800 did, however, have between 300 and 400 cities with over 10,000 inhabitants, and some 2–3000 urban centres in total – both figures well above the likely totals for the Roman world. The rank-size curve for the Roman empire would thus be very much *steeper* than for early modern Europe, much more like those compiled by Rozman (1973; 1976) for Japan and Russia in the nineteenth century (Fig. 5).

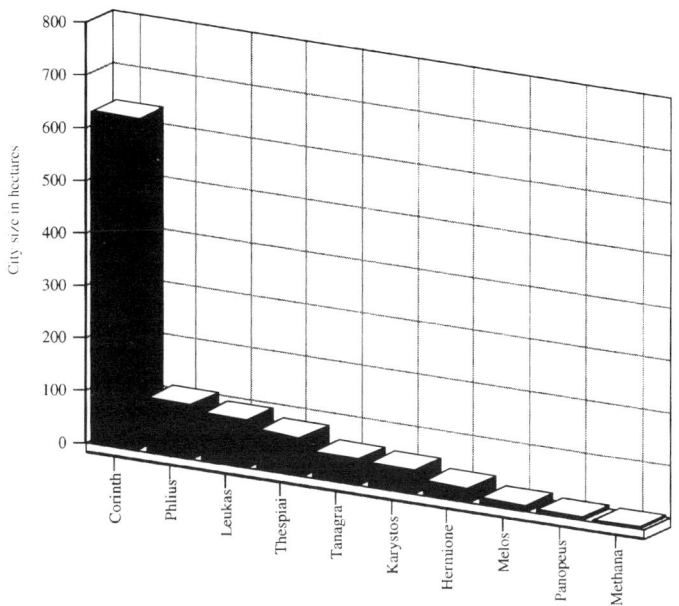

Fig. 4. Distribution of city sizes in Roman Achaia (after Alcock 1993: 162)

Steep primate distributions of this sort have been thought to be typical of imperial systems, of colonial urbanism and of the urban systems of most Third World countries today. Essentially the size of the largest cities is inflated in those circumstances either by the proceeds of empire or by their participation in global or regional systems of exchange. Non-primate distributions indicate that the size of the largest cities is determined more by their function in local, rather than global, exchange systems, possibly resulting from such factors as low levels of trade or obstacles to communications. The latter was certainly true in late imperial China, where Skinner (1977) sees a series of urban systems, each effectively contained within its own geographically circumscribed basin. The flatness of the upper reaches of the European settlement hierarchy partly reflects similar constraints imposed by the continental interior. Even today there are a number of German cities with hundreds of thousands of inhabitants, but none that compete in size with cities like Beijing, London or New York. However a second factor intervenes in modern Europe, and especially Germany, and that is the effect of a decentralised political structure. Early modern Europe too, unlike late imperial China or the Roman empire, was divided into a number of polities and religious circumscriptions, the effects of which are quite clear from the identity of de Vries' largest cities in 1800. Listed in order of size they are: London, Paris, Naples, Vienna, Amsterdam, Lisbon, Dublin, Madrid, Rome, Berlin, Palermo, Venice, Barcelona, Copenhagen, Hamburg and Lyon. Empires enhance hierarchy, in other words, and political pluralism diminishes it.

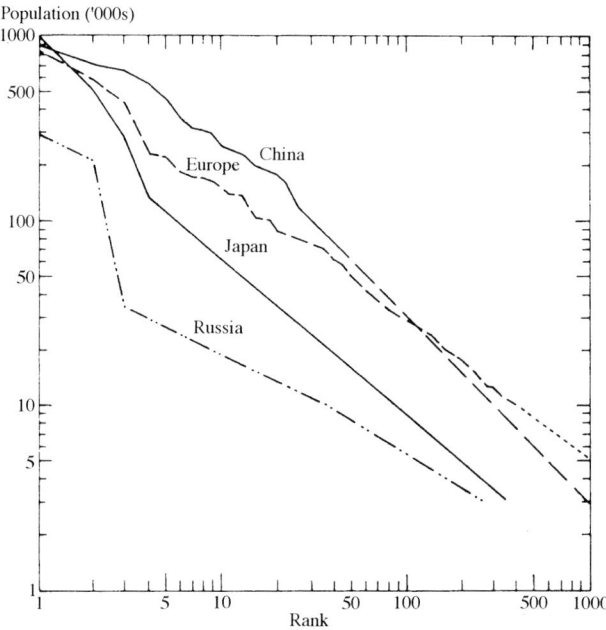

Population ('000s)

Fig. 5. Rank-size distributions: Europe, 1800; China, 1843 (Skinner); Russia, ca. 1800 (Rozman); and Japan, ca. 1800 (Rozman) (after de Vries 1984: 262)

These comparisons are suggestive of explanations for the hierarchical form of the Roman imperial urban network. First, we might expect hierarchy to be enhanced by the fact of empire, if only in inflating the size of the imperial metropolis. Second, the superior communications provided by the Mediterranean will have enhanced hierarchy in comparison to that of urban networks in landlocked areas such as central Anatolia and Rome's temperate empire. It remains to be asked, however, why the urban hierarchies of the west and east Mediterranean basins seem to differ, both in the mean size of urban settlements and in the number of very big cities.

Communication and Urban Networks in the Roman East

Communication, understood in the broadest sense, is the key to understanding how any urban network functions and is sustained. A settlement pattern in which each city simply services its own hinterland and barely communicates with other centres – the kind of system idealised as *polis autarky* in other words – would display no hierarchy between urban settlements, other than those variations generated by disparities in the territories of cities located anywhere other than on an undifferentiated isotropic plain. The existence of large cities in the ancient world can thus be attributed to one or both of two factors. First the larger cities may have been sustained because they provided higher-order services to regions greater than their own territories, regions within which smaller cities only supplied lower-order services. Those higher-order services might include markets where exotic manufactures or imports could be purchased; centres of rhetorical and philosophical teaching; major festivals and cult centres; tourist attractions and perhaps access to justice and potential patrons. Lower-order services included those that cost less and were needed more often: places where peasants could sell agricultural surpluses, buy tools or have them repaired, visit a temple and so on (cf. Hohenberg and Lees 1985: 47–59; Wagstaff 1986). Naturally, urban centres were not the only means of providing these lower-level services in the ancient world; rural shrines, itinerant craftsmen and periodic markets were also important. But the larger cities of the Roman world may not have owed their success only to their provision of services (*pace* Engels 1990). The second potential source of support for the larger cities was the willingness of the politically and economically powerful to direct additional revenue to them. Potential benefactors included the emperor and his connections, but also those private citizens whose wealth might now be drawn from land in the territories of many cities, yet spent elsewhere. Athens is perhaps the most obvious example of a city that attracted, through her cultural and religious prestige, benefactions from emperors and other outsiders, but the same was also true of Ephesos and Smyrna and probably of most of the larger cities.

Either way, additional resources were needed by larger cities not simply as 'start-up capital' but throughout each city's period of prosperity. Death rates in the largest cities of the ancient world will have outstripped birth rates, making these cities dependent for their continuing prosperity on in-migration from the countryside, from other cities, and through the purchase of slaves. Larger cities also needed supplies of food and other commodities from areas beyond their own territories, supplies that had to be paid for or acquired through the generosity of the powerful. For every ancient city that over-reached the capacity of its hinterland, then, we are entitled to ask how far its additional revenue was *earned*, for example by supplying educational, religious, financial, recreational, legal or commercial services to a wide region, or (less likely) by manufacture, and how far it was *underwritten* by political power, whether that of the empire or that of its élite benefactors.

Urban hierarchies may be seen as among the more tangible and certainly the most visible manifestations of extensive exchange systems and complexes of domination (Abrams 1978). The political contribution to the Roman urban hierarchy is relatively easy to isolate from other components. Most marked is the elevation of those settlements chosen to be the centres of *poleis* in relation to those relegated to the rank of *komai* (*civitas* capitals or *municipia* versus *vici* in the west). But Roman government also acted to distinguish some *poleis* from the rest, for example by making some assize centres, licensing some to host major festivals, or bestowing on the favoured few tax immunities, neocorates (the honour of possessing the provincial temple of a deified emperor) and other *beneficia*. Governors toured their provinces and had no administrative capitals as such, yet some cities were treated as effectively provincial or regional centres and some were made permanent centres of provincial cult. The importance of all these distinctions is demonstrated by the energy devoted by cities and their élites to obtaining and retaining them (Millar 1977: 394–434). That activity was in part a competition for honour, but hosting festivals or assizes was also of considerable economic benefit to a city because of the large number of visitors attracted for the occasion (Dio Chrysostom 35.16). Competition was often explicitly framed in terms of vying for position with a powerful neighbour, as in the rivalries of Ephesos and Smyrna or Prusa and Nicomedia. Older rivalries of the kind that typify the history of the *polis* were doubtless one factor in these squabbles, but these cities might also be regarded as 'niche competitors', struggling for desirable positions in the local hierarchy.

Imperial politics also acted in less direct ways to promote hierarchies of cities. Alongside Rome's use of some features of the *polis* went an erosion of its autonomy that affected far more than the right of *poleis* to go to war with their neighbours, although peace was of course important for the continued prosperity of the very large cities. Antioch and Alexandria may have first achieved prominence as capitals of Hellenistic empires, but their survival after the collapse of those empires depended on uninterrupted communications and exchanges with regions far greater than their immediate hinterlands. But the end of *polis* autonomy affected cities in more subtle ways, for example by allowing individuals to accumulate property within the territories of a number of *poleis* and to spend the income from it wherever they wished. The emergence of the super-rich is a marked feature of this period, as is the increase in benefactions beyond their 'home-cities' (Veyne 1976). Cities like Athens could expect to attract euergetism not only from rich Athenians but from numerous foreigners including Greek plutocrats, Hellenistic kings, Roman aristocrats and even emperors. Migration between *poleis* was also much easier. Again Roman Athens, with its large population of rich and prominent metics, is a case in point. Intra-city migration was equally possible for those of lower status and probably accounted in large part for the growth of large centres at the expense of small ones, although rural-urban migration was probably also significant (Rathbone 1983: 49–50, Alcock 1993: 160–64).

Yet political factors alone cannot provide a sufficient explanation for the form taken by the urban network of the Roman East. If imperial power was the main determinant of urban growth we might expect a more even distribution of cities of all sizes at least throughout the Mediterranean parts of the empire, yet a glance at the west shows that this was not the case. Parts of Italy and north Africa certainly had dense urban networks and substantial centres (including Rome itself) existed, but on the whole the level of urbanization was much higher in the Aegean region and in the eastern Mediterranean in general. On first reckoning the existence of Hellenistic empires might seem to provide an explanation, yet many of the larger Aegean centres were never imperial capitals. Besides, urban networks reflect *present* configurations of power, not past situations, and whatever their cultural and religious prominence these centres were not (with the partial exception of Alexandria) used by Rome as regional capitals during the early empire. Nor can the distribution of the larger centres be explained in terms of the fiscal geography of the empire. It has been suggested that urban growth occurred primarily in areas which exported more coin as tax than they acquired from imperial expenditure, the argument being that cities grew in such areas as centres manufacturing goods for long distance trade designed to earn back coin (cf. Hopkins 1978; 1980). Yet if Athens, Corinth and Ephesos must have seen as little of Roman troops as any cities did, Alexandria had a garrison and was capital of a province that included troops while Antioch, like many other cities in the Roman Near East, was a major military centre (Isaac 1990: 269–82). The implication of these arguments is that we should take seriously the possibility that the urban systems of the east at least were self-sustaining, that is to say they did not depend for their existence or form on the uses the state made of them.

The frequency and nature of communications between cities in this period lends support to this hypothesis. In modern empires, people, goods and information commonly move up and down an urban hierarchy rather than between cities at the same level. Petitioners and tribute move from village to town to provincial centres and then to the imperial metropolis; imperial orders or envoys follow the reverse route (Anderson 1991: 53–56). Subjects clamber up the hierarchy until they find the services they seek, rulers reach down through it until they make contact with their subjects. The Roman empire did not entirely conform to this pattern. Emperors and governors moved around within their respective circuits, partly perhaps because poor communications inhibited the efficient working of an administrative hierarchy, partly too because the patrimonialism of Roman culture led them to think in terms of central persons as much as central places. Nevertheless we might still expect traffic between centres at the same level to be relatively slight if the network was mainly articulated around political needs. Why move from one *polis* to another, or between provincial centres, if the object is to locate services not available at home? Yet it is abundantly clear that a great deal of traffic did take place between cities that were *politically* equivalent. Certainly ambassadors and litigants journeyed from periphery to centre (and then had commonly to chase the emperor or governor about on his travels) but there was also a constant flow of others moving between the cities of the Greek East, sophists and missionaries, students and pilgrims, doctors and those seeking cures, tourists and craftsmen, and the performers of all kinds who moved between the great festivals of especially the Antonine age. The travels imagined for St. Paul by the author of *Acts* and for Apollonius of Tyana by Philostratus make clear not only how common and easy travel was, but also how it was organised, with passengers making use of a dense web of commercial transport moving back and forwards across the whole region. Take, for example, the description of Paul's return to Jerusalem from Miletus:

> When we had parted from them and set sail, we made a straight run and came to Cos; next day to Rhodes and thence to Patara. There we found a ship bound for Phoenicia, so we went aboard and sailed in her. We came in sight of Cyprus and, leaving it to port, we continued our voyage to Syria, and put in at Tyre, for there the ship was to unload her cargo.....We made the passage from Tyre and reached Ptolemais where we greeted the brotherhood and spent one day with them. Next day we left and came to Caesarea. We went to the home of Philip the Evangelist, who was one of the seven, and stayed with him.....At the end of our stay we packed our baggage and took the road up to Jerusalem (*Acts* 21.1–3, 7–9, 15).

The journey consisted of three stages, the first and the last in ships that worked local routes, moving from port to port around south-west Asia Minor and along the Levantine coast respectively. The central, longer stage was in a cargo ship sailing across the open sea from Lycia to Syria. Other journeys, for example the visit to Cyprus and the diaspora communities of Pisidia and Lycaonia related in *Acts* 13, show how journeys along the main Roman roads of the region might be dovetailed with rides on short and long haul vessels.

These evidently commonplace movements of goods and merchants are difficult to reconstruct in detail; the use of artefact studies combined with underwater archaeology, which has revealed the development of regional systems of exchange in the west (cf. Duncan-Jones 1990: 30–58; Woolf 1992), has not progressed so far in the east. First signs are, however, suggestive of an even denser web of communications in this region, where the epigraphy of commerce is already well known (Fulford 1987; Pleket 1983). That network of communication was old (Purcell 1990) and to some extent a precondition for urbanism in such an ecologically precarious region as the Mediterranean (Garnsey 1988). But it is also clear that traders carried much more than staples to cities that had outgrown the carrying capacity of their hinterlands and to those struck by food crisis in any given year.

The rival forces of commerce, education, pilgrimage and so forth did not combine to diminish the degree of hierarchy in the system. Rather each created its own hierarchizing effects as travellers flocked to centres like Corinth, Athens or Claros, taking advantage of the imperial peace and the weakening of the bonds of the *polis*. Although some centres attracted visitors for one reason above all – to hear oracles at Claros or Ionopolis or to study law at Beirut, for example – the greatest cities ranked high on a number of criteria. Some travellers came to Antioch to find the governor and because it was a major military centre. Others came because it was en route to the caravan cities of the east, or in order to buy the rich grain surpluses of the Tetrapolis and to sell poor man's luxuries to one of the biggest urban markets in the Roman world. Yet others came to study with the sophists of the city, to visit the shrine at Daphne and eventually to hear the bishop preach and see the shrines of the martyrs. The result was that the urban hierarchies generated by political power were modified, rather than annulled, by other kinds of social power.

Support for this view of an urban system articulated by commerce and culture as much as by imperial power is offered by the observation that the urban system of the east preceded Roman rule in time and extended beyond it in space. The appearance of hierarchy within the urban growth of the east is attested for a number of areas in the Hellenistic period. Recent work on the Syrian Tetrapolis has shown how the urban system established by the first Seleucos continued to develop in the direction of hierarchy over the course of the third and second centuries BC (Grainger 1990: 91–136). Similar trends appeared in Alcock's (1993) study of the area that ultimately became the Roman province of Achaia. Neither the chronological nor quantitative dimensions of this trend can be established with precision, but rural-urban and inter-urban migration certainly began before Roman rule was secure. Hellenistic imperialism may have played some part in these developments, but it may equally be the case that asymmetries in urban development were already appearing for other reasons.

It may even be preferable to situate this growth in the context of the long-term trends towards an increase in the size of both cities and political units that is evident in the Mediterranean region throughout the last millennium BC, and which were not reversed until the late empire. Even then, it seems likely that urban networks could survive the loss of their political functions wherever cultural and commercial activity persisted, so that the end of empire in the west did not mean the immediate collapse of urbanism in the region (Wickham 1984). That line of argument cannot be pursued here, except to make two observations. First, that the same pre-Roman developments had also had an impact on the various societies of south-west Asia. The Roman-period urban network used by traders and missionaries, among others, extended well beyond the eastern limits of the empire through a complex of cities with a variety of origins (Millar 1993b: 437–45; see Potts, this volume). Second, that we should not be too quick to invoke 'economic growth' as the prime mover or central component of these processes. To be sure urbanization had immense economic consequences (especially for patterns of consumption and the distribution of markets) and, like all social change, was only possible when certain economic preconditions were in place. Yet other factors do need to be invoked in any realistic account of the genesis and expansion of ancient Mediterranean urbanism. Ecological constraints, the means by which first the state and then imperial structures were created in the region, and the integration of notions of urbanism into many ancient definitions of civilization: all may prove to be as important as economic growth in accounting for ancient urbanism.

Conclusions

What is to be concluded from this brief survey of urbanization in the eastern provinces of the early Roman empire? Rome's impact on the urban systems of the region was profound, extending the area of urban settlement and making use of new and old cities alike as tools of imperialism. As has long been realised, the extension of the empire itself was in effect the extension of a system of power in which *poleis* and their ruling classes were allocated an important place, and the growth of the main urban settlement in each *polis* was a natural consequence. Roman rule also generated a new degree of hierarchy in the system, partly by overtly 'ranking' urban settlements and distributing governmental functions among them, partly by weakening the bonds of the *polis* in general so that competition between them for resources, material and human, came to generate consistent winners and consistent losers. Yet Roman rule cannot alone account for the dynamics of the urban network or even for the hierarchy within it. The distinctiveness of the experience of eastern cities within the empire rests largely on the density of interaction and communication within an urban network older and wider than the empire itself, and cultural and commercial activities played an important part in these interactions.

Bibliography

Abrams, P. (1978) "Towns and economic growth: some theories and problems," in P. Abrams and E.A. Wrigley, eds., *Towns in Societies: Essays in Economic History and Historical Sociology*, 9–33. Cambridge.
Alcock, S.E. (1993) *Graecia Capta: The Landscapes of Roman Greece*, Cambridge.
Anderson, B. (1991) *Imagined Communities. Reflections on the Origin and Spread of Nationalism* (revised edn.), London.
Bowman, A.K. (1992) "Public building in Roman Egypt," *JRA* 5: 495–503.
Bowman, A.K. and D.W. Rathbone (1992) "Cities and administration in Roman Egypt," *JRS* 82: 107–27.
Cartledge, P. and A. Spawforth (1989) *Hellenistic and Roman Sparta. A Tale of Two Cities*, London.
Duncan-Jones, R.P. (1990) *Structure and Scale of the Roman Economy*, Cambridge.
Engels, D. (1990) *Roman Corinth: An Alternative Model for the Classical City*, Chicago.
Frézouls, E. (1987) "Du village à la ville: problèmes de l'urbanisation dans la Syrie hellénistique et romaine," in E. Frézouls, ed., *Sociétés urbaines, sociétés rurales dans l'Asie Mineure et la Syrie hellénistiques et romaines*, 81–93. Strasbourg.
Fulford, M.G. (1987) "Economic interdependence among urban communities of the Roman Mediterranean," *World Arch* 19: 58–75.
Garnsey, P. (1988) *Famine and Food Supply in the Graeco-Roman World: Responses to Risk and Crisis*, Cambridge.
Grainger, J.D. (1990) *The Cities of Seleukid Syria*, Oxford.
Harper, G.M. (1928) "Village administration in the Roman province of Syria," *YCS* 1: 105–68.
Hohenberg P.M. and L.H. Lees (1985) *The Making of Urban Europe 1000–1950*, Cambridge, Mass.
Hopkins, K. (1978) "Economic growth and towns in classical antiquity," in P. Abrams and E.A. Wrigley, eds., *Towns in Societies: Essays in Economic History and Historical Sociology*, 35–77. Cambridge.
_____(1980) "Taxes and trade in the Roman empire (200 B.C. – A.D 200)," *JRS* 70: 101–25.
Isaac, B. (1990) *The Limits of Empire: The Roman Army in the East*, Oxford.
Jones, A.H.M. (1940) *The Greek City from Alexander to Justinian*, Oxford
Jones, R.F.J. (1987) "A false start? The Roman urbanization of western Europe," *World Arch* 19: 47–57.
Levick, B.M. (1967) *Roman Colonies in Southern Asia Minor*, Oxford.
Lloyd, J.A. (1991) "Forms of rural settlement in the early Roman empire," in G. Barker and J. Lloyd, eds., *Roman Landscapes: Archaeological Survey in the Mediterranean Region* (Archaeological Monographs of the British School of Rome 2), 233–40. London.

MacMullen, R. (1959) "Roman imperial building in the provinces," *Harvard Studies in Classical Philology* 64: 207–35.

Macready, S. and F.H. Thompson, eds. (1987) *Roman Architecture in the Greek World* (Society of Antiquaries Occasional Papers 10), London.

Millar, F.G.B. (1977) *The Emperor in the Roman World*, London.

————(1990) "The Roman *coloniae* of the Near East: a study of cultural relations," in H. Solin and M. Kajava, eds., *Roman Eastern Policy and Other Studies in Roman History* (Proceedings of a Colloquium at Tvärminne 2–3 October 1987, Societas Scientiarum Fennica Commentationes Humanarum Litterarum 91), 7–58. Helsinki.

————(1993a) "The Greek city in the Roman period," in M.H. Hansen, ed., *The Ancient Greek City State*, 232–60. Copenhagen.

————(1993b) *The Roman Near East: 31 B.C. – A.D. 337*, Harvard.

Millett, M. (1990) *The Romanization of Britain: An Essay in Archaeological Interpretation*, Cambridge.

Mitchell, S. (1984) "The Greek city in the Roman world: the case of Pontus and Bithynia," in *Acts of the 8th International Conference of Greek and Latin Epigraphy*, 120–33. Athens.

Mitchell, S. (1987) "Imperial building in the eastern Roman provinces," in S. Macready and F. H. Thompson, eds., *Roman Architecture in the Greek World* (Society of Antiquaries Occasional Papers 10), 18–25. London.

————(1993) *Anatolia. Land, Men and Gods in Asia Minor I: The Celts in Anatolia and the Impact of Roman Rule*, Oxford.

Morris, I. (1991) "The early polis as city and state," in J. Rich and A. Wallace-Hadrill, eds., *City and Country in the Ancient World*, 24–57. London.

Pleket, H.W. (1983) "Urban élites and business in the Greek part of the Roman empire," in P. Garnsey, K. Hopkins and C.R.Whittaker, eds., *Trade in the Ancient Economy*, 131–44. London.

Pounds, N.J.G. (1973) *An Historical Geography of Europe, 450 BC-AD 1330*, Cambridge.

Purcell, N. (1987) "The Nicopolitan synoecism and Roman urban policy," in. E. Chrysos, ed., *Nikopolis I (Proceedings of the First International Symposium on Nicopolis, 23–29 Sept. 1984)*, 71–90. Preveza.

————(1990) "Mobility and the polis," in O. Murray and S.R.F. Price, eds., *The Greek City from Homer to Alexander*, 29–58. Oxford.

Rathbone, D.W. (1983) "The grain trade and grain shortages in the Hellenistic east," in P. Garnsey and C.R. Whittaker, eds., *Trade and Famine in Classical Antiquity*, 45–55. Cambridge.

————(1990) "Villages, land and population in Graeco-Roman Egypt," *Proceedings of the Cambridge Philological Society* 216 (n.s. 36): 103–42.

Rozman, G. (1973) *Urban Networks in Ch'ing China and Tokugawa Japan*, Princeton.

————(1976) *Urban Networks in Russia, 1750–1800, and Pre-Modern Periodisation*, Princeton.

Sartre, M. (1991) *L'Orient romain. Provinces et sociétés provinciales en Méditerranée orientale d'Auguste aux Sévères (31 av. J.-C. – 235 apr. J.-C.)*, Paris.

Skinner, G.W. (1977) "Urban development in imperial China," in G.W. Skinner, ed., *The City in Late Imperial China*, 3–31. Stanford.

Swain, S. (1996) *Hellenism and Empire. Language, Classicism and Power in the Greek World, AD 50–250*, Oxford.

Veyne, P. (1976) *Le pain et le cirque: sociologie historique d'un pluralisme politique*, Paris.

Vries, J. de (1984) *European Urbanization 1500–1800*, London.

Wagstaff, M. (1986) "What Christaller really said about central places," in E. Grant, ed., *Central Places, Archaeology and History*, 119–22. Sheffield.

Wickham, C.J. (1984) "The other transition: from the ancient world to feudalism," *PastPres* 103: 3–36.

Woolf, G.D. (1992) "Imperialism, empire and the integration of the Roman economy," *WorldArch* 23: 283–293.

2. Roman Colonies in the Province of Achaia: Territories, Land and Population

A.D. Rizakis

Introduction

The foundation of Roman colonies in Greece and Macedonia was part of a project conceived by Caesar and his lieutenants and further developed, in many respects, by Augustus. Founded on strategic inland or coastal sites, linking Italy with Greece, Macedonia, and Asia Minor, these colonies, together with a number of free cities, were to form the backbone of the Hellenic policy of the Roman Empire (Fig. 1).

The *deductio* of the colonies, especially the Augustan settlements, led to changes and even upheavals in political and economic life. The new administrative, economic, and cultural Hellenic policy of the *princeps* would be focused on these peripheral centers, which would themselves be the basis of, and the driving force behind, regional development (Alcock 1993: 93–115; Rizakis 1995b: 221–22). The creation of regional administrative centers, urban nuclei closely tied to Rome either by commerce or by the privileged status such ties lent them, gave Rome complete control of both people and territories (Lepelley 1993: 13–23). A chain of allied cities scattered strategically throughout the countryside was thus created, and this countryside was itself centuriated and dominated by a complex system of roads (Fig. 2), the largest of which connected these cities to each other (Rizakis 1996: 262–65). Augustus strengthened his settlements by granting them large territories belonging to neighboring cities, which thus ceased to be *poleis*, instead becoming *kômai* of the new centers. Colonial territory was restructed and reorganized in ways corresponding to the new political and social reality. This new system of organization took into account political, legal, and other constraints, creating a diversity of statuses across the land and among the people who occupied it. Variations in status can also be detected within the territory of a colony, as in the colony of Patras.

Colonization and Rural Space: Overturning the Order of the Land

Colonization has, in principle, an agrarian motivation, insofar as it is often the need for land that leads people to emigrate far from their homelands. Roman colonists, both soldiers and workers,

Fig. 1 . Caesarian colonies and Augustan foundations in Macedonia and Achaia

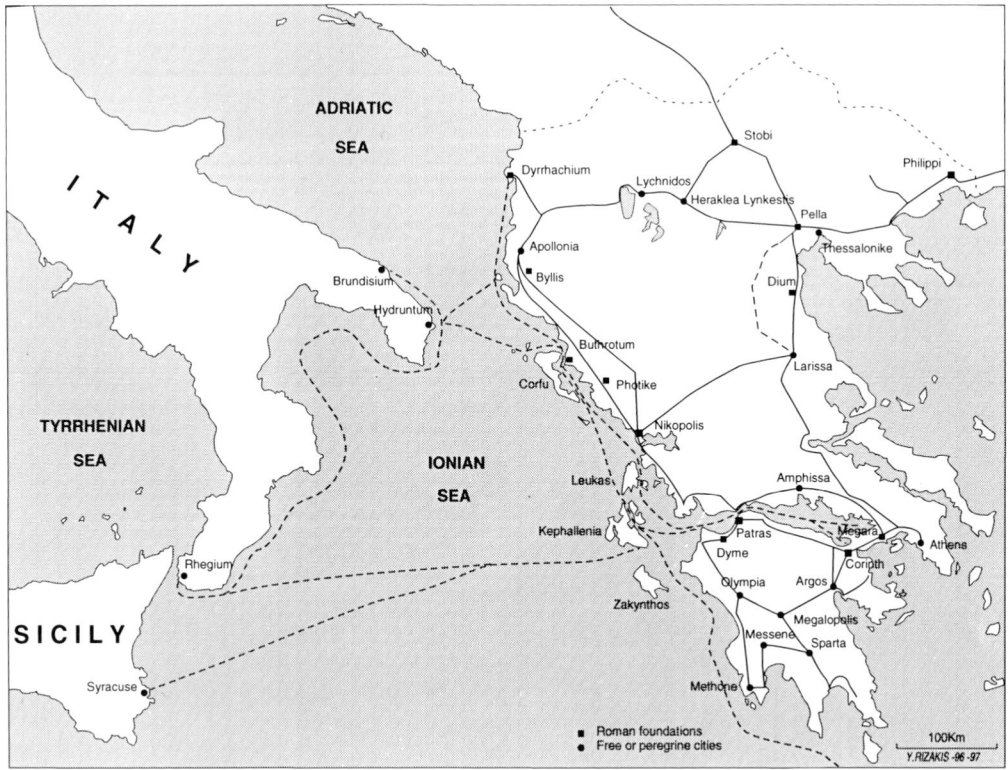

Fig. 2. Map of major maritime and land routes of the imperial period

were already or were to become farmers in their new lands. The forms colonial settlement took differed according to *deductor coloniae* plans, and the overall and local conditions particular to each site; such settlement in turn provoked important changes in the areas of land ownership and other property systems.

As a general rule, Caesar used those colony lands that were part of the *ager publicus*, but he did not hesitate to confiscate land belonging to peregrine cities, which were often loyal to Pompey. This type of quite severe oppression is very old, and it is well described by Livy (26.34; 28.46.4). In the region with which we are concerned, the clearest case is that of Corinth. Following its destruction by Mummius, its lands were confiscated and turned into *ager publicus;* part was given to Sikyon (Strabo 8.6.23). According to the *lex agraria* of 111 BC, the territory of Corinth was divided, some *termini* were set up and partly sold (*CIL* I².585; Crawford 1996: 42ff., ll. 96–105; cf. Johansen 1971: 396–98). Several years later, this project was probably included in the unfinished colonization projects in Achaia by Appuleius Saturninus, during his Tribunate of the Plebs of 103 BC. Two generations later, Caesar decided, after Pharsalus, to distribute some of these *agri capti* (*Dig.* 49.15.20, 21) to Roman workers. Corinth was to become the new great regional center: its foundation was to fill the void created a century earlier by its disappearance. This colonization was not expensive (D'Hautcourt in press) and, above all, it posed no complex legal or political problems – much like, for example, the colonization of Buthrotum. Land confiscation in that city was justified by the fact that its inhabitants owed taxes they were incapable of paying. T. Pomponius Atticus, a main land owner in the region, hastened to loan the sum owed, but the dispatching of colonists was only briefly postponed (Deniaux 1975; 1987).

This episode clearly shows the scale and the depth of the antagonism colonization provoked in the Roman ruling classes: the choice of settlement sites for new colonists often instigated disagreement and even conflict, which literature often fails to echo. The colonization plan for Patras, for example, may not date from the period following Actium; some evidence shows that it was part of the dictator's plans, but that it was rejected at the last minute as a result of Cicero's interventions on the part of his powerful clients in Patras. Roman colonists were later sent to neighboring Dyme, which was chosen because it presented fewer legal obstacles and provoked fewer political reactions (Rizakis 1990b).

We do not know what city previously owned the territory of the colony of Photike in Epirus, to the southwest of Buthrotum and near the present city of Paramythia. According to epigraphic and philological sources, Photike was a flourishing center during the Late Empire (Oberhummer 1941: 660–62; Traiantaphyllopoulos 1984), but the foundation of the colony most probably dates back to the Caesarian or Augustan period (Rizakis 1996: 271–72). The city possessed a vast and fairly fertile territory of which a large area was swampy (Samsaris 1994: 27); this is why Justinian later moved Photike and Phoinike (Procopius, *Aed.* 4.1.37–38; cf. Triantaphyllopoulos 1984: 577–84). The status of these lands prior to the *deductio,* like the pretexts invoked to justify sending colonists there, are not known. It is possible that the *Epirotici homines* Cicero mentioned (*Att.* 1.13; cf. Varro, *Rust.* 2.5.1) owned lands in this region, and they were, perhaps, compromised by loyalty to Pompey. The region was also, like so many others, uninhabited, and it lent itself to settlement by Italian colonizers.

Dyme, in the northwestern Peloponnese, was in a somewhat different situation. Pompey had forced some of the pirates defeated in 67 BC to settle there, and they had since transformed themselves into peaceful peasants (Appian, *Mith.* 96, 444; Strabo 14.3.3). Their loyalty to Pompey may have been the pretext for their violent expropriation by Caesar, although he had asserted that he would not confiscate land for these colonists, but would instead make use either of the *ager publicus* or of lands whose ownership seemed to him uncertain (Cicero, *Att.* 16.1.1–3; Suetonius, *Caesar* 38.1).

We know even less about the conditions under which the Macedonian colonies were founded. Philippi and Cassandrea certainly date from the triumviral period, but in the cases of Dium and of Pella, dates are more ambiguous (Papazoglou 1988: 407–408, 425 nn.56, 109, 137). Part of the lands given to colonists, formerly royal lands, had been part of the *ager publicus* since Pydna (167 BC), while others had perhaps been confiscated following the battle of Philippi.

Unfortunately, we know even less about the procedure Rome followed during Augustan colonization. Like the colonization of the previous period, this was implemented after a civil war whose outcome had been disastrous for the Hellenic peoples; in many cases (e.g. Patras), they had allied themselves with Antony. Quite naturally, they feared that the most brutal form of vengeance the winner might choose would include confiscation of their lands and forced displacement. The sources, however, indicate that the emperor did not pursue the brutal expropriations of the triumviral period, and the *Res Gestae* vaguely suggest that he compensated the former inhabitants of those colonies for the loss of lands given to colonists (Bowersock 1965: 106; 1964: 120–21). For example, some Italian property owners in cities that had supported Antony received, following their expropriation, lands in Macedonia, while others received money (*Res Gestae divi Augusti* 3.16; Cassius Dio 51.4; Hyginus 1.142 in Thulin 1913). Roman settlements, both old and new, were given new land, and their economic scope and political space grew via the attribution of lands belonging to neighboring cities that had found themselves, after wars, in disastrous economic and demographic situations.

Colonial Territory and the New Hierarchy of Space: The Example of Patras

Colonization introduced a new hierarchy at the level of territories and populations; colonial territory became a window onto Roman conquest and occupation. The combinations of various elements inscribed in the landscape thus constitute a reflection of the society of that period, of its day-to-day life and its organization. This organization can only be understood through its man-society-space-time relational systems (Bailly and Beguin 1995: 62–63); during the *deductio,* it took into account pre-colonial situations in many ways. A double hierarchy, spatial and social, is observed, as well as a diversity of organization and status corresponding to diverse social situations. The territory thus included many *ager,* the centuriated lands as well as others that remained outside of the new organization; the legal and political status of populations living there were likewise varied. This situation was neither fixed nor definitive; if at first the extension of colonial territory was achieved at the expense of more ancient populations (and not always legally), changes were later made according to imperial plans, priorities, or preferences (Clavel-Lévêque in press).

In contrast to Caesarian settlements (Buthrotum, Photike, Dyme), which were purely agricultural and whose territories, with the exception of Corinth, did not extend beyond those of the traditional cities, the primary characteristic of Augustan settlements was their vast dimensions (Strabo 8.6.22; cf. Engels 1990: 27 and n. 28; Rizakis 1996: 275–86). Patras and Nikopolis in Greece, and Dium, Cassandrea and Philippi in Macedonia were given the territories of several neighboring cities which became their *attributi* (for Greece, Kahrstedt 1950; for Macedonia, Papazoglou 1982: 89–106; 1988: 405–13). The new Roman foundations became veritable colossi, economic giants, compared to traditional cities or colonies with limited resources. This situation was entirely new, for it overturned the physical barriers between the territories of neighboring cities, whose definitions more or less obeyed natural barriers, constituting what geographers refer to as 'natural regions' (Aristotle, *Pol.* 1328b). Overthrowing the traditional situation was the result of a political decision; what concerned the Roman state during this period was providing new foundations with lands sufficient to maintain their economic balance and reflect their status. Often, the new lands attributed to colonies seem more suited to pasture-lands, which were not available within the *pertica,* that is, the centuriated territory (Flaccus 124–125 in Thulin 1913).

The acquisition of all these new lands was not accomplished speedily; often, the process was fairly long, and setbacks were not unknown. There are two Greek examples, studied by Kahrstedt (1950), of this notion of territorial mobility: the Augustan settlements of Patras and Nikopolis. The former extended throughout western Achaea, southern Aetolia, and the cities of West Lokris; the latter included the territories of other Aetolian cities and of the *koinon* of the Akarnanians. Extension underwent different chronological phases over the period from Augustus to Nero. According to Kahrstedt, the last change was made during the latter's reign, and in the context of an overall decree of the border between the province of Achaia and the new province of Epirus. No changes were made after that date.

While the schema proposed by Kahrstedt remains broadly valid (Rizakis 1996: 276–86), some recent documents, as well as a new approach to, and interpretation of, older ones, could change it or change certain details of it. One of the most delicate problems, concerning the fate of the cities of West Lokris, is the only point upon which I wish to insist here. Pausanias reports (10.38.9; cf. 7.18.8) it is probable that, during settlement of the Patras colony, the cities of West Lokris – with the exception of the city of Amphissa, which became *civitas libera et immunis* – were awarded to the Achaeans of Patras, that is, the Greek inhabitants of the city: 'the others, but not Amphissa, are under the government of the Achaeans of Patras, the emperor Augustus having granted them this privilege.' The traveller was aware of four cities in this region: Amphissa and Myania, to the interior, and Oiantheia and Naupaktos on the coast. His affirmation that there were not, during his time, cities other than Oiantheia and Naupaktos in this latter area is inaccurate, because at least two others, Physkeis and Chaleion, appear in documents of the imperial period as *poleis* (Rizakis 1996: 295).

The date of attachment of the West Lokrian cities is unclear. Kahrstedt (1950: 560–61) saw, in the presence of Latin inscriptions at Oiantheia and Naupaktos (*CIL* III. 569–570), an important argument in favor of their attribution to Patras as early as the Augustan period. He found it strange, however, that Strabo, who mentions the cities of the region (9.4.7), makes no allusion to these two, while informing us that the lake of Kalydon was possessed by Roman colonists of that city (10.2.21). In his eyes, moreover, the attribution of these two Lokrian cities to Patras during the *deductio* of the colony contradicted the fact that the ethnicity of people native to these cities was mentioned in Delphic documents of the Augustan or post-Augustan period (Oiantheia: *FD* III.6, 126; Naupaktos: *FD* III.1, 576). Kahrstedt thought this to be inconceivable given the new situation of dependence, and concluded that the attachment of the cities of West Lokris to Patras must have been later than the *deductio* of the colony. Others adopted his doubts, going perhaps too far in thinking that Naupaktos, like Amphissa, had been an exception to the attribution of the cities of West Lokris to Patras (Meyer 1979: 13). These arguments have since been disproven by the discovery of the funeral stele of a veteran of the twelfth legion *Fulminata* at Naupaktos (Rizakis 1995a: 389–90). The city, therefore, took in Roman colonists, as Kalydon perhaps did too; but this seems not to have had consequences, at least not lasting ones, on its status. Indeed, the attachment of the territory of a small city to a large urban center did not automatically or always lead to the loss of its identity. Thus, during the reorganization of Thracia by Trajan, small cities attributed to larger neighboring ones ceased to be *poleis* in becoming *kômai* of new centers, but their citizens continued to mention their *origo* along with that of their new city (Gerov 1973: 492–95).

The attribution of West Lokris to the Greek Achaeans of Patras at the moment of the colony's *deductio* could only be justified if it were a means of compensating them for losses suffered owing to the colonization and confiscation of their lands. The example would not be unique; the sources of revenue for a city harmed by colonization could sometimes come from quite far away (Rizakis 1996). The best-known example is that of Capua: in 36 BC, Augustus allocated to this city the revenues of a part of the territory of Knossos, in Crete, in order to compensate for losses caused by his veterans' settlement (Velleius Paterculus 2.81.2; Cassius Dio 49.14.4–5; Rigsby 1976: 311–30; Corbier 1991: 343–45). Such a territorial extent allowed local notables to consolidate their fortunes in land and enabled them to take their place among the elite of the empire; in this way, it played an important role in forging new levels of social inequality.

The fates of Nikopolis and Patras had been decisively set during the reign of the first sovereign, and the changes made after his death hardly altered the new regional balances of power that he had established. In this case, Pausanias was wrong to affirm that the attribution to Patras of the neighboring western Achaean colony of Dyme was made, like the others, during the reign of Augustus. This affirmation is contradicted by the minting of that small city's colonial currency, which continued, although sporadically, until the beginning of the reign of Tiberius. The absorption of Dyme by its powerful neighbor could, in fact, have occurred long after its money ceased to be minted (Amandry 1981); it may have coincided with the last phase of colonial territory extension, which Kahrstedt dates to the reign of Nero.

It was, in fact, on that occasion that new borders were drawn, making the course of the Achelous the dividing line between Achaia and the new province of Epirus. Kahrstedt (1950: 558 n. 60) associates this new imperial decree with the creation of the province of Epirus, and he believes that the decree favored the colony of Patras at the expense of the *civitas libera* of Nikopolis, which became the capital of the new province. In fact, Nikopolis kept only the territories of the cities of the former *koinon* of the Akarnanians, while the whole of the Aetolian coast, some of the interior, and the city of Thermon went to Patras. Such a solution explains, according to Kahrstedt, the presence of *duoviri* in two acts of emancipation by consecration to Artemis Hagemone found at Thermon. The association of the collegial magistracy of the *duoviri* with Nikopolis (a *civitas libera*) is in fact unlikely; a more likely one would be with the Roman colony of Patras. Unfortunately, the names preserved are unknown in the prosopography of that city and do not permit confirmation of this hypothesis. The abbreviation CN, which follows the initial phrase, is even more enigmatic. Rhomaios (1927: 5), the first editor of the document, thought these were Greek characters, and suggested they be read as either *e(n) N(omois)*, i.d. iure dicundo or as *e(n) N(ikopolei)*. Dessau (*ILS* 5518) understood them to mean *c(oloniae) n(ostrae)*, while Wilamowitz preferred *c(oloniae) N(ikopolis)* (*IG* IX.i² 92). Levy, in a recent study of the coinage of Patras in the Neronian period, sees in the CN of the Thermon inscription the abbreviation of *c(olonia) N(eronia)* and relates it to contemporary mintings from the colony which bore the legend *Col(onia) Ner(onia) Pat(renses)* (1989: 67ff.). This interpretation seems more plausible than the others, and it confirms Kahrstedt's hypothesis that under Nero, the territory of Patras, then limited in the Aetolian coastal area to the south, expanded into the country's inland regions.

Unfortunately, there remains a problem regarding the date. Basing his argument on paleography, the first editor placed it in the first century AD. Kahrstedt, in contrast, proposed the more precise chronology of approximately 100 AD, but neither the broken-bar form of the *alpha* nor the lunar letters permit such precision. If the interpretation of *C(olonia) N(eronia)* is correct, the document could hardly date from after the reign of Nero: not many years after his fall, Patras returned to minting coins (under Galba) with its former denomination CAAPATR (Burnett *et al.* 1992: 261 n. 1282).

The Legal Status of Reallocated People and Land

Determining the exact legal status of the lands and peoples of regions assigned over to cities is a very interesting problem. Generally, the decline of a city and its attachment to a powerful neighbor were rather badly taken by the Greeks. Dio Chrysostom (31.125; 31.101) considered the dependence of Kaunos, attributed to Rhodes, to be a *diple douleia*, a double servitude to Rome and to the patron city. His statement, however, must not lead us to believe that there was but a single model of such attribution. Relations between the patron city and the regions allocated to it differed according to degrees of opposition, the overall balance of power, and the interests and goals of Roman policy. There was a genuine complexity in these relations; simply reading Siculus Flaccus may convince us of that. While in general the *attributi* were of lower status than the patron city, certain populations could nevertheless have their legal and political status improved by the emperor's specific concession (Laffi 1966: 99). In some cases, they could even secede from the patron city's community. In this way, the *vicus* Orcistos of Phrygia, assigned to Nacoleia, obtained autonomy and the status of *civitas* from the Emperor Constantine (*MAMA* VII 1956 n. 305; cf. Chastagnol 1981: 373–79). Sometimes, Rome tried to clarify the obligations of regions to their new patron centers. In all cases, it is clear that the 'attributee' could not make use of the conceded territory entirely at will (Bertrand 1987: 104–105; 1991:154–58). Unfortunately, in the majority of cases, further details are unknown.

Ancient authors, in this case Strabo and Pausanias, refer to the allocation of different territories to the colony of Patras in the following terms: *prosnemein, telein, didonai, echein* (Pausanias 7.17.5; 7.22.1, 6; 10.38.8; Strabo 10.2.21). These terms relate specifically to such attribution and were in use in certain sources, such as Polybius, from Hellenic times on (Bertrand 1991: 148–50 n. 129). The primary meaning of attribution was political, in that such cities lost their independence: no longer autonomous *poleis,* they became *kômai* administratively linked to the colony. This is precisely the meaning that must be given to the verbs *telein, prosnemein* and *didonai*, which were used, for example, in reference to the attribution to Patras of the ancient cities of the north-western Peloponnese (Dyme, Pharai, Tritaia and Rhypes) and those of southern Aetolia and West Lokris, located on the northern coast of the Gulf of Corinth. They are, in fact, synonyms expressing dependence, although they are vague: only *telein* seems to be more precise, in that it implies the payment of certain taxes. This term can be related to *syntelein*, which we even find in certain imperial documents concerning the fulfillment of tax-related or other obligations toward Rome (Corbier 1991: 641–43). The verb is also used with reference to contributions made by one city to another, for example, in the guise of payments toward the cost of various festivals (*BullEpigr* [1958] 438). The meaning of *syntelein* with a complement in the dative seems more ambiguous: if Strabo's famous passage (4.1.12) concerning the 24 villages (*kômai*) of the Arecomisci subject to Nîmes – κώμας … συντελούσας εἰς αὐτήν – has been rendered by some translators as 'they pay him a tribute' (Goudineau 1976: 105–114; Christol-Goudineau 1987/88: 87–103), others see a territorial meaning in συντελούσας. This meaning is not absent from documents (Robert 1948: 29), and some translators understand it to mean that the *kômai* of the Arecomisci located in the same territorial and financial district (the *civitas* of Nîmes) 'paid to the benefit of Nîmes local charges handled centrally by the urban administrative center, by this intermediary also fulfilling their financial obligations toward Rome' (Corbier 1991: 642). The centralization of taxes in urban centers, as under the empire, highlights – among other things – the inferiority of the village relative to the *polis* (Dio Chrysostom 40.10).

This type of dependence did not necessarily concern the whole of the territories belonging to a city; the imperial state did not simply want to attach *kômai* or neighboring cities to their territory in order to create a large financial *synteleia*. The empire made much use of its urban structures and tried, in many cases – those of Nikopolis and Patras are well known – to broaden the basis of their prosperity by conceding new resources or privileges to them. We have seen that sources of compensatory revenue for certain cities compromised by colonization sometimes came from places that were quite far away.

The case of the West Lokrian cities and their relationship to the Achaeans of Patras, for example, shows that cities' economic space was larger than their political space, that is, than the territory over which they exercised administrative authority. This means that political, economic, and even social dependence varied in ways that are unknown, even incomprehensible, within the framework of a traditional Hellenic city. One primary distinction can be made between the territories included in the colonial *pertica,* thus centuriated land, and those not included; the territories of cities located in the northern part of the Gulf of Corinth seem to belong to this latter category. In contrast to the southern cities, which definitively ceased to be independent *poleis,* becoming instead *kômai* of the colonial territory, the northern ones seem to have kept a kind of administrative autonomy relative to the colony. This status allowed them to control some of their own affairs and to organize their economic and social existence. West Lokrians preserved the individuality of their *ethnos,* for they had kept a voice equal to that of East Lokrians in the Amphictiony reorganized by Augustus (Lerat 1952: 109); indeed their citizens maintained their ethnicity far from their homeland. This rather lax type of dependence could include the transfer of certain revenues, but it included absolutely no property rights and was, in any case, ephemeral. Somewhat later, in fact, the cities of West Lokris entirely regained their independence. Such an interpretation gives meaning to Pliny the Elder's affirmation (4.8) that the cities of that region had been *immunes.* The example is not unique; Rome could regulate relations between partners bit by bit and, if necessary, take back allocated lands from their former beneficiaries (Bertrand 1991: 153–54).

In conclusion, it can be said that there were, broadly, four different types of territories within the colony's *territorium* (Fig. 3), which included territories one might call internal (#1) or external to its *pertica* (#2–5).

(1) The territory of the city of Patras itself, which formed the heart of the colonial *territorium* and was home to the majority of veterans who settled in the urban center and in a few surrounding villages; these lands were integrated into the colonial *pertica* and, in part, centuriated;

(2) The territory of the neighboring western Achaean cities (Pharai, Tritaia, and possibly the territory of Rhypes, which bordered on that of Pharai) that were attributed to Patras, most likely at the time of the *deductio* or shortly afterward, during the reign of Augustus;

(3) The former territory of the Caesarian and Augustan colony of Dyme in western Achaea; it was fully integrated into the colonial *pertica* and once again centuriated (Rizakis 1990a);

(4) The territories of the cities of southern Aetolia, such as Kalydon and Naupaktos, which were dealt with in the colony's *deductio;* in contrast to the other cities thus assigned (#2 and 5), some veterans settled there. The legal and gromatic situation of these lands is more complex. Perhaps

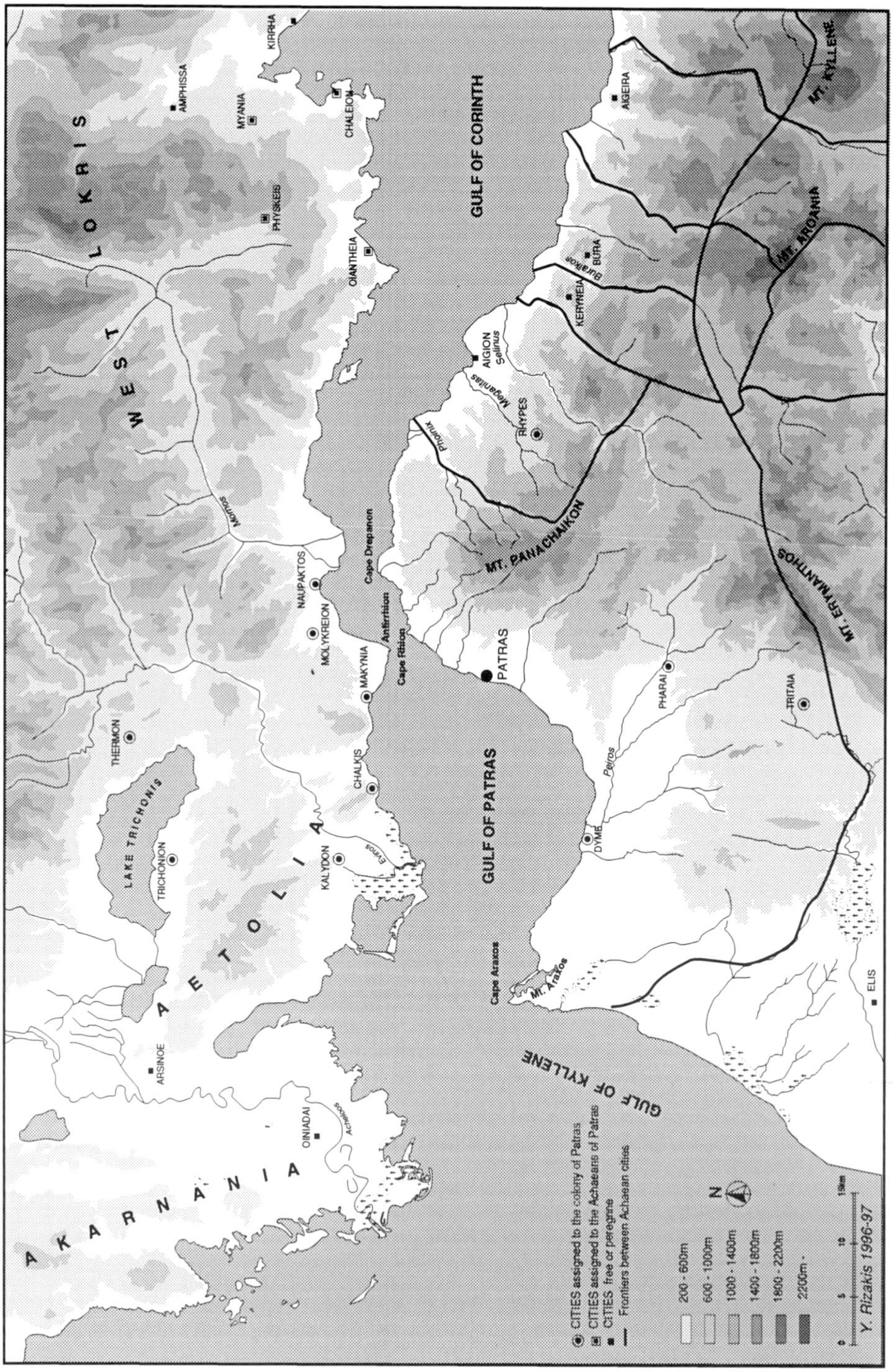

Fig. 3. Cities and territories assigned to the colony of Patras

these *agri ex alienis territoriis sumpte* constituted another category; they have their own cadastral framework (*forma*), and they appear on separate maps (Flaccus 159.29–160.3); such colonial lands are known as *praefecturae*.

(5) And lastly, the territory of the West Lokrian cities given over to the Achaeans of Patras – by way of payment of farm rent – as compensation for losses suffered due to the settlement of veterans. The legal status of inhabitants of these territories is more complex.

Political and Legal Rights of Free or Reallocated Populations

One may deny that classes, in the Marxist sense of the word, existed in Roman society, but it is difficult to deny the existence of a very hierarchical social stratigraphy. This stratigraphy broadly reflected the complexity of territorial status. To be more explicit, the colonists, οἱ ἐν Πάτραις Ῥωμαῖοι, settled in the city of Patras and the surrounding region, constituted the dominant group which, by its political position and social hegemony, was able to organize society in such a way as to serve its own interests. All other groups – the former inhabitants of the colony, and those of the neighboring cities attached to the colony – occupied subordinate roles in power relations. The Achaeans of Patras, though deprived of some of their lands, continued to live in the same city as the colonists; Augustus gave them back their liberty and showered them with so many privileges, according to Pausanias, that their situation was no different than that of the colonists: 'he granted freedom to the Patraeans, and to no other Achaeans; and he granted also all the other privileges that the Romans are accustomed to bestow on their colonists' (7.18.7). This assertion is an exaggeration, and in any case, we have no contemporary epigraphic or numismatic proof of the existence of an exceptional status; it is extremely difficult to know, in precise legal terms, the status of the earlier inhabitants of Patras. Perhaps it should be believed that the colonization of Patras brought about neither the total annihilation of its former free citizens, nor the withering away of their civil rights (examples in Laffi 1966: 204–205). These citizens, in fact, continued to enjoy rights which could only be accorded to foreigners by public decree: the rights of residence and of property, the *ius commercium* and perhaps the *ius connubium*. There can be no doubt that the Greeks of Patras enjoyed advantages that made their position clearly different from that of their compatriots in other Achaean cities, and more closely resembling that of the colonists; but it would be naïve to believe that the two groups were equals. In all cases, their political and legal status had to be inferior to that of *Romani Patrenses;* it could be compared to that of citizens of oligarchal cities, who had no political rights and who wrongly used the term *politai*, that is, citizens (Lotze 1981).

Fewer doubts exist about the legal status of those cities of the northwestern Peloponnese and southern Aetolia awarded to the colony of Patras; their inhabitants did not have the status of *coloni* or that of *incolae*, but rather, most probably, that of *peregrini*. Their legal condition was thus inferior to that of members of the community on which they depended (Laffi 1966: 87–98). In contrast, at Dyme, the change had no consequences for the status of descendants of Roman colonists nor for that of natives: the former remained full citizens, as we can see from inscriptions; the latter remained *peregrini*. Such a situation corresponds better to the term *contributio*, which is used when one small city merges with a larger one. Theoretically, this integration was sometimes advantageous even for native populations (Laffi 1966: 34 n. 71). The reasons behind the fusion of Dyme and Patras were quite different: in fact, the coexistence of two Roman colonies in such a small region proved difficult, as antagonism between the two autonomous cities could lead to the economic and demographic decline of the poorer of the two – that is, Dyme. *Contributio* with the more powerful of the cities – i.e. Patras – had as its goal only the administrative and economic reorganization of the northwestern Peloponnese. One must assume that Dyme, while displaced in an administrative sense, maintained a certain autonomy in the management of its day-to-day affairs, although higher-level political and legal matters were administered by the authorities of the dominant community – Patras. The citizens of Dyme, in contrast to those of neighboring *civitates attributae,* took on the status of the citizens of the central community: those who were Romans remained so, and *incolae* and *peregrini* likewise remained what they had been. Romans, of course, could become civil magistrates, and they had financial obligations *(munera).*

Finally, the populations of West Lokris and also, perhaps, those of Aetolia must be placed in a different political and legal category. The former, above all, were not dependent on the colony but on the Achaeans of Patras, to whom they were most likely obliged to pay an annual farm rent. That occasional obligation was not accompanied by political and legal submission to the colony; their cities did not cease to be *poleis,* did not become *kômai* of the colonial territory. They retained a kind of administrative independence that allowed them to have diplomatic relations with other cities; some – Naupaktos, for example – even achieved a certain prosperity despite a situation that was hardly favorable. The legal status of populations living there was no different than that of all the *peregrini* of the empire, and they enjoyed greater liberty and autonomy relative to populations of cities attributed to the colony. In fact, their financial obligations to the Patras Greeks were only temporary: shortly afterward, the cities of West Lokris entirely regained their independence; again, such independence would lend meaning to the passage of Pliny the Elder (4.8) that says they had been *immunes.*

The Arrangement of Rural Space: Roman Centuriation

Roman colonization was normally accompanied by a rearrangement of the countryside via the introduction of centuriation. This was one, and sometimes the most serious, of the consequences of Roman imperialism; it has been rightly said that the cadastral matrices were meant not only to construct and organize the space dominated by Rome, but also to diffuse this domination, to enlarge it (Clavel-Lévêque 1983: 251). It is, therefore, not surprising that a large number of Roman centuriation systems have been found in the provinces of Achaia and Macedonia, most notably in the territorium of Roman colonies such as Dyme, Patras, Corinth and Cassandrea in the Chalkidike, but also in the territories of *civitates liberae,* such as Nikopolis, Elis and Sikyon (Rizakis 1996). The majority of these date from the Augustan period, when imperial settlements and re-settlements in Greece reached their maximum numbers (Vittinghoff 1952: 126–30; Bowersock 1965: 65).

Without a doubt, Corinth was the site of the most ancient of these interventions. Corinth seems to have experienced *limitatio* twice: one was vast, based on a system of centuries of 16 × 24 *actus,* while the other, less extensive, was based on a 16 × 12 (or 24) *actus* system. Both times, a foot equivalent to 0.295 m appears to have been used (Romano 1993: 10–30; Doukellis 1994; see also Romano 1995; Romano and Schoenbrun 1994). One dates probably to the Flavian period, while the other must be contemporary to the *deductio* of the colony by Caesar. This agrarian division is

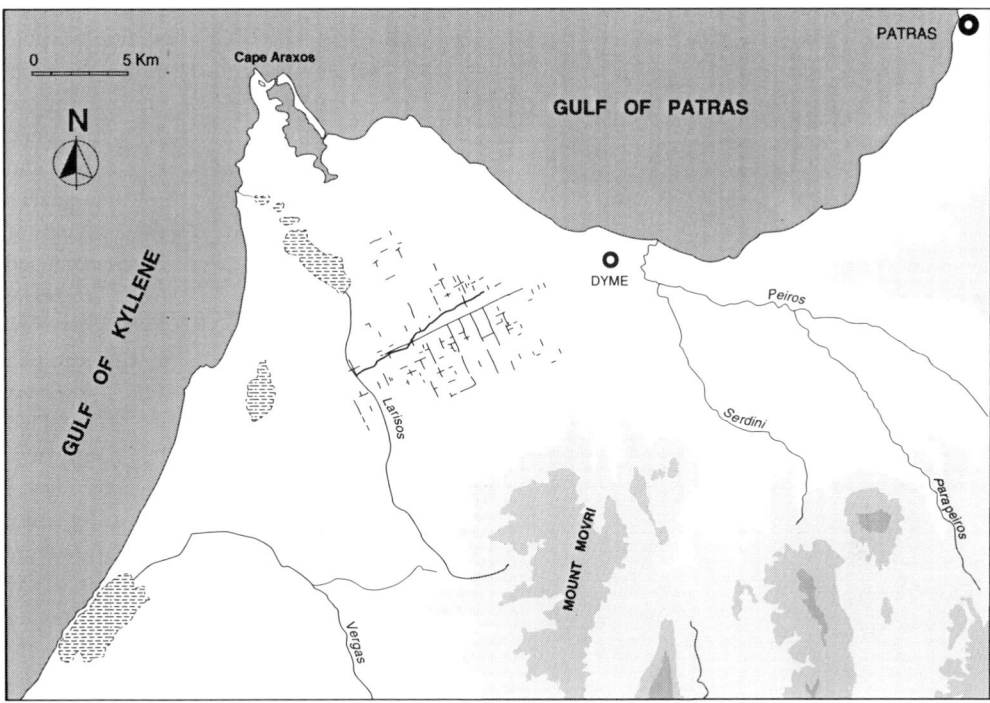

Fig. 4. Cadastral traces in the plain near Dyme in the northwestern Peloponnese

oriented in the same direction as the grid of the colony, and it is highly probable that the two operations were conducted simultaneously. Contemporary with the division of colonial lands in Corinth is that at Dyme (Fig. 4), in the northwestern Peloponnese, which, like Corinth, saw the arrival of Roman workers. After its absorption by its powerful neighbor, Patras, part of its plains were once again rearranged, in centuries of 20 × 20 *actus* (Rizakis 1990a). The cadaster of Cassandrea in Chalkidike dates from the triumviral period; no studies exist regarding the spatial organization of the other Macedonian colonies (Chevallier 1972).

The centuriations of Nikopolis in Epirus, like those of Patras in the northern Peloponnese, date from Augustan times. Settlement of the *civitas libera* of Nikopolis was followed by cadastration of all or part of its territory. Thus, to the south of the city, on the peninsula that encloses the Gulf of Ambracia, a cadastral grid based on 20 × 40 *actus* (707 × 1014 m) has been discovered. The fact that the orientation of the rural network's limits is identical to that of the urban configuration of the city indicates that the design and implementation of both was accomplished simultaneously; this no doubt occurred at the time of *deductio*: that is, in the first years of the reign of Octavian. The 20 × 20 *actus* division of the plain of Arta, to the north of the Gulf of Ambracia, seems to have been contemporary, since this too was part of the territory of Nikopolis (Doukellis 1988; 1990).

It is obvious that, in the Hellenic context, the areas destined for cadastration were not vast. The flat, linear western coast of the Adriatic is in stunning contrast to the rocky appearance of the coast opposite; the most characteristic trait of that latter area is the narrowness of its plains, due, o course, to the imposing mountain chains traversing the region. Nevertheless, despite the narrownes: of these alluvial plains, which are generally situated near the coast, the soil is fertile and rainfall i: as abundant as in certain regions of central Europe, allowing vegetation to grow even in midsummer. The plains' narrowness posed some problems for coastal Roman settlements. As colonies required that a great deal of space be devoted to agriculture, areas of fertile and of less-fertile soils – even arid or swampy zones – were developed. Considerable efforts toward the improvement of the latter zones were undertaken; notably, large drainage canals were dug in the plain of Arta, in Epirus, in the plain of Dyme in the Peloponnese (Doukellis 1990: 275–77; Rizakis 1992: 130–32), and finally at Philippi in Macedonia. It is not known whether or not these great works were successful; one suspects that, in Dyme, they were not. This colony, situated on the plateau to the northeast of the plain, declined rapidly. During the Roman period, few habitation groups developed in this flat region; there is no trace of a villa that might have belonged to an important land owner. It would seem that, despite the efforts made to improve conditions via drainage, the poor quality of the land, which in places consisted of heavy, clayey soils, and the unhygienic conditions characteristic of a humid plain made agriculture difficult. It is therefore not surprising that these lands, given to the earliest colonists, were quickly abandoned (Siculus Flaccus 112–13). Throughout antiquity, this swampy plain remained nearly uninhabited. However, colonization seems not to have disturbed the original inhabitants, who continued to live – as their dwellings prove – in those areas not subject to cadastration. Those areas were, nevertheless, part of the colonial *pertica* (Rizakis 1992: 130–34).

Agricultural Wealth and Exploitation of the Countryside under the Empire

The countryside presents, under the empire, a negative image characterized by the under-exploitation or the abandonment of lands. This is not a literary theme dear to those who are nostalgic for days gone by, but it is a reality of Roman Greece. An authentic agricultural crisis, which was due to the reduction of land use, was a general phenomenon of the period. This situation did not affect all cities or all regions in the same way (Alcock 1993: 33–92; Rizakis 1990c: 433–38). It was not the case, for example, at imperial colonies or settlements (e.g. Nikopolis, Patras, Philippi, Corinth, etc.). Thanks to the addition of new people and to the synoecism of neighboring communities, these cities became economic powerhouses with immense consumption demands for agro-alimentary products (MacMullen 1970; on the typology of cities in the Roman period, see Engels 1990: 43–65; Finley 1981: 3–40; Leveau 1983a; 1983b; Whittaker 1990). The resources of the countryside, subjected to the authority of the new cities, became the source and the reserve of their wealth: a wealth, in turn, proportional to the size of their land and their subject populations, to the revenue produced for these cities by their territories. This reinforcement of the center at the expense of the periphery was linked to the imposition of a hierarchical structure designed to drain agricultural production from the countryside to more powerful areas; these asymmetrical relations favored the growth of urban centers, where the privileged groups resided. It seems that in Patras, as in Caesarea in Mauretania, there was a close link between villas on the periphery of the city and sumptuous urban constructions (Leveau 1984: 465–468; 1983b: 920–42; Petropoulos and Rizakis 1994: 199–201). At Patras, the villas of the littoral constituted the basis of the land wealth of the local elite (Fig. 5). Such villas appeared from the end of the first century AD, when the first great fortunes came into existence (Rizakis 1995b). They worked to ensure the exploitation of agricultural wealth for part of the colonial territory, as well as its economic, political, and social control, for the villa provided the urban market with rural products (Whittaker 1990). This by no means indicates that the *whole* of colonial territory had been subject to this form of economic exploitation. The ongoing presence of groups of traditional dwellings in the *chora* of Patras, as well as in other cities, demonstrates that after colonization, entire regions – even very fertile ones, if only those situated far from urban centers – were left in the hands of their original inhabitants, who continued their own forms of agricultural exploitation (Rizakis 1992: 129–35).

The exploitation of rural wealth was not, certainly, left to chance; agriculture and animal husbandry were, for Greek cities of the period – as for the majority of the empire's cities – the basis of economic prosperity. Despite their incontestable importance, the contributions of commercial and 'industrial' activities to the overall economy must not, however, be underestimated (Hopkins 1978; Pleket 1984). Archeological discoveries show that in certain cases, such as that of Patras, these activities must be associated with cities' economic development from the first century AD onward. In Greece, the best-studied case, which could be used as a model for Patras, is that of Corinth (Engels 1990: 22–42; Williams 1993: 31–46).

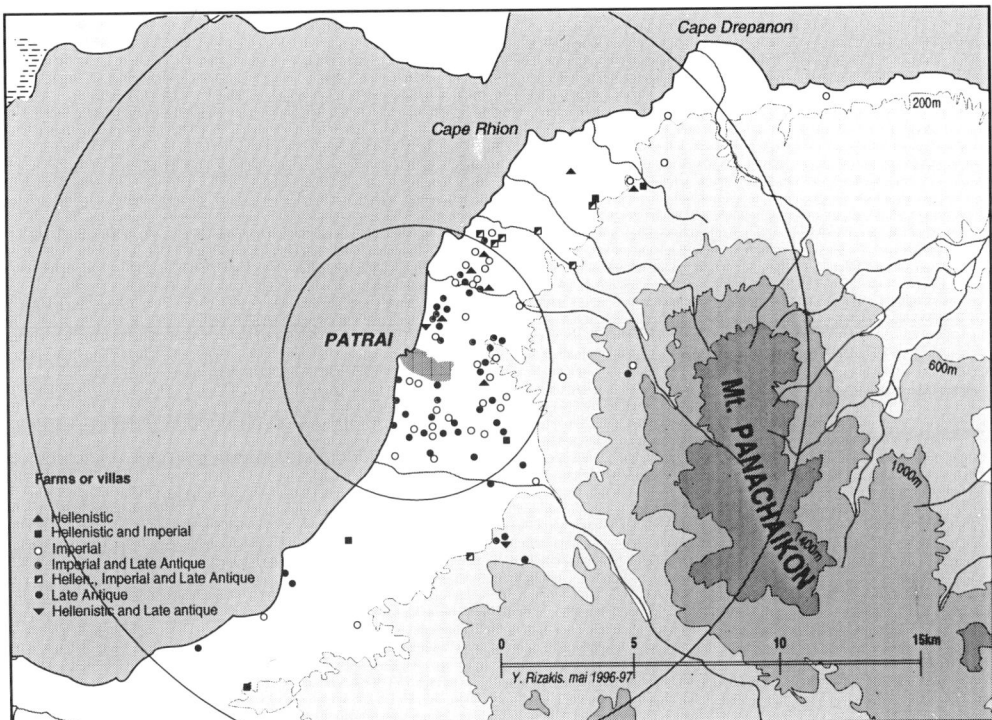

Fig. 5. Distribution of farms and villas in the coastal zone of Patras (concentric circles at 5 and 15 km)

Specific types of agricultural exploitation depended on the precise status of the lands and the populations inhabiting them, on their distance from the city, and on the nature of their produce. The most fertile areas of the 'natural' territory of a colony constituted a sort of 'bread-basket' region, and they were more intensively exploited. The neighboring coastal countryside of Patras was vitally important to the colony, and was occupied by farms of various sizes, agricultural cells designed to feed the city. The rural development of a villa economy shows that an intensive and specialized exploitation developed during the first century BC (Engels 1990: 33–9), when the first great fortunes were constituted (Rizakis 1995b)

The predominant crops were grapes and olives; certain villas featured presses (*torcularia*) and storehouses (*dolia*). In two cases, grouped viticultural facilities of an 'industrial' type have been found in proximity to cities (Petropoulos 1994: 413–14). These discoveries confirm what written sources had already told us, that is, that Achaean viticulture under the Empire was practiced on a large scale. Excavations have, in fact, uncovered only a few oil presses; the cultivation of olives does not seem to have had the same importance as that of grapes, in this region at least (Baladié 1980: 182–85; Pikoulas 1995: 278). It should be noted that the zones more immediately surrounding many Mediterranean cities of the Roman period were devoted to more remunerative activities than the growing of cereal crops, principally vegetable produce and viticulture. The treatises of Varro (*Rust.* 1.8.1) and Columella (3.3.1–2) show that vegetable produce was considered an extremely profitable suburban crop because of the ease of its transportation and sale in nearby cities. At Patras, as in the majority of cases, it is difficult to prove such crops were grown near the city, but their existence can be assumed (Duncan-Jones 1974: 36; Leveau 1984: 465 n. 3). In more distant areas, climatic and pedologic variations introduced some diversity into agricultural exploitation and the rural countryside; in this case one thinks first of the inland Glaucos basin, where the presence of alluvial soils more vulnerable to the unpredictable flooding of the river necessitated seasonal crops and exploitation. Certain parts of the large western plain were, perhaps, reserved for cereal crops (Bingen 1954: 74–82; cf. Rizakis 1995b: 237), while more humid areas were reserved for the cultivation of *byssos* to supply Patras' textile industry, which was quite developed under the Empire (Pausanias 7.21.14; Rizakis 1995a: n. 274). Areas that were less fertile, more arid, and thinly inhabited were most likely reserved for animal husbandry; lastly, the forests, as sources of raw materials and as open spaces, must have played a much more important role than today. Today, the best-known plant life in the area are resiniferous trees; it is possible, however, that the situation was quite different during antiquity. The colony at Patras also operated fishing enterprises (for example, at the lake of Kalydon: Strabo 10.2.21) and a ferryboat for conveyance between the two sides of the Gulf at Rhion-Antirrhion, as well as quarries and salt works most probably in western Achaea and on the opposite coast. In addition to fish from its lagoons and lakes, the latter region possessed flood zones in the lower valley of the Achelous and Evenos rivers that produced green fodder during the summer; the mountains featured, in addition to forests, routes for herds of animals and summering areas necessary to breeding.

Such a schematic layout of the agricultural countryside corresponds more or less to the classic structure of *ager, silva, saltus* (Fig. 6) and to the typical arrangement of the Mediterranean city through the ages (Bailly and Beguin 1995: 104–105). But it goes without saying that such an schema of colonial rural space is nothing more than a working hypothesis that may favor better comprehension of an extremely complex political, social, and economic reality whose complete reconstitution is an

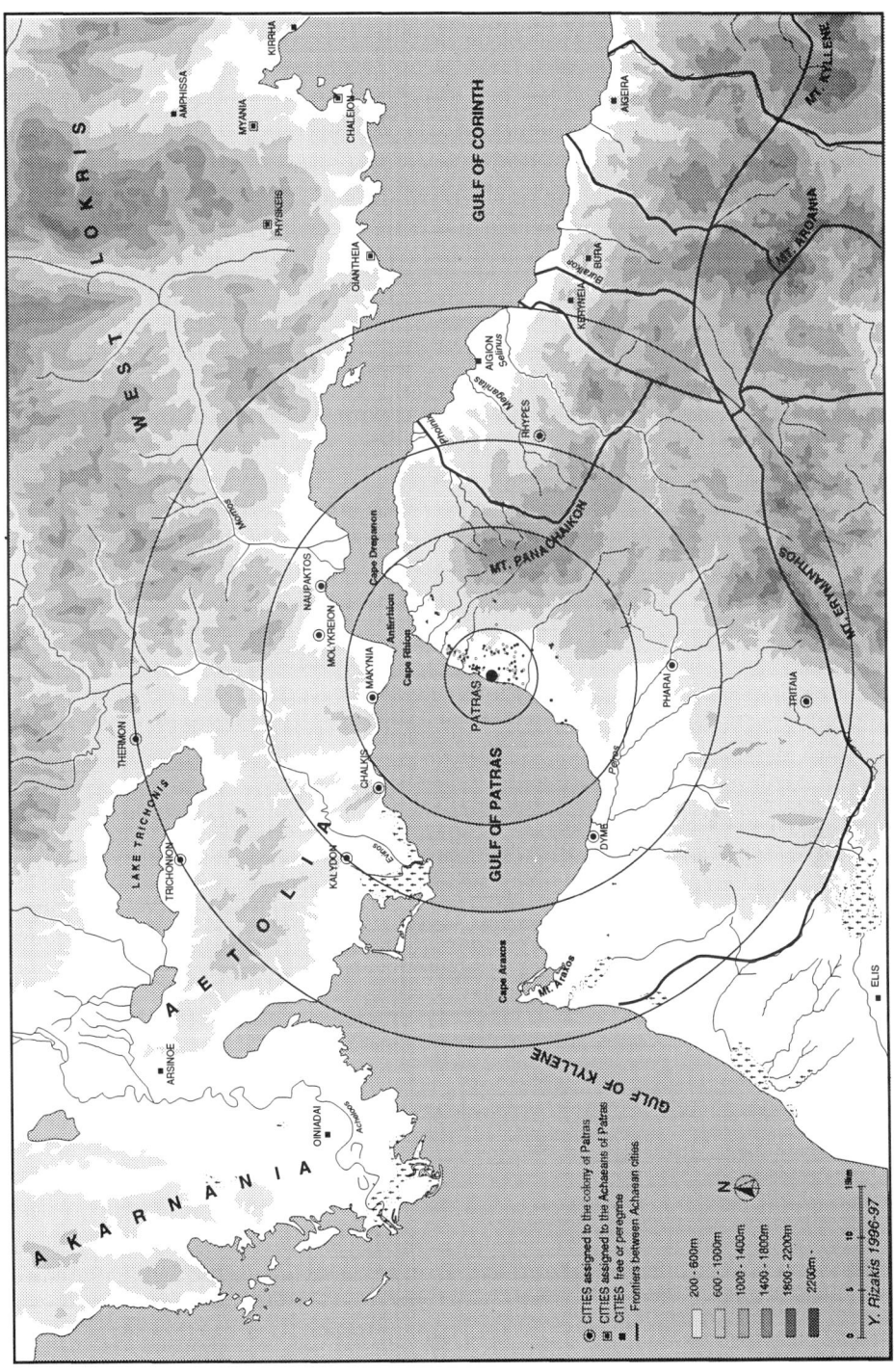

Fig. 6. Assigned cities, territories, and economic zones around the Roman colony of Patras

● CITIES assigned to the colony of Patras
◉ CITIES assigned to the Achaeans of Patras
■ CITIES free or peregrine
— Frontiers between Achaean cities

N

200 - 600m
600 - 1000m
1000 - 1400m
1400 - 1800m
1800 - 2200m
2200m +

Y. Rizakis 1996-97

AKARNANIA

AETOLIA

LOKRIS

W E S T

LAKE TRICHONIS

TRICHONION

THERMON

ARSINOE

ONIADAI

KALYDON

CHALKIS

SOAOS

Cape Araxos

Mt. Araxos

DYME

Peiros

PHARAI

TRITAIA

ELIS

GULF OF PATRAS

GULF OF KYLLENE

PATRAS

MT. PANACHAIKON

Cape Rhion

Antirrhion

Cape Drepanon

MAKYNIA

MOLYKREION

NAUPAKTOS

PHYSKEIS

GIANTHEIA

CHALEION

MYANIA

AMPHISSA

KIRRHA

GULF OF CORINTH

AIGION
Selinus

Meganitas

RHYPPES

KERYNEIA

BURA

BOUKA

SICYON

AGEIRA

MT. ARDANIA

MT. KYLLENE

MT. ERYMANTHOS

almost impossible task. Certainly aerial photos reveal, particularly in flat areas, the existence of Roman centuriations that were most likely occupied by crops, while an analogous organization is not found in mountainous or even semi-mountainous areas; the absence of drystone walls in those areas could suggest that they were reserved for animal husbandry. This division is reminiscent of the classic Mediterranean opposition between *ager* and *saltus*, but often this is only partially true, since the idea that mountainous soil is less fertile is completely false. The majority of Mediterranean mountains feature – beside zones reserved for animal husbandry – lands suited to a wide variety of trees and crops capable of supporting the self-sufficiency of the people living there, often more so than the plains themselves.

Types of Dwelling: The City and Villages

Despite its incontestable inferiority to the city, the village continued to be the structural basis of the Hellenic countryside throughout the Roman period (Rizakis 1996); it continued to serve as the intermediate structure between the city and the countryside until late antiquity (Dagron 1989). If the majority of colonists chose to settle in cities, there are examples of isolated individuals or groups choosing to settle in *vici* and villages (Rizakis 1996). These areas had not, of course, been abandoned by their original inhabitants. The novelty lies in the fact that during this period, a new form of dwelling and rural economy, the Roman *villa rustica,* made its appearance in Greek lands. The breadth of the villa's diffusion in rural space seems to have been limited, except in certain colonies (*contra* Kahrstedt 1954). Agricultural establishments that can be considered villas are spread regularly along the coast of the colony of Patras (Petropoulos 1994; Petropoulos and Rizakis 1994: 199–201). In contrast, at least according to research to date, far fewer are known in the rest of the territory of Patras or in Corinthian colonies (Rothaus 1994) or Dyme (Rizakis 1992: 71). There were two types of village: either the dwellings of small peasants grouped beside these villas, or geographically autonomous communities of rather modest dimensions. At Dyme, the latter groups of dwellings were located on the plateaus formed by the river Peiros; others were near the mountains. At Patras – with the exception of the coast, which was reserved for villas – they can be found throughout the territory; in fact, there, as at Caesarea in Mauretania, the existence of two differently organized rural spaces can be observed. The first, that of the villa, was organized by and in proximity to the city, and was connected to it with roads; this was a constant phenomenon in many colonies (Percival 1976: 157). The second, that of traditional villages, occupied another part of the city's territory (Leveau 1984: 465–68; 1995: 277; Petropoulos and Rizakis 1994: 199–201). Some of these villages seem to have been continuations of more ancient traditions, but there are also cases of new foundations (Rizakis 1996). The survival of more ancient ones is connected to the fertility of lands as well as other resources situated near them (Alcock 1989: 18).

In any case, Roman colonies aside, it was the Greek model that prevailed in the organization of cities. In this model, the *kôme* enjoyed no autonomy from the city; its inhabitants were equal citizens. The city still constituted the smallest administrative unit; in fact, boundaries of the *kôme* within the territory were not marked. The urban agglomeration, the *asty*, was the political and administrative center of the territory (*chora*), but this fact gave it no further rights over the villages and the inhabitants of the countryside (Leveau 1995: 294).

Some variations on this legal and political hierarchy existed in the Roman colonies, for there were several different levels of status applied to lands and people. Broadly, it could be said that one category is that of the villages that previously had been part of the territory of Patras, which were now included in the colonial *pertica* . This category could also include the territory of neighboring cities that were attached to the colony at the time of *deductio* or following colonization; these cities (Tritaia, Pharai, Rhypes and Dyme in western Achaea, like Kalydon, Pleuron, etc. in Aetolia), if they had previously been independent *poleis*, lost that status to become *kômai* of the colonial territory (Rizakis 1996). Their political life was limited to local questions, but the vitality of some of them, such as Pharai, continued to manifest itself in the area of religion (Pausanias 7.22.1–5); the decline of other cities, whether religious in nature or not, is made clear by Pausanias' description as well as by recent archeological discoveries (Rizakis 1995a: 185–230). The situation seems to have been different in West Lokris: those cities continued to be referred to as *poleis;* they had territories, as well as borders separating them from their neighbors. They most likely also had, as we have seen, a form of 'autonomous' administration; this could explain the discovery in the records at Delphi of references to the ethnicities of people native to these cities. One is thus obliged to believe that, from the beginning, these cities enjoyed a superior status, although it is not possible to define their status in precise legal and political terms.

The structure and organization of villages located in colonial *territorium* were not identical throughout the Roman colonies. In the province of Achaia, for example, the Greek tradition of close relations between each city and its surrounding countryside had the effect of endowing *kômai* situated in colonial territory with only a very limited administrative 'independence', of which no trace is found in literary and epigraphic sources. Generally, the situation was one of an urban agglomeration such as Patras or Corinth, in which power was heavily concentrated, dominating the countryside completely in both the political and the economic sense. Even relatively important secondary centers, such as Kenchreai near Corinth, seem not to have had an autonomous organization, analogous to the *vici* in certain other Roman provinces (Strabo 8.6.2; cf. Hohlfelder 1976: 217).

The situation seems to have been somewhat different in Macedonia, particularly in regions bordering on Thrace. At Philippi, for example, beside a small urban center, there was a subdivision of colonial territory into villages (called *vici*) some of which were inhabited by natives, though more often by a mixed population (Collart 1937: 285–912; Rostovtzeff 1957: 287 n. 84). The difference between these and *civitates adtributae* is that they formed communities which were incorporated into the territory of the dominant city, while *adtributae* were external to its actual territory. Although they were hierarchically inferior to the city, *vici* had an administrative and legal status, with their own administrative organization; the *vicani* and *pagani* included in the municipal territory generally had the personal status of *pleni juris* city dwellers (Rostovtzeff 1957: 206). This situation was not exceptional: it marks a territorial structure and organization characteristic of the western provinces. In the east, this organization is found in Thrace and in Syria: in other words, that is, on the periphery of Hellenism. In the Hellenic provinces (Achaia, Epirus, and Macedonia) only the colony of Philippi in eastern Macedonia followed this structure (Rizakis 1996). This organization is closer to the Roman model, whereby the *territorium* is, above all, hierarchical; it includes an urban center administering the territory and its villages, to which Latin sources give names such as *vicus, castellum, oppidum,* etc.. This hierarchy implies neither legal nor administrative independence (Leveau 1984: 459–71).

Translated by Liza Hall

Bibliography

Alcock, S.E. (1989) "Roman imperialism in the Greek landscape," *JRA* 2: 5–34

_____(1993) *Graecia capta: The Landscapes of Roman Greece*, Cambridge.

Amandry, M. (1981) "Le monnayage de Dymé (Colonia Dumaeorum) en Achaïe. Corpus (pl. XIII-XVI)," *RN* 23: 45–67.

Bailly, A. and H. Beguin (1995) *Introduction à la géographie humaine*, Paris.

Baladié, R. (1980) *Le Péloponnèse de Strabon*, Paris.

Bertrand, J.-M. (1987) "Le statut de territoire attribué dans le monde grec des Romains," in E. Frézouls, ed., *Sociétés urbaines, sociétés rurales dans l'Asie Mineure et la Syrie hellénistiques et romaines*, 95–106. Strasbourg.

_____(1991) "Territoire donné, territoire attribué: note sur la pratique de l'attribution dans le monde impérial de Rome," *Cahiers du Centre G. Glotz* II, 125–164. Paris.

Bingen, J. (1954) "Inscriptions d'Achaïe 1. Épigramme honorifique," *BCH* 78: 74–82.

Bowersock, G.W. (1964) "Augustus on Aegina," *Classical Quarterly* 14: 120–29.

_____(1965) *Augustus and the Greek World*, Oxford.

Burnett, A., M. Amandry, and Père P. Ripollès (1992) *Roman Provincial Coinage* I, London.

Chastagnol, A. (1981) "Les *realia* d'une cité d'après l'inscription constantinienne d'Orkistos," *Ktèma* 6: 373–379.

Chevallier, R. (1972) "Note sur la centuriation de Kassandreia," *Caesarodunum* 7: 297–298.

Christol, M. and Chr. Goudineau (1987/1988) "Nîmes et les Volques Arécomiques au Ier siècle avant J.-C.," *Gallia* 45: 87–103.

Clavel-Lévêque, M. (1983) "Pratiques impérialistes et implantations cadastrales," *Ktèma* 8: 185–251.

_____(in press) "Comment penser le territoire," in *Actes du colloque, Colonies, colonisations, paysage (Barcelone, Mars 1993)*.

Collart, P. (1937) *Philippes: ville de Macédoine*, Paris.

Corbier, M. (1991) "Cité, territoire et fiscalité," in *Epigrafia, Actes du colloque international sur l'épigraphie latine*, 629–65. Rome.

Crawford, M. (1996) *Roman Statutes, I-II*, London.

D'Hautcourt, A. (in press) "Corinthe: financement d'une colonisation et d'une reconstruction," in J.-Y. Marc, J.-C. Moretti and D. Viviers, *Constructions publiques et programmes édilitaires en Grèce du IIe s. av.J.-C. au Ier. s. ap. J.-C.*, Athens.

Dagron, G. (1989) "Entre village et cité: la bourgade rurale des IVe-VIIIe siècles en Orient," *Koinônia* 3: 29–52.

Deniaux, E. (1975) "Un exemple d'intervention politique: Cicéron et le dossier de Buthrote en 44 av. J.-C.," *Bulletin de l'Association Guillaume Budé* 2: 283–296.

_____(1987) "Atticus et l'Epire," in P. Cabanes, ed., *L'Illyrie méridionale et l'Epire dans l'Antiquité* I, 245–53. Clermond-Ferrand.

Doukellis, P.N. (1988) "Cadastres romains en Grèce; traces d'un réseau rural à Actia Nicopolis," *Dialogues d'histoire anciennes* 14: 159–66.

_____(1990) "Ena diktuo agrotikon orion sten pediada tes Artas," *Meletemata* 10: 269–86.

_____(1994) "Le territoire de la colonie romaine de Corinthe," in P.N. Doukellis and L.G. Mendoni, eds., *Structures rurales et sociétés antiques*, 359–90. Besançon.

Duncan-Jones, R. (1974) *The Economy of the Roman Empire: Quantitative Studies*, Cambridge.

Engels, D. (1990) *Roman Corinth, An Alternative Model for the Classical City*, Chicago.

Finley, M.I. (1981) *Economy and Society in Ancient Greece*, London.

Gerov, B. (1973) "Die Einteilung der städtischen Territorien im römischen Thrakien in regione (*chôrai*), Phylen und Komarchien," in *Akten des VI. Internationalen Kongresses für Griechische und Lateinische Epigraphik*, 432–35. München.

Goudineau, Chr. (1976) "Le statut de Nîmes et des Volques Arécomiques," *Revue archéologique de Narbonaise* 9: 105–114.

Hohlfelder, R. (1976) "Kenchreai on the Saronic Gulf: aspects of its imperial history," *CJ* 71: 217–26.

Hopkins, K. (1978) "Economic growth and towns in classical antiquity," in P. Abrams and E.A. Wrigley, eds., *Towns in Societies: Essays in Economic History and Historical Sociology*, 35–77. Cambridge.

Johansen, K. (1971) *Die lex agraria des Jahres 111 v. Chr. Text und Kommentar*, München.

Kahrstedt, U. (1950) "Die Territorien von Patrai und Nikopolis in der Kaiserzeit," *Historia* 1: 549–561.

_____(1954) *Das wirtschaftliche Gesicht Griechenlands in der Kaiserzeit*, Berne.

Laffi, U. (1966) *Adtributio e contributio*, Pisa.

Lepelley, Cl. (1993) "Universalité et permanence du modèle de la cité dans le monde romain," in J. Arce and P. Le Roux, eds., *Cité et communauté civique, Actes du colloque de Madrid. 25–27 janvier 1990*, 13–23. Madrid.

Lerat, L. (1952) *Les Locriens de l'ouest* I-II, Paris.

Leveau, Ph. (1983a) "La ville antique, *ville de consommation?*," *Études rurales* 89–92: 275–289.

_____(1983b) "La ville antique et l'organisation de l'espace rural: villa, ville, village," *Annales ESC* 4: 920–42.

_____(1984) *Caesarea de Maurétanie. Une ville romaine et ses campagnes* (*MEFR* 70), Rome.

_____(1995) "La ville romaine et son espace territorial," in *Congrés internacional d'Arqueologia Clàssica (Tarragona 1993)*, 157–65. Barcelona.

Levy, E. (1989) "Nero's 'Apollonia' series: the Achaean context," *NC* 149: 59–68.

_____(1986) "Apparition en Grèce de l'idée de village," *Ktèma* 11: 117–127.

Lotze, D. (1981) "Zwischen Politen und Metöken. Passivbürger im klassischen Athen," *Klio* 63: 159–178.

MacMullen, R. (1970) "Market-days in the Roman empire," *Phoenix* 24: 333–41.

Meyer, E. (1979) "Naupaktos," *Paulys Real-Encyclopädie der classischen Altertumswissenschaft* 16.2, col. 1993.

Oberhummer, E. (1941) "Photike," *RE* 20.1, col. 60–62.

Papazoglou, F. (1982) "Le territoire de la colonie de Philippes," *BCH* 106: 89–106.

_____(1988) *Les villes de Macédoine à l'époque romaine* (*BCH* Supplément 16), Paris.

Percival, J. (1976) *The Roman Villa. An Historical Introduction*, Berkeley.

Petropoulos, M. (1994) "Agroikies Patraikes," in P.N. Doukellis and L.G. Mendoni, eds., *Structures rurales et sociétés antiques*, 404–24. Besançon.

Petropoulos M. and A.D. Rizakis (1994) "Settlements patterns and landscape in the coastal area of Patras. Preliminary report," *JRA* 7: 183–207.

Pikoulas, Y. (1995) "Viticulture in ancient Peloponnesus," *Peloponnesiaka* KA: 269–88 (Modern Greek).

Pleket, H.W. (1984) "City elites and economic activities," *Acts of the 8th International Conference of Greek and Latin Epigraphy*, 134–143. Athens.

Rhomaios, K.A. (1927) "Parartema," *ArchDelt* 1924–25: 455.

Rigsby, R. (1976) "Cnossus and Capua," *Transactions of the American Philological Society* 106: 311–30.

Rizakis, A.D. (1990a) "Cadastres et espace rural dans le nord-ouest du Péloponnèse," *Dialogues d'histoire anciennes* 16: 259–80.

_____(1990b) "Sumbole ste melete tou romaikou apoikismou tes BD Peloponnesou," *Meletemata* 10: 321–37.

_____(1990c) "Romaikes epembaseis sto astiko kai agrotiko topio ton poleon tes Peloponnesou," *Praktika Etaireias Peloponnesiakon Spoudon* D': 433–48.

_____(1992) *Paysages d'Achaïe. Le bassin du Péiros et la plaine occidentale*, Athens.

_____(1994) "E Peloponnesos kata ten autokratorike epoche: poleis, upaithros chora kai koinonike kinetikoteta," in P.N. Doukellis and L.G. Mendoni, eds., *Structures rurales et sociétés antiques*, 397–404. Besançon.

_____(1995a) *Achaie I. Testimonia des cités achéennes*, Athens.

_____(1995b) "Grands domaines et petites propriétés dans le Péloponnèse sous l'Empire," in *Du latifundium au latifondo: un héritage de Rome, un création médiévale ou moderne? (Actes de la Table ronde internationale du CNRS, organisée à l'Université Michel de Montaigne-Bourdeaux III, 17–19 Dec. 1992)*, 219–38. Paris.

————(1996) "Colonies romaines des côtes occidentales grecques. Populations et territoires," *Dialogues d'histoire anciennes* 22: 255–324

Robert, L. (1948) "Un juriste romain dans une inscription de Beroia," *Hellenica* V, 29–34. Paris.

Romano, D.G. (1993) "Post-146 B.C. land use in Corinth and planning of the Roman Colony of 44 B.C.," in T.E. Gregory, ed., *The Corinthia in the Roman Period (JRA* Supplemetary Series 8), 9–30. Ann Arbor.

————(1995) "Remote sensing, GIS and electronic surveying: reconstructing the city plan and landscape of Roman Corinth," in J. Hugget and N. Ryan, eds., *Computer Applications and Quantitative Methods in Archaelogy (BAR-IS* 600), 163–74. Oxford.

Romano, D.G. and B.C. Schoenbrun (1994) "A computerized architectural and topographical survey of Ancient Corinth," *Journal of Field Archaeology* 29: 177–90.

Rostovtzeff, M. (1957) *The Social and Economic History of the Roman Empire II*, (2nd edn.) Oxford.

Rothaus, R.M. (1994) "Urban space, agricultural apace and villae in Late Roman Corinth," in P.N. Doukellis and L.G. Mendoni, eds., *Structures rurales et sociétés antiques*, 391–96. Besançon.

Samsaris, D. (1994) *E romaike apoikia tes Photikes ste Thesprotia tes Epeirou*, Ioannina.

Triantaphyllopoulos, D.D. (1984) "E mesaionike Photike kai e these tes sten palaia Epeiro," in *Praktika tou 10ou diethnous Sunedriou Christianikes Archaiologias*, B': 577–84. Thessalonica.

Thulin, C. (1913) *Corpus Agrimensorum Romanorum* I.i, Leipzig.

Vittinghoff, F. (1952) *Römische Kolonisation and Bürgerrechtspolitik unter Caesar und Augustus*, Mainz .

Whittaker, C.R. (1990) "The consumer city revisited: the *vicus* and the city," *JRA* 3: 110–118.

Williams II, C.K. (1993) "Corinth as commercial center," in T.E. Gregory, ed., *The Corinthia in the Roman Period (JRA* Supplementary Series 8), 31–46. Ann Arbor.

3. The Syrian Desert under the Romans

Michał Gawlikowski

Regional Topography

The land of ancient Syria, being the western half of the so-called Fertile Crescent, borders to the south and the south-east on a band of dry steppe, included approximately between the isohyets of 250 mm and 150 mm of annual rainfall, that is between the dry farming area of western and northern Syria and the true desert of Arabia (Fig. 1). This intermediate area, known in Arabic as *bādiya*, becomes green during some months and can be used for migratory raising of sheep and camels, and even for occasional farming in *wadi* beds in good years. It was the home of some of these 'dimorphic' societies (Rowton 1976) which tend to establish themselves on the ecological borders, to make the best use of the complementary resources offered by two different environments and two contrasting ways of life, in this case nomad pastoralism and sedentary farming.

The area under scrutiny extends over parts of present-day Syria and Jordan, following on the inside the western half of the crescent formed by the agricultural lands in the great river valleys of Syria and Mesopotamia and in the hill country around them (Sartre 1991: 311). The eastern part of the *bādiya* crescent runs along and between the Euphrates and Tigris rivers and does not concern us here. West of the Euphrates this belt is up to 200 km wide near the great bend of the river, to become thinner further south where it runs parallel to the mountains of Lebanon and surrounds the depression of the Dead Sea on the northern side before reaching the Mediterranean near Gaza. East of Palestine, a larger tract of agricultural land extends eastwards over the plain of Ḥawrān, reducing the intermediate zone to the outer slopes of the volcanic Jabal al-Drūz mountains. North from there the *bādiya* encloses the large Ghuta oasis around Damascus and then follows the Anti-Lebanon range and the fringe of the Orontes valley, before turning east to follow the course of the Euphrates, leaving to settled life the limestone hills of northern Syria.

Further south and inside the great arch of the *bādiya*, the steppe becomes gradually the stony desert called *ḥamad*, where only rare wells allow for human life and the seasonal presence of flocks (Fig. 2). On the outer borders of the Ḥawrān, one finds the barren lava fields called *ḥarra*, even less hospitable (Fig. 3). The southern limit of the *bādiya* is roughly marked by the hills crossing from the Anti-Lebanon to the Euphrates, passing through the oasis of Palmyra. Beyond, the desert reaches

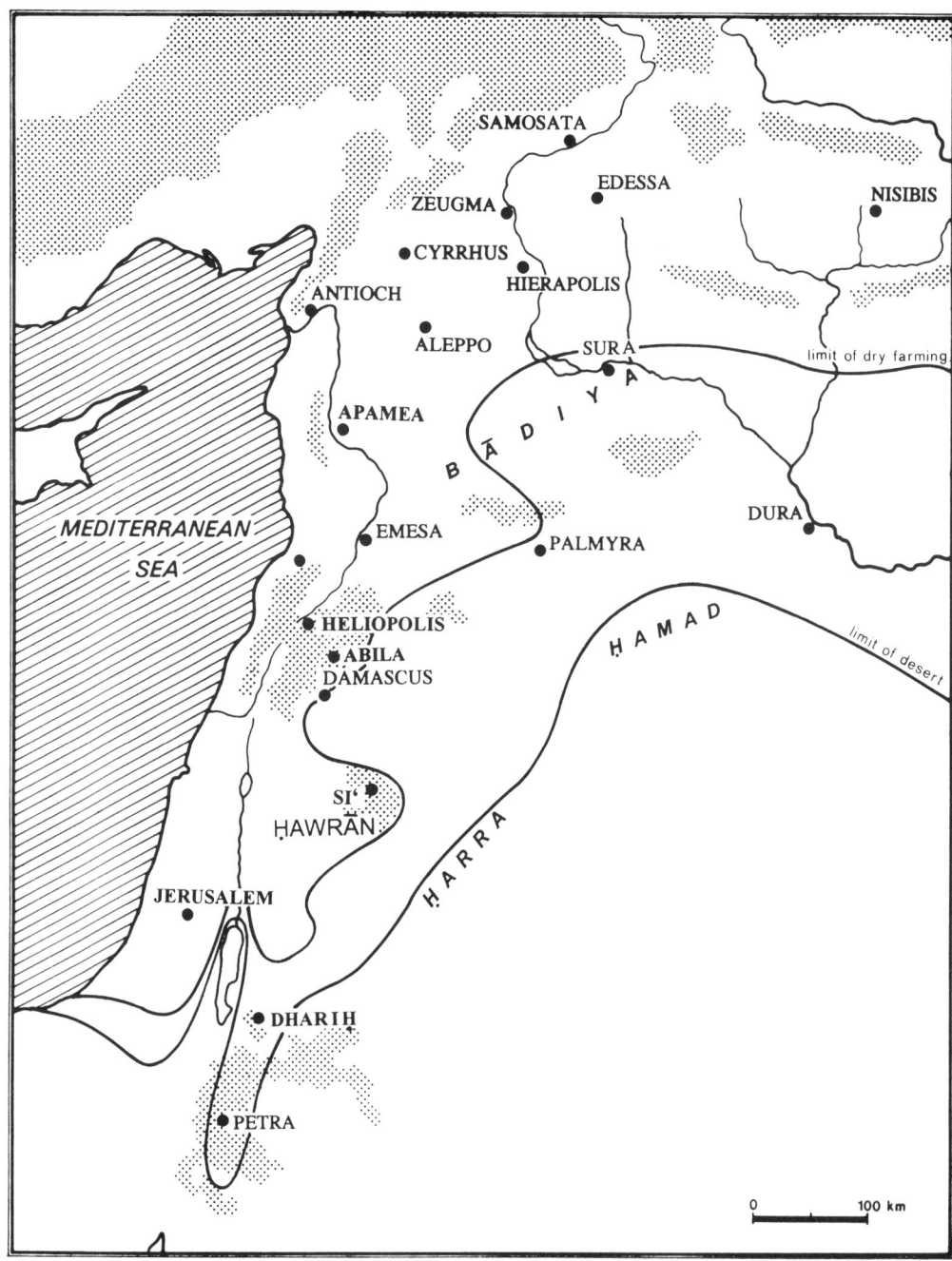

Figure 1. Map of Syria and Palestine, showing the extent of the bādiya *and the sites mentioned in the text*
(Drawn by M. Puszkarski)

Fig. 2. The Syrian ḥamad *with a flock of sheep (Photo M. Gawlikowski)*

from the Euphrates to the borders of Egypt across the Negev and the Sinai. Only the camel-herding Bedouin can sustain themselves in this harsh environment.

Unlike its counterpart in the other half of the crescent, the arid zone of Syria is not crossed by fertile river valleys allowing more intimate relations between peasants and pastoralists. The Middle Euphrates to the east provided opportunities for very limited settlement only, although it constituted an excellent access route to Mesopotamia. The *bādiya* is, therefore, a rather compact domain of nomadic tribes living on their herds of sheep and goats, and moving with them quite close to the surrounding agricultural lands in the dry season. At all times, the settled population tended to regard the nomads with distrust, as primitive and dangerous robbers lurking on the outer margins of the civilized world. Yet this opposition was not as clear-cut as alleged by our sources, both ancient and modern, and a great deal of interaction was usually taking place between the Desert and the Sown (Rowton 1973; Briant 1982: 39–51).

The settled part of Syria is much more varied, including a range of distinct landscapes from high mountains and rocky plateaux to river flatland, often divided into small, well delimited regions. For that reason, the country was never unified under a native ruler in antiquity, while foreign powers controlled not so much a single country as an array of cantons of very different characteristics. Kingdoms, free cities, temple estates, peasant communities, and tribal territories existed side by side at different periods, often confined within specific natural pockets.

Fig. 3. The border between the ḥarra *and the fields in the Ḥawrān (Photo M. Gawlikowski)*

The annexation of Syria by Pompey in 64 BC concerned in the first place the surviving rump of the once proud Seleucid kingdom, which at the time still extended from the Mediterranean to the Euphrates, but hardly beyond the lower Orontes valley. Practically all that remained consisted of the urban territories of Greek cities such as Antioch, Apamea, Seleucia-in-Pieria and Laodicea-on-the-Sea (these four making up the Seleucid *tetrapolis*), Cyrrhus, Beroea (Aleppo), and Seleucia-on-the-Euphrates (later simply Zeugma, i.e. 'Bridgehead'). To this Pompey added the often extensive territories of Phoenician cities of the coast, which had gained recently a large measure of independence, such as Aradus, Berytus, Sidon, and Tyre. He included also a range of small cities in Palestine and Transjordan, some of which claimed Greek origins and became known collectively as Decapolis. By this time, some of these places had been subjugated by the Hasmonean kings of Judaea or local strongmen (Jones 1971: 256–269; Rey-Coquais 1978).

The map of the new province, so far as it could be drawn on existing evidence, would thus resemble a patchwork: between the usually extensive territories of the individual cities there were enclaves of client kingdoms and numerous 'tetrarchies' which in some cases preserved their autonomy to the end of the first century AD. With some exceptions, most notably of Judaea, these were primarily principalities created during the final decay of the Seleucid power by tribal chiefs of definitely, or presumably, nomadic origin. Such principalities were usually located on the brink of the *bādiya*, encroaching on the areas of cultivable land.

Nomads and Sedentaries

Some of the richest cropland of ancient Syria lay in the fertile Beqa' valley between the Lebanon and Anti-Lebanon ranges, and along the Orontes river further north. From the first century BC these parts were under the sway of the Ituraeans, a tribe whose original homeland can be vaguely situated somewhere in northern Transjordan and who had first occupied the slopes of Mt. Hermon, and then of the Lebanon ranges (Schotroff 1982). The kingdom of another tribe, the Hemesenians, had been carved out north of the Ituraean possessions, with the capital at Emesa on the middle Orontes, on land settled and tilled for millennia (Sullivan 1977). If both these tribes had apparently once been nomadic, this had ceased to be the case by the time they are first mentioned as already in control of their conquests. We do hear, in passing from Strabo (16.1.28; 16.2.10), of nomad chieftains in the desert along the middle Euphrates as far as Babylonia, including one Alchaidamnus, a volatile ally of the Romans and king of the Rhambaeans. By that time, some form of civic organization must have existed in the oasis of Palmyra. A score of other principalities and tribal districts, most of them apparently in the mountains of northern Syria, are recorded by name alone in Pliny, who also mentions wholesale some seventeen more 'tetrarchies with barbarian names'(*HN* 5.23).

All of the nomads involved in sharing the spoils of the moribund Seleucid kingdom are usually described as Arabs, and indeed many, if not all, seem to have spoken a dialect close to the later Classical Arabic. This does not mean, as is usually maintained (e.g. Dussaud 1955), that they emerged at some point as conquerors from the depths of Arabia. This deep-rooted general theory is not, in fact, supported by any real evidence. On the contrary, the fact that the nomads of the outer desert in the *ḥarra* and the Ḥijāz spoke a more conservative variant of Arabic seems to preclude such a migration (Gawlikowski 1995a). The ancestors of the Ituraeans, Hemesenians, Rhambaeans, and others were most probably living in the Syrian *bādiya* from times immemorial, moving according to season between the steppe and the fringe of the settled land, only establishing themselves and subjugating the local peasant populations when such a course became feasible.

A similar situation prevailed in Mesopotamia, where nomads roamed the desert between the Euphrates and the Tigris. A part of this country was known as 'Arabia' to Xenophon in 401 BC (*An.* 1.5.1). Later, according to Strabo, some of the tribesmen turned to catering to caravans (16.1.27). In due time they came under the control of the cities and the settled rulers of that country: an *arabarches* resided in the Parthian-dominated Dura-Europos, and his counterpart was appointed over Arabs subject to the kingdom of Edessa further north. The city of Hatra in the desert west of the Tigris grew up around a major sanctuary whose high-priests in the second half of the second century AD were given, presumably by the Parthian rulers, the title of 'kings of the Arabs' or 'of Arabia' (Aggoula 1995). Yet the inscriptions left in Hatra and in or around Edessa are conceived in Aramaic, and there is no doubt that this was the spoken language of these cities, as shown by the later development of Syriac literature out of the dialect of Edessa (notwithstanding the Arab-sounding names of the Abgar dynasty there). In Hatra, the texts clearly distinguish between the 'Hatraeans' and 'Arabs', that is between the city dwellers and the nomads (Dijkstra 1990). It is by no means sure that the term of *'Arab* referred always and everywhere to the speakers of the language so called. It certainly referred to the nomadic way of life, as in the common usage of the Near East where until very recently *'Arab* means simply 'nomads', corresponding to the ancient Greek *Scenitae*, or 'tent-dwellers' (Briant 1982: 113–125) – not necessarily speakers of a particular language.

Remarkably enough, the inscriptions of Palmyra – Aramaic or Greek – never use the term, even though the oasis was surrounded by nomadic territory and though people of nomadic origin must have accounted for an important part of the population. While no Arabic etymology can be ascertained for the rare toponyms in the area around Palmyra which have come down to us, including the name of Tadmor for Palmyra itself (Gawlikowski 1995b), a high proportion of Arabic personal names appear among the most frequently used, and several typically Arab deities found their way into the local pantheon. While there is no reason to doubt that some tribesmen in the Syrian desert in Roman times could have been native speakers of Aramaic, as they certainly were in the Iron Age, most of them must by that time have spoken Arabic, even if Aramaic remained the means of communicating with their settled neighbors.

A convincing case has been made for Arabic as the spoken idiom of the Nabataeans (Cantineau 1934/35), yet even they used Aramaic in writing. From the earliest description of the Nabataeans, referring to events in 311 BC, it is clear that they were then a tribe of tent-dwellers, having already acquired a notable position in the caravan trade (Diodorus 19.94–100). Settling at Petra in the fourth century BC, they preserved many features of their nomadic origins, while managing to control a large area east and south of the Dead Sea, extending northwards as far as the rich corn lands around Bosra. The Nabataean kings, attested sparingly from the second century BC and known better only in the following century, apparently presided over a motley collection of nomadic tribes and farming communities in the marginal lands of southern Syria (Starcky 1966; Bowersock 1983). Controlling vast expanses of the desert as far as Egypt and deep into Ḥijāz, the Nabataeans mastered the art of employing the extremely scarce water resources of their country for agriculture and settled life. Many of their settlements, including the capital Petra itself, survived either solely or chiefly on rainwater collected with considerable skill by means of dams and cisterns (Dentzer and Zayadine 1992; Graf 1992).

The Nabataeans never succeeded in long controlling any of the Greek or Hellenized cities of the region, although they managed to take and keep Damascus for a short time in the first century BC. The only urban centers of the kingdom were those developed by the Nabataeans themselves: Petra, Bostra, and a score of lesser townships in Transjordan and the Negev. While an unprecedented blossoming of settled life would later transform their lands and last into the Byzantine times, it nonetheless remained marginal, and nomadism continued there as a constant and prevailing mode of existence. Deep to the south, the trading stations on the principal caravan tracks, such as Ḥegra in the Ḥijāz or Jawf at the head of the Wadi Sirḥān, marked the Nabataean presence in a region where settled life is found only in some oases.

From Pompey to Trajan, the Nabataean kingdom remained one of Rome's clients, more or less on par with the realm of Herod and some other petty principalities of Syria, if perhaps less dependent owing to its peripheral position. Perhaps briefly annexed from 3–1 BC (Bowersock 1983: 54–56), it was finally transformed into the Roman province of Arabia in AD 106: the last client of the Augustan period to be annexed. Rome inherited thus a desert frontier, or rather the control of a vast desert area where no fixed line would be conceivable (Gatier and Salles 1988).

Other clients disappeared earlier. This was the fate of the tetrarchy founded about 70 BC by a certain Ptolemy son of Mennaeus (Arabic Maʿnai) in the Beqaʿ Valley (ancient Massyas) and in southern Syria. He styled himself a high-priest, possibly of the sanctuary at Heliopolis which was later developed to colossal proportions under the regime of the Roman colony. In the first instance, however, Ptolemy appears to have been a tribal chief of the Ituraeans. In 23 and 20 BC, after the reign of his second successor Zenodorus, the Ḥawrān and the adjoining districts were given to King Herod, and the Beqaʻ assigned about the same time to a newly established colony of Augustan veterans. Small Ituraean tetrarchies survived around Arca in northern Lebanon and Abila to the west of Damascus until AD 53. Under Vespasian, the kingdom of Commagene on the upper Euphrates was annexed to the province of Syria, about the same time as Emesa on the middle Orontes. The former Ituraean districts in southern Syria remained largely under the control of the Herodian princes as late as AD 93, when they were finally placed under direct Roman rule, a few years before the Nabataean kingdom.

The ease with which the Roman government pushed all these dynasts around, giving and taking their estates in an apparently capricious way, resulted partly from features common to these lands. Leaving aside the special case of Judaea, determined by its religious singularity, and to some extent the Nabataean kingdom as it evolved during the first century, the districts left to local rulers shared the characteristics of being non-urban and little Hellenized. By comparison, the territories of the Greek and Phoenician cities in the area, with which these kingdoms and tetrarchies were intermingled (especially in southern Syria and Transjordan) in a kind of jigsaw puzzle, belonged to the province from the beginning. It seems that the Romans considered the cities of the Decapolis as a part of the civilized Mediterranean world, whereas they simply left – for the time being – tribal areas to native rulers. Indeed, the Greek names and the Hellenic education of many of these local dynasts do not reflect the general cultural situation in their domains. Long after their annexation, the activities of the land-surveyors of AD 297 show that villages remained the basic administrative units in the parts of southern Syria outside of the Decapolis, in contrast to the much larger city territories elsewhere (Millar 1993: 535–544).

The nomadic population on the margins of the village zone no doubt participated to some extent in the slow process of acculturation (Villeneuve 1989). For instance, the *strategoi nomadôn* attested in some villages on the eastern slopes of the Ḥawrān were styled at the same time as 'ethnarchs' or 'phylarchs': these were recognized tribal chiefs in charge of the auxiliary units provided by their people. Some of these men were buried in sedentary communities, commemorated in Greek, and could well have taken root in the Ḥawrān villages, together with some of their folk (Sartre 1982b: 123; Grushevoi 1985). Definite facts remain, however, extremely scarce.

Some nomads certainly did settle down at one time or another. In some cases this could have been a result of conquest, as for the Ituraeans in the Beqaʻ and the Anti-Lebanon or Hemesenians on the middle Orontes; the plain fact remains, however, that we know next to nothing about these tribes except their names and the names of their chiefs. While the names of the Ituraean Ptolemy and his successors Lysanias and Zenodorus suggest their being Hellenized, another Ituraean prince bears the name of Sohaemus (Arabic Suḥaim), which was also used by the dynasty of Emesa along with those of Sampsigeramus (Šamšigeram) and Jamblichus (Yamliku). Most probably, the tribesmen soon melted into the settled population of the districts they occupied thanks to the Seleucid decline.

Further north, the territory of Apamea reached near the Euphrates, but there is no hint how this large nomadic area, called Parapotamia (Strabo 16.2.11) was administered by the Greek city. Matters seem clearer in the case of Palmyra. A few inscriptions and some early architectural monuments demonstrate the beginnings of urban life in this isolated oasis during the first century BC. It appears that, about the turn of the Christian era, Palmyra formed a native polity (Aramaic *gebal*, translated as *polis* or *demos*) administered by elected 'treasurers' (Gawlikowski 1973: 41). There is no way of telling how far back in time these institutions reached. This entity was incorporated into the province of Syria, most probably by Germanicus in AD 17, apparently leaving the ancestral institutions in place. By the second half of the century, however, inscriptions already reveal a city council, elected archons, and foreign freedmen acting as publicans: in other words, as far as we know, the standard régime of a provincial city (Will 1992: 39–41). Unlike other provincial cities, however, Palmyra retained Aramaic for official use, if usually doubling it with Greek.

In spite of its cultural particularity, this 'republic of merchants', as it is sometimes called, remained under the firm control of Roman governors with no hint of independence until the paroxysms of the third century. While its northern and western frontiers (with Emesa and Apamea) were fixed, or confirmed, by the Roman authority in the early first century, the civic territory was practically open to the south, fading into the desert *hamad*. To the east, Palmyra controlled a stretch of the Euphrates valley downstream from Dura-Europos, with the island fortress of 'Ana and grazing lands in the Wadi Ḥawrān by the river, as well as military stations along the desert tracks leading there (Gawlikowski 1983). These outposts thus marked the limits of the Roman empire, but they were apparently not manned by regular Roman troops. In a sense, the territory of Palmyra formed a buffer zone, while the city itself remained solidly a part of the province.

The regular caravan traffic to the great river and down to the Persian Gulf presupposed conditions of security that only a complex web of relations with the nomads could have assured (Will 1992: 58–66). And no one but the nomad tribesmen could have provided the necessary growth potential for Palmyra and for the creation of the desert ranches in the north-western hills, essential for the mass breeding of pack animals for the Palmyrene caravans (Schlumberger 1951). Palmyra appears thus as a case of successful settlement of nomads within the pre-existent frame of civic life, prompted by the opportunities for trade which opened with the Roman peace.

Another oasis, situated to the north and only some 20 km distant from the Euphrates, was Mabbug, known in Greek as Hierapolis. A major sanctuary of Atargatis, it was ruled under the Persian Empire by its high-priests, probably remaining under their control during the Hellenistic period, though the local coins have been minted to our knowledge only about the time of Alexander, and not later. Our principal source, the essay of Lucian on the Syrian Goddess, preserved no trace of the sanctuary's continuing autonomy, but portrays it as the seat of a very fervent cult and the goal of pilgrimages from all over Syria and beyond (see Elsner, this volume). Although Hierapolis was situated on the border of nomadic territory, there is nothing in the extant evidence to suggest special ties with the nomadic tribes of the region, such as made the fortune of that other temple city of the *bādiya*, Hatra in Mesopotamia.

Still another important sanctuary of the border zone lay at Siʻ at the northern edge of the Ḥawrān and close to the city of Kanatha. Built for the god Baʻalšamin by a certain Malikat from 33/32 to 2/1 BC (that is, mainly under King Herod), it is said to have been frequented by the nomads from the *ḥarra*, although no firm proof of such gatherings there and no contacts with the villagers can be adduced (Dentzer 1991). It is also very possible that the origins of the great sanctuary of Heliopolis (Baalbek) can be attributed to the Ituraean princes. Many less important temples in the desert area could have formed attraction points for nomads, such as the Nabataean temples of Wadi Ramm, Khirbet el-Dharīḥ or Khirbet et-Tannūr (Sartre 1991: 494–495), or as Ruwwafa in the Ḥijāz, where the tribe of the Thamudeni marked their allegiance to Rome by building a temple to Marcus Aurelius and Lucius Verus (Sartre 1982b: 130; Bowersock 1983: 96).

Settled nomads could thus develop a highly sophisticated royal court as at Petra (and no doubt in Emesa), a caravan city as at Palmyra, or sustain a sanctuary. Normally, however, remains of the actual nomadic way of life are hard to come by. Fortunately, there is one massive exception to that rule. Nomads of the *ḥarra* in north-eastern Jordan and southern Syria have left thousands upon thousands of graffiti while keeping their herds or mounting guard among the basalt stones (Macdonald 1993). Written by unschooled hands, apparently as a mere pastime, these short texts reflect a tribal society hardly touched by any western influence. These populations, known collectively today under the entrenched misnomer of Safaites, in fact represented various Arab tribes living east and south of the Ḥawrān. They used a South Arabian alphabet rather than the Aramaic letters of their settled neighbors, which surely would have been more useful if the chief intention was communication with the outside world. As far as we know, the response to Hellenism on the part of these people was minimal. No more than half a dozen Greek-Safaitic bilinguals are known to date, and these are composed almost entirely of proper names (Milik 1985). Nor is there any reason to suppose that those tent-dwellers of the Syrian desert who had *not* come to the eccentric idea of writing on loose stones were different in any significant respect from these literate shepherds.

The degree of conflict between the nomads and the sedentary, and the nature of the response of Roman authorities to this threat, has recently become a matter for lively dispute. While some see the desert tribes as potential aggressors requiring a constant military presence on the fortified *limes* (Parker 1986; 1987), others consider them as practically innocuous (Banning 1986; Graf 1989; Isaac 1990: 68–77), and the Arabian *limes* of the second century first and foremost as a military road. What is clear is that there is simply no record of serious nomadic incursions under the early empire (Sartre 1991: 332). Whether this resulted from a salutary awe, or from positive steps taken by the Romans, seems a moot question.

The Roman road, traced by the legate Traianus in the time of Vespasian, ran to the fortress of Sura on the Euphrates by the way of Palmyra (Bowersock 1973). It served the obvious military aim of facilitating troop transfers from southern Syria and from the heavily garrisoned Judaea to the Parthian front. Its extension across the new province of Arabia all the way to Aqaba (called by modern scholars *via nova Traiana*) completed this scheme, whatever its other functions might have been. While the dating of those stations along this line which lie in modern Syria remains largely uncertain, it seems that only from the time of Diocletian did this part of the road become a real *limes*, protected with frequent military forts which could, if need be, keep the nomads in check. This *strata Diocletiana* was apparently the answer to the power vacuum left by the demise of Palmyra (Bauzou 1993).

Arts and Architecture

The authors of the Safaitic inscriptions show no inclination for settled life (Villeneuve 1989: 135). The villages of the Ḥawrān were inhabited by people writing chiefly in Greek. Some Aramaic inscriptions have been found in the southern part of that region, that is within the borders of the Nabataean kingdom (Starcky 1985), but none in Safaitic, even though the tribal structure of society is very prominent among these sedentary people (Sartre 1982a; 1985; Macdonald 1993: 352–367). Since their proper names are mostly Semitic (but not necessarily Arabic), it would appear that this region possessed a stable indigenous population, not necessarily of nomadic origin, strongly attracted to the Greek way of life. Their temples, their sculpture, their art clearly illustrate such ambitions from the second century AD onwards (Dentzer 1986). As there are few traces of life in the Ḥawrān in Hellenistic times, it is just possible that these country folk might have originated from other parts of Syria, settling the area with encouragement from the Herodian rulers (Sartre 1985).

Considering the artistic production of Roman Syria, Ernest Will (1965) long ago distinguished three rough geographical zones, each of which responded differently to the stimulus of Hellenism. In the first place, in addition to the Seleucid foundations of northern Syria, there were thoroughly Hellenized Phoenician and Palestinian cities of the coast. The artistic expression of these is entirely in a Greek idiom, and so is their epigraphic record during the Roman period. Such native traditions as did survive can be traced there, strongly altered, only in religious iconography. The re-emergence of Aramaic in late antiquity forces us to admit, however, the continuous, if concealed, presence of a non-Hellenized rural population around Antioch and other urban enclaves.

Will's second zone includes primarily the southern part of Syria, perceived as an area where rural isolation led to schematic and often naive rendering of borrowed Greek themes, such as the ever-present statues of winged Victories in the Ḥawrān. This provincial art is represented chiefly in the collections of the Suwaydā Museum, peopled with rather rudimentary squarish, frontal statues (Bolelli 1985). Similar isolated finds have also been made, for instance in Emesa or Aleppo. New research has both enriched the repertory of monuments and refined their understanding. In the early architectural decoration of the Ḥawrān, beginning with the Siʿ sanctuary (Dentzer 1991) but also in Gerasa and elsewhere (Dentzer-Feydy 1992), the traditions of Seleucid art and architecture can now be recognized, surviving in local, simplified forms. The progressive replacement of 'heterodox' capitals, and other idiosyncratic solutions, by the standard Corinthian order took place during the first century AD in Palmyra and Gerasa, somewhat later in the Ḥawrān – coinciding with the annexation to the empire (Dentzer-Feydy 1986; 1988). Some typical Syrian features, such as covering of door frames with scrolls, persisted throughout the Roman period.

Finally, the third zone of Will covered the domain of so-called Parthian art, including Palmyra, Dura-Europos on the Euphrates, and Hatra in Mesopotamia. According to Will and Schlumberger (1970: 67–144), this is a more remote offshoot of Hellenism, stemming from a selective assimilation of the classical repertory. Generalized frontal representations in sculpture and painting are thought to result from the exclusive imitation of a single posture observed in Greek art, one particularly striking to an unaccustomed and unsophisticated Oriental observer. Whether the origin of this convention is indeed to be sought in the Parthian lands is debatable: the basalt sculpture of the Ḥawrān displays similar attitudes, while Iranian influence there is improbable. A Syrian origin for this artistic expression has been recently claimed (Ploug 1988).

Whatever the origins of 'Parthian art', the tripartite system of Will basically still stands some thirty years later. Our present subject excludes the first two zones: the cities of the coast and the rural world of southern Syria. We are concerned with the third less documented area, the belt running parallel to the settled land of the Fertile Crescent, stretching from the Red Sea to the Middle Euphrates and beyond. Here only certain points, such as Petra or Palmyra, provide reasonably ample information. The rest of the desert was the exclusive domain of the nomads and, in this sequence of regions defined by the decreasing influence of Greek art, is perhaps best considered as a fourth zone, one defined by the sheer absence of such influence.

The variety of art and architecture current in the lands of Nabataean settlement is now much better documented. Sites such as the currently excavated Khirbet el-Dharīḥ above the Wadi Ḥesā, or the previously uncovered neighboring sanctuary of Khirbet Tannūr – together with many others in Negev and Transjordan – show an intensive new village life based on elaborate water catchment procedures. The temples usually contain, behind a profusion of niches and scrolls on the façade, inner shrines in the form of a solid cube with a niche, as at Tannūr, or enclose a raised platform adorned with columns, as at Dharīḥ or in the capital city Petra, where it has been interpreted as the throne of the deity. The niches in the walls of these temples, disguised as Classical decoration, in fact reproduce independent votive tabernacles in the form of a shallow recess within a moulded frame (Arnaud 1986).

The square temple plan (owing nothing to a once-alleged Persian influence), together with the peculiar use of Greek decorative elements, the tendency to cover the walls, door-frames, and even thresholds with running ornaments, and the placement of heads or busts on the capitals, can be found across the Ḥawrān in the first century AD (Dentzer-Feydy 1986). These 'pre-provincial' features, quite often rendered with a degree of clumsiness not entirely owing to the difficulties of working the local basalt stone, disappear gradually during the second century, when this relatively isolated region became annexed for good as part of a Roman province (first of Syria, then of Arabia). These features can also be found in the early manifestations of art in Palmyra, if disappearing earlier there (Seyrig 1940).

It seems to be generally accepted, following Henri Seyrig, that the Arab desert tradition contributed to the common body of religious beliefs of Roman Syria the popularity of the Sun god (Seyrig 1971; cf. Tubach 1986), as well as the habit of conceiving various deities as warriors, often represented in Roman legionary gear (Seyrig 1970; cf. Gawlikowski 1990b). In both cases, novelty is a matter of degree: solar gods and armed gods were always present in the pantheon of the ancient Near East. They are, however, especially prominent in places where Arab settlement and influence was paramount or can be assumed as important. Seyrig linked this with the warlike customs of the nomads, as distinct from the traditions of farming and urban societies who worshipped, among others, the weather-god Hadad or Ba'alšamin (known in the Roman period as Zeus in many local varieties, including Zeus Belos of Apamea or Palmyra) and the goddess Atargatis (often called simply Dea Syria). The old gods never lost their leading position, while admitting among them a new generation of desert warriors (Fig. 6). There is not much evidence for the latter being imported from the Arabian peninsula, and none for any movement of populations which could have brought them to Syria.

The avoidance of the human form as cult object is one common, though by no means general, feature of Nabataean iconography claimed to have emerged from the desert tradition (Pietrzykowski 1985; Patrich 1990). Rectangular blocks, plain or provided with facial features, can be seen represented on many a rock relief; one stele of this form was found in the 'Temple of the Winged Lions' in

Fig. 4. The square-faced idol of a Nabatean goddess in an architectural frame, from the 'Temple of the Winged Lions' at Petra (After Gawlikowski 1990a, pl. 1)

Fig. 5. Head of Dionysos, fragmentary panel from Petra (After Gawlikowski 1990a, pl. 4)

Petra (Fig. 4). We know from elsewhere that such a stone represented the main Nabataean god Dušara in his Petra temple (*Suda* 2.713). The famous betyl of Elagabal, venerated in Emesa and carried to Rome in the third century in the train of its imperial priest and namesake, belongs in the same tradition (Seyrig 1971: 340–345). The idea of gods being better impersonated by plain stones than by human figures certainly goes back to the remote Oriental antiquity of Bronze Age betyls.

On the other hand, the presence of the royal court at Petra favored the introduction of Hellenistic art at its finest (McKenzie 1990). A series of busts of divinities from the entrance to the great Qasr el-Bint temenos at Petra is by no means provincial (Fig. 5). The stucco work on the walls of the Qasr, and above all the imposing series of eighteen, certainly royal, rock tomb façades, directly reflect the architecture of the Greek East, and of Alexandria in particular (in a similar way, the Pompeian painting of the second style reflects these same models). On the other hand, over six hundred other tombs in Petra, and more in Hegra and elsewhere, remain attached to older traditions of the Near East, such as the use of crowsteps and of a cavetto cornice, employing Greek elements only sparingly. After long debate, there is no doubt today that all these monuments should be dated in the first centuries BC/AD – that is under the Nabataean kings and before the Roman annexation (Schmidt-Colinet 1980). The rock-cut tombs, the square temples, the non-figurative idols: all represent indigenous developments stemming from uncertain antecedents and perhaps, in spite of some modern speculation, not of great antiquity. But the royal court imported the metropolitan art of Alexandria and applied it to the tomb façades. Paradoxically, the architecture of that great Hellenistic capital survives most completely on the cliffs of Petra.

Around the turn of the millennium, the city of Palmyra borrowed urban features from rather closer home, most probably from Antioch. While the great temple of Bel, consecrated but not finished in AD 32, is outwardly a Hellenistic pseudo-dipteros, the building retains particularities such as two opposite chapels at the short ends, best explained by the idiosyncrasy of the local cult (see Schmidt-Colinet, this volume). The temple of the Arab goddess Allat, built outside the town about 50 BC, was originally a small shrine, wider than it was deeper, with a statue of the goddess seated in a niche framed with vine scrolls. This original chapel was then enclosed, in the second century, within a Vitruvian cella, quite similar to the contemporary temple of Ba'alšamin, which must likewise have replaced a similar archaic building and which contained an elaborate architectural screen framing a cult relief (Gawlikowski 1989: 339–345). Although no royal patronage was available, Palmyra managed to channel the profits of the caravan trade into temples, colonnades and other buildings, slowly making the desert city akin to any of the more typical coastal centers in Syria (Will 1992: 120–151). As at Petra, this process of acculturation was never quite completed.

This statement is especially true when one considers the plastic art of Palmyra (Colledge 1976). Many hundreds of sculptures depict strictly frontal figures, carved with a love of linear detail in the rendering of costume and jewelry, and most often with an entire indifference to physiognomic truth. While these funerary busts find parallels elsewhere in Syria and in other parts of the Roman world, the Palmyrene style is unmistakable (Parlasca 1985; 1988). Religious relief sculptures, clearly preferred to statues, are striking in their contempt for narrative and in their prefiguration of Byzantine icons (Fig. 6).

The frontal convention appears about the turn of the Christian era in Palmyra, and can be found later in Dura-Europos and in Hatra, when sculpture and painting appear there in the second century. No doubt other urban centers of the *bādiya* shared in this particular style (Schlumberger 1970: 194–

Fig. 6. The desert gods in arms being offered frankincense by the Palmyrene commander of 'Ana (AD 225).
From Umm eṣ-Ṣalabiḫ on the track from Palmyra to Hit on the Euphrates (Photo J. Starcky)

207). The hieratic aspect of figures facing the spectator, the linear, highly realistic approach to the
rendering of detail, but disregard for movement, action, or emotion: all betray an outlook very
different from that of Hellenistic art. This technique conjures the gods and people represented,
forcing through their fixed straightforward glance the feeling of the actual presence of the deities
worshipped or of the deceased commemorated. Hence also the marked preference for relief (and
painting) rather than sculpture in the round: the statues, when they occur, remain strictly frontal
and were intended to turn their roughly finished backs against a wall.

All these manifestations of so-called Parthian art are known from the Aramaic-speaking cities
of the steppe of Syria and Mesopotamia and from isolated find-spots obviously within the range
of these cities (Drijvers 1977). In spite of the name it is commonly given, there is no reason to
attribute the inception and practice of this style to the Parthian court at Ctesiphon (whose art
remains unknown), and even less to the Parthians as a people (Ploug 1988). The masculine fashions
favored in these representations could, however, be described as Iranian, while the Greek himation
was also worn in Palmyra (Will 1992: 106–109). The ample trousers and sleeved tunics, sometimes
richly embroidered and set with stones and usually worn with arms, indeed stem from the Iranian
tradition, but they had become the common garb of the townsfolk in Mesopotamia and parts of
Syria (Fig. 7). Simple camel-drivers, on the other hand, used a kind of apron (none other than the

Fig. 7. A man in Iranian dress being served at a banquet. Funerary monument from Palmyra (Photo: Polish Mission to Palmyra)

loincloth of Arabs of old, as depicted in the Assyrian sculpture) bound around the waist and over a tunic, and sported a small round shield and a spear (Fig. 6). No evidence suggests anything like Parthian sympathies being expressed in the use of the Iranian dress, nor should they be sought for in the style of the plastic arts.

Conclusion

Cultural and ethnic self-consciousness in Roman Syria has recently been the subject of reflection by Fergus Millar (1987; 1993). All nomads were considered Arab in antiquity, although they always used narrower tribal identities to describe themselves. Insofar as the written evidence allows us to see, it is clear that there was no feeling of Arab identity of any kind in Palmyra, whose citizens call themselves Palmyrene and nothing else. The inhabitants of Emesa thought of themselves as

'Phoenicians' in the third century: perhaps simply because the city was part of the province of Syria Phoenice from the time of Septimius Severus, at any rate not because of any demonstrable affinity with Phoenicia proper. In the same way, the inhabitants of the province of Arabia were called Arabs (for example, the emperor Philip the Arab), inheriting the name from the Nabataeans who were commonly called this by Greek and Roman authors and by their Jewish neighbors – no doubt in reference to their nomadic origins.

We know nothing, as Millar observed, of the means employed to hand down literary culture in the vernacular. While there must have been schools teaching Aramaic, at least at an elementary level, and while there must have been a formal chancery tradition in the Nabataean kingdom and in Palmyra, the prestige of Greek remained paramount in higher forms of education. The tombstone for the tutor of Gadimat, king of the Arab Tannūḥ in the late third century, bears a bilingual inscription in illiterate Greek doubled with Nabataean (Millar 1993: 433): bilingualism is typical once some sort of formal culture appears. At the same time, at the sophisticated court of Zenobia, whom the Arab tradition considers as the enemy of the Tannūḥ tribal confederacy, the Greek philosopher Longinus might have seen missionaries from Mesopotamia carrying with them the Manichaean message, probably in the original Aramaic (Will 1992: 202). On the other hand, the curious phenomenon of general literacy among the tribes of the *ḥarra* seems to have been propagated in informal ways and for private use, resulting in no fixed order of letters and indifferent direction of script (Macdonald 1993: 382–388).

The Syrian desert under the Romans saw a development of settled life unprecedented until modern times, the result of a long reign of peace and of growing opportunities for the caravan trade. New sedentary communities did not simply assimilate the Hellenistic civilization of the Syrian coast. Their hybrid culture retained many distinctly native elements, and yet remained conversant with a Hellenic heritage, as expressed in Greek forms of architecture and partly in the use of the Greek language. This desert frontier of the Classical world witnessed the variable absorption of Greek and Roman values, imperfect but not reticent. The early imperial civilization was making steady progress in time and space. It did not recede until several centuries later, as a result of the nomadic intrusions in late antiquity.

Bibliography
Aggoula, B. (1995) "Arabie et Arabes en Mésopotamie (du IIIᵉ siècle av. J.-C. au IIIᵉ siècle ap. J.-C.)," in H. Lozachmeur, ed., *Présence arabe dans le Croissant fertile avant l'Hégire*, 73–79. Paris.
Arnaud, P. (1986) "Les naiskoi en Syrie méridionale," in J.-M. Dentzer, ed., *Hauran I. Recherches archéologiques sur la Syrie du sud à l'époque hellénistique et romaine*, II, 373–86. Paris.
Banning, E.B. (1986) "Peasants, pastoralists and *Pax Romana*: Mutualism in the southern highlands of Jordan," *BASOR* 261: 25–50.
Bauzou, Th. (1993) "Epigraphie et toponymie: le cas de la Palmyrène du sud-ouest," *Syria* 70: 27–50.
Bolelli, G. (1985) "La ronde-bosse de caractère indigène en Syrie du Sud," in J.-M. Dentzer, ed., *Hauran I. Recherches archéologiques sur la Syrie du sud à l'époque hellénistique et romaine*, II, 311–72. Paris.
Bowersock, G.W. (1973) "Syria under Vespasian," *JRS* 63: 133–140.
———(1983) *Roman Arabia*, Cambridge, Mass.
Briant, P. (1982) *Etat et pasteurs au Moyen-Orient ancien*, Paris.
Cantineau, J. (1934/35) "Nabatéen et arabe," *Annales de l'Institut d'Etudes Orientales* 1: 77–97.

Colledge, M.A.R. (1976) *The Art of Palmyra,* London.

Dentzer, J.-M. (1986) "Développement et culture de la Syrie du sud dans la période préprovinciale (Ier s. avant J.-C. – Ier s. après J.-C.," in J.-M. Dentzer, ed., *Hauran I. Recherches archéologiques sur la Syrie du sud à l'époque hellénistique et romaine*, II, 387–420. Paris.

_____(1991) "Hellénisation et cultures indigènes dans la Syrie intérieure: l'exemple du sanctuaire de Si'," in European Cultural Centre of Delphi, ed., *O ellinismos stin Anatoli. International Meeting of History and Archaeology, Delphi 1986*, 269–75. Athens.

Dentzer, J.-M. and F. Zayadine (1992) "L'espace urbain de Pétra," *Studies in the History and Archaeology of Jordan* IV, 233–51. Amman.

Dentzer-Feydy, J. (1986) "Décor architectural et développement du Hauran du Ier siècle avant J.-C. au VIIe siècle après J.-C.," in J.-M. Dentzer, ed., *Hauran I. Recherches archéologiques sur la Syrie du sud à l'époque hellénistique et romaine*, II, 261–310. Paris.

_____(1988) "Frontières et matériel archéologique en Syrie du sud: politique et culture du Ier siècle av. notre ère au IVe siècle de notre ère," in P.-L. Gatier, B. Helly, and J.-P. Rey-Coquais, eds., *Géographie historique au Proche-Orient (Syrie, Phénicie, Arabie grecques, romaines, byzantines)*, 219–239. Paris.

_____(1992) "Le décor architectural en Transjordanie de la période hellénistique à la création de la Province d'Arabie en 106," *Studies in the History and Archaeology of Jordan* IV, 227–32. Amman.

Dijkstra, K. (1990) "State and steppe. The socio-political implications of Hatra inscription 79," *JSS* 35: 81–98.

Drijvers, H.J.W. (1977) "Hatra, Palmyra und Edessa. Die Städte der syrisch-mesopotamischen Wüste in politischer, kulturgeschichtlicher und religionsgeschichtlicher Beleuchtung," *ANRW* II 8: 799–906.

Dussaud, R. (1955) *La pénétration des Arabes en Syrie avant l'Islam*, Paris.

Gatier, P.-L. and J.-F. Salles (1988) "Aux frontières méridionales du domaine nabatéen," in J.-F. Salles, ed., *L'Arabie et ses mers bordières*, 173–87. Lyon.

Gawlikowski, M. (1973) *Le temple palmyrénien. Etude d'épigraphie et de topographie historique*, Warsaw.

_____(1983) "Palmyre et l'Euphrate," *Syria* 60: 53–68.

_____(1989) "Les temples de la Syrie à l'époque hellénistique et romaine," in J.-M. Dentzer and W. Orthmann, eds., *Archéologie et histoire de la Syrie* II, 323–46. Saarbrücken.

_____(1990a) "Les dieux de Nabatéens," *ANRW* II 18.4: 2659–2677.

_____(1990b) "Les dieux de Palmyre," *ANRW* II 18.4: 2605–2658.

_____(1995a) "Les Arabes de Syrie dans l'Antiquité," in K. van Lerberghe and A. Schoors, eds., *Immigration and Emigration within the Ancient Near East (Festschrift E. Lipiński)*, 83–92. Leuven.

_____(1995b) "Les Arabes en Palmyrène," in H. Lozachmeur, ed., *Présence arabe dans le Croissant fertile avant l'Hégire*, 103–108. Paris.

Graf, D.F. (1989) "Rome and the Saracens: reassessing the nomadic menace," in T. Fahd, ed., *L'Arabie préislamique et son environnement historique et culturel. Actes du Colloque de Strasbourg (1987)*, 341–400. Leiden.

_____(1992) "Nabataean settlements and Roman occupation in Arabia Petraea," *Studies in the History and Archaeology of Jordan* IV, 253–60. Amman.

Grushevoi, A.G. (1985) "The tribe 'Ubaishat in Safaitic, Nabataean and Greek inscriptions," *Berytus* 33: 51–54.

Isaac, B. (1990) *The Limits of Empire: The Roman Army in the East*, Oxford.

Jones, A.H.M. (1971) *The Cities of the Eastern Roman Provinces* (2nd edn.), Oxford.

Macdonald, M.C.A. (1993) "Nomads and the Hawrān in the late Hellenistic and Roman periods. A reassessment of the epigraphic evidence," *Syria* 70: 303–413.

McKenzie, J. (1990) *The Architecture of Petra*, London.

Milik, J.T. (1985) "Epigraphie safaïtique," in J.-M. Dentzer, ed., *Hauran I. Recherches archéologiques sur la Syrie du sud à l'époque hellénistique et romaine*, II, 183–88. Paris.

Millar, F. (1987) "Empire, community and culture in the Roman Near East: Greeks, Syrians, Jews and Arabs,"

Journal of Jewish Studies 38: 143–164.

_____(1993) *The Roman Near East 31 BC – AD 337*, Cambridge, Mass.

Parker, S.T. (1986) *Romans and Saracens: A History of the Arabian Frontier,* Winona Lake.

_____(1987) "Peasants, pastoralists and *Pax Romana*: a different view," *BASOR* 265: 35–51.

Parlasca, K. (1985) "Das Verhältnis der palmyrenischen Grabplastik zur römischen Porträtkunst," *RM* 92: 343–356.

Parlasca, K. (1988) "Die Palmyrene – ihr geographischer Rahmen im Lichte der bildenden Kunst und Epigraphik," in P.-L. Gatier, B. Helly, and J.-P. Rey-Coquais, eds., *Géographie historique au Proche-Orient (Syrie, Phénicie, Arabie grecques, romaines, byzantines),* 241–48. Paris.

Patrich, J. (1990) *The Formation of Nabataean Art. Graven Image Prohibition among the Nabataeans,* Jerusalem.

Pietrzykowski, M. (1985) "The origins of the frontal convention in the arts of the Near East," *Berytus* 33: 55–59 (illustrations in *Berytus* 34 [1986]: 135–138).

Ploug, G. (1988) "East Syrian art of 1st century BC–2nd century AD," *Acta Hyperborea* 1: 129–139.

Rey-Coquais, J.-P. (1978) "La Syrie romaine, de Pompée à Dioclétien," *JRS* 48: 44–73.

Rowton, M.B. (1973) "Urban autonomy in a nomadic environment," *JNES* 32: 201–215.

_____(1976) "Dimorphic structure and topology," *OA* 15: 17–31.

Sartre, M. (1982a) "Tribus et clans dans le Ḥawrān antique," *Syria* 59: 77–91.

_____(1982b) *Trois études sur l'Arabie romaine et byzantine* (Collection Latomus 178), Bruxelles.

_____(1985) "Le peuplement et le développement du Hauran antique à la lumière des inscriptions grecques et latines", in J.-M. Dentzer, ed., *Hauran I. Recherches archéologiques sur la Syrie du sud à l'époque hellénistique et romaine,* II, 189–204. Paris.

_____(1991) *L'Orient romain. Provinces et sociétés provinciales en Méditerranée orientale d'Auguste aux Sévères (31 avant J.-C. – 235 ap. J.-C.),* Paris.

Schlumberger, D. (1951) *La Palmyrène du Nord-Ouest. Villages et lieux de culte de l'époque impériale. Recherches archéologiques sur la mise en valeur d'une région du désert par les Palmyréniens,* Paris.

_____(1970) *L'Orient hellénisé. L'art grec et ses héritiers dans l'Asie non méditerranéenne,* Paris.

Schmidt-Colinet, A. (1980) "Nabatäische Felsarchitektur," *BJb* 180: 189–230.

Schottroff, W. (1982) "Die Ituräer," *ZDPV* 98: 125–152.

Seyrig, H. (1940) "Ornamenta Palmyrena antiquiora," *Syria* 21: 277–337.

_____(1970) "Les dieux armés et les Arabes en Syrie," *Syria* 47: 77–112.

_____(1971) "Le culte du Soleil en Syrie à l'époque romaine," *Syria* 48: 337–373.

Starcky, J. (1966) "Pétra et la Nabatène," in L. Pirot, A. Robert, H. Cazelles, and A. Feuillet, eds., *Supplément au Dictionnaire de la Bible* 7, coll. 886–1017. Paris.

_____(1985) "Les inscriptions nabatéennes et l'histoire de la Syrie méridionale et du nord de la Jordanie," in J.-M. Dentzer, ed., *Hauran I. Recherches archéologiques sur la Syrie du sud à l'époque hellénistique et romaine,* II, 167–81. Paris.

Sullivan, R.D. (1977) "The Dynasty of Emesa," *ANRW* II. 8: 189–219.

Tubach, J. (1986) *Im Schatten des Sonnengottes. Der Sonnenkult in Edessa, Harran und Hatra am Vorabend der christlichen Mission,* Wiesbaden.

Villeneuve, F. (1989) "Citadins, villageois, nomades: le cas de la *Provincia Arabia* (IIᵉ-IVᵉ siècles ap. J.-C.)," *Dialogues d'histoire ancienne* 15: 119–140.

Will, E. (1965) "La Syrie romaine entre l'Occident gréco-romain et l'Orient parthe," in *Le rayonnement des civilisations grecque et romaine sur les cultures périphériques* (Actes du VIIIᵉ Congrès d'archéologie classique, Rome 1963), 511–26. Rome.

_____(1992) *Les Palmyréniens. La Venise des sables,* Paris.

4. The Syrian Countryside during the Roman Era

Georges Tate

Our knowledge of the Syrian countryside during the Roman era has made great strides thanks to archeological research done in the region over the last century, and particularly since the nineteen seventies. When one tries to understand what is meant by the rural countryside, by its demography, economy, and society, these data – which are, in some cases, copious – allow one to put into perspective the vast but scattered information of textual sources, of which Heichelheim (1938) offered us a capable and ever-useful synthesis.

The Extension of Peasant-Occupied Territories

Beyond the permanent features marking rural countryside and its economic and social structures (Fig. 1), to which we will later return, the most notable aspect of the history of the countryside in Roman Syria is the considerable extension of the area occupied by sedentary peoples between the first century BC and the end of the third century AD.

The Starting Point

Archeology provides us with hardly any information about the starting point of this process, because no remains of that era have survived. Strabo and Pliny (in Books 7 and 5, respectively), however, are sources of information on the Augustan era and on the first half of the first century AD, respectively. Their writings are difficult to interpret in detail, but they agree that Syrian territory was divided between sedentary peoples on the one hand, and nomads and bandits on the other. What comes out of this is that peasant populations were confined to the areas around cities. On the littoral plains bordered on the east by the Ansariye mountains, there were few nomads, if any (Dussaud 1927; Jones 1972; Millar 1993; Sartre 1991). In contrast, on the interior plateau, cities were only found in the valleys of the Orontes (Lysias, Apamea, Larissa, Arethusa, Laodicea ad Libanum), the tributaries of the Afrin (Cyrrhus), the Qoueiq (Beroea-Aleppo, Qinnesrin, Chalcis) and the Euphrates (Seleucia, Zeugma-Apamea, Europos Amphipolis, Hierapolis, Barbalissos, Zeugma). The valleys

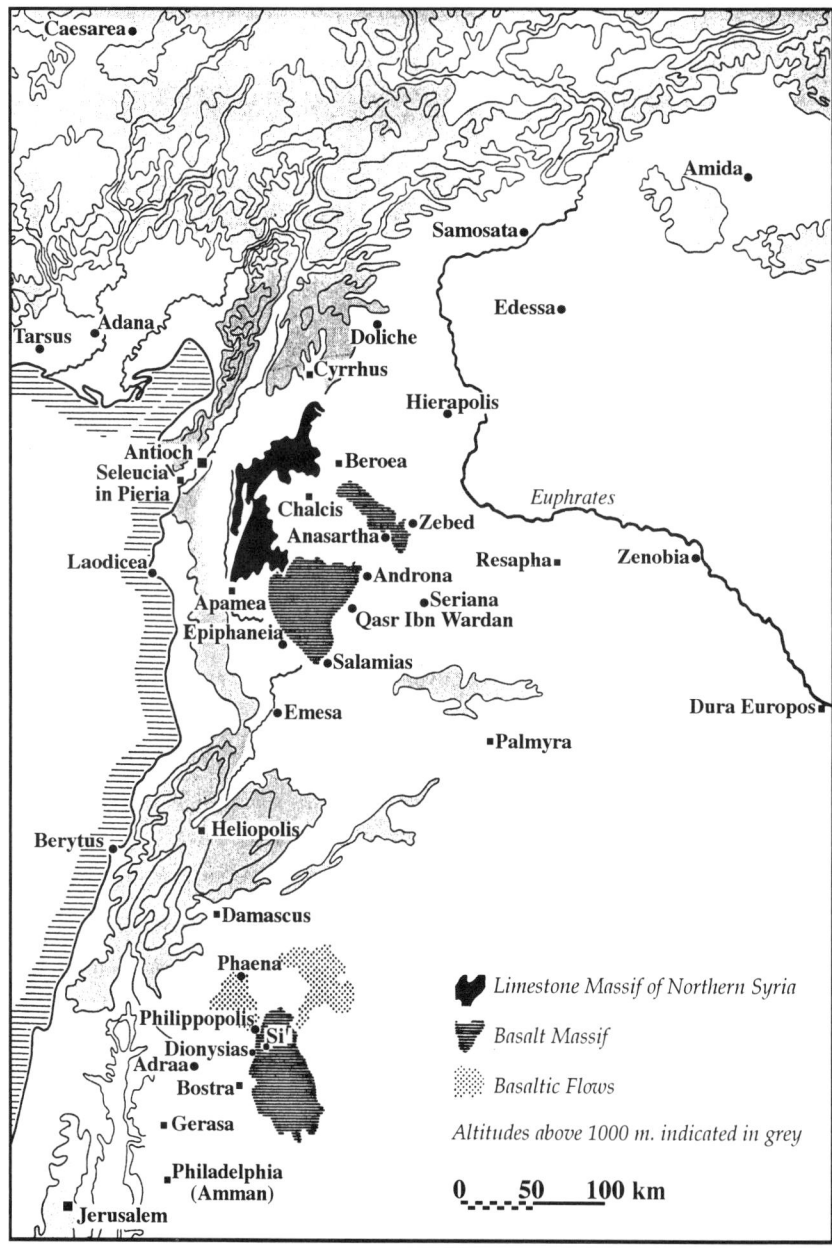

Fig. 1. Map showing Syrian cities in relation to geological features (after Tchalenko 1953–58)

were not, however, completely occupied: the city of Emesa, on the Orontes, was not yet a city, but a modest village on the Tell. The region was inhabited by the tribe of Emisenoi, whose chiefs, the Sampsigerams, lived in Arethusa (Sullivan 1977; 1990).

Throughout Syria before lived 'tribes' whose names became the names of cities or regions: Tardytenses, Nosaris, Gabini, Emisenoi, Rhambei, etc. The exact territories they occupied are not known with certainty, but there is no doubt that they had penetrated the territories of certain cities all the way to the Orontes valley and that they had reached the Ansariyeh. These tribes were not sedentary, for, if we are to believe Strabo, the regions they occupied were known as Skenarchia, which means that the inhabitants lived as true nomads, as tent-dwellers (*Skenitai*). They were governed by phylarchs or tetrarchs who had in some cases managed to impose their authority on cities: Sampsigeram in Arethusa and Denys in Beroea, among many others, are examples. With Rome's return to control following the arrival of Pompey, and particularly after Actium, these tribes were pushed back into their territories, but they continued to impose a climate of insecurity. Strabo underlines the point that, as one moved westward, sedentarization could be seen to progress among these people. During the Augustan era, however, the process was far from advanced: the region of Emesa and the area between the Euphrates and Beroea-Aleppo contained no sedentary peoples. Between the two, the Parapotamie-Skenarchia tribes still moved near the towns of the Orontes.

Nor did sedentary peoples occupy more extensive territories in the south. Two great principalities consisting of Arab tribes were found there: the Ituraeans, whose territory extended from Tripoli, to the north of modern Lebanon, to the Bekaa, spilling over into modern Jordan to the north, all the way to Abila; and the Nabateans, who held the Transjordanian plateau and the south of Syria all the way to Bostra, and even, for a time, to Damascus. The arrival of Pompey pushed the Nabateans to the south and brought about the installation of Roman government, which was in part direct, and in part delegated to Herodian princes. Throughout the first century BC, the region was marked by poverty and banditry. By bandits, ancient writers meant rebels to the established order and to the peasants' sedentary way of life. These bandits lived in Trachonitis, modern Ledja, a vast basaltic plateau filled with grottoes that were used as places of refuge (Villeneuve 1986; Dentzer 1986). Despite the fertility of the soil, Syria was thus a region impoverished by anarchy and fragmentation. In southern Syria, only Damascus and its oasis benefited from agricultural prosperity.

It is possible that this overall situation of the Syrian countryside was the result of a recent evolution of some kind. We lack information on the cities and, to an even greater extent, the countryside of Hellenistic Syria. Even if we admit that the material wealth of both has at times been exaggerated, it is impossible not to recognize the disastrous effects that the crumbling of Seleucid power, civil wars, foreign intervention and the rise of dissidence and separatism had on the rural economy. It may therefore be the case that this situation had not existed prior to the latter half of the second century BC.

The Trajectory of Evolution Prior to AD 400

Extension

From the time of Pompey's conquest of Syria, particularly after Actium, Syria experienced a period of near-total peace under a government which was particularly careful to maintain order and security. This period ended only with the Persian invasion of AD 260. In contemplating rural life at the end of the Roman era, in the middle of the third century, we see a great contrast with the situation that had prevailed even under Augustus. The whole region, between the Euphrates on the one hand and Cyrrhus and the eastern cities on the other, had been sedentarized (Frézouls 1977). Whereas Roman armies had once been obliged to take the road to Antioch at Cyrrhus, then ride to Zeugma to reach the Euphrates, taking a long detour to avoid less secure areas, Cumont notes that in the third century they took the direct route via Beroea and rode straight east to the Euphrates (Cumont 1917:17). Further to the south, the valley of the Orontes was occupied entirely by sedentary peoples; nomadic ways were nowhere in evidence. The dividing line between sedentary and nomadic peoples which, during the first century BC, had held close to the territories of the cities in the Orontes valley, was pushed quite far to the east, although its location cannot be determined with precision. All of the region Strabo designates as Parapotamia was criss-crossed with a dense network of roads connecting military posts; the Peutinger Table and the Antonine Itinerary indicate the principal axes (Mouterde and Poidebarde 1945). Village life was beginning to develop; it eventually thrived during the Byzantine era, in the fifth and sixth centuries covering all this territory up to the 200 mm isohyet. In the middle of the third century, however, villages remained scattered. The domination of sedentary peoples extended to Seriana (Isriye), whose temple Gogräfe studied (Gogräfe 1993), dating it to the beginning of the third century. Further south, the city of Emesa and the surrounding region experienced significant development; in the first century, its territory had been no more than an area traversed by nomadic people (Seyrig 1954). In southern Syria, finally, the bandits of Trachonitis were no longer mentioned after their last revolt (in 12 BC) and village life developed in the region; archeological remains studied by the team of J.-M. Dentzer are an impressive reflection of this fact.

Density

At the same time it began to extend outward, the territory of sedentary peoples also grew in density. In the north, the east, and the south, marginal regions – so defined by their low rainfall or the relative infertility of their soils – began to be developed. This was the case with the limestone massif of northern Syria, as well as with the mountains northeast of Palmyra and those of southern Syria; this point will be discussed in greater detail later.

The Problem of Pace

To understand the pace, or rate, at which this extension of cultivated territories occurred, we must have recourse to dated inscriptions. The inventory of *IGLS* (volumes II, III, IV), which covers the region between Emesa and the border of Turkey and gathers together (somewhat randomly) all the inscriptions discovered up to the 1950s, counts 682 dated inscriptions and that without any more thorough exploration of particular regions (Jalabert *et al.* 1939; 1955; 1959; Tate in press). With just a few rare exceptions, these inscriptions commemorate the construction of an edifice, house, or tomb, the result of building construction. The variations in number of these inscriptions over time reflects broad demographic and economic tendencies, since buildings are constructed only when it is necessary and possible to do so. A graph drawn to represent distribution of inscriptions dated by decades shows that growth was at its maximum between 100 and 350. Different results, however, are obtained when the regions of Emesa and Epiphania or Apamea and Antioch are examined: the degree of growth was far greater in the former zone than in the latter. If the following period, the fourth and fifth centuries, is considered, the opposite result is obtained. This difference may be due to the fact that the Emesa became a true city only during the course of the first century, and that its territory was at that time taken over by a sedentary peasantry. This development could be linked to the construction of a dam on the Orontes, upstream from modern-day Homs, if it were confirmed that construction did in fact take place during the Roman era and that it constituted a decisive element in the development of the region. In Apamea and Antioch, in contrast, development occurred earlier, beginning at least during Seleucid times, though probably well before that (Bowersock 1973; Tchalenko 1953–58; Tate in press). Whatever one is to make of these regional differences, diachronic distribution of dated inscriptions shows that growth here began under the Flavians and reached its zenith under the Antonines; it slowed only around AD 250.

The Question of Causes

Peace

This significant and generalized growth can be attributed primarily to the peace that Roman government established in Syria, in complete contrast to the prevailing situation at the end of the Hellenistic era. There was peace with neighboring lands, for Syria did not experience a single invasion between the defeat of Crassus at Carrhae and the attack of Shapur in the third century AD; more significantly, there was peace within Syria, because Rome had been able to pacify the area and prepare it for unification. The first step Rome took to achieve this was to establish direct government over areas occupied by cities and sedentary peasants. Areas held by nomadic or semi-nomadic tribes were confided to client princes whose missions were to establish order and a regular lifestyle on their subjects; this meant an urban lifestyle with certain territories being designated as agricultural. The fate of the independent peoples Pliny listed after having consulted the province's *forma* is unknown, but, since they completely disappeared afterwards, we must assume that they were conquered and forced to become sedentary. Southern Syria was placed in the hands of Herod the Great; he pacified Trachonitis and suppressed the banditry that had made a more stable lifestyle, be it through agriculture or commerce, impossible. He achieved this by surrounding Ledja with military colonies and by implementing a policy of agricultural colonization and urban development. A century later, security reigned, villages had multiplied, cities had developed, and Hellenized local notables had become capable of carrying out the cities' administration. Upon the death of Agrippa II (AD 92 or 93), his possessions in southern Syria were integrated into the province of Syria. Farther north, the governing of Emesa was confided to kings. Of these populations, Strabo writes, 'as they approach Syria, nomadic populations become more civilized; they seem less like Arabs or *Skenitai*, and the power of their chiefs, the power of a Sempsigeram at Arethusa... takes on more and more of the character of a regular government' (16.2.16). We know nothing of modes of urban and rural development in the region during the course of the first century AD. In any case, however, it is certain that Emesa became an important city whose wealth was based as much on the prosperity of its countryside as on the caravan traffic that came from Palmyra when it was incorporated into the empire at the end of the first century AD (prior to AD 78–79, the date of the pyramidal tomb of Gaius Iulius Sampsigeramos).

The Role of the State and of Cities

LEGISLATION

In the development of the Syrian countryside, the imperial government also played an indirect but decisive role in two and perhaps three domains: legislation, the establishment of cadasters, and perhaps the construction of dams. It has been mentioned that in several regions of Syria, marginal areas that were uninhabited or sparsely inhabited before the arrival of Pompey were gradually developed from the beginning of the Roman era. Cases in point are the limestone massif of northern Syria, the territory of Emesa, and certain parts of southern Syria. There can be no doubt that the limestone massif was virtually uninhabited during Hellenistic times. It is true that non-stratified ceramic material of that period was discovered at Dehes, in the Gebel Barisa, and that third-century Seleucid coins have been discovered, but no structures, neither houses nor tombs, have been dated to before the Christian era. It seems clear, then, that in Hellenistic times, the inhabitants of the region were few in number and scattered: perhaps a few peasants, some animal breeders, and some hunters. In the Achaemenid era, the limestone massif may have been part of the king's domain, some parts of which, texts indicate, were situated in northern Syria. It would thence have passed into the domain of the Seleucid kings. During the Roman era, in any case, there is no evidence of private properties that would have been divided and rented to peasants to work. The first inhabitants of the limestone massif were free peasants, and they behaved like landowners. There is, however, one exception to this generalized phenomenon: the great temples of Mount Koryphe, Gebel Srir, Borg Baqirha and Qalaat Kalota owned several villages. These temples played an important role in the region's early development, but this role was geographically limited (Tate 1992). In all other areas, landless peasants from the neighboring plains settled spontaneously in the harsh lands, which had to be cleared of the rocks that covered them and divided into irregular fields of unequal sizes cut into the barren rock. It is likely that the provisions of the *Lex Manciana* (end of the first century) and of the *Lex Hadriana* were applied to them. These provisions allowed peasants to occupy uncultivated land and to become its owners once they had developed it and paid the necessary tax. The legal conditions under which land was appropriated in Emesa and in southern Syria, however, are unknown. We know that in southern Syria, land was distributed to colonists by Herod. But what was the extent of this policy?

CADASTERS

Another aspect of the Roman government's intervention was the implantation of cadasters in several parts of Syrian territory. In the north of Syria, there seem to have been numerous cadasters, but their study is still in its early stages and it is not possible to arrive at reliable conclusions on all points (Tchalenko 1953–58; Dodinet *et al.* 1990; for an alternative view, see Will 1995; Dodinet *et al.* 1994; Tate 1994). Cadasters have been discovered in the regions of Laodicea, Beroea, Chalcis ad Belum, Apamea, Epiphania, Arethusa, Emesa, and in the limestone massif of northern Syria. In the latter region, drystone walls run for several kilometers in orthogonal networks that are not troubled by the idiosyncrasies of a variable topography. Whatever the case may be, in their current state, they go back to the era of village abandonment, that is the eighth and ninth centuries AD. The narrowness of the plots whose borders they define prove that these primitive networks underwent numerous

*Fig. 2. Aerial view of the cadastration of Gebel Sim'an
(Courtesy Institut Français d'Archéologie du Proche-Orient)*

reconfigurations. It is therefore difficult to identify the earliest forms and determine whether these were centuriations or the 'scamnations' or 'strigations' of the gromaticists. Strangely, these are found only in the Sim'an and Halaqa Gebels and in the Zawiye Gebels (Fig. 2), but not in the center of the limestone massif, in the Barisa and el-'Ala Gebels. Nor do they seem to extend themselves into the plain, whereas ordinarily Roman cadasters were located in the plains, avoiding the mountains. In the Zawiye Gebel, the same networks continue into the territories of Apamea and Antioch. What was the purpose of these cadastrations? I have hypothesized that they did not serve as a framework for the distribution of plots to veterans, since the presence of veterans is attested in surrounding areas and on the interior plains of the massif, but not in the massif itself. The apparent cadasters of the massif seem to have been implanted after a general expropriation of the local peasantry, in order to allow land distribution in favor of veterans; the remaining land was left for previously dispossessed peasants. Under such conditions, the cadasters would have served the purpose of establishing state control, in particular its fiscal control, over a spontaneous appropriation of vacant territory.

Among the other cadasters of northern Syria, only that of Emesa has been referred to in a note, by Van Liere (1958–59). Situated to the southeast of the city, it seems to have been a 30 × 30 *actus* centuriation dating from the time of Caracalla. In his short note, the author expresses the opinion that the implantation of this cadaster occurred within the context of a policy of settlement and development of the countryside.

In southern Syria, near Bostra, M. Dodinet, J. Leblanc and J.-P. Vallat noted four types of property division, two of which are probably Roman. The first, not very extensive, would seem to have been organized according to the axes of the Roman camp; it apparently dates from the beginning of the second century AD. The other, quite extensive, system seems to have been a 15–*actus* centuriation (square plots measuring 532 m on each side) situated to the east of the city (Dodinet *et al.* 1994).

Despite our lack of certainty and our ignorance, it can hardly be doubted that the implantation of Roman cadasters in Syria was part of a rural development policy undertaken principally for fiscal reasons.

HYDRAULIC IMPROVEMENTS

The last type of state intervention, unless it was in fact accomplished by individual cities, consisted of hydraulic works. Such improvements were necessary everywhere: in wet areas, in order to regularize the flow of rivers and tributaries and make irrigation possible; and on the steppes, as a means of collecting water and organizing its distribution. Whatever their origins may have been, these improvements were beyond the scope of small, rural communities. Their achievement could only have been made possible by the intervention of either the imperial government or the city. Archeology has provided us with several examples.

The most impressive of these works is situated near Palmyra. It included a dam (Harbaqa) in the mountains, and a garden and a system for collecting and distributing water in the plain (Schlumberger 1986). The dam, placed where the steep-sloped Ouadi el-Barde widens in a broadening valley, is a rectilinear wall, 345 m wide by 30 m tall and 18 m thick. It consists of a mass of stones and stone fragments encased in a mortar, then enclosed in two huge facings: the blocks are laid out along a regular course, set back from each other and at the base are three outlets. The dam created an artificial lake, now filled in, and enabled the population to regulate the supply of water to the reservoir downstream. Numerous diversions leading from this reservoir provided water for irrigation of the valley and watering of the garden. Between the reservoir and the garden was a mill. Schlumberger dates this dam to the first century AD, attributing its construction and maintenance to Palmyra. The need for land was so great that one did not hesitate to invest considerable means in the construction of works of this size, with the sole purpose being the creation of an artificial oasis in the middle of the steppes. Many such works, of a more modest scale but comparable in their purpose, were constructed farther north on the steppe, to the east of the Aleppo/Epiphania line. Poidebarde gives the examples of Qdeym, and of Amsareddi which he dates to Roman times (Mouterde and Poidebarde 1945). At Qdeym, a veritable oasis was created by means of two systems of water collection (Fig. 3). The first was a foggara consisting of four collection galleries with a total length of 1,850 m; this allowed a dozen hectares to be irrigated. The second was a 9 km foggara running into a reservoir (*birke*) measuring 62 m on each side and 3 m deep and capable of storing 11,500 cubic meters of water. This provided sufficient water for a vast domain. At Amsareddi, we find the same system of collection and conveyance of water via foggaras with, moreover, wells. The foggara system was quite widespread in the Syrian steppes. Numerous remains have been found in the regions of Selemias and Andrôna; unfortunately, these cannot be dated, but there is no doubt that a certain number of them belong to the Roman era.

The dam at Emesa had another function: regulating the flow of the Orontes and allowing the

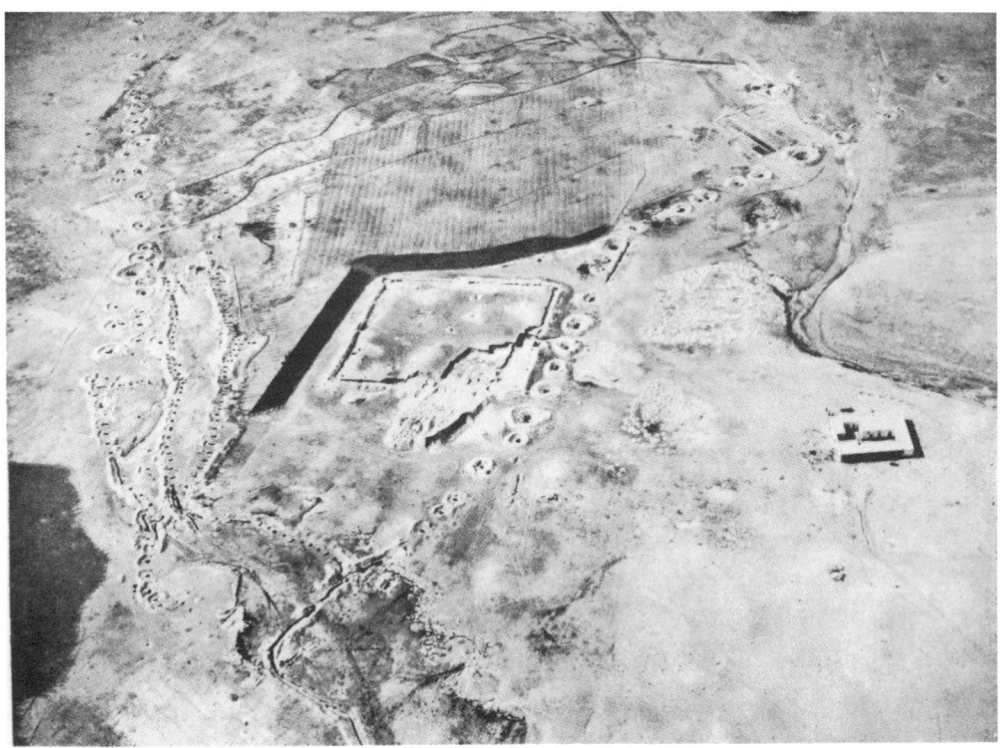

Fig. 3. Aerial view of Qdeym (Acadama) showing the fort, the foggara water collection system,
and cultivated fields (from Mouterde and Poidebard 1945)

valley downstream, in the region of Emesa, to be improved, then irrigated (Seyrig 1954; Weulersse 1940; see also Calvet and Geyer 1992). This dam, 850 m long and 5 m high, was constructed on basalt flows at the point where the river leaves a narrow valley and spreads out into a wider one. Weulersse wrote that as the river enters the plain of Emesa, 'its banks disappear, and at the first obstacle, the river spreads out to become a swampy lake: this is the lake of Homs, on contact with the first basalt flows'. It is not, therefore, an artificial lake, but a natural one whose water level was artificially raised. This dam fed three canals, the first two of which flowed at the rate of 400 liters per second and irrigated the area surrounding the dam. The third, which flowed at the rate of 1,800 liters per second, irrigated the 1,000–hectare gardens of Emesa. The problem of accurately dating this dam has yet to be solved. It is, however, certain that the dam was built or rebuilt during the Roman era, although it is not known precisely when. Seyrig thought that its construction should be attributed to the city of Emesa, whose citizens, made wealthy by caravan trading, could have invested the vast sums necessary for both the irrigation and care of the lush gardens and the improvement of the region. A hypothesis of either whole or partial state subsidy can also be defended.

Whether it was subsidized by the state or by individual cities, the construction of dams falls into the category of an overall system of political intervention. This intervention did not reflect a genuine drive toward economic expansion, of which antiquity does not, in any case, offer other examples, but rather a drive toward organization and control. On the part of the imperial state, this drive reflects a political interest in order as well as the necessity of fixing taxes. On the part of cities, a third motivating factor, that of guaranteeing the availability of food and water for their populations, was added to those.

The Expansion and Enrichment of Cities

Another factor in the growth of the countryside was the rapid expansion and economic growth of cities. Rising urban demand fuelled the development of rural activities. G. W. Bowersock was certainly right to emphasize the role of the countryside and of agriculture in Roman Syria's prosperity, rather than proposing that commercial activity, particularly international trade, was its basis (Bowersock 1989). However, it is true that without the immense profits such commerce supplied, the cities would have been smaller and less prosperous; the countryside would thus have undergone less extensive development.

A striking example of the role played by urban development and prosperity in the development of the countryside is found in D. Schlumberger's study *La Palmyrène du Nord-Ouest* (1951). Palmyra, far from being isolated in the middle of the desert, was in fact at the center of a discontinuous rural area that featured few inhabitants but nevertheless exercised important functions. This rural area consisted of minor oases and small mountain villages, particularly to the northwest of the city. These villages, often just poorly constructed hamlets, featured modest sanctuaries and, above all, cisterns for collecting rainwater. There were no irrigation works to permit farming; animal husbandry was the sole possible activity. Schlumberger hypothesizes, quite reasonably, that it was in these villages that the horses used in Palmyra's famous heavy cavalry were raised and kept; this cavalry performed superbly during the wars fought against the Persians in the second half of the third century. It is to be noted that these villages had not existed prior to the Roman era, and that they disappeared with the fall of Palmyra. In other words, their existence was closely linked to the prosperity of that city.

Although it cannot be demonstrated with the same degree of clarity, the influence of cities on agricultural development in the rest of Syria is no less certain. It is the growth in prosperity of the city of Emesa that explains the conversion of its territory to agricultural production, and it is the development of Antioch, Apamea, Chalcis ad Belum and some other cities that bears witness to the development of harsh regions like the limestone massif.

An attempt to summarize the factors making the development of the Syrian countryside of the Roman period more comprehensible produces a complex model: demographic trends and the economic growth of cities played major roles, but neither of these factors would have existed without the drive toward organization on the part of the state and the urban elite.

Permanent Features of the Syrian Countryside

In examining the more permanent features of the Syrian countryside, we must consider rural living conditions, economic activities, and society.

Rural Living Conditions

In every area where remains survive, a great homogeneity in rural lifestyles can be seen (Dentzer 1985/86; Tate 1992). Grouped settlements and villages predominate. These villages can be seen in northern Syria, on the limestone and basalt massifs, as well as to the south, in the Hauran. Their dimensions vary, and in the vast majority of cases, they are not surrounded by walls. Some exceptions are noted in the basalt Gebel to the north and in Trachonitis to the south; this seems to have been related to the necessity of defending the village from nomads and brigands. It is, however, to be noted that many villages were self-enclosed, owing to the fact that their houses were built very closely together, all overlooking a central courtyard. The layout of villages is characterized by the absence of all organization. No order governed the location of houses; their construction obeyed the limits imposed by topography, but was not influenced by any preliminary plan or by any tendency other than the wish to maintain privacy – inasmuch as this did not involve excessive distance from one's neighbors. There were no public squares, and no networks of roads or pathways, unless one categorizes in that fashion the narrow passages that sometimes separated the windowless walls of two houses over a distance of a few dozen meters, before disappearing into some ill-defined space.

The principal element of the village is the house; some villages included thermal baths, a temple, or an inn, but these cases are fairly rare. The houses, in all the regions where remains survive, consisted of a group of rooms on two stories around a central courtyard. The number of rooms corresponded to the number of nuclear families each house held. These were not villas in the Roman sense of the word, with a *pars urbana* and a *pars rustica,* with one part reserved for the master, his family and his leisure activities and another reserved for slaves and the necessary production materials. These houses are all of a single type (Sodini and Tate 1984; Tate 1981; 1992; Dentzer 1986; cf. Dentzer 1985). They were of a simple model: two storeys, with the ground floor being reserved for utilitarian purposes and the upper floor for living space. As such, they could be expanded or subdivided. Beyond this general uniformity, houses featured regional particularities. The walls were constructed of materials found on site, that is, limestone or basalt; this single fact explains why, despite being based on the same extremely simple design, houses differed in appearance, particularly in the construction of their roofs. The houses of the limestone massif feature peaked roofs; those of the basaltic regions often had terraces made of flat stone slabs placed on transversal arches. Another variable was the structure of the rooms on each storey. In the north, rooms were simple rectangles; some featured a row of pillars dividing the room into 1/3 and 2/3–length sections, which allowed the use of shorter floor beams. In contrast, houses in the south were subdivided into a large front room and a small back room separated by mangers; the latter room was itself divided into two small rooms on separate levels. The origins of this unique layout are not known.

The territorial organization of villages is known only in the limestone massif. These villages were surrounded by a neighboring zone which probably consisted of gardens; further on, two areas overlap: cultivable land and the more rugged terrain of the *saltus*. This mixing was geographic in origin: the countryside consisted of irregularly sized pieces of arable land surrounded by the bare rock that constituted the *saltus*. The latter area was not completely useless from an economic standpoint, for it contained tiny areas of grassy land suitable for grazing. The fields do not appear to have been open. In cadastered areas, in any case, they were not; on the limestone massif, plots were defined by walls that sometimes reached more than a meter in height.

It must not be forgotten, however, that the regions where ruins of ancient villages remain are not necessarily representative of other regions. Whatever the extent of their territory may have been, they represent only a small part of Syrian territory; moreover, they all belong to marginal areas, where peasants were freed from deeply ingrained and restrictive traditions. It is possible that another type of rural house existed on the plains, but no evidence to this effect has been found.

Rural Economy

The rural economy, in contrast to living conditions, is notable for its diversity. The differences are not related to particular agricultural or pastoral methods or techniques. These were the same throughout the Mediterranean region, and they were applied in Syria to crops as diverse as those found elsewhere: wheat, with its biennial rotation; fruit trees; grape vines; vegetables. Animal husbandry occupied an important role everywhere; it was partially stabled, which implies recourse to fodder crops; when this was not the case, it contributed to the fertilization of the land. Irrigation techniques were elaborate, as the examples already discussed demonstrate; it is not certain that norias were known, as the oldest example, pictured in a mosaic, dates from the Byzantine era. The processing techniques employed were olive and grape pressing. As we know, oil was simultaneously an ointment, a raw material used in cooking, and a fuel for lamps. Callot showed that the large oil production sites found in the Roman world from the first century onward, which featured grindstone mechanisms, oil presses, and numerous decantation basins, existed during the same period on the limestone massif; there is one, for example, at Kafr Nabu, in the Gebel Sim'an (Callot 1984). Grape presses were often of the same type as oil presses. In southern Syria, however, Hatoum and Dentzer found an unusual type of grape press: the grapes were pressed in a flagstone-paved area on a slight slope. The grape was processed by use of a screw press on a vertical axis; this axis was fit into a block with a dovetail mechanism.

There was thus variety in Syrian agricultural and pastoral production (on the textual sources, Heichelheim 1938; see Rostovtzeff 1935 for the Byzantine situation). Five types of region, each defined by its principal crops, can be distinguished. The littoral plains, which were naturally well supplied with water, were able to grow both grains and trees. On the interior plains, the plain of Chalcis and that of Hauran (Batanea), grains were predominant, although animal husbandry may also have been practiced. There is reason to wonder whether some land on the Chalcis plain may have been irrigated, because ancient underground conduits have been found in certain areas; however, it is not clear whether their purpose was to irrigate land or simply to fill the cisterns that provided people and animals with water. In drier regions, agriculture's importance diminished while that of animal husbandry grew (Lauffray 1983). The Osrhoene, for example, was devoted to the cultivation of wheat, as was the Tauric Piedmont region to the north, while animal husbandry played a greater role in more easterly regions. The research of Lauffray and Van Liere showed that the valleys of the Euphrates in the region of Sura, of the Balissos (Balikh), of the Chaboras (Khabour), and of its tributary the Mygdonios (Djaghdjagh) were irrigated and thus belonged to the third type of region mentioned above. We have seen that the valley of the Orontes was probably irrigated at the site of Emesa, Arethusa and Epiphania, but nothing of certainty can be said of the Ghab: according to Strabo, the city of Apamea was surrounded by a large lake formed by the Orontes. Weulersse doubts that the people of antiquity were capable of fully regularizing its course (Weulersse 1940), although it is likely that they discovered a means of doing so later, since ships could sail from Seleucia in Pieria to Apamea. One last type of agricultural region must be mentioned: the forests of Mount Lebanon, of which Roman authorites made extensive use (Breton 1980). Beyond the sedentary world of the peasants, were nomads progressively pushed toward the desert, or must it be assumed, by contrast, that it was their own settling down that explains the expansion of the sedentary lifestyle? The debate remains open. Let us simply note that, while peasants and nomads inhabited two different worlds that were in every sense opposites, contacts existed between them which could at times be peaceful and complementary (see Gawlikowski, this volume).

Societies

In discussing rural societies, the qualifications expressed on the subject of the rural economy still apply: the archeological evidence available to us relates to only one type of region, the marginal type, where the degree of freedom was always greater than the norm. As such, the rural houses mentioned here belonged for the most part to a landed peasantry. The rustic format of the houses of the limestone massif prior to the fourth century AD suited a society made up of pioneer peasants who had cleared stones from the fields and who practiced, in most cases, an agriculture poor in food crops, which did not permit them to accumulate a significant surplus. Among them, however, were richer peasants. In the case of the 'basilica-type' building of Dehes studied by Bavant – entirely unique as it is on the limestone massif – there was without any doubt an important landowner involved who did not, perhaps, reside there (Bavant in press). The 'villas,' actually houses, of Bamuqqa and Benebil (Tchalenko 1953–58; Tate 1992), the third-century house at Kimār (Figs. 4, 5), and the beautiful houses, faced with polygonal stones, of the second and third centuries certainly belonged to wealthier peasants, but not to important landowners: there seems to be nowhere the numerous workers necessary to cultivate a large domain could have been housed. The peasants' greatest wealth was, therefore, relative; it is clear that the most prosperous of them were far from owning all the village land, for each village contains several houses of this type, and moreover, the presence of these houses did not prevent the development of the poorest dwellings. Perhaps the wealth of the most prosperous peasants came from rents paid to them for other land? I believe it more likely that they grew more remunerative crops, such as olives, and that they produced oil of which part was sold.

The main landowners in villages were the temples; it is notable that the Karf Nabo press, which dates from AD 238, belonged to a sanctuary. Aside from villages with temples, the only village to have belonged to a single landowner was Baziher, in the Gebel Sim'an: it was surrounded by a wall, and the entire holding did not exceed the size of a small village (a few dozen hectares). In the vast majority of cases, the villages of the limestone massif were poor and each house corresponded to a nuclear family or at most to a group of two or three couples. The situation was probably the same in the basaltic region to the east. Knowledge of the situation in southern Syria remains conjectural.

From an institutional standpoint, however, the villages of northern and southern Syria resembled each other. They were governed by magistrates of various titles: *decaprôtes, presbytes,* and *strategoi* in the limestone massif; *pistoi, pronoètoi, episcopoi* elsewhere (Villeneuve 1986; Sartre 1991; Tate 1992). This variation in titles could be due to the difficulty of translating ancient local institutions into Greek, although in Aramaic their names were clear. The role of these officials is, in any case, known:

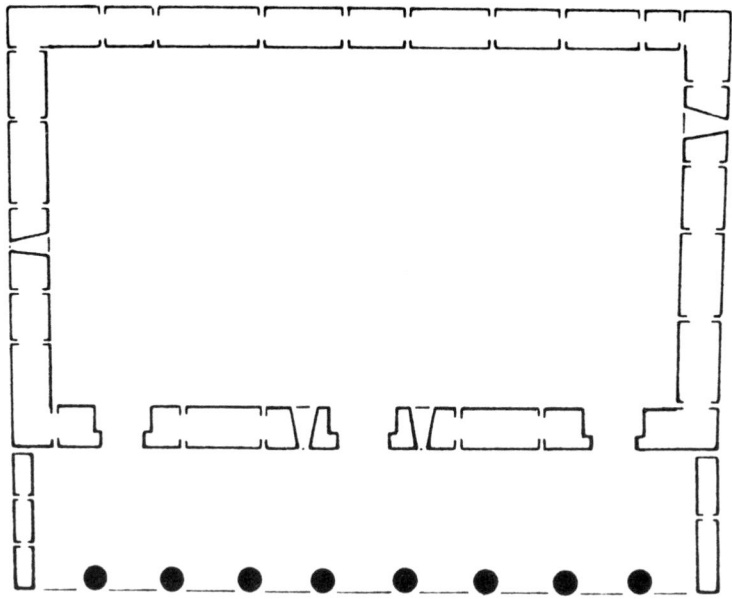

Fig. 4. Plan of House 1 at Kimār (Courtesy Institut Français d'Archéologie du Proche-Orient)

Fig. 5. Façade of House 1 at Kimār (Courtesy Institut Français d'Archéologie du Proche-Orient)

they were responsible for distributing the tax burden and mediating conflicts within the community.

In considering the whole of Syrian territory, it is clear that there were large domains, but they are difficult to identify, and uncertainties remain as to their nature: were they large contiguous domains with a single tenant, to which the term *latifundium* would apply? Or were there, rather, important landowners who did not own a single property, but instead gained their wealth through ownership of individual scattered villages? Considerable differences exist between these two types of large properties, from a social as well as an economic standpoint.

One type of large property is represented by the sanctuaries; we have seen this in the case of the limestone massif. Besides these modest sanctuaries, those of Damascus, Emesa, Baetocaece and Hierapolis must be considered. The best-known case is that of Baetocaece (Seyrig 1951). It did not head a large domain; it owned several villages in the area, but the system of rental charges to which they were subjected is entirely unknown. One might reasonably assume that the other great sanctuaries operated similarly.

Imperial holdings were another type of large property. The forests of Mount Lebanon belonged to this category, but there were certainly others, since we know the name of a freedman who, under the Flavians, became procurator of the Syrian domains (Sartre 1991: 324). According to Rey Coquais, the Herodian principalities of southern Syria became imperial domains after the annexation of the principality of Agrippa II in AD 92–93. This would explain the presence of numerous veterans, but Sartre correctly notes that the veterans may in fact have purchased their lands, which makes the previous proposition hypothetical. If these imperial domains did exist in this region, they must have been rapidly alienated, perhaps via the *Lex Hadriana*. The names of three *saltus* are given in texts: the Bataneos in southern Syria, the Eragizenon in the region of the Euphrates, and the domain of Bab-el-Hawa, which is mentioned during the time of Constantine, but must have existed before then. The term *saltus* normally refers to land held by a single owner; this was probably also the case in Syria.

The last type is that of large properties belonging to individual owners. Such domains certainly existed; how else can we explain the existence of *boule* in the cities and the ability of *bouleutes* to undertake constant liturgies? It is clear that their properties were in the plains, where the constant human occupation since antiquity explains the disappearance of antique remains. Libanius tells us, however, that these properties rarely consisted of a single holding, but rather of villages or parts of villages that were geographically dispersed. It should be noted that after the riot of the 'statues,' the curial classes had nowhere to take refuge in the countryside.

Syria's social situation was therefore notable in its sheer variety, but there can be no doubt that, however important the structure of large properties may have been, a vigorous and free peasantry remained.

The 'Crisis' of the Third Century: Structural or Cyclical?

From AD 250–260 onward, Syria experienced, at the very least, a slowing of economic activities which is generally considered part of the context of the 'crisis of the third century.' What, realistically, should we make of this? Was it a cyclical crisis, or a structural one following a long period of expansion? (Tate in press).

First of all, it should be noted that the evidence of inscriptions indicates that the cessation of activity was brief, lasting no longer than twenty years, and that from the return of unity and peace under Constantine, ca. AD 330, onward, expansion resumed with even more vigor than before. Therefore, to think that the 'crisis of the third century' – which hardly merits such a name – was a structural one would be incorrect. It was simply a question of temporary difficulties caused by the 'plague of Saint Cyprian,' and perhaps also monetary disorder. Rural growth in the Roman era had not yet reached its absolute limit.

There was certainly growth, but can we in fact speak of economic *progress* in the sense of structural change? I have emphasized for the most part the quantitative aspects of growth. It should be noted that the development of uncultivable land and growth in the amount of produce reserved for cities constitute qualitative changes associated with economic progress; however, in the Roman era, this 'progress' was slow.

Translated by Liza Hall

Bibliography
Bavant, B. (in press) *Déhès* II, Paris.
Bowersock, G.W. (1973) "Syria under Vespasian," *JRS* 63: 133–140.
_____(1989) "Social and economic history of Syria under the Roman empire," in J.-M. Dentzer and W. Orthmann, eds., *Archéologie et histoire de la Syrie II: La Syrie de l'époque achéménide à l'avènement de l'Islam* (Schriften zur Vorderasiatischen Archäologie 1), 63–80. Saarbrücken.
Breton, J.-F. (1980) "Les inscriptions forestières d'Hadrien dans le Mont Liban," *Inscriptions grecques et latines de la Syrie* VIII.3, Paris.
Callot, O. (1984) *Huileries antiques de Syrie du Nord*, Paris.
Calvet, Y. and B. Geyer (1992) *Barrages antiques de la Syrie*, Paris.
Cumont, F. (1917) *Études syriennes*, Paris.
Dentzer, J.-M. (1985) "Les villages de la Syrie romaine dans un tradition d'urbanisme oriental," in *De l'Indus aux Balkans: Recueil Jean Deshayes*, 213–48. Paris.
_____(1986) "Développement et culture de la Syrie du sud dans la période préprovinciale (Ier s. avant J.-C. – Ier s. après J.-C.," in J.-M. Dentzer, ed., *Hauran I. Recherches archéologiques sur la Syrie du sud à l'époque hellénistique et romaine*, II, 387–420. Paris.
Dentzer, J.-M. ed. (1985/86) *Hauran I. Recherches archéologiques sur la Syrie du sud à l'époque hellénistique et romaine*, I-II, Paris.
Dodinet, M., J. Leblanc, and J.-P. Vallat (1994) "Étude morphologique des paysages antiques," in P.N. Doukellis and L.G. Mendoni, eds., *Structures rurales et sociétés antiques*, 425–42. Besançon.
Dodinet, M., J. Leblanc, J.-P. Vallat and F. Villeveuve (1990) "Le paysage antique en Syrie: l'exemple de Damas," *Syria* 67: 339–67.
Dussaud, R. (1927) *Topographie historique de la Syrie médiévale*, Paris.
Frézouls, E. (1977) "Cyrrhus et Cyrrhestique jusqu'à la fin du Haut-Empire," *ANRW* II.8: 164–97.
Gogräfe, R. (1993) "Die Datierung des Tempels von Isriye," *DM* 7: 45–61.
Heichelheim, F.M. (1938) "Roman Syria," in T. Frank, ed., *An Economic Survey of Ancient Rome IV*, 121–257. Baltimore.
Jalabert, L., R. Mouterde and Cl. Montdesert (1939) *Inscriptions grecques et latines de la Syrie* II. *Chalcidique et Antiochène*, Paris.
_____(1955) *Inscriptions grecques et latines de la Syrie* III. *Laodicée et Apamène*, Paris.
_____(1959) *Inscriptions grecques et latines de la Syrie* IV. *Emésène*, Paris.

Jones, A.H.M. (1971) *The Cities of the Eastern Roman Provinces* (2nd edn.), Oxford.

Lauffray, J. (1983) *Halabiyya-Zenobia* I, Paris.

Millar, F. (1993) *The Roman Near East 31 BC – AD 337*, Cambridge, Mass.

Mouterde, R. and A. Poidebard (1945) *Le Limes de Chalcis*, Paris.

Rostovtzeff, M. (1935) "La Syrie romaine," *RHist* 175: 1–40.

Sartre, M. (1991) *L'Orient romain. Provinces et sociétés provinciales en Méditerranée orientale d'Auguste aux Sévères (31 avant J.-C. – 235 ap. J.-C.)*, Paris.

Schlumberger, D. (1951) *La Palmyrène du Nord-Ouest*, Paris.

_____(1986) *Qasr el-Heir el Gharbi*, Paris.

Seyrig, H. (1951) "Aradus et Baetocaece," *Syria* 28: 101–123 (reprinted in *Antiquités syriennes* 4 [1953], Paris).

_____(1954) "Caractères de l'histoire d'Émèse," *Syria* 36: 184–92 (reprinted in *Antiquités syriennes* 6 [1966], Paris).

Sodini, J.-P. and G. Tate (1984) "Maisons d'époques romaine et byzantine (II-VIèmes siècles) du Massif calcaire de Syrie du Nord, étude typologique," *Colloque Apamée de Syrie* III, Brussels.

Sullivan, R.D. (1977) "The dynasty of Emesa," *ANRW* II.8: 732–98.

_____(1990) *Near Eastern Royalty and Rome, 100–30 BC*, Toronto.

Tate, G. (1981) "Assetto del villagio in la civilta byzantina ogelti e messagio," Rome (paper delivered).

_____(1992) *Les campagnes de la Syrie du Nord*, Paris.

_____(1994) "À propos des cadastres romains du Nord de la Syrie," in P.N. Doukellis and L.G. Mendoni, eds., *Structures rurales et sociétés antiques*, 443–51. Besançon.

_____(1995) "Le latifundium en Syrie: mythe our réalité?," in *Du latifundium au latifondo: un héritage de Rome, un création médiévale ou moderne? (Actes de la Table ronde internationale du CNRS, organisée à l'Université Michel de Montaigne-Bourdeaux III, 17–19 Dec. 1992)*, 243–252. Paris.

_____(in press) "À titre de comparaison: les manifestations économiques de la crise dans le nord de la Syrie," in *Le IIIème siècle en Gaule Narbonaise*.

Tchalenko, G. (1953–58) *Villages antiques de la Syrie du Nord* (three volumes), Paris.

Van Liere, W.-J. (1958/59) 'Ager centuriatus of the Roman colonia of Emesa (Homs)," *Annales Archéologiques de Syrie* 8/9: 55–58.

Villeneuve, F. (1986) "L'économie rurale et la vie des campagnes dans le Hauran antique," in J.-M. Dentzer, ed., *Hauran I. Recherches archéologiques sur la Syrie du sud à l'époque hellénistique et romaine*, II, 63–136. Paris.

Weulersse, G. (1940) *L'Oronte: étude du fleuve*, Tours.

Will, E. (1995) "Damas," *Syria* 72: 3–4.

5. Jewish Rural Settlement in Judaea in the Early Roman Period

Yizhar Hirschfeld

Introduction

Rural settlement has always figured prominently in ancient Jewish society. Josephus describes this phenomenon as follows:

> Well, ours is not a maritime country; neither commerce nor the intercourse which it promotes with the outside world has any attraction for us. Our cities are built inland, remote from the sea; and we devote ourselves to the cultivation of the productive country with which we are blessed (*Ap.* 1.60).

Jewish cities proper, in the sense of the Greek polis, were few: Jerusalem, Sepphoris, Tiberias. The rest of the population dwelled in provincial towns, large and small villages, and farmhouses scattered over the country.

The determinant event that changed the face of this period, and of Jewish history, was the Great Revolt against Rome (67–70 CE), which, together with the Second Revolt (130–135 CE), engendered a grave change in the Jewish population, both urban and rural. In the period preceding the Great Revolt, i.e., the early Roman period (first century BCE/first century CE), we find – side by side with cities and villages – quite a few farmhouses that were settled by Jews. In contrast, in the period following the Second Revolt, i.e., the late Roman-Byzantine period (second/seventh centuries CE), the Jewish population, as far as I can tell, was concentrated in cities and villages only. This stands in contrast to the non-Jewish pagan population and its Christian successor, whose settled areas contain many sites that may be defined as farmhouses. In other words, from the Second Revolt onward there was a change in the settlement patterns of the Jewish population (and perhaps also of the Samaritans) which distinguished it from the non-Jewish population.

This article will attempt to clarify the nature and essence of this change. The beginning of the article will present the archaeological data corroborating my assumption that this change in settlement was indeed a fixed pattern characteristic of the Jewish population of Palestine at the time. I will then discuss the significance of this change, pinpoint the reasons which brought it about, and determine its possible impact on Jewish communal life in Palestine in the period under discussion.

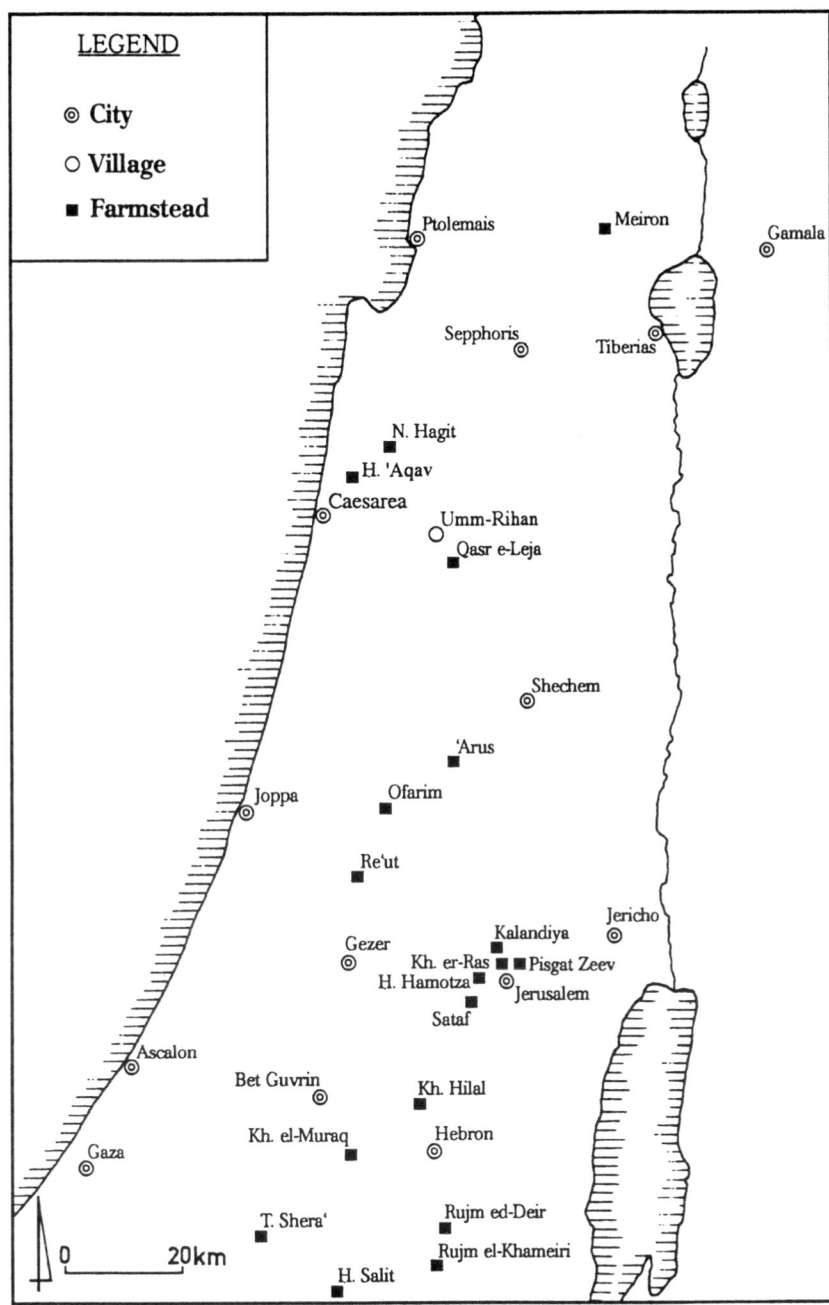

Fig. 1. Distribution of Early Roman farmsteads in Judaea

The Early Roman Period

The farmhouse, or the estate manor – which is similar in function but larger in its physical dimensions and superior in its quality of construction – may be defined as a self-sufficient structure in an agricultural area serving residential and agricultural needs.[1] These structures, known to us in a wide variety of shapes and sizes, were for the most part occupied by landowners or, at times, farmers/land tenants; both of these groups chose to live within the bounds of the worked land of their estate due to considerations of comfort and expediency. The decision of landowners to leave the protective environment of the city or village and settle in farmhouses or estate manors on open agricultural land is a direct outcome of prevailing conditions of security.[2]

The possibility of identifying the inhabitants of the early Roman farms discovered in Judaea as Jewish is based upon two types of archaeological evidence: ritual baths (*miqva'ot*) and stone vessels. In recent years, it has become evident that stepped bathing facilities, cut into rock or dug into the ground and covered with a grayish plaster characteristic of the early Roman period, are ritual baths used by the Jewish population during this period for purification purposes (Reich 1990). Ritual baths of this type have been found on strictly Jewish sites such as Jerusalem, Gezer, Jericho, Gamala, and elsewhere, and thus their discovery on early Roman sites attests to the Jewish origin of their inhabitants. Similarly, it has been proven that the use of typical stone vessels (bowls, cups, etc.), which do not impart impurity, was widespread among the Jewish population at the time (Magen 1984a), and this serves as well as an indication of Jewish presence on these sites.

The sites that are best preserved and most definitively identifiable as Jewish estate manors from the early Roman period are Kalandiya, north of Jerusalem, and Horvat 'Aqav at Ramat Hanadiv, northeast of Caesarea (Fig. 1, and for the other sites discussed). The site exposed at *Kalandiya* is a large complex (1200 m²) containing living quarters, storerooms, and industrial installations for the production of oil and wine (Fig. 2). The structure was built at the end of the Hellenistic period and was used continuously until 70 CE. In the complex's living quarters (Building F, according to the excavator's terminology), two ritual baths were discovered cut into rock. The finds on the site include various types of stone vessels, thereby conclusively identifying the inhabitants of this estate manor as Jews (Magen 1984b; 1993c).

The large estate manor exposed at *Horvat 'Aqav* (2800 m²) is surrounded by a wall and contains living quarters and various agricultural installations, including two winepresses (Fig. 3). Among the remains found in the living quarters of the complex was a ritual bath cut into rock and covered with grayish Herodian plaster (Fig. 4). On the basis of the excavated remains, it has been determined that this was a Jewish estate manor built at the end of the first century BCE and in use until 70 CE (Hirschfeld and Birger-Calderon 1991: 87–100).

Another site whose remains may be interpreted as a Jewish farmhouse from the early Roman period is *Nahal Hagit*, which was recently exposed on southern Mt. Carmel (Seligman 1995a: 55–56). Remains of the first level at the site include walls of a rectangular structure, next to which were found various installations and four stepped pools that were used as ritual baths (*miqva'ot*).

A large group of Jewish farmhouses from the early Roman period was discovered recently in salvage excavations carried out around Jerusalem (Greenhut 1994: 142–47). In *Pisgat Zeev*, in northeastern Jerusalem, a single structure on the top of a hillock was discovered next to a ritual bath, winepress, and subterranean oilpress (Fig. 5; Shukron and Savariego 1994). The finds on the

Fig. 2. Aerial view of Kalandiya, looking south

Fig. 3. Aerial view of H. 'Aqav at Ramat Hanadiv, looking west

Fig. 4. The miqveh at H. 'Aqav, looking east

Fig. 5. Aerial view of the farmstead at Pisgat Zeev, looking south (Courtesy E. Shukron, Israel Antiquities Authority)

*Fig. 6. The miqveh at H. Hamotza,
looking north (Courtesy Y. Billig,
Israel Antiquities Authority)*

site include typical stone vessels (bowls and cups), as well as coins of Alexander Jannaeus (104–76 BCE). In another neighborhood in Pisgat Zeev, east of Tel el-Ful, the remains of a large farmhouse with three ritual baths covered with gray Herodian plaster were exposed (Seligman 1994).

Not far from there, at *Khirbet Ka'kul*, two isolated structures were discovered adjacent to cisterns and ritual baths (Seligman 1995b).[3] The finds in both of these structures attest to their use in the late Hellenistic and early Roman periods, until 70 CE. At *Khirbet er-Ras*, north of Jerusalem, a complex that existed already in the Iron Age was discovered, but its main use was in the early Roman period (Onn and Rapuano 1995). The complex contains living quarters and storerooms arranged next to a courtyard, in which a ritual bath was found. Remains of structures and ritual baths from the early Roman period were also found at *Hurvat Hamotza* (Fig. 6), northwest of Jerusalem, and at *Giv'at Hamatos*, south of Jerusalem.[4]

The remains of farmhouses with ritual baths from a similar time period were also discovered in

Fig. 7. Early Roman remains at Kh. Hilal, looking southeast (Courtesy D. Amit, Israel Antiquities Authority)

the Hebron hills. At *Khirbet Hilal*, west of Gush Etzion, a complex composed of a dwelling, storerooms, and a large ritual bath was found (Fig. 7).[5] The finds at the site, which also included stone vessels, allowed the excavator to date the structure from the first century BCE until the second century CE, and thus he concluded that this was a 'Jewish farmstead built in Herod's reign and destroyed in the Bar-Kokhba war' (Amit 1992b: 151).

In southern Judaea, remains of fortified farmhouses were recently found which contained a courtyard surrounded by structures next to a well-built tower. At several of these sites, such as *Rujm ed-Deir*, north of Yatta, the discovery of ritual baths is indicative of the owners' Jewish origins. There, a tower surrounded by an inclined stone glacis was preserved, and next to it an entranceway leading to a ritual bath cut into rock.[6] Another, better-preserved example is *Horvat Salit*, on the southern slopes of the Hebron hills. This site yielded a tower, next to which was a courtyard containing rooms, storerooms, cisterns, and two ritual baths cut into rock.[7] The rich finds at the site (including stone vessels) date their use to the period between the two revolts, i.e., from the end of the first/ beginning of the second centuries CE.

The complex from the early Roman period exposed at *Khirbet el-Muraq*, southeast of Bet Guvrin, is outstanding in its dimensions and richness (Fig. 8). This is a large complex (37 × 42 m), built around a peristyle courtyard and containing, *inter alia*, halls, rooms, and a small bath house (Damati 1982; Hirschfeld 1995: 88–90). On the basis of its splendor and luxurious structures on the one hand, and the existence of a massive tower on the other, the complex may be defined as a fortified estate manor. The identification of its inhabitants as Jews is based on an inscription mentioning the name of 'Hilkiya son of Simeon' incised on one of the building stones, as well as the discovery of various stone vessels on the site. The results of the excavation indicate that the site was destroyed in the Great Revolt of 70 CE.

Additional remains of dwellings and ritual baths from the early Roman period were also discovered in the area of Modi'in (the foothills between Jerusalem and Tel Aviv). At a site next to the settlement of *Re'ut*, the remains of a Hasmonean-Herodian farmhouse were discovered next to winepresses, a cistern, and agricultural terraces (Hizmi 1990). The finds at the site include stone vessels, indicative of the Jewish origins of its inhabitants. At *Horvat Hermeshit*, also located in the area of Modi'in, remains were found of an early Roman period structure next to two ritual baths cut into rock.[8]

The above examples are indicative of a widespread phenomenon among the Jewish rural population of the early Roman period: that is of families living out on estates and farms.[9] It is clear that this kind of settlement was widespread not only among Jewish farmers. Estate manors and farmhouses from this period, and even earlier, were found in various parts of the country. In western Samaria, a large group of farmhouses dating from the late Iron Age and continuing into the Persian and Hellenistic periods was surveyed.[10] Further north, at *Qasr e-Leja*, impressive remains of a fortified courtyard house from the late Hellenistic/early Roman periods were also discovered through survey (Dar *et al.* 1986: 109–13; Hirschfeld 1995: 52–53). Qasr e-Leja presents additional fortified farmhouses found in western Samaria, among which we should mention the structure that was exposed near *Ofarim*. This structure, which is dated to the early Roman period, includes a tower surrounded by

Fig. 8. Peristyle courtyard in the fortified estate manor at Kh. el-Muraq, looking south (Courtesy E. Damati, Israel Antiquities Authority)

an inclined stone glacis next to a courtyard surrounded by rooms (Riklin 1995). In form and structure, it resembles the fortified farmhouses of southern Judaea.

Sources from the late Hellenistic/early Roman periods refer to estate manors and farmhouses in general terms only. For instance, Josephus (*AJ* 16.278) mentions 'settlements and villages' (*choria kai komai*) that were destroyed by bandits in Tarichaeae and Batanaea; 1 Maccabees 5:65 mentions the 'satellites' (*tougateres*), the 'fortresses' (*ochouromata*), and the 'towers' (*purgoi*) of Hebron. The villages of this period are mentioned in the sources either by the term 'village' (*kefar, kome*), or by the familiar biblical term 'city' (*'ir, polis*). It should be noted that the use of this last term is no more than a familiar reference and has no relevance to the term *polis* in its Greco-Roman sense (Schürer 1979: 196–97). The mishnaic term for estate manor is, most probably, 'town having a single owner' (M 'Eruvin 5:6; Applebaum 1976: 641–43). This definition of the term explains the discussion in M 'Eruvin 5:6 regarding the process by which 'a city of one becomes a city of many.' This process, whereby estate manors formed the nucleus for the creation of a village, may be substantiated archaeologically (Dar 1986: 22–23).

Other terms relating to elements in this type of rural settlement are spelled out in the *Mishnah* as well: 'If a man sold a town (i.e., an estate), he has sold also the houses, cisterns, trenches, vaults, bath houses, dovecots, olive presses, and irrigated fields...' (Bava Batra 4:7); this corresponds with the elements of the early Roman period estate manor found at sites such as Kalandiya, north of Jerusalem, and Horvat 'Aqav at Ramat Hanadiv. We may conjecture that the discussion of the term 'town having one owner' and its application to everyday reality – as it appears in tannaitic literature – reflects an early Roman period setting. In the later, amoraic sources there is no practical discusssion of this term.[11] It seems that, by then, Jewish estate manors had become a thing of the past.

The Late Roman-Byzantine Period

In April, 1995, I was invited to lecture on 'Farms and Villages in Byzantine Palestine' at a Dumbarton Oaks symposium entitled 'Palestine and Transjordan in the Period before Islam' (Hirschfeld, forthcoming). While compiling the archaeological data for that lecture, I came across a phenomenon in settlement which is worthy of mention. Farmhouses and estate manors from the late Roman-Byzantine period were found throughout the country *except* in the eastern Galilee and the western slopes of the Golan, where the Jewish population concentrated at that time. Aided by the site map pinpointing the remains of ancient synagogues, one could outline with greater precision the said area: the eastern upper Galilee; parts of the lower Galilee, between Sepphoris and Tiberias; and the northern drainage basin on both sides of the Jordan River (Tsafrir *et al.* 1994: Map 4). Although many excavations and surveys have been conducted in these areas (Yeivin 1971; Dauphin and Schonfield 1983; Dauphin and Gibson 1994; Ma'oz 1993: 538–45; Stefanski 1995: 13–14), to date no sites have been found that can be defined as farmhouses or estate manors.[12]

The absence of such structures in the areas of Jewish settlement in the Galilee and Golan is especially pronounced in light of the abundance of sites of this type found in other parts of the country. Among many examples, we may mention the farmhouses whose remains were documented on the southern slopes of Mt. Hermon (Dar 1993b: 93–103 [Qal'at Bustra], 104–44 [Nahal Govta], and elsewhere); in the western Galilee (Frankel 1992: 40–42 [Horvat Zabadi], 49–56 [Khirbet el-

Quseir], and elsewhere); on Mt. Carmel (Dar and Siegelmann 1995; Seligman 1995a); south of Mt. Carmel at Horvat 'Aqav (Hirschfeld and Birger-Calderon 1991: 100–109), where the remains of a late structure actually lie on top of the ruins of an early Roman building; on the coastal plain (Porath *et al.* 1985: 65–66; Hizmi 1984; Porath 1988; Israel 1993 [Byzantine estate manor and industrial site north of Ashkelon]). Remains of farmhouses and/or estate manors were also found in Judaea (e.g., Onn and Rapuano 1995 [Khirbet er-Ras, north of Jerusalem]; Feig 1995 [Bet Safafa, south of Jerusalem]; Gat 1982 [Khirbet 'Ein et-Tut, west of Jerusalem]; Sion 1995 [Adam, northeast of Jerusalem]; Amit 1992b [Khirbet Hilal, in the Hebron hills]; Navon 1991: 57–58 [Sansanara Forest, on the southern slopes of the Hebron hills]), and in the Negev.[13]

This period, which is characterized by a markedly long era of peace and security, allowed farmers to leave the village framework and live on their open tracts of land. This is especially pronounced in the Negev, where hundreds of farmhouses of different sizes and types were found, even in the remotest of areas. There was a very important economic advantage to living on land distant from the village: it reduced the amount of time needed to get from the house to the field and back, and by doing so farmers could also significantly broaden the territory to be worked, exploiting land reserves in previously unsettled areas. Many of the farmhouses formed the nucleus for the development of satellite villages, thereby creating diversity and complexity, the picture of settlement as we know it in Byzantine Palestine.

And yet, despite these apparent advantages, on the basis of the archaeological finds it appears that the Jewish farmer in this period preferred to continue living in his native village even if his fields were distant from it. This begins to explain the absence of farmhouses in the Jewish areas of settlement in the Galilee and the Golan on the one hand, and, on the other, the existence of 'large villages of Jews' (*kome megiste Ioudaion*), as they are referred to by the early fourth-century church father Eusebius.[14] It appears that the processes of decentralization, that brought about a diverse settlement pattern in other areas of the country, passed over the Jewish villages of the Galilee, the Golan, and probably over southern Judaea as well.[15] The inhabitants of these villages continued to live in their village confines, despite the economic prosperity and processes of demographic growth which elsewhere had led to the establishment of farmhouses and smaller satellite villages. As a result, the extended village, which was termed by rabbinic literature according to the biblical word 'city' (*'ir*, pl. *'ayyarot*), became the widespread form of settlement amongst the Jewish rural population in the period under discussion.[16]

This phenomenon and the explanation for it were carefully examined by Ronny Ellenblum (1991: 307–10), whose study essentially treats Frankish settlement in Crusader Palestine. Ellenblum believes that the area of Jewish settlement in the eastern Upper Galilee in the Byzantine period is characterized by relatively large settlements of over 5–10 *dunams* (0.5–1 ha); he rightly rejects explanations based upon economic, climatic or security considerations, as the conditions relevant to the existence of the Jewish community at this time would have been no different than those of the non-Jewish population living in other parts of the country. The explanation for this phenomenon, he opines, lies in the Jewish lifestyle, which was dependent upon the accessibility of various communal services and the proximity of the dwelling to the synagogue. Dwelling near the synagogue, then as now, gained especial importance on the Sabbath and on holidays, when the walking distance between synagogue and home was limited by the Sabbath boundaries (*'eruv*), boundaries set by tannaitic halakha at 2000 cubits, that is, no more than 1.2 km around the houses in the settlement.[17] Later on, the rabbis added another 2000 cubits from the point of the settlement's *'eruv* – but not in every direction. This restriction practically prevented observant Jews from living outside a settlement.

If this assumption is correct, then quite a few Jewish farmers whose fields lay far from the village encountered not only inconvenience but real economic loss. Thus, one may understand the words of Rav, the famous early third-century Babylonian sage: 'Blessed are you [who lives] in the city (*'ir*), whose house is near the synagogue, blessed are you [who lives] in the field, whose property is close to the city...' (B Bava Metzia 107a; Aberbach 1994: 176). As a result, we may assume that farmers whose tracts of land were especially remote, and thus not viable to work, were forced to restrict their agricultural occupation and pursue other activities such as commerce or industry.[18]

In summary, there was a substantial upheaval in the settlement patterns of the rural Jewish population in the late Roman-Byzantine period. In contrast to the early Roman period, when there were many Jewish estate manors, in this later period the Jews abstained from living on isolated farms or in small satellite villages. This, in turn, was contrary to the practice of rural non-Jewish populations living in farmhouses and hamlets. As a result, the Jewish villages in the period under discussion expanded both in area and number of inhabitants.

When Did This Change Occur and How May It Be Explained?

The roots of this settlement phenomenon characterizing the Jewish population should be examined against the background of the direct and indirect results of the two revolts against Rome. The destruction caused by the First Revolt, and subsequently by the Second Revolt, led to a massive abandonment of Judaea and the migration of much of the Jewish population to the Galilee. Those who escaped from Judaea were destitute refugees, who were forced to join an established settlement, city or village inhabited by members of their own people.

It should be understood that the possibility of acquiring a tract of land upon which to build a farmhouse would not have been practical in the Destruction generation, or in that following it. However, one should ask why this did not happen in subsequent generations, after the Jewish population in the Galilee, the Golan, and southern Judaea had recovered from the repercussions of the revolt, and even after it had known a prolonged and flourishing period of prosperity.

The answer to this question may be sought in two possible directions. One is a sense of insecurity within the Jewish settlement, which lived as a minority among Palestine's non-Jewish population. It may also be assumed that the destruction caused in the course of the two revolts against Rome perhaps precipitated a personal sense of insecurity among Jewish farmers which discouraged them from abandoning their villages and living in isolated farmhouses.

The second direction of inquiry, which appears to be more significant, is the impact of the Jewish nation's religious leadership, who – in reaction to the physical and spiritual ruin incurred by the revolts against Rome – wished to create an active and vibrant communal framework. Increasing communal activity, through a routine of prayer, study in the synagogue, and observance of Jewish laws according to the *Mishnah*, which had been compiled and edited not long after this time, created a new, and heretofore unknown, situation. The relationship between the individual and this communal framework made it difficult for a Jewish farmer to leave the village and settle on a remote tract of land. This process continued – as is evident from the archaeological remains – in the late Roman/Byzantine period, despite the growth of the Jewish rural population and the expansion of their property holdings. It appears, then, that the Jewish farmer preferred to make the long trek to his tract and back rather than leave the collective society of his village. This pattern of behavior would be markedly in contrast to that of his non-Jewish pagan and, later, Christian counterparts, who often chose to abandon the village and settle in the heart of his tract of land.

This process, which created a clear distinction between the Jewish and non-Jewish rural societies of Palestine, raises a question regarding the Samaritan population. Was the pattern of this community, which was also essentially rural, closer to the Jewish or the non-Jewish model? Archaeological studies conducted in Samaria are inclined to favor the former. Surveys and excavations in western Samaria have yielded only a handful of sites that may be defined as farmhouses dating to the late Roman/Byzantine period – in contrast to the abundance of farms and towers from the period preceding the destruction of the Second Temple (Dar *et al.* 1986:105–14 [area of Umm-Rihan, in northwestern Samaria]; Dar 1986 [western Samaria]). In contrast, in the same area a large number of contemporaneous villages have been studied and excavated (Dar *et al.* 1986 [Umm-Rihan]; Dar 1984 [Khirbet el-Burak]; Dar and Safrai 1984 [Khirbet el-Bireh]; Magen 1993a [Qedumim]). These studies of Samaria have shown that the Samaritans, like the Jews, preferred to settle in villages.

This interesting phenomenon raises a number of further questions. What motivated the Samaritan farmer to behave like his Jewish counterpart? Did the Samaritans undergo processes similar to those that shaped Jewish settlement patterns after 70 CE? The fate of the Samaritans in the period when the Jews rebelled against Rome is unknown. On the one hand, we have evidence of destruction and ruin incurred upon Samaria in the period of the Great Revolt; on the other, it is clear from the sources that the Samaritans built themselves up in the wake of the Jewish destruction in the Second Revolt (Safrai 1982: 257). Later on, in the fourth century, the Samaritan population experienced a revitalization movement, a return to religion, headed by their legendary leader, Baba Rabbah. It appears that, from the days of Baba Rabbah onward, the Samaritans adopted the Jewish purity laws, as well as the concept of assembly around the synagogue as a place of prayer and Torah-study.[19] As a result, the Samaritan farmers required a network of services to be furnished by their community.

The remains of a number of magnificent synagogues from this period were discovered recently in various villages in Samaria (Magen 1993b: 66–90). It is thus possible that the same factors that motivated the Jewish farmers not to leave their villages were at play among the Samaritans as well. This supposition, as well as its corroboration by archaeological data, await further examination.

Summary

The destruction and ruin caused by the Jewish revolts against Rome, and the subsequent activity of convalescence and rebuilding, had far-reaching effects on the shaping of the Jewish people's profile. Jewish – and apparently also Samaritan – rural society developed differently from that of the non-Jewish rural population. The more usual process, which led to abandonment of villages and settlement on remote tracts of land, did not occur in Jewish society. The Jewish farmer – either due to his sense of insecurity or to halakhic stipulations and religious observance – preferred to remain within the village limits, even if his property lay a considerable distance away. This preference has far-reaching ramifications, attesting to the extraordinary place the Jewish community and its institutions held in the life of the individual – not only in large cities, but also in relatively remote villages. This may possibly mark the beginning of a long process which led, on the one hand, to the abandonment of agriculture as a primary source of income among the Jews and their transition to a more intensive occupation in commerce and industry. On the other hand, this process might have turned the Jews from a more rustic way of life and made Judaism a more urban-oriented religion.

Notes

1   Shimon Dar (1986: 1) defines the farmhouse as 'a structure surrounded by cultivated area, the former used by the cultivators for habitation and handicrafts.' Israel Finkelstein (1981: n. 5) offers a similar definition. The majority of farmhouses and estate manors found throughout the country are characterized – in contradistinction to the Roman villa – by their modest dimensions and lack of luxurious structures; the use, therefore, of the term 'villa' by Shimon Applebaum (1989: 124) is unacceptable.

   On the distinction between villa – a planned structure designed to bring pleasure to its owners, and farmhouse – intended to fulfill agricultural needs, see Ackerman 1990: 9–10. The model of the rural villa in the West, which is described in detail by Varro, Cato, Columella, and others, is practically almost unknown in Roman Palestine. For these reasons, Safrai's (1994: 82–83) use of the term to describe the Palestinian villa is unsubstantiated.

2   On the economic advantages that motivated villagers to leave the village and move to dwellings on worked tracts of land, see Safrai 1986: 30–31. Farmhouses often went on to form a nucleus for the creation of satellite villages.

3   In the area east of Khirbet Ka'kul, a 'fortress' from the Persian period was discovered, which continued to be used into the early Roman period and until the Great Revolt (Nadelman 1994). I believe that it would be more reasonable to view the Persian 'fortress' as a structure on a fortified farm which continued to be used until the Great Revolt. A similar Persian 'fortress,' which was in use until the Hellenistic period, was found on Har Adar in northwestern Jerusalem (Dadon 1995).

4   At Hurvat Hamotza, the remains of structures, ritual baths, and stone measuring utensils were found (Billig 1995). At Giv'at Hamatos, south of Jerusalem, remains of a structure were found next to a ritual bath inside a cave (Kogan-Zehavi 1995: 86). Remains of a farmhouse and ritual bath from the early Roman period were surveyed at Sheikh 'Ubeid, near Sataf, west of Jerusalem (Gibson 1992: 28). At Khirbet el-Marmita, near Bet Shemesh, remains were discovered of a structure from the Second Temple period containing stone vessels, potsherds, and coins from the end of the second century BCE until the first century CE (Gershuny 1992). A farmhouse or estate manor from the early Roman period was surveyed at Rasm Dihna, southeast of Bet Guvrin (Kloner 1987; cf. another site, Qasr Firjas, 202–203).

5   Amit 1992a. In addition to Khirbet Hilal, we should mention the ritual bath discovered at Horvat Hazzan on the Judaean coastal plain (Avni *et al*. 1987: 115–27). Besides a ritual bath, finds – including stone vessels – found at the site attested to its use in the early Roman period. These finds are indicative of Jewish presence; due to the absence of architectural remains, however, it is impossible to determine whether the site functioned as a satellite village or farmhouse at this time. Remains were also found of a elaborate estate manor from the Byzantine period.

6   Amit 1991. This site may be compared with another, better-preserved site, Rujm el-Khameiri, located southeast of Yatta. The remains of Rujm el-Khameiri include a courtyard surrounded by rooms and a tower surrounded by an inclined stone glacis. The site was surveyed by the author as part of a regional study of the eastern frontier (Hirschfeld 1979: 83–84), and was dated to the Byzantine period; however,

it has become evident from Yuval Barukh's recent excavations that the site dates to the early Roman period. I would like to thank the excavator for his personal communication of this important information.

7   Alon 1987a. The excavator interprets the site as a fortress, but, on the basis of the finds and by comparison with other sites, it appears more reasonable to view it as a fortified estate manor from the end of the early Roman period (Hirschfeld 1995: 71–72). Horvat Salit may be compared with a similar site, Nahal Yattir, which was also destroyed in the Bar-Kokhba war (Alon 1987b: 154–58). The absence of ritual baths does not necessarily indicate that the inhabitants at the Nahal Yattir site were not Jewish. Remains of a single structure from the first century CE were discovered on Tel Sera', northwest of Beersheba (Oren 1993: 1335). Chalkstone measuring cups found at the site are suggestive of its inhabitants' Jewish origins.

8   Greenhut 1990. On the Byzantine remains at Horvat Hermeshit, see Greenhut 1991. Early Roman pottery was found in the excavations of the terraces near the site (Yron-Lubin 1995: 85). The remains from the early Roman site there do not as yet permit its definition as a village or estate manor. In this context, we should mention Horvat Zikhrin on the inner coastal plain, north of Horvat Hermeshit and southeast of Tel Aphek. Remains of farmhouses that were abandoned in the Great Revolt were discovered at this location (Fisher 1994: 43–44). Later on, in the second/third centuries, these farmhouses were the nucleus for the creation of a Byzantine village at the site (its population, on the basis of the discovery of the church in the center of the village, was Christian).

9   Recently, the remains of a large estate in Samaria, identified with the estate of Herod's court minister Ptolemy, were published (Dar 1993a). In this context, we should mention the royal estates belonging to the Hasmonean and Herodian dynasties in Jericho. The early Roman period is characterized by the existence of large estates that were awarded in lieu of either military or royal service (Sperber 1978: 187).

10 Finkelstein 1981. According to Finkelstein, these farms ceased to exist during wartime and the political upheavals that accompanied the Hasmonean battles. To these finds we should add the 'fortified' agricultural farm, which, according to the excavators, was uncovered in Tirat Yehudah (Yeivin and Edelstein 1970: 67). The farm at Tirat Yehudah emerged in the Iron Age (8th/7th centuries BCE) and flourished mainly in the Hellenistic period (3rd/2nd centuries BCE). Two more farmhouses were surveyed in northwestern Samaria (Dar, Safrai and Tepper 1986: 107–109 [the Moshav Rihan farm], 113 [the Ziqzuq farm]). In the region of Judaea, southwest of Jerusalem, three Iron Age farms were surveyed (Amit 1992a: 147), while at Har Adar, northwest of Jerusalem, we have mentioned the Persian 'fortress' that was converted into a Hellenistic farmhouse (Dadon 1995). The structure of a Hellenistic farm was discovered next to Moshav Aderet on the foothills of Judaea (Yogev 1984).

11 Barring a single reference in the Jerusalem Talmud (Yevamot 8, 8d), which appears to be within the context of a story and thus not necessarily a reflection of reality: 'There was an incident of one who took a private estate (= '*ir*) of uncircumcised slaves from a non-Jew in order to circumcise them and they reconsidered.' I would like to thank Z. Safrai for referring me to this source.

12 In Ma'oz's discussion of Jewish settlement in the Golan, he mentions villages only; moreover, in a personal communication dated August 13, 1995, he states: 'In the area of the synagogues in the Golan I do not know of any farms.'

13 Rubin 1990. Surveys in the Beersheba Valley and southward, until Makhtesh Ramon, have yielded hundreds of farmhouses, some in remote places with poor access. Information about the Negev surveys has been published in several volumes by the Archaeological Survey of Israel.

14 Eusebius, *Onomastikon*, Engaddi, Estemoa, and Iutta (Klostermann 1904: 86.16; 86.20; 108.8 respectively). See also Thomsen (1903): 57–62.

15 From the archaeological work done in southern Judaea, I do not know of remains from any site that could be defined as a farm belonging to Jews – in contrast to the large sites, such as Horvat Susiya or Eshtemoa, which were decisively Jewish villages. For the historical background of the 'South,' see Schwartz 1991.

16 The term 'city' ('*ir*) in the sense of village is common in rabbinic literature. From an analysis of its occurrences,

it can be proven that it refers to villages differing from one another in size ('large city' – *'ir gedola*, and 'small city' – *'ir qetana*), as it appears, for example, in the M 'Eruvin 5:8 or J Makkot 2.7.31b, but not in their definition as rural settlements. The term in rabbinic literature reserved for a city proper, i.e., a city in the Greco-Roman sense of polis, is *kerakh*. For an up-to-date discussion, with summary and references to modern studies, see Safrai 1994: 17–19. On the various components of the talmudic 'city,' i.e., the extended village, see Yeivin 1987. A common error found in the studies of Safrai, Yeivin, and others is the interpretation of the talmudic term 'city' (*'ir*) as a small city (i.e., the modern-day town). The error has many ramifications vis-à-vis the perception of the village, its planning, and the activities conducted therein.

17   Tannaitic halakha is the Jewish law of early rabbinic traditions organized in the *Mishnah* and redacted by Rabbi Judah the Prince ca. 200 CE (Fine 1991).

18   Rabbinic sources mention many Jewish villages that excelled in various production industries, such as mats from Usha, pottery from Kefar Hanania, Shikhin, and Netofah, a type of sandal from 'Amuqa, etc. (Safrai 1994: 78–79). On village pottery production centers in the Galilee, see Adan-Bayewitz 1993: 23–41. It is, of course, possible that this phenomenon is not unique at all to the Jewish village, but was common to large villages elsewhere throughout the country.

19   On the Samaritan ritual baths discovered at Qedumim and their significance, see Reich 1988.

Bibliography

Aberbach, M. (1994) *Labor, Crafts and Commerce in Ancient Israel*, Jerusalem.

Ackerman, J.S. (1990) *The Villa: Form and Ideology of Country Houses*, Princeton.

Adan-Bayewitz, D. (1993) *Common Pottery in Roman Galilee*, Ramat Gan.

Alon, D. (1987a) "Horvat Salit (Kh. Salantah)," *Excavations and Surveys in Israel* 5: 94–96.

_____(1987b) "Nahal Yatir Site," in A. Kloner and Y. Tepper, eds., *The Hiding Complexes in the Judean Shephelah*, 154–59. Tel Aviv. (in Hebrew)

Amit, D. (1991) "Yatta, Survey," *Excavations and Surveys in Israel* 9: 165–166.

_____(1992a) "Farmsteads in Northern Judea (Betar Area), Survey," *Excavations and Surveys in Israel* 10: 147–148.

_____(1992b) "Khirbet Hilal," *Excavations and Surveys in Israel* 10: 150–151.

Applebaum, S. (1976) "Economic life in Palestine," in S. Safrai and M. Stern, eds., *The Jewish People in the First Century*, II, 631–700. Philadelphia.

_____(1989) *Judaea in Hellenistic and Roman Times*, Leiden.

Avni, G. et al. (1987) "Ahuzat Hazzan," in A. Kloner and Y. Tepper, eds., *The Hiding Complexes in the Judean Shephelah*, 115–27. Tel-Aviv. (in Hebrew)

Billig, Y. (1995) "Horvat Hamotza," *Hadashot Arkheologiyot* 103: 71–72. (in Hebrew)

Cohen, J.M. (1981) *A Samaritan Chronicle*, Leiden.

Dadon, M. (1995) "Har Adar," *Excavations and Surveys in Israel* 14: 87–88.

Damati, E. (1982) "The Palace of Hilkiya," *Qadmoniot* 15: 117–120. (in Hebrew)

Dar, S. (1984) "Khirbet al-Burak," *Excavations and Surveys in Israel* 1: 13–14.

_____(1986) *Landscape and Pattern: An Archaeological Survey of Samaria 800 B.C.E.-636 C.E.*, I-II (BAR International Series 308), Oxford.

_____(1993a) "The estate of Ptolemy, Senior Minister of Herod," in I. Gafni et al., eds., *Jews and Judaism in the Second Temple, Mishna and Talmud Period*, 38–50. Jerusalem. (in Hebrew)

_____(1993b) *Settlements and Cult Sites on Mount Hermon, Israel* (BAR-IS 589), Oxford.

Dar, S. and Z. Safrai (1984) "Khirbet el-Bireh," *Excavations and Surveys in Israel* 1: 11–13.

Dar, S., Z. Safrai, and Y. Tepper (1986) *Um Rihan: A Village of the Mishna*, Tel Aviv. (in Hebrew)

Dar, S. and A. Siegelmann (1995) "Survey on Mt. Carmel," *Excavations and Surveys in Israel* 14: 49–50.

Dauphin, C.M. and S. Gibson (1994) "Ancient settlements in their landscapes: the results of ten years of survey on the Golan Heights (1978–1988)," *Bulletin of the Anglo-Israel Archaeological Society* 12: 7–31.

Dauphin, C.M. and J.J. Schonfield (1983) "Settlements of the Roman and Byzantine periods on the Golan Heights," *IEJ* 33: 191–206.

Ellenblum, R. (1991) *Frankish Rural Settlement in Crusader Palestine* (Ph.D. thesis, Hebrew University). (in Hebrew)

Feig, N. (1995) "Jerusalem, Beit Safafa," *Excavations and Surveys in Israel* 14: 99–102.

Fine, S. (1991) "Entry into rabbinic literature," *Biblical Archaeology Review* 17: 54.

Finkelstein, I. (1981) "Israelite and Hellenistic farms in the foothills and in the Yarkon Basin," *ErIsr* 15: 331–348. (in Hebrew)

Fisher, M. (1994) "Horvat Zikhrin: 1987–1989," *Excavations and Surveys in Israel* 12: 40–44.

Frankel, R. (1992) "Some oil presses from Western Galilee," *BASOR* 286: 39–71.

Gat, J. (1982) "Khirbet 'Ein et-Tut," *Excavations and Surveys in Israel* 1: 52.

Gershuny, L. (1992) "Khirbet el-Marmita," *Excavations and Surveys in Israel* 10: 29–30.

Gibson, S. (1992) "Sataf: 1989," *Excavations and Surveys in Israel* 10: 27–28.

Greenhut, Z. (1990) "Horvat Hermeshit (Ne'ot Qedumim)," *Excavations and Surveys in Israel* 7/8: 81–83.

————(1991) "Horvat Hermeshit (Ne'ot Qedumim): 1989," *Excavations and Surveys in Israel* 9: 141–143.

————(1994) "Renovations of the archaeological research in the periphery of Jerusalem," *Ariel* 100: 133–147. (in Hebrew)

Hirschfeld, Y. (1979) "A line of Byzantine forts along the eastern highway of the Hebron Hills," *Qadmoniot* 12: 78–84. (in Hebrew)

————(1995) *The Palestinian Dwelling in the Roman-Byzantine Period*, Jerusalem.

————(forthcoming) "Farms and villages in Byzantine Palestine," *DOP* 51 (1997).

Hirschfeld, Y. and R. Birger-Calderon (1991) "Early Roman and Byzantine estates near Caesarea," *IEJ* 41: 81–111.

Hizmi, H. (1984) "Giv'at Ehud (Yehudit)," *Excavations and Surveys in Israel* 3: 32–33.

————(1990) "Re'ut (Kh. Abu Saris)," *Excavations and Surveys in Israel* 7/8: 155–156.

Israel, Y. (1993) "Ashqelon," *Excavations and Surveys in Israel* 13: 100–105.

Kloner, A. (1987) "Rasm Dihna," in A. Kloner and Y. Tepper, eds., *The Hiding Complexes in the Judean Shephelah*, 209–16. Tel Aviv. (in Hebrew)

Klostermann, E. (1904) *Eusebius Onomastikon der biblischen Ortsnamen*, Leipzig.

Kogan-Zehavi, E. (1995) "Jerusalem, Giv'at Hamatos," *Excavations and Surveys in Israel* 13: 85–89.

Magen, Y. (1984a) "Jerusalem as the centre for stone-ware production in Herodian times," *Qadmoniot* 17: 117–120. (in Hebrew)

Magen, Y. (1984b) "Kalandia: a vineyard farm and winery of Second Temple times," *Qadmoniot* 17: 61–71. (in Hebrew)

————(1993a) "Qedumim: a Samaritan site of the Roman-Byzantine period," in F. Manns and E. Alliata, eds., *Early Christianity in Context*, 167–80. Jerusalem.

————(1993b) "Samaritan synagogues," in F. Manns and E. Alliata, eds., *Early Christianity in Context*, 193–230. Jerusalem.

————(1993c) "Qalandiyeh," in E. Stern, ed., *New Encyclopedia of Archaeological Excavations in the Holy Land* 4: 1197–1200.

Ma'oz, Z. (1993) "Golan," in E. Stern, ed., *New Encyclopedia of Archaeological Excavations in the Holy Land* 2: 534–546.

Nadelman, Y. (1994) "Jerusalem, Pisgat Ze'ev (H. Zimri)," *Excavations and Surveys in Israel* 12: 54–56.

Navon, A. (1991) "Sansanara Forest," *Excavations and Surveys in Israel* 9: 68–69.

Onn, A. and Y. Rapuano (1995) "Jerusalem, Kh. er-Ras," *Excavations and Surveys in Israel* 13: 71.

Oren, E. (1993) "Sera', Tel," in E. Stern, ed., *New Encyclopedia of Archaeological Excavations in the Holy Land* 4: 1329–1335.

Porath, Y. (1988) "Mishmar David," *Excavations and Surveys in Israel* 6: 81–82.

Porath, Y., S. Dar and S. Applebaum (1985) *The History and Archaeology of Emek-Hefer,* Tel-Aviv. (in Hebrew)

Reich, R. (1988) "A note on Samaritan ritual baths," in D. Jacoby and Y. Tsafrir, eds., *Jews, Samaritans and Christians in Byzantine Palestine*, 242–44. Jerusalem. (in Hebrew)

_____(1990) *Miqwa'ot (Jewish Ritual Immersion Baths) in Eretz Israel* (Ph.D. thesis, Hebrew University).

Riklin, S. (1995) "Ofarim," *Excavations and Surveys in Israel* 13: 53–54.

Rubin, R. (1990) *The Negev as a Settled Land*, Jerusalem. (in Hebrew)

Safrai, Z. (1982) "The Samaritans," in Z. Baras et al., eds., *Eretz Israel from the Destruction of the Second Temple to the Muslim Conquest*, 252–64. Jerusalem. (in Hebrew)

_____(1986) "The influence of demographic stratification on the agricultural and economic structure during the Mishnaic and Talmudic Periods," in A. Kasher et al., eds., *Man and Land in Eretz-Israel in Antiquity*, 20–48. Jerusalem. (in Hebrew)

_____(1994) *The Economy of Roman Palestine*, London and New York.

Schürer, E. (1979) *The History of the Jewish People in the Age of Jesus Christ (175 B.C. – A.D. 135)*, II, Edinburgh.

Schwartz, J. (1991) *Lod (Lydda), Israel* (BAR-IS 571), Oxford.

Seligman, J. (1994) "Jerusalem, Pisgat Ze'ev (East A)," *Excavations and Surveys in Israel* 12: 52–54.

_____(1995a) "Nahal Hagit," *Hadashot Arkheologiyot* 104: 55–57. (in Hebrew)

_____(1995b) "Jerusalem, Kh. Ka'kul," *Excavations and Surveys in Israel* 13: 69–70.

Shukron, A. and A. Savariego (1994) "Jerusalem, Pisgat Ze'ev (Villa Quarter)," *Excavations and Surveys in Israel* 12: 56–58.

Sion, O. (1995) "Adam," *Excavations and Surveys in Israel* 14: 86–87.

Sperber, D. (1978) *Roman Palestine 200–400: The Land*, Ramat Gan.

Stefanski, Y. (1995) "Rosh Pinna Map, Survey – 1992," *Excavations and Surveys in Israel* 14: 13–15.

Thomsen, P. (1903) *Palaestina nach dem Onomasticon des Eusebius*, Tübingen.

Tsafrir, Y., L. Di Segni and J. Green (1994) *Tabula Imperii Romani – Iudaea – Palaestina – Eretz Israel in the Hellenistic, Roman and Byzantine Periods – Maps and Gazetteer*, Jerusalem.

Yeivin, Z. (1971) *Survey of Settlements in Galilee and the Golan from the Period of the Mishnah in Light of the Sources* (Ph.D thesis, Hebrew University). (in Hebrew)

_____(1987) "On the 'medium sized city'," *Eretz-Israel*, XIX (Avi-Yonah Volume), 59–71. Jerusalem. (in Hebrew)

Yeivin, Z. and G. Edelstein (1970) "Excavations of Tirat Yehuda," *'Atiqot* 6: 56–69. (in Hebrew)

Yogev, O. (1984) "Aderet," *Excavations and Surveys in Israel* 1: 1.

Yron-Lubin, M. (1995) "Horvat Hermeshit (Ne'ot Qedumim)," *Excavations and Surveys in Israel* 14: 83–85.

6. The Roman Relationship with the *Persicus sinus* from the Rise of Spasinou Charax (127 BC) to the Reign of Shapur II (AD 309–379)

D.T. Potts

Introduction

There are at least two, very different contexts in which to pursue an analysis of the Roman relationship with the communities inhabiting the islands and shores of the *Persicus sinus* (Fig. 1). For the sake of simplicity we may set these out in the form of the following thesis and antithesis:

Thesis: There is no *a priori* reason to believe that the Roman relationship with the *Persicus sinus* differed fundamentally from that of any of Rome's imperial predecessors or successors in the region. Hence, it will be helpful to place Rome's relationship in the context of earlier and later patterns of imperial 'behaviour' (in the most all-inclusive sense of the term) towards the region, from the Old Akkadian (ca. 2350–2100 BC) through the British colonial (1820–1970) era. Material culture in the Gulf region can be expected to reflect both patterns and levels of integration with the Roman world.

Antithesis: Because Rome never physically controlled any of the territories adjacent to the *Persicus sinus*,[1] its relationship with the area cannot be compared with that of the Akkadians, Kassites, Assyrians, Achaemenids, Parthians, Sasanians, western Arabs, Portuguese, or British. The Roman empire represented a non-Oriental, physically remote power, and Rome's relationship with the region must therefore be analysed along completely different lines than that of its predecessors or successors. Material culture in the Gulf region cannot be expected to reflect either patterns or levels of integration with the Roman world.

The archaeological irony of these two positions is that they pave the way for a series of diametrically opposed interpretations based on one and the same data set. If we accept the Thesis, then Roman imports and Roman-inspired local products from the region may be interpreted as positive indicators of integration with the Roman world. If we follow the Antithesis, then such goods may be dismissed as having little or no bearing on the question of integration with Rome.

I have stated the case here in intentionally exaggerated, black and white terms, in order to underscore how very different interpretations can be reached from the same body of material. Yet I propose to follow neither of the positions stated above. In fact, the seemingly intractable difference

89

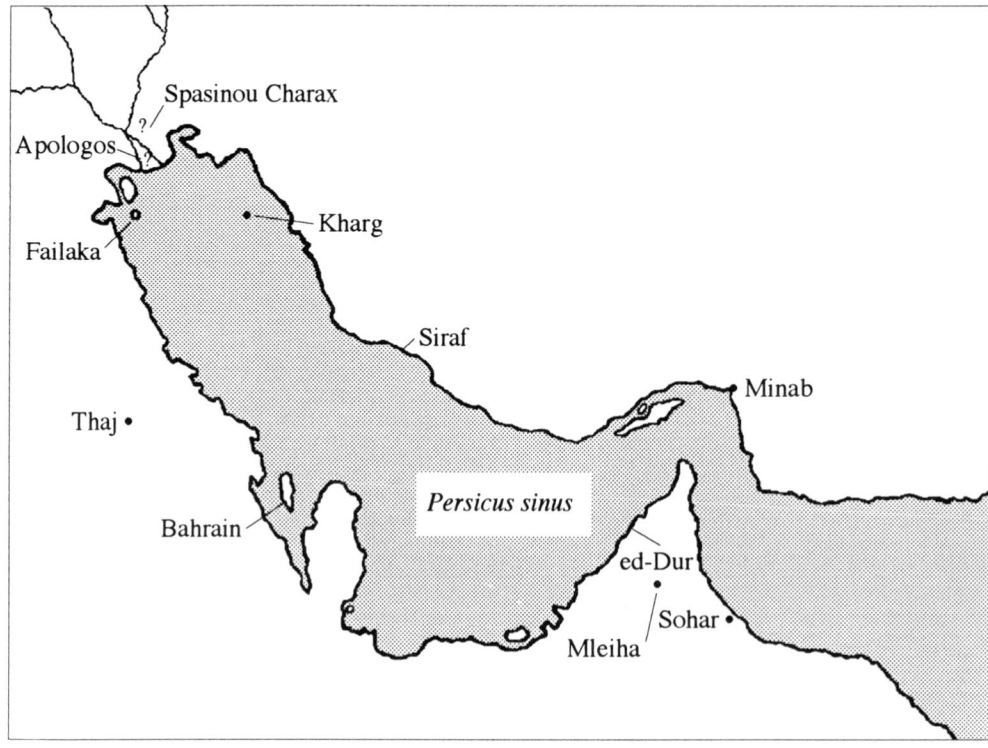

Fig. 1 . Map of the region showing the principal sites mentioned in the text

between these two positions can be resolved if we consider the following proposition, which will be adopted throughout the course of this chapter.

Synthesis: For a plethora of reasons, the Roman empire was structurally unlike any empire which had preceded it in the East. In the *Persicus sinus*, Roman imperial 'behaviour' was never once displayed in a direct fashion. No Roman equivalent of a British gunboat ever sat off an Arabian or Iranian port to intimidate an intractable local ruler, and no merchant vessel from Alexandria ever dumped its cargo on the quay at Teredon or Bahrain. Nevertheless, a wide range of archaeological material attests to the popularity of Roman styles (in glass, ceramics, bronze, etc.) in the region, styles which reached the area through the mediation of economic mechanisms generated both by Rome and by those neighbours interacting either directly or indirectly with the Roman economy. In this way, an extra-imperial region like the *Persicus sinus* was integrated into the Roman world in spite of geographically intervening political boundaries and hostile relationships. Political realities notwithstanding, it was this penetration by Rome of a region where its armies never set foot which characterised the Roman relationship with the *Persicus sinus*. In a multicultural, multilingual world where Indian, Iranian, Babylonian, Central Asian and native Arabian symbols all circulated freely, Roman-manufactured and Roman-inspired goods in the *Persicus sinus* became powerful 'symbols in action', to borrow a phrase from Ian Hodder, symbols of the metropolitan, cosmopolitan West (Hodder 1982). Thus, the presence of Roman goods and their derivatives in the *Persicus sinus* reflected neither the integration implied above in our Thesis, nor the lack of integration implied by the Antithesis, but a penetration of symbols which were transformed in their new context, becoming imbued with a symbolic value which was not always inherent in their original locus of manufacture and use.

State of Research

It should be stressed at the outset that the archaeological basis for undertaking the sort of analysis proposed here is far from ideal. A series of factors, many of them political, has meant that the coverage available for the different geographical areas bordering the *Persicus sinus* is highly discontinuous and imbalanced. In particular, the western, Arabian side of the *Persicus sinus* is much better investigated than the eastern, Persian side. Although some work has been done by both Western expeditions along the Iranian coast (e.g. survey by Vanden Berghe in coastal Fars [Mostafavi 1978: 63]; survey by Prickett and Williamson in coastal Fars and Kerman [Williamson 1987]; survey on Kish island [Whitehouse 1976]; excavations on Kharg island by Ghirshman [Ghirshman 1959] and at Siraf by Whitehouse [Whitehouse 1974; Lowick 1985]) and by Iranian scholars (e.g. excavations on Hormuz island by Bakhtiari; survey by Chamlou [1972]; observations on historical monuments by Mostafavi [1978] and Nurbash [1979/80]; see Eqtedari 1969/70; Carls 1982 and Piacentini 1988 for good summaries of the literature pertaining to Minab and Hormuz), the sum total of that work and the literature generated by it is far less than that which is available from surveys and excavations in Kuwait, eastern Saudi Arabia, Bahrain, Qatar, the United Arab Emirates (U.A.E.) and Oman (see Potts 1990 for an indication of the quantity of data available ca. 1990). Major excavations on Failaka (Kuwait), Qalat al-Bahrain and a dozen or more cemeteries on Bahrain; large-scale exposures at ed-Dur and Mleiha in the U.A.E.; and test excavations at Thaj and Ayn Jawan in eastern Saudi Arabia, along with surveys in all of these areas, have yielded material dating to between the first century BC and the fourth century AD which far surpasses anything known on the Iranian side of the Gulf.

As for the head of the Gulf (southernmost Iraq and southwesternmost Iran), if we limit ourselves strictly to the coastal region (i.e. ignoring Susiana and southern Babylonia) then very little information is available, apart from that collected during surveys in the Hor al-Hammar by Roux (1960) and along the Shatt al-Arab by Hansman (1967; for summaries of the historical evidence see Brinkman 1993).

In conclusion, we are very unequally informed about the populations inhabiting the shores and islands of the *Persicus sinus* during the early Roman era. Nevertheless, certain points are clear.

Climate, Subsistence and Other Economic Activities

The particular climate, topography and hydrography of the Gulf region meant that during the period of our concern its inhabitants were engaged principally in four primary subsistence-related activities:

fishing; shellfish-gathering; stock-breeding; and horticulture. Other important economic activities included pearling, textile manufacture, ceramic production, stoneworking, metallurgy and maritime trade. Let us first consider the natural conditions of the region before looking at the economic bases for life there.

Without going into great detail on the climatic history of the region, suffice it to say that the present hyper-arid regime (with rainfall generally under 100 mm *per annum* and temperatures in the range of 11–22° C. in winter and 30–40° C. in summer) has been in place since roughly 1000 BC (Sanlaville 1992: 23). Nevertheless, this aridity must not be misconstrued, for the region is as rich in groundwater (cf. Potts 1990: 27–31), not all of which is brackish (Willcox 1990: 43), as it is short of rainfall. It is this water source, rather than precipitation, which has permitted the sustenance of permanent human, animal and plant communities throughout the region during most of its history.

The evidence from sites of the early Roman period, such as ed-Dur (van Neer and Gautier 1993), shows that fish accounted for the largest portion of the faunal inventory in the first centuries AD. Both open water species, such as tuna, as well as denizens of the coastal lagoons (e.g. mullet, groupers, emperors) were caught. While bronze fish hooks are well known from earlier sites in the region (e.g. Tell Abraq), none have been recovered at ed-Dur, where an abundance of fish-net sinkers (Boucharlat *et al.* 1988: Fig. 9) leaves little doubt that nets were used. Fish-traps, well-attested in later periods in the Gulf (Serjeant 1968), may have been used on Failaka, where a type of weight peculiar to the fish-trap (Chavane 1988: 293) has been found.

After fish, shellfish were the second most important source of protein for the Roman-era inhabitants of the *Persicus sinus*. Out of the ca. 20 species represented at ed-Dur, *Terebralia palustris*, *Murex kusterianus*, *Pinctada*, *Ostrea* and *Marcia hiantina* were the most significant. All are edible, and most inhabited the mangrove lagoons found along northern Bahrain[2] and the present-day coast of Saudi Arabia (near Tarut) and the U.A.E. (Van Neer and Gautier 1993: 111–12).

Sheep was the most important animal herded at ed-Dur, followed by goat. Cattle and pig, though present, were numerically insignificant. The importance of sheep and goat in an arid environment like eastern Arabia cannot be overestimated. Not only do they provide secondary products such as fleece and hair for textile manufacture, they serve as walking water purification systems by turning brackish water, otherwise unpotable by the human population, into drinkable milk (Lancaster and Lancaster 1992: 345) which can in turn be transformed into *ghee* (clarified butter), cheese and yoghurt.

Garden horticulture was practiced both on the major islands (e.g. Tarut, Bahrain) and in coastal settlements. Known as *bustan* in Arabic, this system is predicated upon the cultivation of date-palm groves with inter-cropping of cereals and smaller fruit trees. Date-palms were essential for they provided not only dates (for human consumption) and date-stones (used as animal fodder), but secondary products such as fronds (for mats and palm houses) and fibre (for making rope) as well (for a complete treatment of the date-palm and its by-products, see Landsberger 1967). Equally important, however, was the *shade* created by the date-palm, since this was the *sine qua non* for the cultivation of cereals and fruit trees in such an arid environment.

By the Roman period a wide array of cultivars was being raised in eastern Arabia, including various types of wheat and barley, melon, date, lentil and chick-pea, all attested archaeologically, as well as tamarind, grape and fig, attested in literary sources (Theophrastus, *Hist. Pl.* 4.7.7–8; cf. Potts 1990: 135–36). In addition, apricot, peach, millet and possibly alfalfa (lucerne) may have been introduced into the Gulf region as early as the first centuries AD (Potts 1994b: Table 1 and 263). *Bustan* cultivation is often by hand, and it is interesting to observe that a bronze hoe-blade of Seleucid or early Roman date, very similar to those still in use, was found at Al Midra ash-Shamali in eastern Saudi Arabia (Potts 1994a: 160).

On the fertile gravel plains of the U.A.E., where water is abundant and drainage excellent, more extensive cultivation of larger plots would have been possible. At Mleiha, the best-known site of the Seleucid and Roman periods in this area, an iron ard-share has been recovered in a context datable to the first or second century AD (Mouton 1992: 84–85). This find suggests that bullock-drawn ards (a 'sliding plough' which loosens only the topsoil) were being used here by the Roman era (Potts 1994a: 162).

Pearling, an activity which writers including Theophrastus (*De Lapidibus* 36), Strabo (16.3.6–7), Isidore of Charax (in Athenaeus, *Deipnosophistai* 3.146), and Philostratus (*VA* 3.57) associated with the Gulf, was practised off Bahrain and almost certainly along the coast of the U.A.E. (viz. the Great Pearl Bank off Abu Dhabi). At ed-Dur, a bell-shaped weight made of lead, with an iron ring attachment on top, was found in a house dating to the first century AD (Boucharlat *et al.* 1989: Fig. AA). This weight is identical to the stone weights used by pearl-divers in the region in the recent past. The recovery of large pearl oyster shells in graves at ed-Dur also suggests that the pearl was a highly valued commodity of this period, and Tabari, one of our best sources for the Sasanian period in the region, confirms that when the Arab conquerors entered the palace of the last Sasanian emperor, Yazdagerd III at Ctesiphon in Iraq, they found pearls from Bahrain amongst the many luxury goods stored there (Nöldeke 1879).

Evidence for textile manufacture during the Seleucid period exists for Bahrain where, according to Theophrastus, tree cotton (*Gossypium arboreum*) was grown (*Hist. Pl.* 4.7.7). Undoubtedly, goat hair and sheep fleece were also used locally to manufacture textiles as well.

During the Roman era, local centres of ceramic production existed throughout the area. Mainland eastern Saudi Arabia produced red, black, and white-slipped wares which were exported to the north (Failaka), east (Bahrain), and south (ed-Dur). Domestic and storage-jar wares were manufactured somewhere near the sites of Mleiha and ed-Dur, while certain exotic wares were imported from Mesopotamia, southwestern Iran, southeastern Iran, and the Indian sub-continent (see below).

The U.A.E. and Oman, which had a long tradition of stoneworking in soft-stone (steatite, chlorite, talc), produced shallow, lathe-turned bowls suitable for holding unguents and other liquid substances (Haerinck 1994: Fig. 9.1–7). At the same time, alabaster vessels from South Arabia were imported as well.

The Oman peninsula, rich in both copper and iron, and with gold and silver present as well, saw a flourishing metals industry which specialised in the manufacture of weaponry and metal vessels. Equally, it should be stressed that the sources in this region probably provided the ore from which its earliest coinage, native to eastern Saudi Arabia and the area of Mleiha in the U.A.E., was minted (Potts 1991; 1994c).

We thus have a picture of a region which was fully self-sufficient. All of its subsistence needs were met locally, and all of the requisite crafts existed which could provide for the material wants of its inhabitants. That foreign goods were imported as well, however, should hardly come as a surprise, for there are few economies and societies in which extra value is not attached to the exotic.

Roman goods circulated alongside indigenous products and those acquired from other neighbouring regions. Before examining them, however, let us consider how they reached the *Persicus sinus*.

The Characene Corridor

All students of the early Roman empire are familiar with the commercial maritime corridor which linked the Mediterranean to India via the Red Sea and the Indian Ocean. Enshrined in the *Periplus of the Erythraean Sea*, this route was but one of several trans-Asian 'highways' in existence during the first centuries AD. The Indian Ocean-Red Sea route was not well-placed to service eastern Syria, southern Mesopotamia, coastal Iran, or the Arabian littoral. Rather, these were the areas served by what I propose to call the 'Characene corridor'. As has often been observed, the author of the *Periplus* was largely ignorant of conditions in the *Persicus sinus*, noting only the existence there of two significant ports, Apologos and Omana. In fact, these two sites, the former identical with early Islamic Ubulla near modern day Basra, and the latter perhaps to be identified with ed-Dur on the coast of Umm al-Qaiwain (Potts 1988), represented the two most important staging points within the *Persicus sinus*, along a route which began at Palmyra and ended in India.

Palmyra, both in its independent form and as a dependency of Roman Syria, was a caravan city linked to the east by an overland route which struck east through a series of desert halting posts located at the modern sites of Umm al-Amad, Umm as-Salabikh, Qasr Swab, Qasr Helqum, Muhaiwir (where the overland route from Damascus joined the route), Qasr Amij, and Qasr Khubbaz (see Gawlikowski 1983: 54). Striking the Middle Euphrates at Hit (Mouterde and Poidebard 1931; Gawlikowski 1987), caravans originating at Palmyra proceeded southeast along the river,[3] arriving at the lower Mesopotamian cities of Forat, Teredon, Ampa, Digba, Apamea-of-Mesene, Spasinou Charax and Apologos, the metropoleis of the kingdom of Characene (Drouin 1890: 133–36). This small state, comprising the southernmost reaches of what is today Iraq, had become independent under Hyspaosines (hence the chief city's *cognomen*, 'Spasinou') in 127 BC, two years after the death of Antiochus VII (Potts 1988: 137–38). In spite of their proximity to Parthia, the leaders of the kingdom of Characene — some of whom were in fact members of leading Parthian royal families — functioned with an uncanny degree of independence until the state was finally absorbed into the Sasanian empire ca. AD 224.[4] The commercial importance and juridical status of Spasinou Charax is well-illustrated by the terminology used to describe it in the *Periplus* (§35) where it is called 'a market-town designated by law'. Judging by the available epigraphic information from Palmyra, a significant share of the city's commercial life was owing to the presence there of Palmyrene merchant groups. Let us examine briefly how these groups functioned.

It has long been recognised that Palmyra was characterised by a quadripartite tribal social structure (Schlumberger 1971) to which Teixidor has attributed the particular form of civil and fiscal administration which characterised the city. Between AD 25 and 114 four 'treasurers' (*argyrotamiai*), representing each of the four tribal divisions, played the leading role in Palmyrene administration (Teixidor 1984: 11, 61), and it is from this period that we see the establishment of Palmyrene merchant colonies (*fonduqs*) in southernmost Mesopotamia, colonies which were to survive at least until the mid-third century AD. The seeds of this commercial expansion eastward, however, had probably been sown several years earlier, as the following texts reveal.

According to a Palmyrene text Germanicus (GRMNQS), the Roman *proconsul* and nephew of Tiberius who was present in the Near East from AD 17 to 19 (when he died there) sent a Palmyrene merchant named Alexandros ('LKSNDRWS) to southern Mesopotamia (Bowersock 1973: 136; Cantineau 1931: 139). Teixidor considers Alexandros a Palmyrene financier with his own commercial agency in Mesene, i.e. southernmost Iraq, who was sent to Mesopotamia in order to care for and develop Roman interests in the region (Teixidor 1984: 11). On the other hand, a bilingual Greek-Palmyrene inscription (Cantineau 1939: no. 6 = *CIS* II 3924) from the Bel temple at Palmyra dating to AD 19 honours the 'Palmyrenes and Greeks of Seleucia [-on-the-Tigris]'. Rostovtzeff interpreted this as commemorating a commercial alliance between an inexperienced group of Palmyrene merchants and their more competent Greco-Babylonian counterparts (Rostovtzeff 1932: 797; cf. Gawlikowski 1983: 63). By AD 24, as another text (Cantineau 1939: no. 11) from the Bel temple at Palmyra reveals, we see one Malikho being honoured 'by the merchants who are in the city of Babylon' because of the aid which he rendered them (Rostovtzeff 1932: 797; cf. Teixidor 1984: 11).

From the earliest text of AD 19, discussed above, the catalogue of Palmyrene caravan inscriptions extends through to AD 269, no less than four decades after the rise of the Sasanian empire.[5] From AD 50/1 or 70/1 until 193, according to the extant sources, much of that overland caravan traffic took place between Palmyra and Spasinou Charax, as documented by a series of Palmyrene inscriptions (Table 1) which once adorned the bases of statues erected at Palmyra to honour the more eminent leaders of the caravans (*synodiarchs*) and trading companies (*archemporoi*) (Rostovtzeff 1932; Will 1957; Teixidor 1984: 11). Although Babylon and Vologesias were also mentioned as destinations of Palmyrene caravans (Rostovtzeff 1932: 797ff), Spasinou Charax, the capital of the kingdom of Characene, and its port Apologos[6] were the principal outlets for the seaborne trade with India which proceeded down the *Persicus sinus* and across the Arabian Sea.

Spasinou Charax was more than a commercial port-of-trade, however. In the second century AD the king of Spasinou Charax, Meredat (a Parthian prince put on the Characene throne), extended his political control at least as far south as the central Gulf. A Greek-Palmyrene bilingual caravan inscription from AD 131 (Seyrig 1941: 254–55 for the Greek; Starcky 1949: 25 for the Palmyrene version) honouring 'Yarhai (son of) Nebozabad (son) of Shalamallât (son) [of] 'Aqqadân (?) citizen of Hadriana Palmyra' (Table 1) tells us that the merchant served Meredat as 'satrap' of the Thilouanoi (*satrapes Thilouanôn*). This ethnic designation for the inhabitants of TLWN leaves us in no doubt that the governorship exercised by Yarhai was based on the island known to the Greeks as Tylos, modern Bahrain. Characene control of Kharg, another important island off the coast of Iran near Bandar Bushire, is suggested by the presence there of rock-cut tombs in Palmyrene style (Ghirshman 1959). As there is no epigraphic or literary evidence for the existence of a Palmyrene merchant colony on the island, it might well be that a Palmyrene was established there in a political capacity, like Yarhai on Bahrain. Finally, Meredat may also have extended his authority as far south as the coast of the U.A.E. A series of coins (Potts 1988: Figs. 2.11–12) minted by Meredat in AD 142 calls him BACILEYC OMAN which has been interpreted by F. Pennacchietti as 'king of the Omani' (Potts 1988: 147). Given the particular significance of Omana in the trade network linking Spasinou Charax with the east (viz. the testimony of the *Periplus*), it is likely that Meredat's interest in controlling this strategic southern port would have been great.

The Characene interest in Omana is perhaps reflected by the fact that ed-Dur, which I have

D. T. Potts

Date	Summary	References
50/1 or 70/1 A.D.	Statue honouring Zabdibol, son of Obayhan, by the Palmyrene traders of Spasinou Charax (here called by its Parthian name, Aspasinkart)	Cantineau 1930: 25; Gawlikowski 1983: 63
81 A.D.	Zabdibol, son of Ogilo, honoured for conducting a caravan from Spasinou Charax to Palmyra	Cantineau 1930: 8
88 or 188 A.D.	Honours a Palmyrene trader living at Spasinou Charax	*Inv* X 19; Gawlikowski 1983: 63
131 A.D.	Statue honouring Yarhai, son of Nebozabad, citizen of Palmyra Hadriana, satrap of the Thilouanoi for Meredat king of Spasinou Charax, erected by the merchants of Spasinou Charax, at Palmyra	*Inv* X 38; Gawlikowski 1983: 63
135 A.D.	Inscription on a statue erected to honour the centurion Julius Maximus, a legionnaire stationed at Palmyra, by the members of a caravan which had travelled from Charax	*Inv.* X 81; Seyrig 1941: 242; Teixidor 1984: 30
138 A.D.	Yarhibola honoured for services rendered to the merchants of Spasinou Charax	*Inv.* X 114; Gawlikowski 1983: 64
c. 140 A.D.	Inscription honouring Soados, who frequently assisted the traders, caravans and fellow citizens established at Vologesias, for whom four statues were erected at Palmyra, and three others were set up by the senate and people at Spasinou Charax, at Vologesias and at the caravanserai of Gennaes, probably the site of Umm al-Amad where the text was found	Mouterde & Poidebard 1931: 106-108
154/5 A.D.	Marcus Ulpius Yarhai honoured for aiding a caravan which travelled from Spasinou Charax to Palmyra	*CIS* 3928; Rostovtzeff 1932: 802
193 A.D.	Taimarsou, son of Taime, honoured by the caravaneers who travelled with him from Spasinou Charax	*CIS* 3948 = *Inv.* III 28; Teixidor 1984: 17

suggested is ancient Omana, is the only site in southeastern Arabia at which Characene coins have been discovered (Potts 1988: Fig. 2.1–10). Other evidence of Characene contact may be provided by a particular type of glazed ceramic which differs from standard Parthian glazed wares. Known as BI-ware after the area on Failaka where examples of it were first recognised (Hannestad 1983: 14), this ceramic has been recovered not only on Failaka but on Bahrain and at ed-Dur as well. Given the fact that it does not seem to have been manufactured in either Iran or Mesopotamia, J.-F. Salles has suggested that it may have been a Characene product (Salles 1990: 329), a suggestion which can only be verified when a site like Spasinou Charax, possibly to be identified with the mound of Naisan on the Shatt al-Arab (Hansman 1967), is eventually excavated. Eggshell ware, a product of Seleucia-on-the-Tigris during the Seleucid and Parthian periods, has similarly been found on Failaka, at Thaj in eastern Saudi Arabia, and at ed-Dur, but while this is a Mesopotamian import, it is not known whether it was ever produced in Characene or only in central Babylonia.

In many ways the positions of Palmyra and Spasinou Charax were strikingly comparable. Each city existed with remarkable financial independence in the shadow of a more powerful neighbour, Palmyra in the shadow of Rome, Spasinou Charax in the shadow of Parthia. Both of those powers, of whom it was said by Pompeius Trogus that they divided the world between them (Justin 41.1.1), recognised that a *laisser-faire* attitude towards these trading centres would be more profitable than a heavy-handed attempt at imposing too rigid controls upon them. There were, of course, differences as well. As Pliny noted (*HN* 5.88), Palmyra enjoyed a privileged role between Rome and Parthia. Palmyrene trading groups were established in Spasinou Charax, but to the best of our knowledge, no Characene companies ever existed at Palmyra. What kind of profit-sharing arrangements existed between Palmyra and Spasinou Charax for their overseas ventures is difficult to assess. It is by no means clear that, from southern Mesopotamia eastwards, all trade proceeded in Characene hands, for an inscription dating to AD 157 from Palmyra speaks of 'the merchants who have returned from Scythia [viz. India] in the fleet of Honainu (HNYNW), son of Haddudan (HDWDN) (Starcky 1949: no. 96). Did both Characene and Palmyrene ships operate on this route? Does this inscription reflect a unique event or a late development in the trade? Was Honainu, a name attested at Palmyra only in this inscription (Stark 1971: 23), in fact a Characene entrepreneur, and not a Palmyrene at all? Until Spasinou Charax is excavated, we shall probably have to live with the severe imbalance in reporting, for the Palmyrene-Characene relationship is really only known from the Syrian side, and the Characene voice is largely missing in the extant documentation.

The Movement of Goods and the Circulation of Symbols

It is probable that Anatolian, Levantine, north Syrian[7] and of course Roman goods travelling by caravan to Spasinou Charax penetrated the markets of the *Persicus sinus* as well as reaching India and the East.[8] Indeed the *Periplus* states specifically (§36) that the market towns of Apologos and Omana exported pearls, purple, clothing, wine, dates, gold and slaves to India. Ships sailing from Spasinou Charax to India almost certainly stopped along the way, possibly calling in at Kharg, Siraf, Bahrain, Omana (ed-Dur), and a host of smaller ports on the coasts of Kerman and Baluchistan, creating a kind of maritime equivalent to the 16th century overland peddling trade so well-documented by Steensgaard (Steensgaard 1974: 15ff.). This pattern of trade diffused a wide array of goods from the metropolitan centres of the West to communities with social and economic structures completely dissimilar to those in which the goods had originated. At the same time, it introduced a range of commodities which operated on a completely different symbolic plane from those locally manufactured ones, which undoubtedly moved down and across the Gulf via completely different, domestic networks of trade and on vessels owned by local entrepreneurs rather than Palmyrene or Characene capitalists. In the case of the *Periplus* trade from Roman Egypt to India we have an extensive (if not necessarily comprehensive) catalogue of the goods being traded. In the case of the Characene corridor, we have, in addition to the testimony of the *Periplus* cited above (§35), a fair amount of archaeological evidence as well. Does there somewhere exist, waiting to be discovered, a *Periplus of the Persicus sinus*? Not necessarily. Commenting on the fact that only a handful of the hundreds of accounts of journeys through Asia published in the 16th-18th century were written by merchants, Steensgaard noted: 'This secrecy was probably intentional, the routes and market conditions constituting part of the merchants' *misterio*' (1974: 22).

As the thrust of this volume is on the early Roman empire, let us begin with Roman products. Quantitatively the best-represented category of Roman manufacture is undoubtedly glass. Even if Salles is partially correct in suggesting that some of the Roman glass found in the Gulf may have been '*Periplus*'-glass sent to India and re-exported into the Gulf (Salles 1995: 136–37), there seems no reason to believe that Roman glass was not amongst the goods moving between Palmyra and India along the Characene corridor. Although it is impossible to provide anything like an accurate estimate of the quantity of Roman glass which eventually reached the *Persicus sinus*, the pillar-moulded bowl from Jidd Hafs on Bahrain (During Caspers 1972–74: Fig. 5a), once the only example of its kind in the region, has now been complemented by many more pieces.

On Bahrain, at least twenty-eight glass vessels have been recovered from the graves at al-Hajjar, most of which are of Roman manufacture (Boucharlat and Salles 1989: 110–22). A wealth of glass has also been recovered at ed-Dur (Figs. 2–3). Alongside the complete examples, which number upwards of two dozen, well over a hundred fragments of pillar-moulded bowls have been found in numerous areas across the site. Most of these, judging by the published comparanda, date to the first and early second centuries AD. In addition to the pillar-moulded bowls (Fig. 2f-g), however, a wide range of other Roman glass types has also been recovered at ed-Dur. An almond-bossed beaker (Fig. 2a); vessels in the shape of a fish (Haerinck 1992: Fig. 11); pear-shaped flasks (Fig. 3f-h), and many other shapes, both moulded (Fig. 2b-e) and blown (Fig. 3a-e), are represented in the ed-Dur glass répertoire. While all of the more complete examples of Roman glass at ed-Dur have been found in tombs (Figs. 4–5; e.g. Haerinck *et al.* 1991: 40–52; Haerinck 1992: 193–95; 1993: Fig. 10), more than enough fragments have been excavated in domestic contexts (e.g. houses in Areas C and E) to confirm that these were objects used in daily life and not merely reserved for funerary, ritual purposes.

Nor is Roman pottery lacking either. *Terra sigillata* has been recovered at ed-Dur (Potts 1993: Fig. 16; Haerinck 1994: Fig. 21), as has a western Mediterranean amphora fragment with incuse letters LNV (Papadopoulos 1994). The influence of Roman *sigillata* forms, moreover, can be detected in the so-called 'Nabataean' or Ayn Jawan bowls manufactured in eastern Saudi Arabia. As discussed elsewhere (Potts 1993: 92–93; Fig. 17), carinated *sigillata* bowl forms provided the model for the modification of an indigenous, Arabian bowl type during the late first century BC or early first century AD. The surface finish of these local products, however, cannot compare with that of true *sigillata*. While Indian Red-Polished Ware *may* have exerted some influence on Gulf ceramics (e.g. Salles 1990: Fig. 7j, which has a rim reminiscent of Indian Red-Polished forms), the similarity of forms shows clearly that Roman tableware most definitely served as a model for local potters.

An agate intaglio depicting Athena and a frit Aphrodite (Haerinck *et al.* 1991: Figs. 21, 28–29) have been recovered at ed-Dur as well. Roman coinage, however, is rare. An *aureus* of Tiberius from ed-Dur (Howgego and Potts 1992: Fig. 17) and four later Roman issues from Thaj and Jabal Kenzan are among the few which can be cited (these include a Constantinian bronze [PROVIDENTIAE CAESS Camp gate, from AD 324–330]; an Alexandrian issue [GLORIA EXERCITVS, from AD 335–337]; a coin of Constans [AD 347–348]; and a GLORIA ROMANORUM type [AD 364–375]; Howgego and Potts 1992: 185–87).[9]

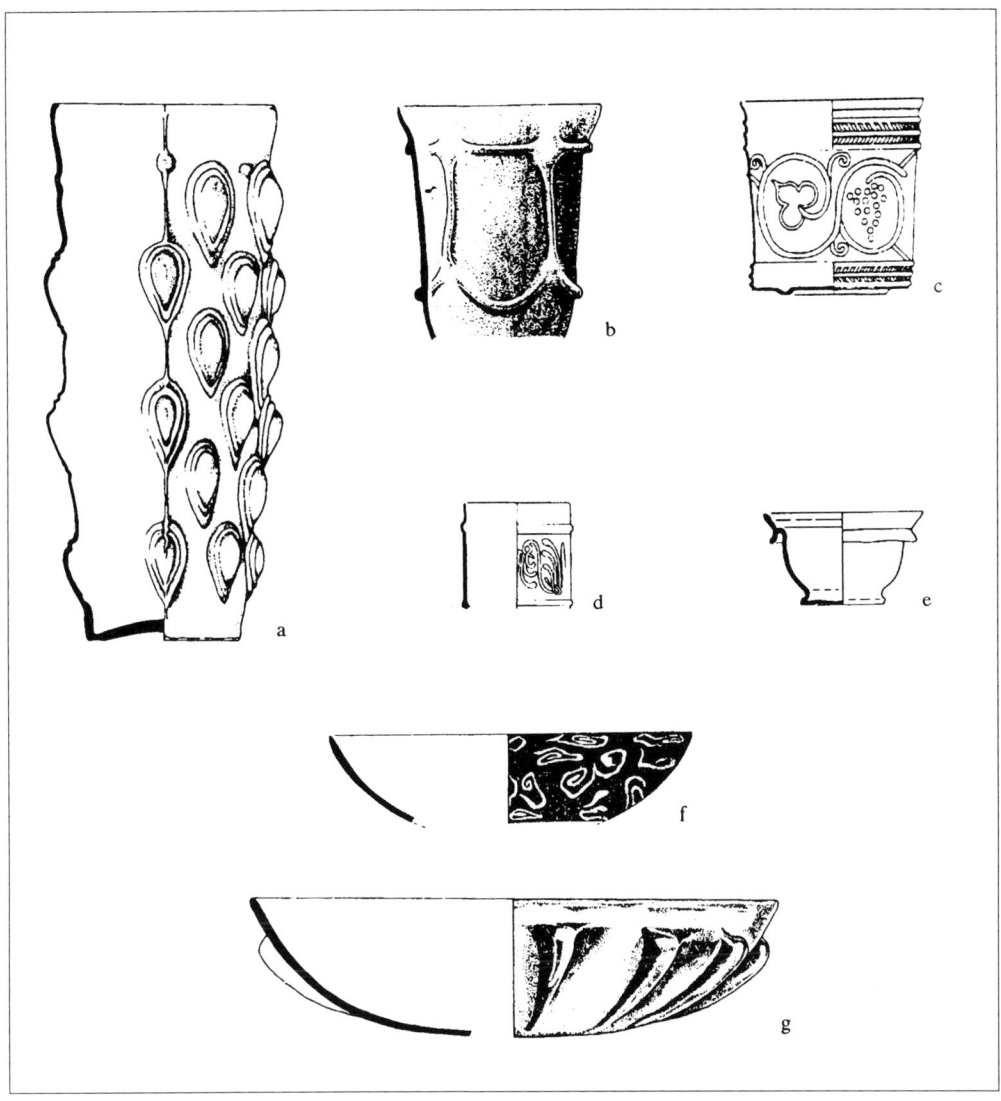

Fig. 2. Roman glass from ed-Dur (after Potts 1990: Fig. 22; Haerinck 1992: Fig. 2; 1993: Figure 10)

Roman goods such as these rubbed shoulders, as it were, with commodities originating in Mesopotamia, such as oil, sesame, textiles, and luxury ceramics (viz. glazed BI-ware, eggshell ware). Material goods undoubtedly moved from east to west along the Characene corridor as well. Examples of Indian Red-Polished Ware have been found at Sohar on the coast of Oman (Kervran and Hiebert 1991: Fig. 4.16–19, Fig. 5.14–15), at ed-Dur on the Gulf coast of the U.A.E. (Haerinck *et al.* 1993:

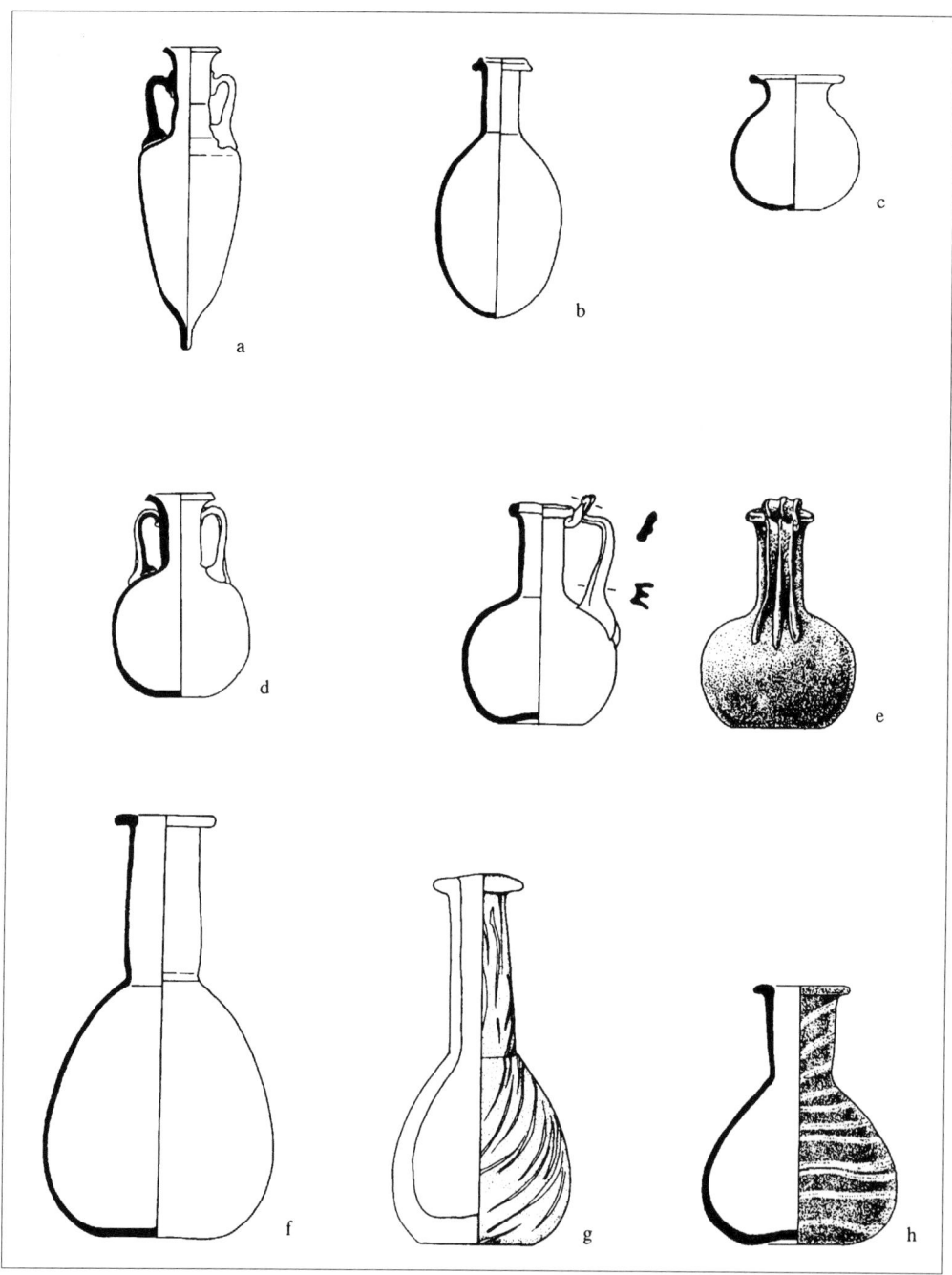

Fig. 3. Roman glass from ed-Dur (after Haerinck et al. 1991: Fig. 32; Haerinck 1992: Fig. 2)

187) and at numerous sites along the Iranian coast of Fars (Whitehouse and Williamson 1973: Fig. 7). Some of this dates securely to the first century AD, for at ed-Dur it has been found in association with Roman pillar-moulded glass bowls. In addition to an undescribed 'poorly preserved square Indian base-metal coin' from ed-Dur (Haerinck *et al.* 1993: 186), a bronze tribal coin (3.18 g; 13 x 14 mm) with a swastika on its reverse as been found on the surface of Mleiha. From north/central India, the coin dates to somewhere between the fall of the Mauryan and the beginning of the Gupta empire (ca. 184 BC – AD 319). Although it originated nearly in the centre of India, Helen Brown believes it may well have reached the Gulf via the Indian port of Barygaza/Broach,[10] where the merchants of Spasinou Charax and Palmyra travelling the Characene corridor met those from Alexandria who had come via the Red Sea route (Teixidor 1984: 39; Liu 1994: 8–9).

As indicated above, a vernacular trade in locally-produced goods undoubtedly went on within the Gulf as well, in some cases following the same trajectories as the Characene trade, in other cases moving between smaller ports of call which were off the beaten track of the Palmyrene and Characene merchants. Trade of this sort was probably responsible for the circulation of northeast Arabian coinage in what is now the U.A.E. (Potts 1991; 1994c), moving from sites such as Thaj, Jabal Kenzen and ash-Sha'aba in what is today the Eastern Province of the Kingdom of Saudi Arabia to Omana (ed-Dur) and Mleiha. Along with coinage, pottery from centres such as Thaj undoubtedly moved around the Gulf as well, for it is well-represented at ed-Dur (Haerinck *et al.*

Fig. 4. Typical tomb (Area O) at ed-Dur, viewed from the west, showing the corbelled entrance

Fig. 5. Roman pillar-moulded glass bowl found just above the floor of the Area O tomb

1993: Fig. 4.7–12), and on Bahrain (Herling and Salles 1993: Figs. 3, 5) and Failaka (Hannestad 1983: 49–50). On the other hand, contact across the Straits of Hormuz certainly accounted for the appearance at ed-Dur and Mleiha of so-called 'Namord ware' from southeastern Iran — fine orange pottery painted with black decoration (Haerinck *et al.* 1993: Fig. 5; cf. Sajjadi 1989; Potts n.d.).

More distant contacts penetrated the region as well. The use of the epigraphic South Arabian script to write monumental stone inscriptions in both eastern Saudi Arabia and at Mleiha in the U.A.E. (Potts 1990: 69–85) attests to the impact of South Arabian contact, as does the appearance in both areas of typically South Arabian alabaster jars with lids surmounted by couchant lions (Potts 1990: Fig. 18a-b, d-e; cf. Boucharlat 1989: Fig. 6). South Arabian coinage has also been found at Mleiha (Sedov 1995), while a single coin of the sort minted there has been recorded as coming from a site in the Hadramawt, possibly Shabwa (Munro-Hay 1991: Fig. 16.33).

The short conclusion to be drawn from this pattern of circulation is that the goods concerned were mainly luxury goods, none of them necessary for life in the region in a strictly utilitarian sense. Symbolically, however, they were anything but luxuries. Rather, they were absolutely necessary, required by the elites of the *Persicus sinus* to display a cosmopolitan veneer which local goods simply could not impart. The differential distribution of these foreign goods at ed-Dur is instructive, for while Mesopotamian (i.e. glazed Parthian) pottery, Indian Red-Polished ware, Namord ware from southeastern Iran or Baluchistan, and Roman glass are all attested in domestic habitation contexts, it is only the Roman glass and the glazed Parthian pottery which found its way into the graves. Judging by the high frequency of Parthian pottery in most settlement areas, Roman glass was certainly the rarer of the two types of goods. The elite graves at ed-Dur in which Roman glass vessels were placed reveal a reverence for this particular foreign item which was not enjoyed by domestic ceramics, stone or metal vessels. Whether or not they were interred as part of a food offering for the dead, their selective presence points to a symbolic value far greater than anything else available in the marketplace. Thus, without the loss of a single Roman soldier, Rome managed to impact on a region far removed from its principal sphere of influence in a manner which went to the core of local tradition. It is this pattern, and not one of political, religious, or economic integration in the usual senses of the term, which distinguishes the Roman penetration of the *Persicus sinus*.

The Characene Corridor Becomes a Sasanian Lake

The collapse of the independent kingdom of Characene occurred soon after Ardashir's rise to power in the early third century AD. A Sasanian overstrike of Shapur II on a Roman coin found at Thaj (Howgego and Potts 1992: Figs. 2–3) is eloquent testimony to the change in political dominance within the *Persicus sinus*. Moreover, it is echoed at ed-Dur, where the later occupation areas (notably Area F) show an abundance of Sasanian, rather than Roman glass (Lecomte 1993: Fig. 14). Over twenty years ago Whitehouse and Williamson speculated on the extent of Sasanian maritime trade in the Gulf (Whitehouse and Williamson 1973), but what they failed to realise at the time was that the Sasanian rise to prominence mirrored the downfall of the earlier Characene influence in the area. The relatively small number of Sasanian coins found in the area (Potts and Cribb 1995) belie the massive political influence of an Iranian empire which, from Ardashir to Yazdegerd III, exerted more than nominal control over the area, both directly and through the mediation of its Lakhmid vassals. By the time the armies of the Prophet entered eastern Arabia, the appeal of Roman luxury goods had long since given way to different, more eastern symbols of status and rank.

In charting the history of Roman penetration in this area, I have conspicuously avoided playing what I consider 'chronological games' with the evidence. The data we currently possess, both literary and archaeological, are highly discontinuous. Teixidor has stressed that it would be unwise to read too much into the presence of caravan inscriptions in some years, and their absence in others (Teixidor 1984: 49). The fact is, as is so often the case, absence of evidence is not evidence of absence, and it would be rash to pile the narratives of Pliny and other authors onto the skeletal epigraphic record, the history of Roman-Parthian and early Roman-Sasanian political relations, and an archaeological record of only approximately datable finds, in order to present a more textured picture of the micro-fluctuations which must have affected trade in the Characene corridor. This is not to deny that such fluctuations did not occur, merely to warn against reading too much into what is, admittedly, a very fractured database. Aware of the difficulties of painting a picture with a broad brush, such as I have consciously done here, I prefer, for the moment, to let the fullness of the evidence speak, and to try to convey, however impressionistically, one account of what that evidence *might* be telling us, rather than beoming bogged down in speculations on data which, with the best will in the world, cannot be tightly dated and made to conform to a clear-cut chronological framework. I leave it to others familiar with this material, and to readers with a better grounding in traditional Roman-era archaeology and history, to decide whether the picture sketched out here is at all serviceable. One thing is certain, however. The present chapter could not have been written twenty, even ten years ago, prior to the excavations at ed-Dur. We can be certain that much remains to be discovered in this region which will undoubtedly challenge and refine some of the ideas put forward above.

Notes

1   Trajan's brief visit to the head of the Gulf in AD 116, recently discussed by Millar (1993: 101), certainly does not equate to Roman control over the area, and in the later periods Roman control never extended below northern Mesopotamia.

2   The mangroves of Bahrain, ancient Tylos, were substantial enough to warrant extended comment from Theophrastus (*Hist. Pl.* 4.7.7–8). See the discussion in Potts 1990: 129–33.

3   I doubt very much that the caravans only travelled as far as the Euphrates or Vologesias (Teixidor 1984: 36), at which point their cargo was put into boats headed for the south. This may have sometimes occurred, but I find it difficult to believe that this was the norm, particularly as — in the other direction — caravans definitely originated in the south, e.g. at Charax. This is shown clearly by the wording of the caravan inscriptions which were generally erected by the caravaneers who *ascended* the Euphrates with their chief, the *synodiarch*, on the way from Spasinou Charax to Palmyra, or *descended* from Palmyra to Vologesias. Cf. Schlumberger 1961: 258 and n. 5.

4   The precise date of Ardashir's conquest of Mesene, the southern Mesopotamian province in which Charax was located, is uncertain. Piacentini (1984: 176) puts it at ca. AD 224 but could it have occurred in the course of Ardashir's Mesopotamian campaign two years earlier? For the sources see Felix 1985: 32–33. Much secondary literature could be cited on this point but none of it is very conclusive.

5   Texts are known from the years 19, 24, 70, 81, 86, 131, 132, 135, 138, 140, 142, 150, 155, 156–59, 161, 193, 199, 210, 247, 257 and 269. See Teixidor 1984: 49.

6   Groom (1995: 188) emphasises that Pliny (*HN* 6.140, 148) mentions the port of Teredon rather than Apologos, implying that Apologos, named as a port in the *Periplus* (which Groom dates to ca. AD 45) had ceded its position of prominence to Teredon by the AD 70's. I do not believe that Pliny can be relied on, for in most matters Arabian he notoriously confused matters.

7   Seyrig (1941: 261) suggested that the Palmyrene merchants brought textiles (particularly purple-dyed ones) from the Levant; precious metal vessels from an unnamed source; and storax from Asia Minor to Charax for the sea-borne trade to India.

8   In discussing the Roman glass found at Begram, in Afghanistan, Whitehouse (1989: 155) has suggested that it probably came from India via the *Periplus* trade, not overland through Mesopotamia. I do not think that an export of the sort of glass found at Begram through Palmyra and Charax, down the Characene corridor to India, and thence up to Begram, should be ruled out, for the very existence of this route has scarcely been acknowledged in most of the literature pertaining to Roman interests in the east. So few contexts in Mesopotamia and Iran dating to the first few centuries AD have been excavated that any exclusion of the Palmyra-Charax-India route seems highly premature at this point.

9   These coins, however, must not be misinterpreted. The Tiberius issue is typical of the coinage minted prior to Nero's monetary reform of AD 64. This coinage was consciously sought out by Roman traders with India for use in making payments in the east, for there it was far overvalued in relation to its intrinsic value within the Roman empire, where lighter gold *aurei* and debased silver *denarii* circulated following the reform (Potts 1994d: 219; cf. MacDowall 1968: 137–38). The late Roman issues, on the other hand, are all base-metal coins, unlikely to have served in commercial transactions.

10   I would like to thank Mrs. Helen Brown, Heberden Coin Room, Ashmolean Museum, Oxford, for this information (letter of 22.7.1992). Mrs. Brown compares the Mleiha coin with *BMC Ancient India* 253/82–84 and 254/85 (not illustrated), and feels it should be dated 'earlier rather than later' within the time span of ca. 184 BC to AD 319.

Bibliography

Boucharlat, R. (1989) "Documents arabes provenant des sites 'hellénistiques' de la péninsule d'Oman," in T. Fahd, ed., *L'Arabie préislamique et son environnement historique et culturel* (Travaux du Centre de Recherche sur le Proche-Orient et la Grèce antique 10), 109–126. Leiden.

Boucharlat, R., E. Haerinck, C.S. Phillips, and D.T. Potts (1988) "Archaeological reconnaissance at ed-Dur, Umm al-Qaiwain, U.A.E.," *Akkadica* 58: 1–26.

Boucharlat, R., E. Haerinck, O. Lecomte, D.T. Potts and K.G. Stevens (1989) "The European archaeological expedition to ed-Dur, Umm al-Qaiwayn (U.A.E.): An interim report on the 1987 and 1988 seasons," *Mesopotamia* 24: 5–72.

Boucharlat, R. and J.-F. Salles (1989) "The Tylos period," in P. Lombard and M. Kervran, eds., *Bahrain National Museum Archaeological Collections Vol. 1. A Selection of Pre-Islamic Antiquities from Excavations 1954–1975,* 83–131. Bahrain.

Bowersock, G.W. (1973) "Syria under Vespasian," *JRS* 63: 133–140.

Brinkman, J. (1993) "Meerland," *RlA* 8: 6–10.

Cantineau, J. (1930) "Inscriptions palmyréniennes," *RAssyr* 27: 27–51.

_____(1931) "Textes palmyréniens provenant de la fouille du temple de Bel," *Syria* 12: 116–141.

_____(1939) *Inventaire des inscriptions de Palmyre,* IX, Damascus.

Carls, H.-G. (1982) *Alt-Hormoz – ein historischer Hafen an der Straße von Hormoz (Iran)*, Munich.

Chamlou, G. (1972) "Explorations archéologiques dans la région de Minab," *Bastan Chenasi va Honar-e Iran* 9–10: 84–88.

Chavane, M.-J. (1988) "Petits objets de la forteresse," in Y. Calvet and J. Gachet, eds., *Failaka, fouilles françaises 1986–1988* (Travaux de la Maison de l'Orient 18), 285–302. Lyon.

Drouin, E. (1890) "Notice historique et géographique sur la Characène," *Le Muséon* 9: 129–150.

During Caspers, E.C.L. (1972–74) "The Bahrain Tumuli," *Persica* 6: 131–156.

Eqtedari, A. (1969/70) *Athar-e sharha-ye bastani-e sawahel wa jaza'yer-e Khalij-e Fars wa Dariya-ye Oman,* Teheran (in Farsi).

Felix, W. (1985) *Antike literarische Quellen zur Außenpolitik des Sasanidenstaates* (Österreichische Akademie der Wissenschaften, phil.-hist. Kl. Sitzungsberichte, Bd. 465), Vienna.

Gawlikowski, M. (1983) "Palmyre et l'Euphrate," *Syria* 60: 53–68.

_____(1987) "The Roman frontier on the Euphrates," *Mesopotamia* 22: 77–80.

Ghirshman, R. (1959) "Ile de Kharg dans le Golfe Persique," *Arts Asiatiques* 6: 107–120.

Groom, N. (1994) "Oman and the Emirates in Ptolemy's map," *Arabian Archaeology & Epigraphy* 5: 198–214.

_____(1995) "The *Periplus*, Pliny and Arabia," *Arabian Archaeology & Epigraphy* 6: 180–195.

Haerinck, E. (1992) "Excavations at ed-Dur (Umm al-Qaiwain, U.A.E.) – Preliminary report on the fourth Belgian season (1988)," *Arabian Archaeology & Epigraphy* 3: 190–208.

_____(1993) "Excavations at ed-Dur (Umm al-Qaiwain, U.A.E.) – Preliminary report on the fifth Belgian season (1991)," *Arabian Archaeology & Epigraphy* 4: 210–225.

_____(1994) "Excavations at ed-Dur (Umm al-Qaiwain, U.A.E.) – Preliminary report on the sixth Belgian season (1992)," *Arabian Archaeology & Epigraphy* 5: 184–197.

Haerinck, E., C. Metdepenninghen and K.G. Stevens (1991) "Excavations at ed-Dur (Umm al-Qaiwain, U.A.E.) – Preliminary report on the second Belgian season (1988)," *Arabian Archaeology & Epigraphy* 2: 31–60.

_____(1992) "Excavations at ed-Dur (Umm al-Qaiwain, U.A.E.) – Preliminary report on the third Belgian season (1989)," *Arabian Archaeology & Epigraphy* 3: 44–60.

Haerinck, E., C.S. Phillips, D.T. Potts and K.G. Stevens (1993) "Ed-Dur, Umm al-Qaiwain (U.A.E.)," in U. Finkbeiner, ed., *Materialien zur Archäologie der Seleukiden- und Partherzeit im südlichen Babylonien und im Golfgebiet,* 183–93. Tübingen.

Hannestad, L. (1983) *The Hellenistic Pottery from Failaka* (Ikaros: The Hellenistic Settlements 2:1), Aarhus.

Hansman, J.F. (1967) "Charax and the Karkheh," *IrAnt* 7: 21–58.

Herling, A. and J.-F. Salles (1991) "Hellenistic Cemeteries in Bahrain," in U. Finkbeiner, ed., *Materialien zur Archäologie der Seleukiden- und Partherzeit im südlichen Babylonien und im Golfgebiet*, 161–182. Tübingen.

Hodder, I. (1982) *Symbols in Action: Ethnoarchaeological Studies of Material Culture*, Cambridge.

Howgego, C. and D.T. Potts (1992) "Greek and Roman coins from eastern Arabia," *Arabian Archaeology & Epigraphy* 3: 183–189.

Kervran, M. and F. Hiebert (1991) "Sohar pré-islamique," in K. Schippmann, A. Herling and J.-F. Salles, eds., *Golf-Archäologie: Mesopotamien, Iran, Kuwait, Bahrain, Vereinigte Arabische Emirate und Oman* (Internationale Archäologie 6), 337–348, Buch am Erlbach.

Lancaster, W. and F. Lancaster (1992) "Tribe, community and the concept of access to resources: territorial behaviour in south-east Ja'alan," in M.J. Casimir and A. Rao, eds., *Mobility and Territoriality: Social and Spatial Boundaries among Foragers, Fishers, Pastoralists and Peripatetics*, 343–63. Providence and Oxford.

Landsberger, B. (1967) *The Date-palm and its By-products according to Cuneiform Sources* (Archiv für Orientforschung Beiheft 17), Graz.

Lecomte, O. (1993) "Ed-Dur, les occupations des 3e et 4e s. ap. J.-C.: contexte des trouvailles et matériel diagnostique," in U. Finkbeiner, ed., *Materialien zur Archäologie der Seleukiden- und Partherzeit im südlichen Babylonien und im Golfgebiet*, 195–217. Tübingen.

Liu, X. (1994) *Ancient India and Ancient China: Trade and Religious Exchanges AD 1–600,* Delhi.

Lowick, N.M. (1985) *The Coins and Monumental Inscriptions* (Excavations at Siraf, Fascicle 15), London.

MacDowall, D. (1968) "Numismatic evidence for the date of Kaniska," in A.L. Basham, ed., *Papers on the Date of Kaniska* (Australian National University Centre of Oriental Studies Oriental Monograph Series IV), 134–149. Leiden.

Millar, F. (1993) *The Roman Near East 31 BC – AD 337*, Cambridge, Mass.

Mostafavi, M.T. (1978) *The Land of Párs (The Historical Monuments and the Archaeological Sites of the Province of Fárs)*, Bath.

Mouterde, R. and A. Poidebard (1931) "La voie antique des caravanes entre Palmyre et Hit au IIe siècle ap. J.-C. d'après une inscription retrouvée au s.-e. de Palmyre (Mars 1930)," *Syria* 12: 101–115.

Mouton, M. (1992) *La péninsule d'Oman de la fin de l'Âge du Fer au début de la période sassanide (250 av.-350 ap.JC)*, unpubl. PhD diss., University of Paris I (Panthéon-Sorbonne).

Munro-Hay, S. (1991) "The coinage of Shabwa (Hadhramawt), and other ancient South Arabian coinage in the National Museum, Aden," *Syria* 58: 393–418.

Nöldeke, T. (1879) *Geschichte der Perser und Araber zur Zeit der Sasaniden, aus der arabischen Chronik des Tabari,* Leiden.

Nurbash, H. (1979/80) *Bandar Lengeh dar Sahel-e Khalij-e Fars,* Bandar Abbas (in Farsi).

Papadopoulos, J.K. (1994) "A Western Mediterranean amphora fragment from ed-Dur," *Arabian Archaeology & Epigraphy* 5: 276–279.

Piacentini, V.F. (1984) "La presa di potere sassanide sul Golfo Persico tra leggenda e realtà," *Clio* 30: 173–210.

————(1988) "La fascia costiera del Harmuzgan: Storia e territorio," in V.F. Piacentini, ed., *Gruppi socio-tecnici e strutture politico-amministrative della fascia costiera meridionale Iranica* (Biblioteca della "Nuova Rivista Storica" 37), 117–156. Rome.

Potts, D.T. (1988) "Arabia and the kingdom of Characene," in D.T. Potts, ed., *Araby the Blest* (Carsten Niebuhr Institute Publications 7), 137–167. Copenhagen.

————(1990) *The Arabian Gulf in Antiquity, Volume II*, Oxford.

————(1991) *The Pre-Islamic Coinage of Eastern Arabia* (Carsten Niebuhr Institute Publications 14), Copenhagen.

————(1993) "The sequence and chronology of Thaj," in U. Finkbeiner, ed., *Materialien zur Archäologie der Seleukiden- und Partherzeit im südlichen Babylonien und im Golfgebiet*, 87–110. Tübingen.

————(1994a) "Contributions to the agrarian history of eastern Arabia I. Implements and cultivation techniques," *Arabian Archaeology & Epigraphy* 5: 158–168.

_____(1994b) "Contributions to the agrarian history of eastern Arabia II. The cultivars," *Arabian Archaeology & Epigraphy* 5: 236–275.

_____(1994c) *Supplement to the Pre-Islamic Coinage of Eastern Arabia* (Carsten Niebuhr Institute Publications 16), Copenhagen.

_____(1994d) "Augustus, Aelius Gallus and the Periplus: A re-interpretation of the coinage of San'â' Class B," in N. Nebes, ed., *Arabia Felix: Beiträge zur Sprache und Kultur des vorislamischen Arabien, Festschrift Walter W. Müller zum 60. Geburtstag*, 212–222. Wiesbaden.

_____(n.d.) "Namord ware in southeastern Arabia," in C.S. Phillips, D.T. Potts and S. Searight, eds., *Arabia and her Neighbors: Essays on Prehistorical and Historical Developments Presented in Honour of Beatrice de Cardi (Abiel III)*, Turnhout.

Potts, D.T. and J. Cribb (1995) "Sasanian and Arab-Sasanian coins from eastern Arabia," *IrAnt* 30: 123–137.

Rostovtzeff, M. (1932) "Les inscriptions caravanières de Palmyre," *Mélanges Gustave Glotz*, ii, 793–811. Paris.

Roux, G. (1960) "Recently discovered ancient sites in the Hammar Lake district (southern Iraq)," *Sumer* 16: 20–31.

Sajjadi, M. (1989) "A class of Sasanian ceramics from southeastern Iran," *RdA* 13: 31–40.

Salles, J.-F. (1990) "Questioning the BI-Ware," in Y. Calvet and J. Gachet, eds., *Failaka, fouilles françaises 1986–1988* (Travaux de la Maison de l'Orient 18), 303–334. Lyon.

_____(1995) "The Periplus of the Erythraean Sea and the Arab-Persian Gulf," in M.-F. Boussac and J.-F. Salles, eds., *Athens, Aden, Arikamedu: Essays on the Interrelations between India, Arabia and the Eastern Mediterranean*, 115–146. New Delhi.

Sanlaville, P. (1992) "Changements climatiques dans la péninsule Arabique durant le Pléistocène supérieur et l'Holocène," *Paléorient* 18: 5–26.

Schlumberger, D. (1961) "Palmyre et la Mésène," *Syria* 38: 256–260.

_____(1971) "Les quatre tribus de Palmyre," *Syria* 48: 121–130.

Sedov, A. (1995) "Two South Arabian coins from Mleiha," *Arabian Archaeology & Epigraphy* 6: 61–64.

Serjeant, R.B. (1968) "Fisher-folk and fish-traps in al-Bahrain," *BSOAS* 31: 486–514.

Seyrig, H. (1941) "Antiquités syriennes 38. Inscriptions grecques de l'agora de Palmyre," *Syria* 22: 223–270.

Starcky, J. (1949) *Inventaire des inscriptions de Palmyre*, X, Damascus.

Stark, J.K. (1971) *Personal Names in Palmyrene Inscriptions*, Oxford.

Steensgaard, N. (1974) *The Asian Trade Revolution of the Seventeenh Century*, Chicago.

Teixidor, J. (1984) "Un port romain du désert, Palmyre et son commerce d'Auguste à Caracalla," *Semitica* 34: 7–125.

Van Neer, W. and A. Gautier (1993) "Preliminary report on the faunal remains from the coastal site of ed-Dur, 1st-4th century AD, Umm al-Quwain, United Arab Emirates," in H. Buitenhuis and A.T. Clason, eds., *Archaeozoology of the Near East: Proceedings of the First International Symposium on the Archaeozoology of Southwestern Asia and Adjacent Areas*, 110–118. Leiden.

Whitehouse, D. (1974) "Excavations at Siraf: Sixth interim report," *Iran* 12: 1–30.

_____(1976) "Kish," *Iran* 14: 146–147.

_____(1989) "Begram reconsidered," *KölnJb* 22: 151–157.

Whitehouse, D. and A. Williamson (1973) "Sasanian maritime trade," *Iran* 11: 29–49.

Will, E. (1957) "Marchands et chefs de caravanes à Palmyre," *Syria* 34: 262–277.

Willcox, G. (1990) "The plant remains from Hellenistic and Bronze Age levels at Failaka, Kuwait," in Y. Calvet and J. Gachet, eds., *Failaka, fouilles françaises 1986–1988* (Travaux de la Maison de l'Orient 18), 43–50. Lyon.

Williamson, A. (1987) "Regional distribution of Mediaeval Persian pottery in the light of recent investigations," in J. Allan and C. Roberts, eds., *Syria and Iran: Three Studies in Medieval Ceramics* (Oxford Studies in Islamic Art 4), 11–22. Oxford.

Section 3: Images and Identities

7. The Imperial Image in the Eastern Mediterranean

Charles Brian Rose

Scholars have been writing about Roman portraits since the Renaissance, and portrait scholarship has consistently occupied a central place in ancient art history ever since (Wegner 1939: 7–8). Nearly all of the literature, however, has concentrated on identification and cataloguing, leaving the social and political function of Roman portraits largely unexplored. In this essay I would like to examine two things: the administrative process involved in the production of the Imperial image in the eastern Mediterranean, specifically Greece and Asia Minor, and the extent to which early Roman portraits of the Imperial family represent a change from Hellenistic royal portraits. In keeping with the general theme of this volume, I will confine my comments to the first century AD, and especially to the Julio-Claudian and Flavian dynasties.

Before looking at what a portrait meant in early Imperial society, it is legitimate to ask why scholarship has continually separated the images of men and women from the societies which set them up. The beginning of the study of Roman portraiture is linked to museums and private collections, and the goal was to provide dates and attributions for the masses of portraits which had accumulated over the centuries. Many of the portraits under consideration had either no provenance or a shaky one, and the writers of the books and articles about portraits usually had no excavation experience. There was consequently a disinclination to move past the museum context of the portraits and view them, along with other classes of material culture, as components of a society. Standard portrait methodology has not changed substantially since then: similar portraits are assembled in a group, compared with securely identified numismatic portraits, and associated with a member of the Imperial family. Once the group has been assembled, the locks of hair on the forehead are numbered and drawn, and the portraits are subdivided into types, each of which is often arbitrarily linked to key events in the life of the man or woman in question.

Within any group of portraits, of course, there is considerable variety, and many portraits resist placement in one of the pre-conceived types, but scholarly demand for order has resulted in the appending of recalcitrant portraits to one type or another. Since the whole process is driven by collecting and connoisseurship, the portraits used to represent the types are usually those which are the best preserved, rather than those with the best archaeological context. Such a system obviously

108

favors inductive analysis and represents the reverse of what our methodology should be. Yet this model is generally used for all of Roman Imperial portraiture, with little regard for the ways in which the process varied by region and with a tacit assumption that the system was controlled by Rome (for more regional groupings of Roman portraits, see Inan and Rosenbaum 1966; 1979; Pekary 1978; Kiss 1979; Price 1984: 170–206).

One issue in particular must be kept in mind: emperors did not set up portraits of themselves; provincial cities set up portraits of the emperor in gratitude for or in anticipation of Imperial benefactions.[1] To understand the function of portraits in a given region or city one therefore has to start with the political relationship between that area and Rome, and then look at how the portraits fit into that relationship. Statuary bases provide extremely useful information since they often include the date, the name of the dedicator, and the reasons for producing the statue. In the eastern Mediterranean these dedications constitute our best evidence for Imperial portraits, since the portraits themselves were frequently made of bronze or precious metal and consequently do not survive. Unfortunately the bases have not been systematically investigated very often since scholars tend to focus on extant portraits, rather than on the dedications for portraits which are no longer preserved, and this has resulted in a very uneven treatment of the subject (exceptions include Stuart 1938; Hanson and Johnson 1946; Tuchelt 1979; Pekary 1978; 1985).

By the beginning of the Julio-Claudian dynasty the practice of setting up honorific portraits in the eastern Mediterranean was over three centuries old, and the procedure followed in the early empire was basically the same as that which had been used during the Hellenistic period. I have therefore included a brief description of Hellenistic portrait production so that the Roman practice can be viewed in a broader context.

Here too the most valuable evidence is epigraphic. Beginning in the fourth century BC cities produced portraits to thank their benefactors for political and/or economic assistance (Gauthier 1985; Price 1984: 23–52; Henry 1983: 294–310; Veyne 1976: 185–373; Blanck 1968; Poland 1909: 425–445; Welsh 1904–1905: 32–43). At first the most common honors were a golden crown and bronze portrait statue, but, beginning in the second century, men often received portraits in several different media – bronze, marble, and gold, or paintings set within a gilded shield.[2] The decrees continually specified that the images should be erected in the most visible spot in the area (Gauthier 1985: 27; Tuchelt 1979: 66–68; Pekary 1978: 739–41), although as these kinds of honors became more frequent, cities devised new methods to distinguish more recent images from the older ones (Gauthier 1985: 45).[3]

Honors became even more elaborate in Asia Minor during the first century BC, especially for ambassadors to Rome. Artemidorus of Knidos, for example, seems to have secured freedom for his city from Rome, and in response he was voted nine portraits: three each in bronze, marble, and gold, as well as another gilded painted portrait set up in the temple of Artemis (*GIBM* 4.1, 787).[4] Statues of both kings and non-royal benefactors were regularly placed in temples or precincts of the Olympian gods (Nock 1972: 235ff.; Price 1984: 23–52), and they were occasionally shown crowned by personifications of the Demos, Virtue, and Honor.[5]

There were also attempts to involve the benefactor more closely in the composition of his honors by soliciting his opinions on the matter. In formulating honors for Attalus II, for instance, the Boule and Demos of Aptera (Crete) decreed a bronze statue for the king and gave him the choice of whether it would be standing or equestrian (*OGIS* 270; Robert 1940: 115–18). Benefactors were also allowed to choose where the image would be erected, and the location permitted varied from one decree to the other. Athens voted to set up a statue of Asandros of Macedon anywhere in the agora he chose, provided it was not next to the Tyrannicides (*IG* II, ed. min., 450, col.B, ll. 10–12; 646, l. 39); but there are examples of cities permitting statues to be erected anywhere the benefactor wanted.[6]

Statues were usually set up after a service had been rendered but occasionally they were intended to encourage the completion of a benefaction. A case in point is the dedication for King Pharnaces of Pontus, and I include here the contents of the decree since the steps involved in the erection of a portrait are summarized so clearly. In the early second century BC Pharnaces had promised funds to Athens which he was unable to pay after an unsuccessful war with Pergamon and Cappadocia, and the promised money, which had begun to arrive in yearly installments, eventually stopped. When Pharnaces married Nysa, the niece of Antiochus II, the Athenians attempted to reactivate the payments by voting statues for the king and his wife on Delos; in the decree the proclamation of the statues was juxtaposed with a message concerning Pharnaces' lapsed obligations (*I. Delos* 1497 [=Durrbach 1976: 73]). The city passed the decree immediately upon receiving the news that Pharnaces married Nysa. An envoy was elected by the Athenians to inform the king of the statues and to discuss a resumption of the promised payment.[7] Three commissioners were appointed to oversee the execution of the statues, and the secretary of the prytany was in charge of inscribing the decree on a marble stele and setting it up in front of the images. The city's military funds were intended to cover all costs relating to the engraving of the decree, the production of the statues, and the envoy's travelling expenses. The decree also contains a clause indicating that Pharnaces will not be honored less than the other benefactors of the city, which in effect places the king's unfulfilled pledge in the context of other completed benefactions and subtly introduces the issue of aristocratic competition for honors and prestige. Even a brief account such as this demonstrates the complexity of the process and the link between portraits and politics. It also indicates the range of costs which had to be considered and the amount of time and correspondence involved.

The same administrative system operated during the Roman empire: statues of the emperor were voted by a town or region, the decree was transmitted to the emperor by one or more envoys, and the emperor then had to decide whether to accept the proposed honors, modify them, or reject them. The practice of voting portraits in several different media simultaneously – bronze, marble, gold, and paintings on shields – disappears after the Augustan period and is never used for members of the Imperial family. Nor do we have any Imperial examples wherein the dedicator offers the emperor a choice of statuary type or of placement, but on occasion the emperors did request modifications regarding number and media. When they were offered statues in precious metals, the emperors usually asked for a change from gold or silver to bronze as part of a general refusal of divine honors, and they sometimes wrote letters requesting a decrease in the number of portraits they had been voted and indicating where the statues should be erected.[8]

The production of statues can be linked to a variety of circumstances, but as in the Hellenistic period they formed part of the framework of Imperial euergetism, and enough correspondence between Rome and the provinces survives for us to see how this relationship worked. Letters began with offers to erect statues of the emperor and continued with appeals to him to provide political or economic assistance to the city. A letter which the Alexandrians wrote to Claudius asking him to intercede in the city's ethnic conflicts is a particularly clear example of this, and one can see the same approach in correspondence between Augustus and Sardis (*I. Sardis* 8; Oliver 1989: no. 7

[Letter of Augustus to the Sardians]; 1989: no. 19 [Letter of Claudius to the Alexandrians]). This system also extended to officials outside the Imperial family: when the Sanctuary of Hera at Samos had its right of asylum renewed in AD 32, the Demos set up statues of the consuls who held office that year (Herrmann 1960: 150, 'h'; *IGR* IV.1724). The impetus for action sometimes came from Rome itself in the form of senatorial decrees disseminated throughout the empire when a member of the Imperial family died. Very few of these have come to light, but a recent discovery in Spain allows us to reconstruct nearly all of the *senatus consultum* following the death of Germanicus in AD 19 (Gonzales 1984; Gonzales and Arce 1988; Lebek 1987; 1991). Statues of him in triumphal contexts were to be set up in Rome, Germany, and Syria, and copies of the decree were to be sent to all colonies and municipalities in the empire and placed in prominent locations. The same procedure was followed after other Imperial funerals, and these decrees would have signalled the most opportune time for the erection of Imperial statues.

Deciding which members of the family to include in these monuments was never easy owing to the constant changes within the Imperial family: a design appropriate one year could be outdated the next. At Ephesos, for example, sometime before 13 BC, two freedmen built a new gateway to the agora and proposed to crown it with statues of Augustus, Agrippa, and their wives, Livia and Julia, respectively (Hanson and Johnson 1946: no. 11; Alzinger 1974: 9ff.; Roddaz 1984: 474ff.). By the time the gateway was finished, nearly ten years later, Agrippa was dead and his wife Julia had remarried the emperor's stepson Tiberius. Such Imperial remarriages, as well as divorces and adoptions, occured with great frequency during the Julio-Claudian period, and the emperor's letter of acceptance was probably often inscribed on stone and set up near the statues in order to verify that their erection was Imperially sanctioned.[9]

Once approval from the emperor had been secured, the dedicators needed to deal with three issues: the text of the inscription to be placed beneath the portrait, the acquisition of the portrait type, and the choice of the statuary type. The first issue was the easiest. The titles of the emperor, or any member of the Imperial family, could have been obtained from the heading of the letter which granted permission for the statues, and whatever epithets seemed appropriate to the local situation could then be added. There is no evidence that the exact wording of the dedication was included in the initial proposal to the emperor, although this had been done consistently during the Hellenistic period (and was still occasionally done for non-Imperial benefactors during the first century AD; Robert 1935: 440, ll. 71–75; *IGR* IV.144, ll. 13–17).

Without more literary or epigraphic evidence we will probably never be able to reconstruct the ways in which official portrait models were disseminated throughout the Mediterranean, but the system was probably more flexible than modern scholarship would indicate.[10] There is an assumption that the dedicators of portraits always ordered the latest models available, and dates are assigned to portraits based on that premise. Yet the changes from one Imperial type to another were usually not substantial – often involving only a slight rearrangement of the bangs on the forehead – and if the city had earlier dedicated one statue of the emperor, they sometimes simply reused the same type rather than ordering a new model from Rome or a regional workshop. This happened, for example, at Lepcis Magna in Tripolitania, where an Augustan type of Livia was used for a Tiberian dedication (Aurigemma 1940: 50–56). Considering the slight variations in type and the elevated positions which statues usually occupied, it is unlikely that anyone would have noticed the use of an older type, and it was undoubtedly also a much cheaper option.

Compiling statistics on the range of Imperial statuary types during the early empire is difficult since so many of those erected in the eastern Mediterranean have disappeared. Based on the surviving examples, however, the standing nude and the cuirassed type were the most popular for men; equestrian and togate statues were extremely rare. Although enthroned types were not uncommon in the west, very few from the first century AD have been excavated in Greece and Asia Minor.[11] The same avoidance of the enthroned type is apparent during the Hellenistic period, and it seems to have been regarded as a format appropriate for humans only in extraordinary cases.[12]

The types chosen for women emphasized their role in the perpetuation of the dynasty. Aphrodite and Demeter types were not uncommon, serving as illustrations of epithets such as *karpophoros* (fruit-bearing) and *kalliteknos* (bearer of beautiful children) which were used in the dedicatory inscriptions.[13] In the Julio-Claudian period Imperial women also appear to have been shown with their newly born children. All such examples are attested by inscription only, but considering the age at which the children were represented, the parents must have been shown holding them in their arms. We should probably imagine these as adaptations of earlier mythological types, such as Ploutos and Eirene, or Leto with Apollo and Artemis; there are a few surviving examples of the type in first century AD sculpture.[14] The advent of the type should probably be connected with the travels of the Imperial family to Greece and Asia Minor during the early empire. On occasion commanders were accompanied by their wives and children, and some of the wives even gave birth while in the east (Halfmann 1986: 163–166 [Agrippa and Julia]; 168–170 [Germanicus and Agrippina the Younger]). Such family travels did not occur in the Hellenistic period, and this is probably one of the principal reasons why the format was not used for royal women.

No extant early Imperial statues survive in which emperors or members of their families are crowned by personifications, although this was the standard format in the Imperial reliefs from the Aphrodisias Sebasteion, and the type was probably more common than the evidence now indicates.[15] The placement of Imperial statues within temples of the Olympians was rare, in both eastern and western regions of the empire, and this stands out by comparison with Hellenistic practice.[16] The change is undoubtedly linked to the Imperial refusal of divine honors, which had not been the custom during the Hellenistic period, but on a purely practical level it also made more sense to place Imperial images in an outdoor setting, where they could more easily be seen.

The problems associated with the dedication of statues did not end once they had been set up in their chosen location. During the first century AD the number of murders and exiles within the Imperial family extended into the double digits, and on four occasions the Senate ordered the destruction of Imperial portraits and inscriptions.[17] A quick examination of early Imperial inscriptions indicates that there was some confusion as to how to handle this in the provinces. Despite the senatorial decree, in none of the cases was there a systematic erasure of names, and even in the same city an emperor's name was sometimes erased from one inscription but left intact in another (e.g. Agrippina the Younger at Epidauros: *AEpigr* 1980: no. 855 [erased]; *IG* ed. min. 4.1, 602 [not erased]). Portraits were regularly recut into images of the next emperor, although cities occasionally found cheaper solutions to the problem. In the Sebasteion at Aphrodisias, for example, the Imperial reliefs were positioned over six meters above the head of the spectator, and this distance, combined with the heavily idealized faces, made the portraits nearly indistinguishable from each other. After Nero's death the city simply erased his personal name and left the portraits untouched (Smith 1987: nos. 7, 11; Reynolds 1981: 324).

We should not be surprised by this haphazard approach to Imperial *damnationes*. Members of the Imperial family who were denounced during one reign were sometimes accorded the highest honors once a new emperor ascended the throne; this was the case, for example, for the brothers and mother of Caligula (Barrett 1989: 60ff.) and for Commodus (Rubin 1980: 212–14). There was also no local tradition in Greece and Asia Minor for this kind of iconoclasm: in the Hellenistic period individual cities or regions had occasionally ordered the destruction of royal inscriptions and portraits, but there had been no centralized system in which decrees mandating the destruction of images were circulated throughout the realm (Smith 1988: 18; Vittinghoff 1936: 18–19).

There was apparently a change in this practice during the second century AD, which can be seen most clearly by looking at the *damnationes* of Domitian (AD 96) and Geta (AD 211). In *IGR* there are over thirty inscriptions which mention Domitian and about the same number which refer to Geta. Domitian's name has been erased in slightly more than half the examples, whereas Geta's name was erased from all but one of his inscriptions (*IGR* I.855 [Olbia]). During the later empire the heads of denounced members of the Imperial family were also chiselled off coins with greater frequency, and the early Imperial ambivalence toward defacement appears to have been replaced by a rapid and relatively uniform response (Harl 1987: 35).

Perhaps the most important question to ask of Imperial statues in the eastern Mediterranean is how anyone would have known they were Imperial. In other words, how easy was it to distinguish Imperial statues from portraits of private benefactors or officials? If the dedicatory inscription were still legible, and if the viewer were literate, there would have been no problem. But inscriptions sometimes wore away and a sizable proportion of the population was unable to read.[18] The question, then, is whether there were other aspects of the statue, or of its context, which made it clear that an emperor or a member of his family was being represented. To explore this issue, I have examined the corpus of Imperial and private portraiture from the eastern Mediterranean with an eye toward their location, size, costume, and attributes.

This was not an easy task, not least since many of the private portraits from the early empire were bronze and we have no idea what they looked like. But enough Imperial and private portraits survive to show that, at least in the early empire, there does not appear to have been any discernible difference between them. The idealizing trends popular during the Julio-Claudian and the later Flavian periods were used for both Imperial and private portraiture, and facial features alone would probably not in most cases have been sufficient to determine whether a portrait was Imperial or private. In both cases the statues were usually slightly over-lifesize (a little more than two meters high; relatively few colossal portraits from Greece and Asia Minor are preserved [Kreikenbom 1992: III.8, 18, 23, 41, 68, 69, 71, 93]). In both cases, they are set up in locations which guaranteed the greatest public exposure – usually agoras or sanctuaries. The same media were also used: either bronze or marble, with the latter considered more valuable than the former, with painted portraits a rarity.[19] In terms of costume and format, so few types survive for this period that it is impossible to determine whether some were more popular than others. In the extant examples, the toga was used for both Imperial and private portraits, while only the emperors and members of their families were shown on horseback, in armor, or nude. Nevertheless, all of these types can be found in both royal and private portraiture from the Hellenistic period, and most of them were probably used for private bronze portraits which no longer survive.[20]

In later periods the emperor was often shown wearing the *corona civica*, which developed into an exclusively Imperial attribute, but in the first century AD it was rarely used for Imperial statues in the east.[21] In women's portraiture the one attribute which would have immediately signalled Imperial rank was the *stephane* or crescent-shaped diadem, which had also been worn by Hellenistic queens. The *stephane*, however, did not become popular in the east until the Flavian period.[22] The heads of Julio-Claudian women were generally bare or covered by a simple veil, as in private portraiture.

A few examples drawn from various reigns in the early empire will demonstrate the difficulties of dealing with Imperial and private portraits in public contexts. The first two photos are of female statues from Olympia. Figure 1, which was found in front of the Temple of Hera, shows Agrippina the Younger, wife of Claudius (Treu 1894: 256–57; Hitzl 1991: no. 3); Figure 2, which portrays a priestess, was discovered within the same temple but was made perhaps two decades later than the first (Treu 1894: 259). They are both approximately the same size; both have fairly idealized facial features. If one were looking for special signs of Imperial rank, one might easily choose the wrong one. It is the private statue which occupied the more prestigious site within the temple, and it is her hair which is bound with the *infula*, the sacred beaded fillet which was used in Imperial women's portraiture primarily during the Julio-Claudian period (Wood 1995: 473–79). Two cuirassed statues from the early second century make the same point. The statue of Ti. Julius Celsus Polemaeanus (Fig. 3), consul in AD 92 and proconsul of Asia in AD 106/7, was featured in his library at Ephesos

Fig. 1. Statue of Agrippina the Younger, wife of Claudius, from Olympia (after Treu 1894: pl. 63.2)

Fig. 2. Statue of a Flavian priestess from Olympia (after Treu 1894: pl. 63.6)

Fig. 4. Statue of Hadrian from the Odeion at Troy (photo by M. Wiebell)

Fig. 3. Statue of Ti. Julius Celsus Polemaeanus from the Library of Celsus at Ephesos (after Wilberg et al. 1953: fig. 101)

(Wilberg *et al.* 1953: 57–9; Inan and Rosenbaum 1966: no. 144). I have here juxtaposed it with a statue of the young Hadrian from the stage building of the Odeion at Troy (Fig. 4; Rose 1994: 90–92). Note that the armor of Celsus is more elaborately decorated than that of Hadrian, and it is Celsus, the private citizen, who wears the laurel wreath, while Hadrian's head is bare.

Contrary to one's expectations, then, it was not always easy to distinguish between private and Imperial portraits in the eastern Mediterranean during the early empire. If one were walking through an agora or sanctuary, the only absolute criterion for identifying an Imperial statue would have been the dedicatory inscription. Any spectator who was illiterate, or at least not literate in Greek, would have needed assistance in separating the images by status, since portraits of kings and non-Imperial benefactors already filled the major public spaces. This too represented a change from the Hellenistic period: although both royal and non-royal dedications had occupied the agoras, the portraits of king and queen had always been immediately recognizable by their diadems. There were, of course, contexts in which Imperial status would have been easily recognized. Sanctuaries of the ruler cult (Sebasteia or Kaisareia) do not appear to have contained any non-Imperial images, at least during the early empire, and the size of some of these statues, such at that of Titus from Ephesos (Fig. 5), would have quickly signalled the superhuman status of the emperor (Daltrop *et al*, 1966: 86; Inan and Rosenbaum 1966: 67, no. 27; Meric 1985).[23] But in large and multi-purpose spaces, eastern cities placed the emperors and their local benefactors in the same category.[24]

During the second and third centuries, increased use of the *corona civica* for men and the *stephane* for women would have made it easier to distinguish between Imperial and private images, but as

Charles Brian Rose

*Fig. 5. Reconstruction of the colossal statue of Titus from the Flavian Sebasteion at Ephesos
(drawing by R. Hagerty after Meric 1985: pl. 24)*

the employment of distinctly Imperial attributes became more common, so too did the mixing of private and Imperial images in façade architecture such as propylons and theater skenes, for example at Olympia (Bol 1984: esp. 88–91), at Perge (Boatwright 1993: 197–98) and at Aphrodisias (Erim 1986: 123–130). We should assume Imperial knowledge and authorization of these groups, even though the letters approving them do not survive, and conclude that there were no local or Imperial strictures against such mixing. Nor should we expect them: the emperors were shown with the local aristocracy who in turn were here linked to the center of power; provincial cities, which had used the honorific statue for centuries as a means of promoting their political and economic strength, would have continued to benefit from both groups.

Notes

1   During the period in question there are references to Caligula and Nero commissioning their own portraits, but this was the exception rather than the rule, and they were not intended for public locations: Cassius Dio 59.4.4; Pliny, *NH* 35.51; Suetonius, *Nero* 25.2. In the eastern Mediterranean there is no evidence that the emperor or the Senate ever ordered the erection of an Imperial portrait.

2   *I. Priene* 109 (120 BC); *I. Priene* 112 (84 BC); *I. Sardis* 27 (ca. 75–50 BC); *CIG* 3085 (Teos); Bérard 1891: 546 (Iasos); Hauvette-Besnault and Dubois 1881: 96 (Mylasa). The following are all Augustan: *I. Sardis* 8; *GIBM* 4.1.787 and 893 (Knidos and Halikarnassos); *I. Kyme* 19.

3   Honorific statues in front of the temple of Apollo at Delphi were raised on pillars to separate them from the mass of images in the area: Courby 1927: 262–65 (Prusias II of Bithynia); 275–77 (Eumenes II); 302–5 (Aemilius Paullus); 269–75 (probably Drusilla, sister of Caligula); 277–81 (Augustus?).

4   The honors for the ambassador Iollas of Sardis were even more elaborate (*I. Sardis* 27; 75–50 BC). He received three gilded portraits, one of which was colossal and another equestrian, as well as three in marble, four in bronze, and four which were painted.

5   *IGR* IV.292, ll. 24ff. (Diodoros Pasparos of Pergamon crowned by the Demos); *I. Kyme* 13.1, ll. 2 ff. (Archippe of Kyme crowned by the Boule, after 130 BC); Smith 1993: 24–42 (Zoilos of Aphrodisias crowned by personifications of the city, virtue, and honor; late first century BC).

6   *OGIS* 763 = Welles 1934: no. 52 (Eumenes II); *IG* 11.4, 1136, 1061 = Durrbach 1976: 75 (200–150 BC); *I. Delos* 1519 = Durrbach 1976: 85 (153/52 BC); *I. Sardis* 8, sections 7–10 (late first century BC). In the first example, the king was given the choice of any location in Ionia for his statue; he selected Miletos. The statuary base was uncovered at the site, and a copy of Eumenes' letter of acceptance was inscribed on the base: Von Gerkan and Krischen 1928: no. 306. The benefactor was sometimes also allowed to dictate where the stele recording his honors would be erected; Lalonde 1971: 166–68.

7   For the process of choosing envoys and the costs involved in their travels, see Lalonde 1971: 108–131.

8   On requests for the use of less precious metals: Charlesworth 1939; Scott 1931: 101–23; Pekary 1985: 66–80; Oliver 1989: no. 196 (Letter of Marcus Aurelius and Commodus to the Athenian Gerousia). It is worth noting that there is no evidence for similar modifications on the part of Hellenistic kings or benefactors. On requests regarding fewer portraits and portrait placement: Oliver 1989: no. 18 (Letter from Caligula to the League of the Achaeans, Boeotians, Locrians, Phocians, and Euboeans); no. 19 (Letter of Claudius to the Alexandrians).

9   See, for example, Oliver 1989: no. 7 (Augustus to Sardis), no. 15 (Tiberius to Gytheion), no. 19 (Claudius to Alexandria). For a good Hellenistic example of this practice, see Von Gerkan and Krischen 1928: no. 306 (Eumenes II at Miletos).

10 For a discussion of the issues, see Stuart 1939. The systematic dissemination of royal portrait models does not seem to have occurred in the Hellenistic period, see Smith 1988: 27–8.

11 During the first century AD in Greece and Asia Minor the only extant examples I have been able to find

are the statues of Augustus and Livia from the Basilica at Ephesos: Inan and Rosenbaum 1979: nos. 3 and 5. An enthroned type was probably used for the statue of Julia Livilla in the Temple of Athena at Pergamon: *OGIS* 474. The enthroned type was used several times during the first century at Lepcis Magna in Tripolitania, see Aurigemma 1940: 80–83; Niemeyer 1968: nos. 89, 90.

12   A survey of the honors conferred on Hellenistic kings and benefactors turns up only two certain examples, both from the first century BC: Antiocho of Commagene at Nemrud Dag (Wagner 1983), and Diodoros Pasparos at Pergamon (*IGR* IV.293, ll. 44f.).

13   For the use of the word *karpophoros*, see Robert 1960: 285–98; Hahn 1994: 134–138; *I. Ephesos* 7.2, 4337. For Julia, daughter of Augustus, as *kalliteknos*, see *I. Priene* 225; Hodot 1982: 174; Hahn 1994: 109. For the links between Imperial women and Aphrodite or Demeter, see Hahn 1994: 44–48.

14   For children-in-arms: *SIG*³ 779 A, B, D (Delphi, the infant Agrippina the Elder probably held by a member of the Augustan family); *AE* 1928: nos. 49–50 (Thespiae, Agrippa with his daughter Agrippina the Elder); *IGR* I.835 (Thasos, Livia holding her granddaughter Julia). For surviving adaptations of mythological types: Andreae 1984: no. 6 (Antonia Minor holding Cupid at Baiae) ; Andreae 1977: pl. 55 (Livia holding Cupid on the Ravenna relief); Kersauson 1986: no. 94 (the Louvre "Messalina" with her infant son). The latter is a private portrait although it has often been associated with the Julio-Claudian dynasty. For Leto with Apollo and Artemis, see Bieber 1977: fig. 469; for Ploutos and Eirene, see Ridgway 1984: pl. 76. The type was frequently used on Antonine coinage for personifications holding the newly-born children of Faustina II, see Bol 1984: 38–45.

15   For the Sebasteion reliefs, see Smith 1987. The same idea was expressed in the decoration of the Library of Celsus at Ephesos, where statues of the virtues of Celsus occupied niches in the facade: *I. Ephesos* 5108–5111.

16   *I. Delos* 1591 (Augustus in the Temple of Apollo on Delos); *IGR* IV.144 (Livia in the Temple of Athena at Cyzicus); *OGIS* 474 (Julia Livilla, sister of Caligula, in the Temple of Athena at Pergamon); Carter 1983: 286–88 (Claudius in the Temple of Athena at Priene). See also Price 1984: 146–156.

17   Tacitus *Ann.* 6.2 (Livilla, the wife of Drusus the Younger, in AD 23); Tacitus *Ann.* 11.38 (Messalina, the third wife of Claudius, in AD 48); Suetonius, *Nero* 49.2 (Nero in AD 68); Suetonius, *Domitian* 23.1 (Domitian in AD 96). For re-cutting of the heads of Nero and Domitian, see Bergmann and Zanker 1981: 317–412.

18   For worn inscriptions, see Oliver 1989: no. 170 (Letter of Marcus Aurelius and Lucius Verus to Ephesos). For a discussion of literacy in the Imperial east, see Harris 1989: 185–190.

19   For the relative value of bronze and marble statues, see Tuchelt 1979: 70–90. For the paintings, *SEG* 11.922–23, l. 34 (Gytheion; paintings of Augustus, Livia, and Tiberius); *I. Ephesos* 4337, ll. 14–24 (Ephesos, paintings of Livia and the twin sons of Drusus the Younger).

20   There is epigraphic evidence for a few private equestrian statues in the east during the first century AD; Bergemann 1990: no. E102 (P. Memmius Regulus at Athens); no. E125 (M. Maecilius Rufus at Olympia). The cuirassed type does not seem to have been used for private portraits in the east during this period; the earliest example dates to the first quarter of the second century, see Inan and Rosenbaum 1966: no. 144 (Ti. Julius Celsus Polemaeanus at Ephesos).

21   Smith 1987: nos. 1, 3, 5 (Augustus and Claudius at Aphrodisias); Inan and Rosenbaum 1979: no. 2 (Augustus at Ephesos); Tölle-Kastenbein 1974: 174, pl. 327 (Claudius at Samos); Hitzl 1991: no. 4 (Titus at Olympia).

22   For Julio-Claudian examples from Greece and Asia Minor, see Smith 1987: no. 11 (Agrippina the Younger at Aphrodisias); Bol 1986 (Octavia or Poppaea at Olympia). For the *stephane* in Hellenistic portraiture, Smith 1988: 43; in Flavian portraiture, see Daltrop *et al.* 1966: 52.

23   Although the portrait was identified as Domitian by Inan and Rosenbaum and by Meric, Daltrop *et al.* are surely correct in attributing it to Titus.

24   The design process for Imperial statues in the east is discussed more fully in my recent book (Rose 1997).

Bibliography

Alzinger, A. (1974) *Augusteische Architektur in Ephesos*, Vienna.

Andreae, B. (1977) *The Art of Rome*, New York.

_____ (1984) "Le sculture," in *Baia. Il ninfeo imperiale sommerso di Punta Epitaffio*, 49–66. Naples.

Aurigemma, S. (1940) "Sculture del Foro Vecchio di Lepcis Magna raffiguranti la Dea Roma e principe della casa dei guilio-claudi," *AfrIt* 8: 1–94.

Barrett, A. (1989) *Caligula: The Corruption of Power*, London.

Bérard, V. (1891) "Inscriptions d'Asie Mineure," *BCH* 15: 538–562.

Bergemann, J. (1990) *Römische Reiterstatuen*, Mainz am Rhein.

Bergmann, M., and P. Zanker (1981) "'Damnatio Memoriae': Umgearbeitete Nero und Domitiansporträts. Zur Ikonographie der Flavischen Kaisar und des Nerva," *JdI* 96: 317–412.

Bieber, M. (1977) *Ancient Copies*, New York.

Blanck, H. (1968) "Porträt Gemälde als Ehrendenkmäler," *BJb* 168: 1–12.

Bol, R. (1984) *Das Statuenprogramm des Herodes-Atticus-Nymphäums* (Olympische Forschungen 15), Berlin.

_____ (1986) "Ein Bildnis der Claudia Octavia aus dem Olympischen Metroon," *JdI* 101: 289–307.

Boatwright, M.T. (1993) "The city gate of Plancia Magna in Perge," in E. D'Ambra, ed., *Roman Art in Context*, 189–207. Englewood Cliffs.

Carter, J. (1983) *The Sculpture of the Sanctuary of Athena Polias at Priene*, London.

Charlesworth, M. (1939) "The refusal of divine honors: an Augustan formula," *BSR* 15: 1–10.

Courby, F. (1927) *Fouilles de Delphes II: Le terrace du temple*, Paris.

Daltrop, G., U. Hausmann, and M. Wegner (1966) *Die Flavier* (Das römische Herrscherbild II.1), Berlin.

Durrbach, F. (1976) *Choix d'inscription de Délos*, Hildesheim.

Erim, K. (1986) *Aphrodisias, City of Venus Aphrodite*, New York .

Gauthier, P. (1985) *Les cités grecques et leur bienfaiteurs* (*BCH* Suppl. 12), Paris.

Gerkan, A. von, and F. Krischen (1928) *Milet I.9. Thermen und Palaestren*, Berlin.

Gonzales, J. (1984) "Tabula Siarensis, Fortunales Siarenses et Municipia Civium Romanorum," *ZPE* 55: 55–100.

Gonzales, J., and J. Arce, eds. (1988) *Estudios sobre la Tabula Siarensis*, Madrid.

Hahn, U. (1994) *Die Frauen des römischen Kaiserhauses und ihre Ehrungen im griechischen Osten anhand epigraphischer und numismatischer Zeugnisse von Livia bis Sabina*, Saarbrucken.

Halfmann, H. (1986) *Itinera Principum. Geschichte und Typologie der Kaiserreisen im Römischen Reich*, Stuttgart.

Hanson, C., and F.P. Johnson (1946) "On certain portrait inscriptions," *AJA* 50: 389–400.

Harl, K. (1987) *Civic Coins and Civic Politics in the Roman East A.D. 180–275*, Berkeley.

Harris, W. (1989) *Ancient Literacy*, Cambridge.

Hauvette-Besnault, A., and M. Dubois (1881) "Antiquités de Mylasa," *BCH* 5: 95–119.

Henry, A.S. (1983) *Honors and Privileges in Athenian Decrees: The Principal Formulae of Athenian Honorary Decrees*, New York.

Herrmann, P. (1960) "Die Inschriften römischer Zeit aus dem Heraion von Samos," *AM* 75: 68–183.

Hitzl, K. (1991) *Die Kaiserzeitliche Statuenausstattung des Metroon* (Olympische Forschungen 19), Berlin

Hodot, R. (1982) "Décret de Kyme en l'honneur du Prytane Kléanax," *GettyMusJ* 10: 165–180.

Inan, J. and Rosenbaum, E. (1966) *Roman and Early Byzantine Portrait Sculpture in Asia Minor*, London.

_____ (1979) *Römische und Frühbyzantinische Porträt Plastik aus der Türkei. Neue Funde*, Mainz am Rhein.

Kersauson, K. de (1986) *Catalogue des portraits romains. Musée du Louvre*, Paris.

Kiss, Z. (1979) *Études sur le portrait impérial romain en Egypte*, Warsaw.

Kreikenbom, D. (1992) *Griechische und Römische Kolossalporträts bis zum späten ersten Jahrhundert nach Christus*, Berlin.

Lalonde, G. (1971) *The publication and transmission of Greek diplomatic documents*. Unpublished Ph.D. thesis, University of Washington.

Lebek, W. (1987) "Die drei Ehrenbögen für Germanicus," *ZPE* 67: 129–140.

_____(1991) "Ehrenbogen und Prinzentod: 9 v. Chr. – 23 n. Chr.," *ZPE* 86: 47–71.

Meric, R. (1985) "Rekonstruktionsversuch der Kolossalstatue des Domitian in Ephesos," in *Pro Arte Antiqua. Festschrift für Hedwig Kenner*, 239–41. Vienna.

Niemeyer, H.-G. (1968) *Studien zur statuarischen Darstellung der römischen Kaiser*, Berlin.

Nock, A. D. (1972) "Sunnaos Theos," in Z. Stewart, ed., *Essays on Religion and the Ancient World* I, 202–251. Cambridge.

Oliver, J. (1989) *Greek Constitutions of Early Roman Emperors from Inscriptions and Papyri*, Philadelphia.

Pekary, T. (1978) Statuen in kleinasiatischen Inschriften, in S. Sahin, E. Schwertheim, and J. Wagner, eds., *Studien zur Religion und Kultur Kleinasiens. Festschrift F. K. Dörner*, 727–744. Leiden.

_____(1985) *Das römische Kaiserbild in Staat, Kult, und Gesellschaft* (Das römische Herrscherbild III.5), Berlin

Poland, F. (1909) *Geschichte des Griechischen Vereinwesens*, Leipzig.

Price, S. (1984) *Rituals and Power. The Roman Imperial Cult in Asia Minor*, Cambridge.

Reynolds, J. (1981) "New evidence for the imperial cult in Julio-Claudian Aphrodisias," *ZPE* 43: 317–32.

Ridgway, B. (1984) *Roman Copies of Greek Sculpture: The Problem of the Originals*, Ann Arbor.

Robert, L. (1935) "Études sur les inscriptions et la topographie de la Grèce centrale," *BCH* 59: 438–452.

_____(1940) "Deux inscriptions d'Aptera," *Hellenica* 1: 113–118.

_____(1960) "Recherches épigraphiques V. Inscriptions de Lesbos," *REA* 62: 285–315.

Roddaz, M. (1984) *Marcus Agrippa*, Rome.

Rose, C. B. (1994) "The 1993 post-Bronze Age excavations at Troia," *Studia Troica* 4: 75–104.

_____(1997) *Dynastic Commemoration and Imperial Portraiture in the Julio-Claudian Period*, Cambridge.

Rubin, Z. (1980) *Civil-War Propaganda and Historiography*, Brussels.

Scott, K. (1931) "The significance of statues in precious metals in emperor worship," *TAPA* 62: 101–23.

Smith, R. R. R. (1987) "The imperial reliefs from the Sebasteion at Aphrodisias," *JRS* 77: 88–138.

_____(1988) *Hellenistic Royal Portraits*, Oxford.

_____(1993) *The Monument of C. Julius Zoilos* (Aphrodisias 1), Mainz am Rhein.

Stuart, M. (1938) *The Portraiture of Claudius*, New York.

_____(1939) "How were imperial portraits distributed throughout the Roman empire?," *AJA* 43: 601–617.

Tölle-Kastenbein, R. (1974) *Das Kastro Tigani* (Samos XIV), Bonn.

Treu, G. (1894) *Olympia III. Die Bildwerke in Stein und Ton*, Berlin.

Tuchelt, K. (1979) *Frühe Denkmäler Roms in Kleinasien I: Roma und Promagistrate* (IstMitt-BH 23), Tübingen.

Veyne, P. (1976) *Le pain et le cirque*, Paris.

Vittinghoff, F. (1936) *Der Staatsfeind in der römischen Kaiserzeit*, Berlin.

Wagner, J. (1983) "Dynastie und Herrscherkult in Kommagene. Forschungsgeschichte und neuere Funde," *IstMitt* 33: 177–224.

Welles, C.B. (1934) *Royal Correspondance in the Hellenistic Period*, New Haven.

Welsh, M. K. (1904–05) "Honorary statues in ancient Greece," *BSA* 11: 32–49.

Wegner, M. (1939) *Die Herrscherbildnisse in antoninischer Zeit* (Das römische Herrscherbild II.4), Berlin.

Wilberg, W., M. Theuer, F. Eichler, and J. Keil (1953) *Forschungen in Ephesos V.1. Die Bibliothek*, Vienna.

Wood, S. (1995) "Diva Drusilla Panthea and the sisters of Caligula," *AJA* 99: 457–482.

8. Greeks and Barbarians: The Black Sea Region and Hellenism under the Early Empire

David Braund

Throughout antiquity there abided a recurrent uncertainty about the relationship between the Black Sea region and Greece, the traditional geographical and cultural homeland of hellenism. While a more inclusive view could accept the 'Greekness' of the Black Sea (or parts of it), there was also a strong tendency to exclude the region as something outside the Greek world, something barbarian and other. As such, it was ripe for geographical disquisition. The power of that exclusive tendency is indicated by the decision of Procopius in the sixth century, when Byzantium had become the imperial centre, to include – as many had done before him – just such a disquisition within the historical narrative of his *Wars*, Book 8. Evidently he was not deterred from launching upon such a discussion either by the close proximity of the Black Sea to the imperial capital or by the fact that many another author had surveyed the region before him: not only geographers, but also historians as disparate as Polybius and Ammianus Marcellinus, in Greek and Latin respectively.

Greek ambivalence towards the region may be illustrated further by juxtaposing three very different writers of different epochs, namely Plato, Euripides and Pausanias. Plato's comparison (through the voice of Socrates) of as it seems Greek cities with frogs and ants around a pond is very familiar to students of the classical world:

> I am convinced that the world is a very large entity and that we, between the Pillars of Heracles and Phasis, live in a particular small section of it, dwelling around the sea like frogs and ants around a pond, while many others dwell in many other such regions (Plato, *Phaedo* 109b).

However, it is seldom observed that the pond in question is described as stretching from the Pillars of Heracles in the west as far as Phasis in the east. The observation matters because it indicates that Plato seems to have understood the Greek world to include not only the Mediterranean, but also the coast of the Black Sea as far as Phasis on its east coast, the destination of 'the farthest voyage' (Braund 1994: 73–74; for the phrase, see Strabo 11.2.16; cf. Braund 1994: 27).

In partial contrast, Euripides seems to have envisaged not Phasis but the Black Sea (Pontus) itself as a terminus, balanced again by the Pillars of Heracles (here described as *Atlas' bounds*). It remains unclear whether he includes or excludes the region from the Greek world, in this case specifically the

Greek religious world in which the goddess Aphrodite receives cult. Aphrodite herself opens the play:

> Great among mortals and not without name, Cyprian goddess am I called, as in the heavens. And all who between Pontus and Atlas' bounds do dwell and look upon the light of the sun... (Euripides, *Hippolytus* 1–4)

Much later, in the second century AD, Pausanias seems to consider the Black Sea region as essentially barbarous, although, as we shall see (and as further points up the ambivalence in question), he is also aware of Greek connections there. Sulla's sack of Athens in 86 BC led Pausanias to speak of Mithridates, whom he describes as the king 'of the barbarians around the Euxine Sea': no mention is made of the Greek cities of the region which formed so much of Mithridates' empire (1.20.4). Pausanias proceeds to explain away Athens' unfortunate decision to support the king against the Romans; not all Athenians, but only society's dregs, the *demos*, and the most unruly of the *demos* at that, chose to support Mithridates (1.20.5). In other words, Pausanias imagines an unholy alliance between a king of barbarians and the worst elements in Athenian society – an enemy without allied to another within. Roman cruelty in this case also had to be considered: Sulla's behaviour in Athens is not excused, but is set aside (remarkably) as atypical of Roman imperialism, as inappropriate to a Roman (1.20.7; cf. Ziolkowski 1993: 85, defending Sulla). Such a claim accords well with a broad tendency in early imperial hellenism which sought to reconcile the principle of Roman imperial rule with the everyday experience of its failings by treating bad governors and the like as rogue exceptions (see further Swain 1996: 240). For Pausanias, it is not Rome but the Mithridatic side that is judged barbarous.

Of course, even (northern) barbarians may be allowed to have their own particular skills, as Pausanias observes with regard to a Sauromatian breastplate dedicated in the sanctuary of Asklepios at Athens (1.21.5), or as Dio Chrysostom implies in his concern with the Getae (see below). Yet the image of the Black Sea region was nonetheless redolent of threats and hostility. For example, it was from here that the Amazons came to invade Attica (Pausanias 1.2.1; 1.15.2; 1.25.2), while Iphigenia's flight from the Tauri accords well with the depiction of the region as dangerous and inimical to hellenic culture (e.g. Pausanias 1.33.1). The myth of Amazons offered a threat to hellenism in all its forms and by that threat helped to shape its identity (cf. Hall 1989); their courage, however, could be approved (Sidebottom 1993: 254–55). The defeat of the Amazons was chosen not only for the shield of the cult statue of Athena Parthenos herself at Athens, but also for the base of the statue of Olympian Zeus (Pausanias 1.17.2).

In what follows, I explore episodes which together serve to illustrate not only Greek ambivalence towards the Black Sea region under the early empire, but also a desire on the part of those within the region who perceived themselves as Greek to forestall and overcome their potential marginalization. The antiquarian tendencies of hellenism under the early empire meant that imperial readings of fifth and fourth century BC texts played a particularly powerful role in conditioning the outlook of Greeks of the imperial age – not least with regard to the Black Sea about which those texts had much to say. In the three sections that follow, I bring together instances of the interplay of past and present in relations between the Black Sea region and the self-consciously 'Greek' world of the eastern Mediterranean under the early empire. These instances encompass both texts and historical events, both realized and unrealized.

I shall first argue that the rulers of the Crimean Bosporus should be given a prominent place in any consideration of Rome's client kings in the east. Further, I shall suggest that at least one Bosporan ruler may very well have participated in the royal scheme of completing the temple of Olympian Zeus at Athens and of dedicating it to the *Genius Augusti*. Secondly, I shall explore the didactic and protreptic use by one early imperial Greek author, Dio Chrysostom, of traditional images of the Black Sea region in general, and of Olbia in particular. We shall see how Dio's account of an Olbian adventure is constructed, for the benefit of Mediterranean 'Greeks', as a committed exploration of how Greeks should live with each other and with Rome, while remaining true to a treasured heritage. Finally, in the third section, I shall stress the particular importance of readings of canonical texts in the formation and confirmation of the hellenic outlooks of the Greeks of the imperial age. Throughout, we find vigorous attempts by Black Sea communities and individuals to share in, and to have themselves acknowledged as sharing in, the Greekness of the eastern empire. At the same time, however, we find a powerful tendency in the eastern Mediterranean to deny, or at least to denigrate, the Greekness of the inhabitants of the Black Sea region. Moreover, that tendency could be validated by the very texts wherein much of the foundation of imperial hellenism was located.

Athenian Zeus, Roman Jupiter and the Bosporan Kingdom

In his *Life of Augustus*, Suetonius has much to say about the emperor's treatment of the so-called client kings of the Roman empire. These included rulers as disparate and distant as chieftains of Britain in the west on the one hand, and the sophisticated royal regimes of the east on the other. However, it was the latter rulers who mattered most in imperial thinking and, by and large, in imperial action (Braund 1996). As we shall see, these included the rulers of the Crimean Bosporus, whose realm embraced not only the eastern Crimea but also the Taman' peninsula across the Straits of Kerch' and even the coastlands of the Sea of Azov.

Suetonius seems particularly to mean the client kings of the Greek east when he stresses Augustus' integration of such rulers within the imperial system, wherein he encouraged their intermarriage and more generally their good relations: 'he cared for them all precisely as limbs and parts of empire' (*Aug.* 48). His imperial *beneficia* found a response in royal *officia*:

> Friendly and allied kings each founded cities in their kingdoms as Caesareas and also they all together decided at common expense to complete the temple of Olympian Zeus at Athens which had been begun in antiquity and to dedicate it to his (*sc.* Augustus') *Genius*. And they often left their kingdoms and paid their daily respects to him not only at Rome but also as he travelled about the provinces, dressed in their togas and without their royal insignia, in the manner of clients (Suetonius, *Aug.* 60)

Suetonius is the only writer to record the scheme to complete the temple of Olympian Zeus, which is also the only specific example he gives of royal response to Augustus. In all probability, the scheme had a particular interest for Suetonius as a figure in Hadrian's regime: after all, it was Hadrian who was finally to complete the temple, among the other benefactions he bestowed upon Athens.

The implications of this royal scheme deserve consideration. Suetonius stresses that it was a joint venture of *all* the rulers; even if we take that to be an exaggeration (as we probably should), it can hardly be doubted that at the very least several rulers were involved. The element of organization is to be noted: this was an appropriately collective response to an emperor who encouraged the co-operation, friendship and intermarriage of client rulers. No doubt the royal participants were predominantly from the eastern empire: their choice of Athens as the site of their dedication suggests as much. The city was the premier show-case of Greek culture, where many a Hellenistic ruler had chosen to bestow royal patronage.

In the first century BC, Sulla had removed columns from the temple of Olympian Zeus for re-use in his restoration of the Capitol's temples at Rome, no doubt especially its principal temple of Jupiter Capitolinus (Abramson 1974: 19–20 seems perverse in denying the use of such a prize in the temple of Jupiter, given the literary evidence he collects, e.g. Pliny, *NH* 36.45; Gellius, *NA* 2.10.2). As Zanker observes, the incident invites exploration of the connection between these two temples, one of the Greek, the other of the Roman manifestation of the king of the gods (1988: 21–22). Sulla had his precedents: we happen to know, for example, that a century earlier T. Quinctius Flamininus had dedicated a statue of Jupiter Imperator on the Capitol at Rome, having seized it in Macedonia (Cicero, *Verr.* 2.4.129; with Gruen 1992: 104–105; cf. 88). More to the point, perhaps, Antiochus IV Epiphanes of Syria had concerned himself both with the temple of Olympian Zeus at Athens and with the construction of a magnificent temple of Jupiter Capitolinus in his kingdom, at Syrian Antioch (Livy 41.20; cf. Polybius 26.1.10; Bringmann 1993: esp. 13). Antiochus was of course a prominent philo-Roman ruler of the second century BC and, as such, a forerunner of the kings of the Augustan age. Nor had the king and his plans been forgotten. Vitruvius takes a keen interest in those plans, designed 'with great care and skill' by Decimus Cossutius, a distinguished architect who was also a Roman citizen (Vitruvius 7.*praef.* 15, 17; Abramson 1974: 3). An honorific statue of Cossutius was erected at the Olympieion: the Roman architect was recognised as a significant figure in his own right (*IG* II/III² 4099 with Rawson 1991: 190–91 on his origins). Whether he was also the architect commissioned to build the temple of Jupiter Capitolinus at Antioch remains uncertain (Rawson 1991: 192–93 offers appropriate caution).

Vitruvius' interest offers some insight into the issue of the reconstruction of the temple of Olympian Zeus in the later first century BC. Such a project was already in the air and recognised as appropriate to relationships between kings, Romans and Rome. We should also note the judgment of another writer of the period. Livy describes the temple of Olympian Zeus at Athens as 'the only one undertaken in the world that is commensurate with the greatness of the god' (*unum in terris inchoatum pro magnitudine dei*: Livy 41.20.8). These contemporary voices indicate that the Augustan royal project was seen to be outstanding indeed.

Insofar as the temple of Olympian Zeus at Athens may be perceived as a Greek counterpart of the temple of Jupiter Capitolinus (see Rigsby 1980: 238), royal interest in the completion of the Olympieion reflects royal concern with the Capitol at Rome, which was the sustained religious and political focus of the relationship between Rome and so-called client kings (Braund 1984: esp. 24–25, 55–56). Another contemporary author, Strabo, for example regards dedications on the Capitol as a key feature of the affiliation of British rulers to Rome under Augustus (4.5.3; cf. 6.4.2; see Syme 1995: 332, criticising Strabo's triumphalism). It seems that Strabo took the trouble personally to inspect such dedications (see also Josephus, *AJ* 14.35–36, where there are textual difficulties). It must be stressed that the temple of Jupiter on the Capitol at Rome was the only place where many (if not all) of the kings and queens of the Roman empire engaged in much the same activities in articulating their relations with Rome, although the nature of their dedications evidently varied. Their collective concern with the Olympieion was a reflection of their common concerns with the temple of Jupiter Capitolinus.

In the end, the Olympieion had to wait for Hadrian. One wonders why the kings failed in their project after going so far in their planning as to leave a record which Suetonius could find, perhaps in the imperial archives, more than a century later (Abramson 1974: 23–24 considers that some work may have been started under Augustus, though he recognises the lack of any evidence for this). It seems inconceivable that the kings themselves would have cancelled the project, bringing a measure of disgrace and imperial displeasure upon themselves. Nor can Athens have enforced any objection. Conceivably one or two kings died, but not all, for significant rulers like Juba II and Archelaus I of Cappadocia outlived Augustus. The most likely obstacle was surely the emperor himself. It may be that Augustus was unwilling to risk the potential obloquy of dedicating the renowned Olympieion to his *Genius* (cf. Livy 41.20.8, quoted above): even Hadrian dedicated the sanctuary to Zeus (though it was replete with images of the emperor, as Alcock [1993: 181] observes; cf. Claudius' reservations elsewhere: *P. Lond.* 1912). Or was Augustus simply at odds with the city of Athens at such a time as to kill the project? (Hoff 1989: 3–6 on the shifting attitude of the emperor to Athens; Bowersock 1987: 298–99)

The identity of the rulers here in question is in part a matter for speculation, but some reasoned inferences are possible. Suetonius' formulation suggests that those kings who built Caesareas were also those who planned to complete and dedicate the temple of Olympian Zeus. Indeed, both the Caesareas and the Olympieion were redolent of the imperial cult, more than simply acts of construction involving the emperor, as I have argued in detail elsewhere (Braund 1984: 107–12). Therefore, one might expect that those rulers who were most energetic in their establishment of Caesareas and in their involvement with the imperial cult were also those who planned to complete the Olympieion and dedicate it to Augustus' *Genius*. Obvious candidates include Herod, Archelaus I, and perhaps even Juba II.

Easily overlooked but also likely candidates are the rulers of the Crimean Bosporus (Braund 1984: 107–12 collects the evidence on their foundations). A ruler of the Bosporus, perhaps Polemo I, refounded Panticapaeum (Kerch') as Caesarea (Gaidukevich 1971: 328; cf. 477; Sullivan 1990: 158–63) and his second city, Phanagoria, as Agrippeia (Braund 1984: 108; Zograph 1977: 309; cf. 304; Tsvetayeva 1979). The Bosporan princes were quite exceptional in the frequency with which they proclaimed their imperial connections within their kingdom. They were exceptional also in naming themselves high priest of the Augusti in their royal titulature, while regularly giving the *tria nomina* that their Roman citizenship permitted them (Braund 1984: 41–42, 112–13). At an uncertain date, a Bosporan ruler also issued copper coins which depict a five-columned temple with the letters KAPE on the obverse, and a royal monogramme on the reverse. It is very tempting to infer that the temple depicted is that of Capitoline Jupiter, although whether such a temple was erected in the Bosporus must remain an open question. The date of these coins is a matter of dispute, but they can be attributed to the first or second centuries AD (see the convenient survey of Golenko [1975] and the literature he lists; cf. Braund 1984: 113). The figurines of (as it seems) Jupiter Capitolinus, which occur in the Black Sea region as well as in the Mediterranean, offer a further, if slight, indication of the currency of his cult there, even at as obscure a site as Myskhako near Novorossiysk on the eastern fringe of the Bosporan realm (Treister 1992).

It is tempting to suggest that the particular enthusiasm of the rulers of the Crimean Bosporus to express their roles in, and connections with, the Roman empire may well be a function of their very location on the margins of the Graeco-Roman world. In what follows, we shall see that such enthusiasm is similarly characteristic of Bosporan and other Pontic engagement with Greek culture. In the Black Sea, a sense of marginality to the Graeco-Roman world was perhaps inevitable, whether to the political and military might of Rome or to the cultural power and identity of Greece and the Greek world of the Mediterranean Sea. To overcome or to compensate for that marginality was to struggle with the very image of the Black Sea region as understood in the Graeco-Roman Mediterranean.

Images of the Black Sea: Chrysostom's Olbia

A temple of Zeus is the dramatic location for much of the action of Dio Chrysostom's *Oration* 36. In this case it is a temple at Olbia on the north-west coast of the Black Sea (see Moles 1995: 186, who notes the symbolic power of that location). Around the turn of the first to second century AD, Dio composed an address to the people of Prusa in Bithynia (his home town) in the form of an extended anecdote about his visit to Olbia. The historicity of his account of Olbia is a matter of some interest. Although it has often been taken to be a precise description of contemporary Olbia, derived from personal autopsy, there seem no grounds for much certainty in Dio's text. While nothing in his account makes an actual visit incontestable, on the other hand neither is there good reason to deny that Dio visited Olbia (perhaps in summer AD 97: Jones 1978: 51). He clearly knew something about the place, however he had come by his information (see Russell 1992: 22, with Birge 1994). There were certainly literary influences upon his account: Moles draws attention to Herodotus and Plato's *Phaedrus* (Moles 1995: 184). It is probably significant that Dio prefers the city's older name, Borysthenes, to the name Olbia. The former occurs only rarely in the inscriptions of the city, although it is well represented in literary sources. In the city itself Olbia was the usual name employed, not least in Dio's day. Even in Dio's choice of name, therefore, there may be an indication of the distance between his account and Olbian actuality.

Dio's purpose in *Oration* 36 is not simply to report what he saw at Olbia, but to develop broad arguments about hellenism, and about civic and cosmic order, for presentation in Prusa and in the Greek world beyond. Jones rightly observes that 'the romantic exaggeration is palpable' (Jones 1978: 61). One might add that, in any case, visitors tend to see what they want and expect to see (see Alcock 1996).

In general, Dio's presentation of Olbia seems far too gloomy, as has been seen to be characteristic of his later writings (Moles 1978: 94–95). Dio offers an Olbia that is in a parlous state, not only in terms of its physical remains, but also in its military difficulties and its isolation from the world of hellenic culture. His Olbia is in a permanent state of war with its non-Greek neighbours (see in general Sidebottom 1993). Although according to Dio its defences are in poor repair, the archaeology actually tends to suggest that Olbia was well enough defended in this period, despite the powerful influence upon archaeologists of literal readings of Dio's account (Buyskikh 1991: 16–30). Of course, the notional weakness of Olbia's fortifications has a purpose. It helps Dio to build a picture of a community on the brink of destruction by its enemies, with its funeral monuments and the ruined statues in its sanctuaries, embodiments of its religious and perhaps historical identity, cut about by war (cf. Sidebottom 1993: 248).

His stated reason for being in Olbia (or Borysthenes) at all, en route to the Getae through Scythia, seems to raise some doubt:

> I happened to be in Borysthenes on a visit in the summer, as then I had sailed there after my exile with the wish of going, if I were able, through the Scythians to the Getae, so that I might see how matters were there (36.1).

This is the opening sentence of the oration and we should note both the vagueness of Dio's claimed rationale for being in Olbia and his reservation, 'if I were able'. If Dio had really wished to visit the Getae, as he says, then a journey through Olbia, and thence through Scythia, seems a difficult and roundabout way of reaching them. The Danube or Tomi might seem to offer a more straightforward line of approach. Indeed the situation which Dio describes at Olbia suggests that he soon discovered his mistake, if such it was. According to the account of his return from the Getae in the so-called *Olympic Oration*, he came back by the direct route, across the Danube (12.16–22). Dio had a penchant for situating his discourse in specific geographical locations: for example, Dio situates other imaginary encounters in Euboea or in the Peloponnese (Alcock 1993: 226). More broadly, Dio's purpose in mentioning a visit to the Getae during his exile requires explanation: one might suspect a reference to Ovid, whose exile had brought him too among the Getae, but the point of any such reference remains obscure. His lost *Getica*, evidently a historical work on the Getae, probably holds the key to an understanding of the episode. Philostratus, who knew the work and seems to have read it, presents the Getic journey especially as a principled withdrawal from the tyrannical power of Domitian (i.e. before AD 96), an act of resistance against Domitian's persecution of philosophy, during which Dio wandered as an Odysseus until the emperor's assassination allowed him to throw aside his rags (Philostratus, *VS* 487–88). The land of the Getae offered Dio another world, it seems, an alternative to the Roman empire; perhaps the land of the Getae served as the end of the earth which he said that Apollo had indicated to him at Delphi (13.1–9 with the cautions of Jones 1978: 46–50).

The barbarians at Olbia are variously identified in Dio's text as Scythians or Sauromatians and perhaps carelessly so, for it was their barbarism that was Dio's concern not their proper nomenclature (esp. 36.7–8). Olbia, stresses Dio, is a city situated not only among barbarians, but among perhaps the most warlike of barbarians at that (36.4). Also important for Dio is the barbarians' lack of a city of their own (though there is a stronghold, 36.3), for their nomadism was the appropriate counterpoint to the civic existence of Olbia; the Scythians seem to have been popular among the sophists of the early empire, not least as a means of exploring through rhetoric the respective merits and demerits of the Greek city (Philostratus, *VS* 572–73; cf. 620; see Dio 13.32 on potential Scythian wisdom). Of course, a city's relations with its neighbours were a theme of significance to Dio and to Prusa, particularly in the rather different context of the petty rivalries of the cities of Roman Asia Minor, with external rivalries between cities and internal within each one (notably, Dio 40.39–41). Depicting Olbia as a community united by the enemies who beset it in real warfare, Dio draws attention by implication to the self-indulgent futility both of Prusa's version of hostilities with neighbours and of the internal dissensions within the city that the lack of a real external enemy permits.

In that context, we can only wonder whether Dio's choice of Olbia as a setting for his remarks may have been encouraged by a traditional view of the city. Indeed, Dio himself stresses that Olbia has been under siege for generations (36.4). Nor is he alone in this; for example, Macrobius mentions

Olbia precisely as a city which famously resisted a siege, that of Zopyrion soon after 325 BC (*Sat.* 1.11.33; cf. Curtius Rufus 2.1.44; Justin 12.1.16; 37.3.2). Further, if Olbia was readily imagined as a city under siege, the siege itself certainly had a place as an image in philosophical discourse (Epictetus 1.28.25). At the same time, Dio's Olbia is presented very much as the sort of unified community that was identified in ancient thought as the most likely to subsist under siege (Whitehead 1990: 25–33, 136–37). As Dio is at pains to stress, Olbia could easily be seen as in danger, exposed at the margins of civilization: Propertius is not alone in choosing to name Olbia as a city at the end of the world (2.7.18; cf. a favorite author of Dio – Demosthenes 35.10 – speaks of travelling to the left bank of the Black Sea 'as far as Borysthenes'). As for historical actuality, warfare was indeed closer to Olbia than to Prusa. We happen to know of warfare at Olbia under Antoninus Pius some fifty years later, but that is evidently an exception, whose very historicity has been wrongly denied (on this Tauroscythian War, *SHA Pius* 9.9; with Braund 1991 against such denials).

Jones rightly stresses that Dio has exaggerated (imagined, one might say) the cultural isolation of Olbia; he documents in detail the vigorous hellenic culture of the city under the emperors (Jones 1978: 63). The recent discovery of an inscribed epigram off Olbia on the island of Berezan serves further to indicate the degree of fantasy in Dio's picture of Olbia as culturally isolated and impoverished in its hellenism. Letter-forms indicate that the epigram was inscribed in the first century AD, probably towards its end; if so, the temporal coincidence with Dio's visit could hardly be closer. Evidently, there were those at Olbia in the late first century AD who wished to compose elegiac verses and were quite capable of doing so to a reasonable standard. Certainly, there is nothing wrong with the quality of the Greek inscribed. A measure of confirmation is given, on the other hand, to the historicity of circumstantial details in Dio's account: the epigram is addressed to the island (of Berezan) and to Achilles (Pontarches, perhaps) and its discovery at Berezan seems to support Dio's report of an Achilles cult there (Shelov-Kovedyayev 1990, with comments and slight improvements by Dubois 1991: 505–506).

The culture of Dio's Olbia, however, is very different in most respects from that which generated the epigram. Dio presents himself as a completely unusual visitor to the city, thereby magnifying his exploit in going there and explaining his outstanding reception by the citizens. The cultural allegiance of Dio's Olbiopolitans is firmly Greek, particularly Milesian, though they have embraced the more familiar aspects of local non-Greek dress and accoutrements. Their isolation, as Dio has it, results in their veneration of Homer and ignorance of most other Greek writers (Plato being the only significant exception). Veneration of Homer is organically connected not only with the key civic cult of Achilles, but also with the warfare that dominates and threatens civic existence in Olbia (36.9, 15–16, 27). Dio's Olbia occupies a time-capsule: its archaism appears not only in its literary tastes, but even in its citizens' sustained preference for beards – they even look like the Greeks of Homeric times (36.17; cf. Podossinov 1987: 157–59 on similarities with Ovid's Tomitans).

Jones emphasises the utopian features of Dio's Olbia, and rightly so. Yet it is also a dystopia, bereft and under military and cultural threat, 'by no means idealized' (Russell 1992: 23). Dio is not inviting Prusa to become another Olbia. It is too limited, not least in its cultural appreciation. So committed are the Olbiopolitans to Homer that 'they do not even wish to hear of any other poet than Homer' (36.9). They almost all know the *Iliad* by heart, although to learn the *Iliad* by heart seems, in Russell's judgment, to have been 'not too uncommon an accomplishment in classical times' (Russell 1992: 217, citing Xenophon, *Symp.* 3.5–6). Much more important, and damning, was their shaky Greek: 'they do not speak Greek clearly as a result of living among barbarians' (36.9). In the hellenic outlook of the eastern Roman empire, as represented by Arrian, Philostratus and the like, there was a tendency to bemoan the deleterious effects of local barbarians upon the Greek language of a city (Arrian, *Peripl. M. Eux.* 1 on Pontic Trapezus; cf. Philostratus, *VA* 1.24). Greeks might even become barbarians, as did the Achaei of the north-east coast of the Black Sea, imagined (by Appian, for example, in the second century AD) as having abandoned their hellenism in reaction to their abandonment by the Greeks who fought at Troy (*Mith.* 102 with Braund 1994: 39). So too their neighbours, the barbarian Heniochi, who could be credited in the early empire with descent from the Spartan charioteers of the Dioscuri (Lucan 3.269; Braund 1994: 33). The phenomenon was by no means imagined to be confined to the Black Sea, of course: Philostratus has Apollonius of Tyana encounter other such cases elsewhere in the east (*VA* 1.16). An unpalatable but intriguing 'fact' for those who saw themselves as the champions of hellenic culture was that the impact of circumstances, attitudes and environment could turn even Greeks into barbarians, or at least into barbarized Greeks. Yet, at the same time, Dio seems to locate the barbarians outside the city, for his model required as much. In this too, that model seems to have been at best an over-simplification, for material remains at Olbia seem to suggest a substantial 'barbarian' presence within the population of the city (Marchenko 1988).

In Dio's imagination, the Greeks of Olbia seem to have lost more than they have retained; even clinging to the *Iliad* (the *Odyssey* was less appropriate), they have lost much of their Greek language. There was little to be applauded in that: their very Greekness required qualification (36.16), while they have failed to appreciate the limits of the ethics of the *Iliad* and Achilles within the community (Russell 1992: 23). The only social practice that is considered as abidingly Greek (specifically, Milesian) and as a potential influence upon the neighbouring barbarians is homosexuality, for which Dio elsewhere expresses his dislike and which he treats here as a source of corruption for the ignorant barbarians:

> Callistratus was about 18 years of age, very handsome and tall, having much of the Ionian about him in appearance. He was said to be brave in matters of warfare – to have killed many of the Sauromatians and to have taken many of them prisoner. He was enthusiastic also for oratory and for philosophy, so that he even desired to sail away with me. For all these reasons he enjoyed a fine reputation among his fellow-citizens, not least on account of his beauty, as he attracted many lovers. For indeed this practice has abided among them from their mother-city – the matter of love-affairs between men. So much so, that they risk converting even some of the barbarians, not for any good, I suggest, but as those people would adopt such a practice, in barbarous fashion and not without hubris (Dio 36.8; cf. 7.148–52, with Russell 1992: 216).

The detail resists explanation: why did Dio see fit to make specific remarks about homosexuality? A detail of heritage would attract his attention, however much he might dislike it. Here, he turns homosexuality into a further area in which Greek and barbarian may be distinguished: if Greek homosexuality is a bad thing, how much worse would be the barbarians' version? Further, one wonders whether Dio may be alluding to the only well-known thinker to have emerged from Olbia, namely Bion of Borysthenes, whom Diogenes Laertius presents as a reprehensible champion of homosexuality (4.46–57). For Dio there was no philosophy at Olbia, save a little Plato and Dio's own visit (36.24–26). The young warrior Callistratus, though martial in name and habits, is an exception who proves the rule. Somehow he had conceived an interest in oratory and philosophy: that interest could not be pursued in Olbia, so Callistratus wished to leave the isolated and embattled community with Dio.

Dio has almost nothing to say about the other Greek foundations of the region. He can only build a picture of Olbia as an isolated outpost of hellenism by inviting his audience to overlook Olbia's Greek neighbours: only Apollonia is named and then as a mark of barbarian conquest (36.4). Particularly striking is the virtual omission of the important city of Chersonesus in the south-western Crimea, though it may be encompassed in Dio's passing allusion in very general terms to the Greeks and Scythians who inhabit the Crimea (36.3). Nor was Byzantium itself so very far away: inscriptions attest Olbian links with Byzantium under the early empire (*IOSPE* i² 40, 41, 79; cf. *IO* 9, for the fourth century BC). Once one considers the large numbers of Greek foundations in and around the western Pontus, the notion of an 'isolated' Olbia looks ever more fantastic. Indeed, Dio himself was not the only citizen of Bithynian Prusa to have dealings with the city (*IOSPE* i² 40, 41; *IO* 47), so that even in his own city Dio's picture of Olbia might well have been understood as a place of the imagination, developed as a setting for philosophical discourse.

Rome is also far away: there is no sign in Dio's Olbia of Roman support against the barbarians at the gates. Only once do Romans occur at all in the speech, when a single individual in Dio's audience is seen as standing out as the only man without a Homeric beard:

> Among them only one was shaven, and they all insulted and hated this man. He was said to maintain such an appearance for no other reason than to curry favour with the Romans and to display his friendship towards them. So that one might see in his case the shamefulness of the matter and that it is in no way fitting for men (36.17).

The passage is an exceptional indication of disharmony within the city. In Dio's imagined Olbia, as in his historical Prusa and elsewhere in the eastern empire, disputes within the community were pursued in the context of Roman provincial and imperial power. In particular, local politicians might pursue their enemies by making allegations to the Roman authorities. Dio, urging unity, expresses distaste for the practice, and was himself the subject of such allegations, but he does not seem to have been above making them in his turn (Jones 1978: 95–103). The negotiation of relationships with governors and emperors was a long-standing problem, rendered more difficult by changes in personnel and attitudes. Elsewhere, addressing the Rhodians, Dio reconciles the assertion of local autonomy and tradition with Roman imperial authority by the claim that the Romans are wise enough to want their subjects to be free: they do not wish to rule over slaves (31.111). Similarly, in his oration at Olympia Dio can credit the Dacians with fighting against Rome for freedom and their homeland, while at the same time avoiding hostility to Rome or even to Roman imperialism (12.20, with Sidebottom 1993: 255–56, 261; contrast Swain 1996: 202, who sees criticism of Rome here). A Roman senator, such as Tacitus, could express much the same view at much the same time, as Russell wisely observes (Russell 1992: 173). As Jones writes of Dio, 'the kind of hellenism he preaches is one that does not conflict with Roman supremacy, but is approved by the Romans' (1978: 35).

Dio's words on the shaven Borysthenite have been taken to be an exception to that general position: 'the apparent anti-Roman tone of this passage is remarkable' (Russell 1992: 220 and the literature he cites); 'an unexpected anti-Roman aside' (Swain 1996: 216). However, it is not an exception, but accords well with Dio's broader position on the best manner of Greek conduct within the Roman empire (see further Moles 1995). The fault of the shaven Borysthenite is not that he is well-disposed towards Romans, but that he 'curries favour' with them inappropriately (*kolakeuōn*, which might better be translated as 'flattering'). His shaving expresses his abandonment of his civic traditions and of his allegiance to his community: his is not the behaviour of a free subject, but of a servile toady. Even the misguided Rhodians, who – for Dio – were mistaken in their approach to Romans, indulged only in *therapeia* ('service', even 'courting'). While *therapeia* might be acceptable enough as an honourable approach to the powerful, *kolakeia* was servility: it suggested both self-interest and disloyalty. Neither Dio nor his imagined Borysthenites hate their shaven fellow-citizen because he is a friend of Rome. On the contrary, although he displays his friendship for Rome, he is a *kolax*, a friend of no-one but himself (and from a philosophical perspective, he is not even a friend of himself). As such, he has much in common with a traitor: the shaven insider represents almost as great a danger to the community as the barbarian outsider (see further Sidebottom 1993: 249).

'Greekness' and the Black Sea

In *Oration* 36 Dio exploits a traditional conception of the Black Sea region as distant and rebarbative. The 'Inhospitable' Sea (*Pontos Axenos*) might have been rendered 'Hospitable' (*Euxeinos*) by the myths of the Argonauts and the process of Greek settlement, but it retained an image of danger, so that 'Hospitable' could be understood as at best a euphemism. The region was both within Hellas and outside it: Dio presents the western Black Sea as part of an extended Hellas, which was exposed to barbarians by its very position on the margins of the Greek world (36.5).

Elsewhere Dio reminds us that the Black Sea might have particular evocations in the local histories of various Mediterranean cities. He reminds the Rhodians, for example, of their old activities there, alluding no doubt to Rhodes' war with Byzantium in the later third century BC (31.103 with Braund 1995; note the otherwise surprising mention of Byzantium a few chapters later, 31. 105). Later, in the second century AD, Pausanias observes particular civic links with the Black Sea region. At Corinth, for example, the myth of Medea and her sons had a particular relevance to cult practice, buildings and other landmarks: Pausanias cites in particular the archaic poetry of Corinthian Eumelus and of the Spartan Cinaethon, as well as Hellanicus and the Naupactian Argonautic epic. Immediately, Pausanias becomes bogged down in a flurry of competing versions culled from this range of sources, and doubtless more besides (2.3). Subsequently, he notes also traditions about the Dioscuri and the Black Sea which were current at Sparta in his day (3.19, 24). The myths of the Argonauts also interacted with colonial histories to generate a series of particular local connections between Greek cities of the Mediterranean and the Black Sea.

In colony and mother-city alike, there was a powerful concern with colonial origins and identities, with almost unlimited scope for the invention and elaboration of mythical connections throughout antiquity. Pausanias relates that in 370 BC the people of Trapezus in Arcadia did not wish to join in the foundation of Megalopolis. In order to escape the wrath of their fellow Arcadians, he claims, they fled to the Black Sea, where they were received generously by the city of Trapezus there. Pausanias states that the reason for their acceptance in Pontic Trapezus was that they came from its mother-city. In other words, Pausanias' story entails the claim that these two cities were related by more than their shared name: Arcadian Trapezus was the mother-city of Pontic Trapezus (8.27.6). Pausanias' story of a settlement in 370 BC and the notion that Pontic Trapezus was settled from Arcadia are unparalleled; all other sources indicate its foundation from Sinope (Kacharava and Kvirkvelia 1991:

282–83). The whole story in Pausanias illustrates the scope for invention – but who believed it? Evidently, Pausanias took it seriously enough to relate it. And perhaps the coincidence of names encouraged the people of Pontic Trapezus to accept some Arcadian role in their foundation. There was nothing for them to lose by accepting the notion and something to gain – most obviously a link with mainland Greece and, through Arcadian Evander, even something in common with the foundation of Rome itself (Pausanias 8.43). Local histories flourished in the second century AD, not least in the Black Sea region where, for example, Memnon of Heraclea Pontica seems then to have composed his history of his native city, viewing the history of the world from a perspective in Heraclea, around which even the greatest events are seen to revolve (cf. Bowie 1996: 210).

There were, however, also broader and more generally influential perspectives. Xenophon seems to have dominated second century conceptions of the Black Sea region. Certainly, Arrian takes close account of Xenophon's *Anabasis* in his own account of the Black Sea region, his *Periplus*. Dio Chrysostom, although rather less devoted to Xenophon than Arrian, nevertheless expresses his admiration for the fifth century author very clearly:

> I think that Xenophon alone of the ancients can meet the needs of a man in public life. Whether one is a general in war-time or leading the city, or speaking before the people or in the council-chamber or in the law-court...the best of all and most profitable in all these regards seems to me to be Xenophon (18.14).

Dio proceeds to recommend in particular the *Anabasis*, by whose speeches, he claims, he could be moved even to tears (18.16). There can be no doubt that Dio's account of Olbia owes much in spirit to Xenophon's account of small Greek communities in the Black Sea region as embattled oases in a desert of barbarism (cf. Plato, *Phaedo* 109b). Xenophon (not unlike Arrian after him) seems ambivalent about the inclusion within Hellas of even as venerable a Greek city as Trapezus. Having travelled all along the south coast of the Black Sea west from Trapezus, Xenophon can claim that it was only at Byzantium that he reached Hellas (Braund 1994: 134). Pausanias, in only partial contrast, seems to envisage, for one travelling north to south across the Black Sea, the Greek sphere as beginning at Sinope (1.31.2): the northern lands are a wondrous place where bees follow the herds (1.32.1).

Whereas the Black Sea of the influential Xenophon was a largely hostile environment, the region could also be imagined more positively. In particular, the region had a reputation as a reservoir of resources from which the Aegean world could and did draw (Polybius 4.38). It also produced the occasional philosopher, such as Heraclides Ponticus or Bion of Borysthenes, not to mention the Scythian Anacharsis, though it was felt necessary to keep him in his place (Pausanias 1.22.8 on his rebuff at Delphi). In particular, the speeches of Demosthenes had much to say about the Black Sea region as a source of grain for Athens. Demosthenes too was an influential figure in second century hellenism – he was Dio's 'great exemplar' (Jones 1978: 25). And Dio could look for an example to Demosthenes' *Against Leptines* wherein much is said of the export of Bosporan grain and the generosity of Bosporan rulers to Athens (31.128; cf. later, Eunapius, *VS* 462).

It was also Demosthenes' *Against Leptines* that served as the starting point for a second century AD rhetorical tour-de-force by Lollianus of Ephesos. Pursuing Demosthenes' arguments, Lollianus imagined the baleful consequences for the Athenian grain supply in a world where Leptines had had his way and where grain no longer reached Athens from the Black Sea. Lollianus' concern with the speech had a particular relevance to his career as a second-century sophist who held a chair of rhetoric at Athens and was also *strategos* there. In his brief biographical sketch of Lollianus, Philostratus stresses that Lollianus' responsibilities particularly included the food-supply of the city; Philostratus mentions his plight in a bread-riot and his raising of funds to pay for a grain-consignment from Thessaly. In that context, the disaster predicted in Demosthenes' speech had come true, in the sense that Athens now indeed had pressing problems of food-supply, with Lollianus himself charged with dealing with them. In an intellectual world dominated by concern with the hellenism of the classical past, the sophist could not fail to find a connection between Demosthenes and himself (Philostratus, *VS* 526–27; cf. in general, Bowie 1996: 215–16).

The sophists of the second century were well aware of the role that the Black Sea had played in the classical Greek world: their reading of Xenophon, Demosthenes and other writers ensured as much. It also shaped their attitudes towards the region: within the world of Hellas the Black Sea remained marginal. Even Byzantium was still considered marginal enough, a place of luxury just outside the Black Sea where the fish, as Dio has it, throw themselves on the shore (33.24–25; cf. 35.25). Philostratus introduces the sophist Marcus of Byzantium with the complaint that he has not gained the reputation he deserves among Greeks of the Mediterranean world; his lack of a great reputation is probably to be explained by his decision to teach in his home city, where he belonged to a family which possessed fishing interests and which traced its descent from the city's founder Byzas. The sophist Polemo, we are told, mistook him for an uncultured man, an *agroikos*. While Philostratus explains the mistake as the result of Marcus' dishevelled beard and hair, we may also wonder whether his origins in Byzantium did not contribute to such a judgment. At any rate, when Polemo heard Marcus speak, he realised who he was by virtue of his Doric accent. In his speech at least (no small matter among sophists), Marcus was something of an outsider (Philostratus, *VS* 529). Bowersock observes that both Marcus and the other sophist whom Philostratus mentions at Byzantium, namely Chrestus (*VS* 590), are each said to be neglected (Bowersock 1969: 19–20). Coincidence is possible, but the marginality of Byzantium in the outlook of early imperial hellenism seems a more satisfactory explanation of their shared fate.

Given such ambivalence towards the hellenism of the Black Sea region, it is hardly a surprise that no city of the Pontus, not even Byzantium, is known to have been a member of Hadrian's Panhellenion, an association founded to link Greek cities, with its headquarters at Athens (the closest is Perinthus; Spawforth and Walker 1985; 1986; Alcock 1993: 167 offers a convenient depiction). Cities of the Black Sea region might be Greek, but not Greek enough: there were too many barbarians there, with too much influence – as in Dio's Olbia. In that light, one wonders whether, when Pausanias states that 'from each city a likeness of the emperor Hadrian was dedicated' in the emperor's completed Olympieion at Athens (1.18.6), any Black Sea cities were among those which made dedications. Given the probable involvement of a Bosporan ruler in the Augustan scheme for completion of the temple, the absence of any Black Sea involvement under Hadrian would be striking indeed, a symptom perhaps of the more exclusive hellenism of the second century AD.

At the same time, the very existence of the sophists Marcus and Chrestus at Byzantium surely indicates a concern in that community with the more esoteric forms of hellenic culture (if that were ever in doubt). The philosophical ambitions of Dio's Callistratus represent a strand of Black Sea hellenism beyond his own imaginary case: there were real people in the Black Sea who wished to leave for the Mediterranean world in search of hellenic culture. The life of Bion of Borysthenes offers a Hellenistic instance of Black Sea, and specifically Olbian, cultural marginality, from the perspective of the Mediterranean Greeks, for Bion's Olbian origins seem to have been a persistent problem for him in the Greek world at large. Diogenes Laertius, about AD 200, recounts Bion's biting responses to sneering queries about his origins, while Diogenes himself describes Borysthenes as if non-Greek, as 'Scythian land' (4.46–57, esp. 55). Bion, Callistratus and the like may be compared with a king of the Crimean Bosporus who, according to Philostratus, made the journey to Ionia. There he encountered the haughty sophist Polemo, an embodiment of mainstream hellenic culture (especially in his own view):

> And when the ruler of the Bosporus, equipped with a full Greek education, came to Smyrna in the course of his study of Ionia, Polemo not only failed to place himself among his entourage, but also kept procrastinating when invited to meet him until the king was forced to come to his house with a payment of ten talents (Philostratus, *VS* 535).

Philostratus tells the story as one among several instances of Polemo's attitude; there may be a conscious echo of the elder Cato's treatment of a Pergamene king on a visit to Rome, as told about AD 100 by the Greek biographer Plutarch (*Cato Maior* 8.8). The wise man may stand aloof from a king and look down upon him, whether the king is Bosporan or Pergamene, but the Bosporan was particularly vulnerable by virtue of the marginality that underpins the anecdote. Major implications arise here for the history of Black Sea colonization. In studying Ionia, the Bosporan king was exploring his own roots and the roots of the cities of his kingdom. He was, says Philostratus, a ruler thoroughly educated in a Greek manner: such a king might very well take a lively interest in the hellenic past of the Black Sea, especially at a time when hellenism was in such vogue (Swain 1996).

Moreover, there was a precedent, even in the texts of classical Athens, of travel from the Bosporan kingdom in search of Greek culture: namely the speaker of Isocrates' *Trapeziticus*. This individual was a member of the Bosporan elite who claimed to have conceived a desire to visit Athens, where he delivered the speech, and the rest of Hellas (*Trapeziticus* 3–4). Whether Philostratus' Bosporan king visited Athens is unclear, but there were others from the Black Sea who did. Philostratus has one Agathion answer a question as to the place of his education:

> The hinterland, Attica's fine school for one wishing to converse. For the Athenians in the city take in for pay a flood of youths from Thrace and Pontus and other barbarian peoples and thereby corrupt their own language rather than imparting fine speech to the visitors. But the hinterland is free from barbarians, its speech flourishes and its tongue attains the highest Attic (Philostratus, *VS* 553).

Who are the Thracian, Pontic and other barbarians who flooded into the city of Athens? Since they are described as paying, they are evidently not slaves but members of the local elites of these regions (Roman visitors too: Alcock 1993: 226). The purpose of their presence seems to have been broadly cultural: Agathion's reply tends to suggest that they had come to improve the purity of their Greek (cf. Philostratus, *VS* 624 on the purity of Aelian's Attic despite his life at Rome). These were forerunners of the pupils of the Armenian Proaeresius, born in Cappadocian Caesarea about AD 276 (Eunapius, *VS* 10.3.12 with *PLRE* I.731). As Dio and Arrian had observed, such young men might benefit from an exposure to 'proper' Greek but, claims Philostratus' Agathion, they had destroyed the object of their quest: as the cities of the Black Sea had had their hellenism corrupted by barbarians, so the hellenism of Athens itself was now at risk through the influx of their youths.

It was easy for the would-be champions and standard-bearers of hellenic culture to draw distinctions between such 'barbarians' and themselves at the Aegean centres of hellenism, which could claim traditional cultural dominance and which could be allowed places within the Panhellenion. By and large, it seems, the Greeks of the Black Sea region spoke dubious and no doubt accented Greek. Their prominence among the subjects of Middle Comedy suggests that, as early as the fourth century BC, there may have been a tendency to mock their versions of hellenism (see Long 1986). It is clear enough, however, that from at least as early a time, Greeks of the Black Sea were conscious enough of their distance from Hellas proper to seek to develop and explore their hellenic identity by visiting and studying in Athens and Ionia. In the eastern Roman empire, familiar categories of 'Roman', 'Greek' and 'barbarian' conceal a wealth of opportunities for differentiation; as we have seen, some were considered to be more Greek than others, and the Greeks of the Black Sea were not allowed the prominence that the antiquity of their civic foundations might have permitted.

About AD 200, Athenaeus reported the sort of Pontic joke that has its counterparts even among the Greeks of today, for whom Pontics remain a favourite butt of humour on the grounds of their alleged stupidity, odd dialect and general lack of culture. Among the anecdotes which Athenaeus gathers concerning *hetaerae* (Hawley 1993), he reports a story of the encounter of a Pontic youth (in Athens, evidently) with the formidable Gnathaena:

> They say that a little chap from the Black Sea went to bed with Gnathaena. And in the morning he asked her to present her rear to him. She replied, 'Wretch ! You ask me to present my rear to you at a time when you should be driving out your pigs to pasture ?' (Athenaeus, *Deipnosophistae* 13. 580f–81a).

The Pontic youth was out of his depth, not simply with Gnathaena, but by his very presence in the city of Athens, in 'Greece proper'. Athenaeus himself, so much the champion of hellenic culture in the context of the Roman empire, was from distant Naucratis in Egypt (Zecchini 1989: esp. 257 for Athenaeus' reservations about Athens). An origin in Naucratis, however, shared with the likes of the grammarian Pollux, seems to have been more broadly acceptable in the Greek society and culture of the world of the eastern empire than were origins in the Black Sea region.

Bibliography
Abramson, H. (1974) "The Olympieion in Athens and its connections with Rome," *CSCA* 7: 1–26.
Alcock, S. E. (1993) *Graecia Capta: The Landscapes of Roman Greece*, Cambridge.
_____ (1996) "Landscapes of memory and the authority of Pausanias," in J. Bingen, ed., *Pausanias historien* (Fondation Hardt, Entretiens 41), 241–67. Geneva.
Birge, D. (1994) "Trees in the landscape of Pausanias' *Periegesis*," in S.E. Alcock and R. Osborne, eds., *Placing the Gods: Sanctuaries and Sacred Space in Ancient Greece*, 231–45. Oxford.
Bowersock, G.W. (1969) *Greek Sophists in the Roman Empire*, Oxford.
_____ (1987) "The mechanics of subversion in the Roman provinces," in A. Giovannini, ed., *Opposition et résistance à l'empire d'Auguste à Trajan* (Fondation Hardt, Entretiens 33), 291–317. Geneva.
Bowie, E.L. (1996) "Past and present in Pausanias," in J. Bingen, ed., *Pausanias historien* (Fondation Hardt, Entretiens 41), 207–30. Geneva.
Braund, D.C. (1984) *Rome and the Friendly King: The Character of Client Kingship*, London.
_____ (1991) "Dion Khrisostom, torgivlya Ol'vii ta ol'viys'ka `tavroskifs'ka viyna'," *Arkheologiya* (Kiev) 3: 25–30 (in Ukrainian).

_____ (1994) *Georgia in Antiquity*, Oxford.

_____ (1995) "Fish from Byzantium," in J. Wilkins, F.D. Harvey and M. Dobson. eds., *Food in Antiquity*, 162–70. Exeter.

_____ (1996) *Ruling Roman Britain: Kings, Queens, Governors and Emperors from Julius Caesar to Agricola*, London.

Bringmann, K. (1993) "The king as benefactor: some remarks on ideal kingship in the age of hellenism," in A. Bulloch, E.S. Gruen, A.A. Long and A. Stewart, eds., *Images and Ideologies: Self-Definition in the Hellenistic World*, 7–24. Berkeley.

Buyskikh, S.B. (1991) *Fortifikatsiya Ol'viyskovo gosudarstva (pervye veka nashey ery)*, Kiev.

Dubois, L. (1991) "Bulletin épigraphique: Pont," *REG* 104: 505–507.

Gaidukevich, V.F. (1971) *Das Bosporanische Reich* (revd. German edition), Berlin.

Golenko, K.V. (1975) "Nördliches Schwarzmeergebiet: Münzen der bosporanische Könige," *Chiron* 5: 603–33.

Gruen, E.S. (1992) *Culture and National Identity in Republican Rome*, London.

Hall, E. (1989) *Inventing the Barbarian*, Oxford.

Hawley, R. (1993) "`Pretty, witty and wise': courtesans in Athenaeus' *Deipnosophistae Book 13*," *International Journal of Moral and Social Studies* 8: 73–91.

Hoff, M. (1989) "The early history of the Roman Agora at Athens," in S. Walker and A. Cameron, eds., *The Greek Renaissance in the Roman Empire* (*BICS* Suppl. 55), 1–8. London.

Jones, C.P. (1978) *The Roman World of Dio Chrysostom*, Cambridge, Mass.

Kacharava, D.D. and G.T. Kvirkvelia (1991) *Goroda i poseleniya Prichernomor'ya antichnoy epokhi*, Tbilisi.

Long, T. (1986) *Barbarians in Greek Comedy*, Carbondale..

Marchenko, K.K. (1988) *Varvary v sostavye naseleniya Berezani i Ol'vii*, Leningrad.

Moles, J.L. (1978) "The career and conversion of Dio Chrysostom," *JHS* 98: 79–100.

_____ (1995) "Dio Chrysostom, Greece and Rome," in D. Innes, H. Hine and C. Pelling, eds., *Ethics and Rhetoric*, 177–92. Oxford.

Podossinov, A. (1987) *Ovids Dichtung als Quelle für die Geschichte des Schwarzmeergebiets*, Konstanz.

Rawson, E. (1991) *Roman Culture and Society: Collected Papers*, Oxford.

Rigsby, K.J. (1980) "Seleucid notes," *TAPA* 110: 233–54.

Russell, D.A., ed. (1992) *Dio Chrysostom: Orations VII, XII, XXXVI*, Cambridge.

Shelov-Kovedyayev, F.V. (1990) "Berezanskiy gimn ostrovu i Akhillu," *VDI* 3: 49–62 (photo opposite 64).

Sidebottom, H. (1993) "Philosophers' attitudes to war under the Principate," in J. Rich and G. Shipley, eds., *War and Society in the Roman World*, 241–64. London.

Spawforth, A.J. and S. Walker (1985) "The world of the Panhellenion: I. Athens and Eleusis," *JRS* 75: 78–104.

_____ (1986) "The world of the Panhellenion: II. Three Dorian cities," *JRS* 76: 88–105.

Sullivan, R.D. (1990) *Near Eastern Royalty and Rome, 100–30 BC* (*Phoenix* Suppl. 24), Toronto.

Swain, S. (1996) *Hellenism and Empire: Language, Classicism and Power in the Greek World, AD 50–250*, Oxford.

Syme, R. (1995) *Anatolica: Studies in Strabo*, Oxford.

Treister, M.Yu. (1992) "Bronzovaya statuetka Yupitera Kapitoliyskovo iz Myskhako," *VDI* 2: 41–53.

Tsvetayeva, G.A. (1979) *Bospor i Rim*, Moscow.

Whitehead, D., ed. (1990) *How to Survive under Siege*, Oxford.

Zanker, P. (1988) *The Power of Images in the Age of Augustus*, Ann Arbor.

Zecchini, G. (1989) *La cultura storica di Ateneo*, Milan.

Ziolkowski, A. (1993) "Urbs direpta, or how the Romans sacked cities," in J. Rich and G. Shipley, eds., *War and Society in the Roman World*, 69–91. London.

Zograph, A.N. (1977) *Ancient Coinage* (*BAR* 33), Oxford.

9. Funerary Monuments and Mortuary Practice in Roman Asia Minor

Sarah Cormack

Introduction

That distinctions in burial practices existed at various times and in various locations in the Roman world has long been recognized. Inhabitants of the eastern Mediterranean generally practiced inhumation in an unbroken sequence from the archaic period on, while in the west cremation of the body was favoured, giving way to the influence of inhumation in the second century AD (Morris 1992: 42–69). In this century certain scholars have attempted to articulate the meanings behind the transformation from one burial ritual to another in the Roman world. Two opposing theories emerged, one viewing the transformation from cremation to inhumation as simply a change in fashion (Nock 1932), the other that it represents a significant cultural change, signalling a shift in religious belief (Cumont 1966). Recently it has been suggested that these discussions will always remain fruitless; we are never likely to rediscover the beliefs of those who, for example, rejected cremation in favour of inhumation (or vice versa) on the basis of burial evidence alone. This is not to say that burials are devoid of what might be termed 'religious' content, but in focussing on belief alone, the relevance of the archaeological material itself is reduced to the level of 'illustrative material.' Instead, it has been persuasively argued, funerary material has much to reveal about social structures and – when analysed in conjunction with other forms of evidence such as texts – can indicate transformations in those structures (Morris 1992: 33, 203).

In this essay I want to sketch the burial practices (in so far as they can be reconstructed) of the inhabitants of Asia Minor in the late Republican and early imperial periods. The wealth of material that is preserved from this vast region will be reviewed, not only as 'illustrative material' providing evidence for how people were buried and what sort of monuments were erected in their honour, but also as indicative of the manner in which local practices were influenced (or not) by contacts with the Roman west. Thus the process of 'romanization' in this context may be defined as the way in which certain inhabitants of Asia Minor responded to their new status as citizens of the empire, and in particular how this transformation was reflected in the burial record. The archaeological evidence may also, ultimately, illuminate underlying belief systems with regard to the relationship between the living and the dead during this time of political and cultural transition. Asia Minor

137

presents itself as an obvious area on which to focus, given the following criteria: the relatively clear history of cultural and political contacts between the east and the west (Magie 1950; Mitchell 1993: 61–69; Strocka 1988: 291–307), the vast amount of funerary material that is preserved from the various provinces and regions of Asia Minor in the Roman period, and last but not least, the obvious importance ascribed to funerary architecture given its prominence in the civic landscape.

I shall not attempt a demographic analysis following the models proposed by others (Hopkins and Letts 1983; Hopkins 1987; Saller 1994), but instead shall rely on the 'illustrative' value of the preserved funerary monuments in order to chart patterns of contact between east and west. Although changes in burial practice (as inferred from variations in types of monument) may not *always* indicate external influence, recent research (for example, at Palmyra in Syria) does indicate that the funerary record can often be revealing about the manner in which architectural styles or decorative motifs were transmitted from one region to another (Schmidt-Colinet, this volume). The ultimate goal of this analysis is to explore what such transmissions reveal about social change. Following a brief introduction outlining pre-Roman burial practices in Asia Minor, the funerary material from the Roman period will be surveyed: not only the free-standing built tombs, but also portable burial containers or markers (sarcophagi, stelai, osteothekai). When posing the question to what extent 'romanization' affected burial practices in Asia Minor, it should be borne in mind that the archaeological evidence must be examined before the 'practice' lying behind it can be extrapolated. In most cases, inscriptions and ancient sources are notoriously silent on the issue of funerary ritual and associated beliefs. There are, however, some exceptions, as we shall see.

Burial Structures Of The Pre-Roman Period

Before discussing the complex picture of funerary practices in Roman Asia Minor, it is necessary to set the scene by outlining the sepulchral evidence of the pre-Roman period.[1] The funerary architecture of Anatolia and the western and southern coastlands of Asia Minor constituted a rich and diverse body of material which cannot have failed to have an impact on such Roman settlers or visitors as came into contact with it, and which certainly continued to exercise an influence on indigenous burial patterns in the Roman period. The generalization can be made that inhumation (as opposed to cremation) was the dominant burial method from the archaic period onwards, as was the norm in other parts of the eastern Mediterranean, such as Greece. Delicately painted terracotta sarcophagi from archaic Klazomene in Ionia, stone sarcophagi carved with mythological scenes from Lycia, such as the "Payava" sarcophagus from Xanthos, monumental sarcophagi of the aristocracy and royalty (for example the sarcophagus from the tomb at Belevi near Ephesos, the tantalising descriptions of the discovery of the burial chamber of Mausolus at the Mausoleum of Halikarnassos, and the inhumation burial of 'King Midas' in the great tumulus at the Phrygian capital, Gordion): all attest to the overriding desire to preserve the body in a structure whose elaboration was equivalent to the status of the deceased (Fedak 1990: 174 [Klazomene]; fig. 267 [Xanthos]; 81–83 [Belevi]; 71–74 [Halikarnassos]; 56–58 [Gordion]). Small areas practicing cremation did exist, but were rare and far from the norm.

In addition to free-standing sarcophagi which might be prominently placed in a necropolis, secreted within a built tomb structure, or interred, Hellenistic Asia Minor saw the development of another burial fashion which was to exert an influence on the region's inhabitants of the Roman period, namely, the construction of 'heroa.' The heroon was the burial location of rulers or of those voted heroic honours by their city in recognition of outstanding civic benefactions, or of superlative athletic or military prowess. A number of such heroa are preserved in Lycia, south-west Asia Minor; these heroa, although clearly revealing the artistic influence of classical and late classical Greece, also suggest strong Persian contacts. Outstanding examples of Lycian heroa from the pre-Roman period are preserved, including a tomb house at Trysa where additional sarcophagi were placed within a temenos wall decorated with mythological reliefs (Oberleitner 1994), the tomb of Perikles at Limyra dating to ca. 360 BC (Borchhardt 1976; Fedak 1990: 68–71), and the Nereid Monument at Xanthos of the early fourth century BC (Coupel and Metzger 1969; Fedak 1990: 66–68). Another outstanding Anatolian tomb of the Hellenistic period is the Mausoleum of Halikarnassos, no longer extant but tentatively restored on the basis of ancient testimonia and surviving fragments. The Mausoleum, one of the Seven Wonders of the Ancient World, was the tomb of Mausolos, a satrap of Caria, completed ca. 350 BC (Jeppesen and Luttrell 1986). The tomb was the location for lavish sculptural display depicting mythological battles; above a tall podium was a peripteral cella of Ionic columns surmounted by a pyramidal roof. The monument's form would influence tomb design not only in Roman Asia Minor but throughout the eastern Mediterranean. Furthermore, heroa and other honorific funerary structures of social élites were often (but not always) erected within the inhabited area of the city, in contrast to the usual practice in the west of separating the residential area from the necropolis; this practice of intramural burial was to have a lingering influence into the Roman period.

Rock-cut tombs were also a prominent feature of the pre-Roman burial picture in Asia Minor, a fact not surprising given the topography of the region. These rock-cut tombs could mimic more elaborate free-standing tombs in their use of columns *in antis* and gabled faìades, as at Kaunos in Caria and Fethiye (ancient Telmessus) on the Lycian coast; or they could be simple cubic hollows in the vertical and inaccessible rock face, resembling a sort of open-air columbarium! (for example, Pinara in Lycia; Roos 1972; Kolb and Kupke 1992: 45–58). In these rock-cut tombs, the presence of klinai (couches on which the deceased were laid, often arranged in a triclinium format mimicking the disposition of ancient dining rooms) carved out of the rock itself suggests that even here cremation was not practiced, but instead the deceased was provided with grave-goods (in general, pottery and other vessels), and laid out to their rest. Clearly there will have been many much simpler burials of the pre-Roman period, including rock-cut sarcophagi (cist graves) frequently located in rocky outcrops surrounding ancient cities, as well as inhumation burials covered by tiles; such non-élite forms of burial continued into the Roman period.

Burial Structures of Roman Asia Minor

Tombs and Necropoleis

Following Rome's initial contacts with Asia Minor, and the establishment of the province of Asia after the bequest of Attalus in 133 BC (Mitchell 1993: 61–69), the burial picture is characterized both by continuity and by change.[2] It is clear that pockets of Roman settlers imported their own burial traditions, or commissioned monuments locally which reflected the styles and motifs of the

Fig. 1. Street of tombs, Arycanda, Lycia

capital city (see below), while in the Hellenized cities, not only those of the Ionian coast but also of the mountainous hinterlands, funerary monuments which drew on well-established indigenous practices continued to be erected. Turning to the form and meaning of necropoleis in the eastern provinces of the empire, it is in the areas of patronage and social advertisement that the impact of 'romanization' is most clearly felt. This Roman influence was not limited to the social and cultural arena, however: the built tombs of Roman Asia Minor also display the tangible architectural influence of contacts with the capital city, for example in the adoption of the western Roman podium temple as an appropriate model for the tombs of those with social aspirations.

A fundamental observation that must be made with regard to the necropoleis of Asia Minor is the seeming disregard for the injunction against intramural burial which obtained in the Roman west. In the city of Rome itself, intramural burial was a privilege only rarely bestowed, for instance upon those who had celebrated a triumph or attained other outstanding honours. In general, burial was forbidden within the *pomerium* or sacred boundary of the city, both for practical and for religious reasons (Cicero, *Leg.* II.58; Frischer 1982/83: 51–86; Scheid 1984: 117–39). Many cities of Asia Minor, on the other hand, are noteworthy for their vast necropoleis which in many instances encroach upon the city of the living; two examples are Hierapolis in Phrygia (Equini-Schneider 1972) and Ariassos in Pisidia (Cormack 1996). Although it has been observed that the presence of monumental tomb buildings lining the approach roads to cities of the east can be viewed as an eastern adaptation of the 'Gräberstrasse' of the Roman west (Fig. 1; von Hesberg and Zanker 1987: 17–18), the intrusion of burial monuments into the inhabited space of the city remains a phenomenon common to Asia Minor. Tombs of prominent citizens were often built within the city itself: at Rhodiapolis in Lycia, the tomb of the leading citizen of the Antonine period, Opramoas, was constructed on a conspicuous

Fig. 2. Ruins of 2nd century AD tomb of Opramoas, with theatre in background, Rhodiapolis, Lycia

terrace adjacent to the theater (Fig. 2). At Oinoanda in Lycia, the Doric building 'Mk2' at the west end of the esplanade below the theater is tentatively identified as a heroon built in the first century AD and honouring a "founder" of the city (Coulton 1982: 45–59). At Aezanoi in Phrygia a tomb of unknown patronage in the form of a small temple was built in the second century AD inside the agora of the city, in a direct axial alignment with the great Temple of Zeus complex ca. 70 m away (Naumann 1973/74: 183–95). The colonnades of the agora in which the tomb stands may have functioned as a visual 'temenos' for the tomb, echoing the vast temenos of the Temple of Zeus itself. The tomb, of slightly later date than the Hadrianic temple which it confronts, also had an altar on its front steps, implying that sacrifices were offered here to the heroized dead within.

Whether inside or outside the city, funerary monuments in Roman Asia Minor provided the opportunity for public advertisement and social display, just as they had done in the preceding era. One obvious manner by which social stratification could be indicated is through the scale of the tomb: at Patara on the Lycian coast, a barrel-vaulted tomb located to the west of the harbour measures ca. 8.3 × 6 m – dimensions comparable to those of contemporary temples (Colvin 1991: 80–82; Adam 1994: fig. 73). Other tombs which appear to be direct 'imports' from the Roman west also differentiated their patrons from the local populace and marked them as belonging to a particular, perhaps even consular or senatorial, class.

One example of this is the so-called Hidirlik Kulesi which dominates the entrance to the harbour at Antalya (the ancient Attaleia, Pamphylia). This is identified as the tomb of a man of senatorial rank but of local origin, dating probably to the mid-first century AD (Fig. 3). The identity of the tomb's patron has been tentatively proposed: M. Calpurnius Rufus, member of the leading family of Attaleia, senator during the reign of Claudius, and eventually *legatus Augusti pro praetore* (Stupperich 1991: 420; Mitchell 1993: 153). The form of the tomb, with quadrangular base and superposed

Fig. 3. "Hidirlik Kulesi," 1st century AD tomb (of M. Calpurnius Rufus?), Antalya, Pamphylia

Fig. 4. Detail of the fasces carved next to the door, tomb (of M. Calpurnius Rufus?), Antalya, Pamphylia

circular element, directly mimics the monumental tombs of the late Republican aristocracy such as those located along the Via Appia outside Rome. In choosing to import an Italian tomb-type to Anatolian soil, the tomb's patron was clearly identifying himself with the ruling elite of Italy; the consular rank of the family of the patron is further indicated by the fasces carved on either side of the tomb's door (Fig. 4; Stupperich 1991: 417–22). Such an obvious example of an import from the Roman west, however, did not have an appreciable impact on indigenous funerary architecture elsewhere; the circular consular tomb at Antalya remains an isolated phenomenon. The patron of the tomb was not, therefore, expressing solidarity with a large group of transplanted settlers (as will be suggested below in the discussion of ossuaries from Ephesos), but rather was proclaiming his allegiance to or association with Roman nobility, and his prominent status via the form of his tomb.

Similar conclusions can be drawn with regard to the late Trajanic Library of Celsus at Ephesos, an elaborate civic structure which became the intramural burial location of the man in whose honour it was built: Ti. Julius Celsus Polemaeanus. The tomb's elaborate exterior architecture is quite at home in the lavish 'marble style' designs of Roman Asia Minor, but its brick inner walls reveal Roman architectural practices: Celsus is known to have held important offices at Rome (Strocka 1978: 893). On the other hand, his burial within a civic building can be viewed as a traditional practice of Asia Minor, marking the civic honours bestowed on Celsus by his home town.

The circular tomb at Antalya is indicative of the manner in which tomb monuments expressed individual will in the area of architectural style – to a much greater degree than was possible in, for example, the construction of public, non-sepulchral architecture. Eclecticism of form characterizes much funerary architecture: a phenomenon not limited to Asia Minor (Schmidt-Colinet, this volume for Palmyra; von Hesberg 1992). The tomb commonly known as the 'Gümüşkesen' at Milas (ancient Mylasa) in western Asia Minor is a second-century AD miniature variation of the Mausoleum of Halikarnassos, located on the coast approximately twelve kilometers away (Fig. 5). Although the identity of the

Fig. 5. 'Gümüşkesen' tomb, Mylasa, 2nd century AD

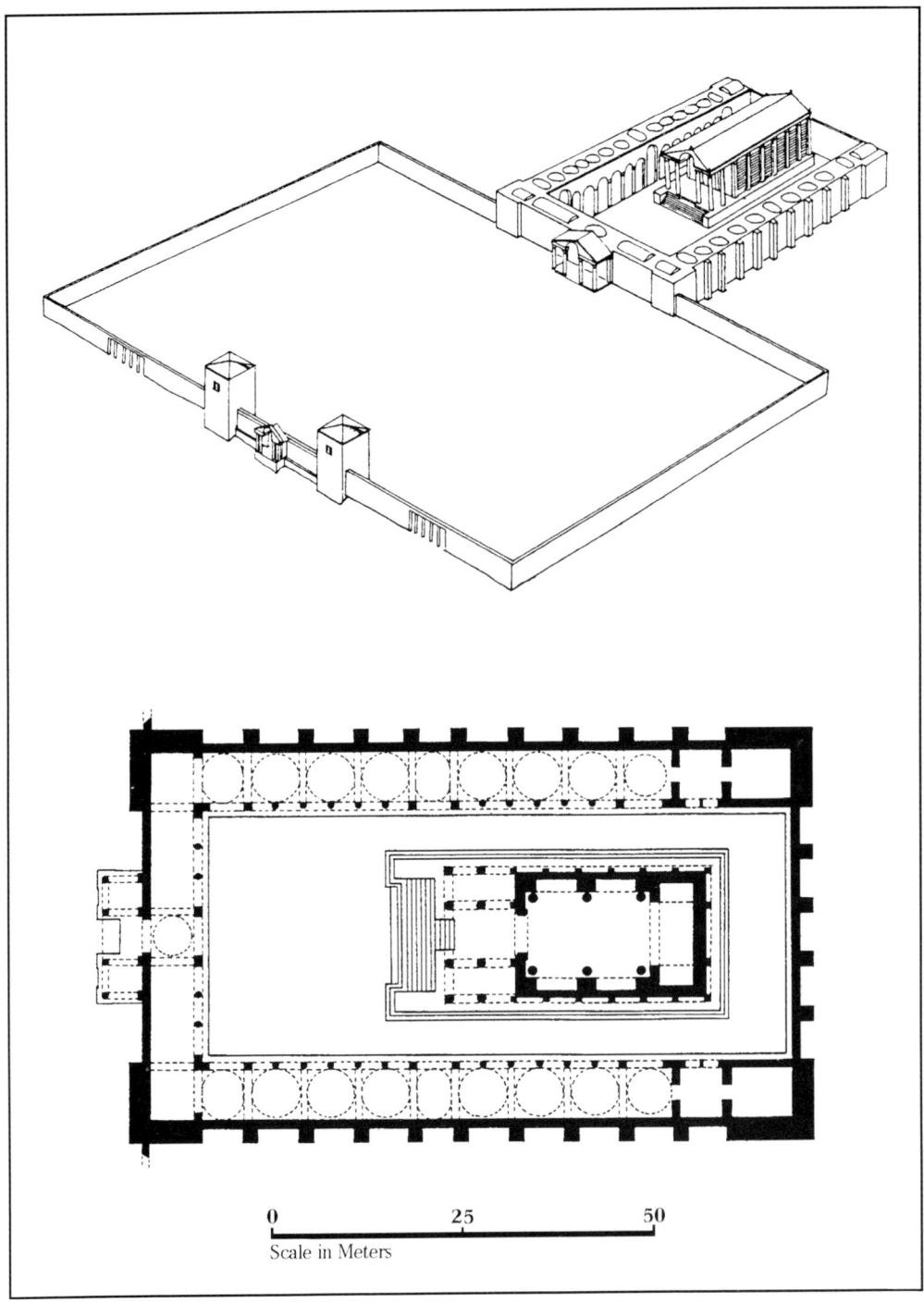

Fig. 6. Plan of temple tomb complex, late 2nd century AD, Side, Pamphylia (after Colvin 1991: fig. 71)

tomb's patron is not known, the choice of a podium tomb with peripteral columns, together with a massive pyramidal or lantern roof, clearly reveals the patron's desire to adopt not only the architectural forms of the great Hellenistic tomb, but possibly its heroizing or even divinizing associations as well. The resulting monument, however, is a unique creation of its time, not a slavish copy.

An additional manner in which the tombs of the Roman period demonstrate a strong continuity with the classical and Hellenistic past is in an increasing emphasis on heroization of the deceased. As already mentioned, heroa (monumental tombs often demarcated from civic space by the erection of a temenos wall) were a fairly common element of the classical and Hellenistic landscape. During the Roman period, the concept of the heroon finds new architectural form; this phenomenon gained momentum in the second century AD and, appropriately, it was the western Roman podium temple which served as the model. The adoption of a religious architectural type may have implied additional connotations of the heroization of the deceased. It is interesting to note that the dissemination of the temple-tomb is a phenomenon characteristic of the eastern empire at large; at Palmyra in Syria temple-tombs replace the indigenous tower-tomb type, and are seen as a direct response to increasing 'romanization' (Schmidt-Colinet, this volume; 1989).

Numerous examples of these 'temple-tombs' are known in Asia Minor, many of them clustered in the south-west (primarily in Lycia, Pamphylia, Pisidia and Cilicia). In general they are built either within the urban fabric itself, or they occupy promontories or other conspicuous locations in order to ensure maximum visibility. At Side on the coast of Pamphylia one such monumental tomb was built in the late second century AD which clearly announced the achievements and aspirations of the deceased (Fig. 6). The tomb took the form of a prostyle podium temple with 'Syrian' gable and frontal staircase. The impressive effect of the building was increased through the construction of a dipteral porch at the facade (an unusual example of this architectural style in funerary architecture), and engaged exterior pilasters. Clearly no expense was spared in the construction of this tomb, whose patron, unfortunately, remains anonymous: the building was faced with marble slabs, and the vaulted roof was lined with marble coffers carved with a variety of decorative motifs (Kramer 1983: 145–166).

Other tombs of temple form employed architectural decoration to reinforce their message of apotheosis, or at very least of elevated status. At Arycanda in Lycia, a tomb was built along one of the main civic arteries, with a door lintel carved with winged victories supporting a bust, presumably of the deceased. Further east, at Demircili near Olba-Diokaisareia in Cilicia, an elaborate two-storeyed tomb of the second century AD displays a gable carved with two semi-naked male busts (von Hesberg 1992: 187). The implications of such decorative schemes are clear: the representation of the deceased in the pediment not only announces high social status, but also suggests divinizing aspirations through the utilization of a space formerly reserved for figures of gods in temple architecture.

Burial Containers

With few exceptions, the tombs discussed above were the repository of sarcophagi, or of stone klinai on which the dead were placed. That the inhabitants of Asia Minor still favoured inhumation over cremation, at a time when the western empire was cremating its dead, reflects a continuity of burial tradition in Anatolia. But what do these portable burial containers – osteothekai, stelai and sarcophagi – reveal about "romanization"? Do locally produced burial containers reflect the influence of imported styles and motifs from the west in the same manner that built tombs adopted architectural elements? And further, are there any instances of 'prefabricated' burial containers imported into Asia Minor from the west, perhaps accompanying settlers and colonists? It has long been recognised that from the second century AD sarcophagi were exported in increasing numbers *from* Asia Minor (and Greece) to the west, and it has often been assumed that this trade influenced burial practice in the western provinces. The suggestion has been made, however, that western examples might in fact have predated the Asiatic imports, and that Anatolian sarcophagi of the imperial period might thus reflect the stylistic influence of western Roman burial motifs (Strong 1978: 677–83). This theory is attractive given the reciprocity of influence already charted in the area of funerary architecture.

In mountainous regions which were far removed from sources of marble, sarcophagi were frequently carved directly into limestone outcrops, or were free-standing. Many of these sarcophagi have gabled lids with simplified acroteria or stylised roof-beams, and are carved with repetitive motifs such as Medusa heads, *tabulae ansatae*, shields, and occasionally eagles (Fig. 7). Some of these limestone sarcophagi, for example in the necropoleis of Sagalassos, Pisidia, were also fitted with lids in the form of klinai. The kline lids, carved with reclining figures (often a husband and wife), reflect similar monuments from the Roman west, drawing on a funerary tradition which ultimately derives from Etruscan burials. Since these sarcophagi with reclining effigies cannot be traced back to early sarcophagus production in Anatolia, it seems plausible that even these relatively simple limestone sarcophagi from remote mountain regions reveal the impact of western Roman prototypes (Strong 1978: 678; Fedak 1990: 173–180).

Fig. 7. Limestone sarcophagus with shield motifs and inscribed tabula ansata, *Termessos, Pisidia*

Given the penetration of such western forms as the kline-lid sarcophagus into remote provincial regions, it is hardly surprising that important centers of marble sarcophagus production (for example Proconessus in the Sea of Marmara, or the southern coastal province of Pamphylia) should also produce objects which display motifs derived from western funerary symbolism. Garland sarcophagi, for example, are common in both east and west in the Hadrianic and Antonine periods; their motifs clearly derive ultimately from cinerary urns and altars, a type of burial marker which is not common in the east. In other words, workmen – who may well have been trained in the west – created lavish marble sarcophagi for an eastern clientele who were already accustomed to inhumation as a burial practice. This scenario does not contradict the more traditional view that Asia Minor was an important creative center for sarcophagi which were often exported to Rome and elsewhere, a phenomenon now proven by detailed marble analysis (Ferrari 1966; Walker 1990: 46).

Common motifs for marble sarcophagi produced in Asia Minor include garlands supported by erotes and bull's heads, the labours of Hercules, and seated philosopher figures attended by Muses (Wiegartz 1965; Walker 1990: 45–55). Asia Minor 'columnar sarcophagi' derive their name from the fact that the figures appear before a framework of columns and aediculae, in an architectonic scheme which transforms the sarcophagus into a miniature house or shrine for the deceased. Again, although it is tempting to view columnar sarcophagi as a natural linear development from pre-Roman Anatolian sarcophagi which were similarly architectural, the architecture of the Roman columnar sarcophagi seems rather to reflect the façades of contemporary elaborate public buildings (such as nymphaea, propylaea and the *scaenae frontes* of theatres) rather than, as one might have expected, temples and tombs (Strong 1978: 677). Yet again, the influence of stone masons perhaps trained in Rome (or in Asia Minor and who then travelled west) is apparent (Strocka 1988: 291–307). What emerges is a fruitful dialogue between east and west in the area of sarcophagus production, a situation which is paralleled in other eastern centers such as Palmyra in Syria.

Not all patrons chose sarcophagi as a burial marker. Stelai, often carved with rich funerary symbolism and inscriptions identifying the deceased, were popular choices, in particular in certain north-western regions of Asia Minor such as Mysia and Bithynia (Corsten 1990; 1993; Cremer 1991; 1992). Although their function is not clear in all cases, it is likely that the stelai were erected upright in the ground, above the inhumation burial (or burials) below. These stelai were produced from at least the fifth century BC onwards, and thus they provide a useful index for the development of funerary iconography and the manner in which it was, or was not, affected by 'romanization.' The picture that emerges here parallels that seen so far in this analysis, with eastern elements gradually enriched by funerary imagery directly imported from the Roman west. Common motifs of late classical stelai which are viewed as originating in Persian iconography include hunting scenes and naval battles (Cremer 1991: 17–27). By the Hellenistic period the funerary banquet was a dominant motif on relief stelai, a banquet which is interpreted, however, as revealing very little about the actual life and status of the deceased but which has instead been transformed into a symbol 'sans relations avec le personnage enterré' (Corsten 1993: 307).

By contrast, during the late Hellenistic period and increasingly into the Roman period, stelai with reliefs reveal an increasing emphasis on the deceased as an individual: late Hellenistic stelai begin to depict the occupation of the deceased, while stelai from the Roman period often stress the personal relationships of the patron. Funerary stelai from Mysia, in particular from the region around

Cyzicus, begin to be decorated during the Augustan period with busts of the deceased represented with other family members, a trend which continues until the Hadrianic era. The model – funerary reliefs with busts of freedmen from late Republican and Augustan Italy – is obvious and provides a striking example of direct iconographic influence from the west. Women sport the coiffures and dress popular in the Imperial court, while juvenile status is symbolized by the wearing of the bulla. Such examples suggest the adoption of the exterior forms of 'romanization,' forms which ultimately reflect the social stratification promoted during the reign of Augustus. Funerary monuments of the Augustan period from the Roman west, in particular those of the freedman class, reveal the importance placed on familial relationships, and this emphasis has been viewed as a response to Augustus' moral legislation promoting marriage and the production of legitimate heirs (Kleiner 1990). Indeed, it has been noted how quickly the Augustan cultural reform was reflected in the funerary monuments of the inhabitants of Asia Minor (Cremer 1991: 96; pls. 17–19).

In spite of the rapid dissemination of the outward trappings of Roman influence in this particular class of funerary objects, the first century AD stelai from Bithynia and Mysia demonstrate subtle yet significant differences from their Roman prototypes. First, they were not built into the architectural fabric of a tomb, but were instead free-standing in a necropolis. This difference is probably related to the fact that the Roman reliefs decorated tombs in which were placed the ash urns of the deceased, while the Asia Minor stelai marked inhumation burials. Secondly, the busts from the Asia Minor stelai do not represent physiognomically accurate portraits of the deceased and other family members, but rather are somewhat stylized or even idealized. Here the motivation seems to have been to emulate the portraits of the Imperial court. This assimilation to the styles of the western nobility is further revealed in the clothing of the Asia Minor figures, who often wear the costume of the Roman élite (the toga for men, the *tunica intima*, palla and stola for women). What iconographical analysis reveals here is that, while the outward form of the funerary monument was adopted from the Roman west by the upper classes of Asia Minor, its underlying social implications were not; these stelai were commissioned by a completely different social class in the east. Thus, and somewhat paradoxically, citizens of northern Asia Minor could express allegiance to the Roman nobility via the adoption of a funerary monument which had its origins in a social sphere quite removed from their own, that of enfranchised slaves in the west.

Ossuaries or urns for cremation burial constitute yet another type of 'portable' funerary monument which has recently and convincingly been viewed as revealing the impact of motifs from the west (Thomas 1996: 393). During the first century BC marble ossuaries from Ephesos were often left uncarved, and their inscriptions indicate that they were commissioned by Greeks and by freedmen. During the late first century BC and the early first century AD, however, these ossuaries began to be decorated with garlands, and their inscriptions reveal that their patrons were now Romans, or at least Latin speakers, new arrivals drawn to Ephesos when it became the capital city of the province of Asia. If the introduction of garland motifs onto cinerary urns was the direct result of Roman patronage, perhaps this substantiates the suggestion above that garland sarcophagi similarly reflect the influence of funerary imagery from Rome. In addition, the existence of cinerary urns is perhaps surprising given the general predisposition towards inhumation burial in Asia Minor. Although the Roman settlers at Ephesos apparently had an impact on the form of the burial marker, at other colonies – for example Cremna in Pisidia where Augustan veterans were settled in ca. 25 BC – inhumation continued to be the normal burial practice.

Ritual and Practice

In addition to tracing the stylistic influence of the Roman west on the funerary art of Asia Minor, both in the areas of architecture and on portable burial containers, the issue of burial practice must also be addressed. Two forms of evidence aid in elucidating not only for whom (and by whom) the monuments were commissioned, but also how they were intended to be used: inscriptions, and archaeological evidence (for example, the carving of libation holes into the object).

The primary function of architectural funerary inscriptions, as far as it is possible to generalize from such a vast corpus of material, appears to have been to announce the name and family of the deceased, and his or her social position. In this regard the inscriptions reaffirm the status aspirations of the citizens represented on the relief stelai from Bithynia and Mysia. This genealogical emphasis seems particularly pronounced in Asia Minor compared to the Roman west; in many cases entire family trees can be reconstructed by linking various inscriptions together from a particular site, as has been demonstrated at Termessos in Pisidia (Lanckoronski 1892: nos. 122, 58, 55; Heberdey and Wilberg 1900: 180–87). In other cases, for instance at the late second century AD mausoleum of Licinia Flavilla at Oinoanda in Lycia, a single tomb might be carved with a lengthy inscription which announces the lineage of its patron, often going back for generations (*IGR* III.500). The implication here is that the announcement of one's noble lineage served as a form of *res gestae* for the deceased.

Another feature shared by the epitaphs from Asia Minor is an insistence on the right of burial in the tomb. Inscriptions are often extremely specific about who may be buried within a particular grave (no matter what its architectural form), and a study of such texts has shown that generally this right is extended to those defined as 'family': be they spouses, nieces, nephews, grandchildren, sisters, brothers, children, freedmen, slaves and occasionally nurses (Kubinska 1968). When offspring are lacking, sometimes *threptoi* (foster or adopted children) will be included.

Funerary inscriptions also often included a formulaic injunction against improper or illegal burial, with appropriate fines imposed for violation of this law. There were nonetheless cases where this proscription was flagrantly violated. For example, at tomb no. 3 at Demircili (Cilicia) the architrave inscription identifies the tomb as belonging to Papylos, son of Papios and states that it should not be disturbed; another inscription, however, presumably carved later on the *anta* (an unusual location for tomb inscriptions) claims that the tomb is the resting place of another family altogether. It should not surprise us that these monumental and expensive structures were reused (Strubbe 1991).

Exactly how effective the threat of the imposition of fines was is hard to discern. Tombs at the Pisidian site of Termessos contain numerous instances of such fines which were to be imposed should the tomb be violated. The inscription at the second century AD tomb of Aurelia Ge states:

> Aurelia Ge, daughter of Hermaios, set forth this proclamation: she has prepared the heroon and no-one may come forward to destroy the burial place, or may bury anyone except her parents Hermaios and Oa, and her brother Hoplos who died an untimely death. Should anyone attempt otherwise, let him pay to the demos of Termessos and to the priestly treasury the sum of 50,000 denarii (Lanckoronski 1892: 122; Heberdey and Wilberg 1900: 187–90).

Clearly if these fines were ever collected, they would have benefited the community or the religious treasury, thereby having the practical effect of continuing the euergetism of the deceased even after death. Many of the more elaborate tombs at Termessos with inscriptions threatening fines for misuse were commissioned by individuals who held the position of priest or priestess of the Imperial cult or other religious cults. A close nexus of relationships between the community, the temple, the patron and the tomb is thus implied. The threat of fines also implies a concept of the tomb as a 'sacred' area, an area which is not to be violated; this concept further underscores the interpretation of certain tombs as 'heroa,' as suggested above (Strubbe 1991).

In some cases the inscription itself served as an intrinsic element of the tomb's decorative scheme, appearing on the socle rather than the architrave. An additional location for inscriptions is on the body of the sarcophagus contained within (or outside) the tomb, often within a demarcated zone, the *tabula ansata*. At Demircili in Cilicia, a sarcophagus in the upper cella of tomb no. 2 identifies those buried within, and warns against additional illegal burial (Fig. 8). The insistence on tomb ownership contained within these funerary inscriptions of Asia Minor during the imperial period not only provides some insight into the degree to which a patron attempted to control who was buried in the tomb, but also indicates that violations must have been fairly frequent – otherwise injunctions and fines would presumably not have had to be threatened.

In addition to defining who had right of burial, the inscription or epitaph often performed the additional function of announcing the social status of the deceased. The walls of the tomb of Opramoas at Rhodiapolis in Lycia were carved with texts announcing Opramoas' many benefactions and offices, serving as a public billboard detailing the wealth of the city's most important citizen and his services as euergetes (Petersen and von Luschan 1889: 76–81). An inscription from Aezanoi in Phrygia, possibly associated with the intramural heroon in the agora, similarly praises one Menogenes son of Meniskos, and refers to his blameless life; the Aezanoi inscription, furthermore, provides a rare instance of directions for the actual burial rite, proclaiming that Menogenes be

Fig. 8. Sarcophagus in upper storey of tomb no. 2, Demircili, near Olba-Diokaisareia, Cilicia

brought in procession into the agora and given a golden crown (Günther 1975: 351). At the Isaurian site of Gölçük Ören (whose ancient name has not been identified), a small building containing statue bases and located in the necropolis area is interpreted as relating to one of the monumental tombs nearby. If this is the case, then here we have an example of a separate structure whose only purpose appears to have been commemorative: the inscriptions on the statue bases found inside honour M. Aur. Demetrios as *proboulos, strategos, eirenarch, eponymous archon, gymnasiarch*, and high priest of the local cult of 'Zeus Nikator in Orokendois.'

Thus, funerary inscriptions reveal much concerning patronage and social status in Roman Asia Minor, but they generally studiously avoid any reference to religious belief, hope for a peaceful and blessed afterlife, or propitiation of the gods. There are exceptions where epitaphs cryptically allude to 'beliefs': an inscription from the tomb of Apollonios Strabonianos at Termessos warns the passer-by: '...take heed, keep your outrages of our limbs away from the tomb; for if someone, without heed for the dead, is thus sinful, truly the vengeance of the dead lives...'; and further, from the tomb of Aurelia Padamuriane Nanelis at the same site: '...nor is it permitted for anyone to place another sarcophagus in the heroon, nor to open it for another burial, nor to bury another corpse; if anyone does this, against this injunction, he will be guilty of impiety against the infernal ones.....' (Cousin 1899: 281 no. 63; *TAM* III.1.648) Such examples suggest the possibility of belief in vengeful deities or the dead themselves; how much these warnings reflect actual belief is hard to gauge, however, and it may be more accurate to interpret these inscriptions as attempting to ensure the protection of the tomb space.

For the interpretation and reconstruction of what ritual activity or practices took place at the tomb we need to turn to archaeological evidence. This evidence for ritual and belief falls into two categories: tangible evidence, such as holes carved into the monument for the pouring of libations, and more allusive evidence, based on the overall design of the monument itself. That libations were poured and banquets eaten in honour of the dead is well attested in the archaeological record from the western empire (Toynbee 1971: 43–64). In Asia Minor, monumental tombs also served as the location for such activity. Outside Pergamon, a second century AD temple tomb was provided with a courtyard and outlying buildings, as well as a water supply. Finds from these rooms, such as ceramic bowls, suggest that banquets of a ritual nature took place here in honour of the heroized dead, whose statue stood inside the tomb in the same location as a cult statue in a temple (Rheidt *et al.* 1986: 99–146). At the 'Gümüşkesen' tomb at Mylasa (discussed above), a hole has been carved in the marble cella floor providing access for libations down to the burials in the *hyposorion*, or lower chamber below. The presence of altars at the tomb site, for example on the steps of the temple tomb at Aezanoi already mentioned, also implies that offerings were made in honour of the deceased.

Such offerings were not only made at the more elaborate tomb sites, however; an interesting and unusual group of stelai from Bithynia also reveals that such ritual practices extended to small-scale monuments as well (Corsten 1991: 93–96). These stelai, dating to the second century AD, resemble miniature temples or built tombs through the addition of such architectural elements as pilasters, gables and acroteria (Fig. 9). What is most interesting, however, is the presence of a depression with a drilled hole in their bases; the hole resembles a patera or libation dish through which offerings would be poured to the dead. This certainly reflects the continuity of a burial ritual attested as early as the Geometric period in Asia Minor. The presence of similar libation holes in sarcophagi, altars,

Fig. 9. Relief stele from Bithynia with busts in gable (Iznik Museum inv. no. 797)

and kline monuments from the Roman west affirms that this ritual was not confined to the early imperial east but was common throughout the empire, indicative of a deep-rooted desire to provide the dead with sustenance.

Conclusions

This study has concentrated on the tombs of the wealthy and the burial markers of the middle classes, at the expense of the tombs of the poor; the latter have traditionally either been excluded from surveys of funerary material in Asia Minor or are not well-preserved in the archaeological record. A survey of even a small sample of the funerary material from early imperial Asia Minor, however, is suggestive in a number of ways about the process of 'romanization.' Although the onset of Roman rule had a profound if subtle impact on the *outward* forms of the sepulchral realm, the picture that emerges is on the whole conservative, with entrenched Anatolian traditions continuing to exert influence. Burial traditions and funerary iconography in the provinces of Asia Minor did not undergo drastic transformations during the imperial period. Its inhabitants did not, either suddenly or gradually, adopt cremation, the *mos Romanus* of the first century AD – adoption of which has been viewed as just one of the ways in which the western provinces signalled 'allegiance to Rome' (Morris 1992: 49). In Asia Minor on the other hand, the effects of contact with the west are seen in less obvious ways. We can summarize some of these now, beginning with the more concrete fashions in which contacts with Rome were made manifest in the funerary record.

Although the mortuary architecture of Asia Minor in this period does display certain characteristics unique to this region, the body of material as a whole exemplifies the reciprocity of ideas and techniques current in other monumental buildings, and typical of the cross-fertilization of architectural ideas which occurred between Rome and the eastern provinces (Ward-Perkins 1978). In certain areas and cases, western architectural influence is notable. At certain sites in Cilicia where a local equivalent of *pozzolano* was readily available (for example Iotape, Elaiussa Sebaste, and Selinus), tombs are constructed with barrel vaults of concrete which are quite distinct from the ashlar vaults of neighbouring mountainous regions. Whether or not these experiments in architectural techniques can be said to be due to the architectural influence exerted by the presence of the Roman army in the region remains open to question, but is an attractive suggestion given the dominance of ashlar masonry in Asia Minor in general.

The organization of the marble trade in Asia Minor, flourishing in the second century AD, had a significant impact both on the structure of the tombs of the elite and on the types of sarcophagi which might be placed within them (Dodge and Ward-Perkins 1992). The monumental tomb complex at Side in Pamphylia is representative of the way in which the decorative potential of marble was exploited, yet the almost total absence of marble at such isolated inland sites as Cremna, Selge and Termessos indicates that its use depended entirely on whether or not there was a local source, or whether it could be transported. If marble was not available, decorative architectural features were executed in limestone instead; the frieze of garlands and bulls' heads on the south tomb at Cremna in Pisidia represents a local limestone version of a motif which elsewhere would have been carved in marble. Sarcophagi, on the other hand, were portable and more easily transported. At numerous sites, marble sarcophagi, either fragmentary or complete, have been discovered *in situ*: at Arycanda, Patara and Xanthos in Lycia, Side in Pamphylia, and Miletos and Pergamon in Asia. Such marble sarcophagi found within tombs attest to the wide-reaching influence of the marble trade in Asia Minor in the second century AD. This is not to suggest, however, that all monumental tombs were equipped with marble coffins; their presence probably implies a wealthier-than-average burial, and at sites such as Ariassos and Termessos in Pisidia, massive limestone sarcophagi, most likely carved on site, were the norm.

In addition to imported construction techniques and the increased quantities of marble in the funerary record, another manifestion of 'romanization' is through transformations in tomb type. Tombs on tall podia with frontal steps and prostyle columns constructed throughout the provinces of Asia Minor (for example at Side, Myra, Patara, Xanthos and Phaselis in Lycia and Pamphylia, Iasos, Pergamon and Aezanoi in Asia, or Selge and Termessos in Pisidia) reveal the penetration of the western Roman podium temple form as a model for funerary architecture. Furthermore, isolated examples such as the consular tomb at Antalya reflect the import of 'undiluted' funerary forms deriving directly from Italy. Western models could be adopted, transformed and given new meaning, as is clear in the case of the relief stelai from Bithynia – carved for an elite of the east but based on the funerary reliefs of freedmen from the west.

Finally, burial methods are certainly relevant to religious belief, but, as suggested above in the discussion of ritual and belief, religious attitudes are often hard to reconstruct from the funerary material. An analogy can perhaps be suggested with the importation of the imperial cult into Asia Minor. Such cult was an obvious manifestation of the way in which indigenous religious practices responded to the Roman presence, but it is hard to argue that the inhabitants of Asia Minor suddenly began to view the emperor 'as' a god, in spite of the broad and rapid dissemination of cult activity throughout the provinces (Price 1984; Mitchell 1993: 100–102). Similarly, when we do see transformations in the funerary record in Asia Minor – for example the importation of new monument types – these are almost certainly the result of local initiative rather than a response to external directives. These initiatives were designed to signal allegiance to Roman power and the status of local elites rather than implying drastic alterations in 'belief.' On the contrary, the presence of hero-cult activity suggested by the numerous intramural tombs and temple tombs would seem to indicate the continued strength of pre-Roman burial practices. Additionally, the failure or unwillingness of the cities of Asia Minor to adopt the western Roman (or even classic Greek) prohibition against intramural burial also suggests that when western rituals *were* adopted – for example the incorporation of the imperial cult into pre-existing sanctuaries – this had far more to do with the recognition of power structures than with underlying convictions on the subject of human mortality. I would suggest that 'romanization' is detectable in the adoption of exterior forms rather than in the transformation of existing, inherent attitudes and beliefs about death and the afterlife. The corpus of funerary material in Asia Minor in the Roman period thus can be characterized in general as a complex tissue of associations constructed over an essentially conservative skeleton.

Notes

Stephen Mitchell and Thomas Corsten have generously given advice, for which I am extremely grateful; all errors which exist, however, are my own.

1   For further reading on funerary material from pre-Roman Asia Minor, see: Asgari (1965); Bruns-Özgan (1987); Bryce (1980); Childs and Demargne (1989); Waelkens (1982).
2   For further reading on Roman sepulchral material from Asia Minor, see the following: Alföldi-Rosenbaum (1971; 1980); Cormack (1989); Coupel and Demargne (1976); Dardaine and Longepierre (1985); Ganzert (1984); Hallett and Coulton (1993); Machatschek (1967); Quagliano Palmucci (1977); Waelkens (1986).

Bibliography

Adam, J-P. (1994) *Roman Building. Materials and Techniques*, Bloomington.
Alföldi-Rosenbaum, E. (1971) *Anamur Nekropolü. The necropolis of Anemurium*, Ankara.
_____ (1980) *The Necropolis of Adrassus (Balabolu) in Rough Cilicia (Isauria)* (*DenkschrWien* 146), Vienna.
Asgari, N. (1965) *Kleinasiatische Ostotheken in sarkophagform*, (Unpublished dissertation, Istanbul).
Borchhardt, J. (1976) *Die Bauskulptur des Heroons von Limyra (IstForsch 32)*, Berlin.
Bruns-Özgan, C. (1987) *Lykische Grabreliefs des 5. und 4. Jahrhunderts v. Chr.* (*IstMitt-BH* 33), Tübingen.
Bryce, T.R. (1980) "Sacrifices to the dead in Lycia," *Kadmos* 19: 41–49.
Childs, W.A.P. and P. Demargne (1989) *Fouilles de Xanthos VIII. Le Monument des Néréides. Le décor sculpté I-II*, Paris.
Colvin, H. (1991) *Architecture and the Afterlife*, New Haven and London.
Cormack, S. (1989) "A mausoleum at Ariassos, Pisidia," *AnatSt* 39: 31–40.
_____ (1996) "The Roman-period necropolis of Ariassos, Pisidia," *AnatSt* 46: 1–25.
Corsten, T. (1990) "Neue Grabstelen mit Totenmahlreliefs aus der Gegend von Prusa ad Olympum," *EpigrAnat* 16: 91–108
_____ (1991) "Neue Denkmäler aus Bithynien," *EpigrAnat* 17: 79–100
_____ (1993) Review of M.-L. Cremer, *Hellenistisch-römische Grabstelen im nordwestlichen Kleinasien, 1. Mysien* (1991), *Topoi* 3.1: 305–20.
Coulton, J.J. (1982) "Oinoanda: the Doric building (Mk2)," *AnatSt* 32: 45–59.
Coupel, P., and P. Demargne (1976) "Un heroon romain à Xanthos de Lycie," in P. Ducrey *et al.*, eds.,*Mélanges d'histoire ancienne et d'archéologie offerts à Paul Collart*, 103–115. Lausanne.
Coupel, P. and H. Metzger (1969) *Fouilles de Xanthos III: Le Monument des Néréides: L'architecture*, Paris.
Cousin, G. (1899) "Inscriptions de Termessos de Pisidie," *BCH* 23: 165–192, 280–303.
Cremer, M.-L. (1991) *Hellenistisch-römische Grabstelen im nordwestlichen Kleinasien, 1. Mysien* (Asia Minor Studien 4.1), Bonn.

_____ (1992) *Hellenistisch-römische Grabstelen im nordwestlichen Kleinasien, 2. Bithynien* (Asia Minor Studien 4.2), Bonn.

Cumont, F. (1966) *Recherches sur le symbolisme funéraire des Romains* (originally published 1942), Paris.

Dardaine, S. and D. Longepierre (1985) "Essai de typologie des monuments funéraires de Sidyma (époques lycienne et romaine)," *Ktema* 10: 219–232

Dodge, H. and B. Ward-Perkins (1992) *Marble in Antiquity: Collected Papers of J.B. Ward-Perkins* (Archaeological Monographs of the British School at Rome 6), London.

Equini-Schneider, E. (1972) *La necropoli di Hierapolis di Frigia* (*MonAnt* Serie Miscellanea I.2), Rome.

Fedak, J. (1990) *Monumental Tombs of the Hellenistic Age: A Study of Selected Tombs from the pre-Classical to the Early Imperial Era*, Toronto.

Ferrari, G. (1966) *Il commercio dei sarcophagi asiatici*, Rome.

Frischer, B. (1982/83) "Monumenta et Arae Honoris Virtutisque Causa: evidence of memorials for Roman civic heroes," *BullCom* 88: 51–86.

Ganzert, J. (1984) *Das Kenotaph für Gaius Caesar in Limyra* (*IstForsch* 35), Tübingen.

Günther, W. (1975) "Ein Ehrendekret post mortem aus Aezanoi," *IstMitt* 25: 351–356.

Hallett, C.H. and J.J. Coulton (1993) "The East Tomb and other tomb buildings at Balboura," *AnatSt* 42: 41–48.

Heberdey, R. and W. Wilberg (1900) "Grabbauten von Termessos in Pisidien," *ÖJh* 3: 177–210.

Hopkins, K. (1987) "Graveyards for historians," in F. Hinard, ed., *La mort, les morts et l'au-delà dans le monde romain (Actes du Colloque de Caen, 20–22 Novembre 1985)*, 113–126. Caen.

Hopkins, K. and M. Letts (1983) "Death in Rome," in K. Hopkins, *Death and Renewal*, 201–256. Cambridge.

Jeppesen, K. and A. Luttrell (1986) *The Maussoleion at Halikarnassos. Reports of the Danish Archaeological Expedition to Bodrum, 2. The Written Sources and their Archaeological Background*, Aarhus.

Kleiner, D.E.E. (1990) "Social status, marriage and male heirs in the age of Augustus: a Roman funerary relief," *North Carolina Museum of Art Bulletin* 14: 20–29.

Kolb, F. and B. Kupke (1992) *Lykien* (Zaberns Bildbände zur Archäologie 2), Mainz.

Kramer, J. (1983) "Zu einigen Architekturteilen des Grabtempels westlich von Side," *BJb* 183: 145–166.

Kubinska, J. (1968) *Les Monuments funéraires dans les inscriptions grecques de l'Asie Mineure*, Warsaw.

Lanckoronski, K. (1892) *Die Städte Pamphyliens und Pisidiens, Vol. II*, Vienna.

Magie, D. (1950) *Roman Rule in Asia Minor* (2 vols.), Princeton.

Machatschek, Alois (1967) *Die Nekropolen und Grabdenkmäler im Gebiet von Elaiussa Sebaste und Korykos in Rauhen Kilikien* (*DenkschrWien* 96), Vienna.

Mitchell, S. (1993) *Anatolia. Land, Men and Gods in Asia Minor, Vol. I: The Celts in Anatolia and the Rise of Roman Rule*, Oxford.

Morris, I. (1992) *Death-Ritual and Social Structure in Classical Antiquity* (Key Themes in Ancient History), Cambridge.

Naumann, R. (1973/74) "Das heroon auf der Agora in Aezanoi," *IstMitt* 23/24: 183–195.

Nock, A.D. (1932) "Cremation and burial in the Roman empire," *HThR* 25: 321–59. (Reprinted in Z. Stewart, ed., *Essays on Religion and the Ancient World* [Oxford 1972], 277–307).

Oberleitner, W. (1994) *Das Heroon von Trysa* (Zaberns Bildbände zur Archäologie 18), Mainz.

Petersen, E. and F. von Luschan (1889) *Reisen in Lykien, Milyas und Kibyratis*, Vienna.

Price, S.R.F. (1984) *Rituals and Power: The Roman Imperial Cult in Asia Minor*, Cambridge.

Quagliano Palmucci, L. (1977) "Architettura funeraria dell'Asia Minore. Rapporti con Aquileia," *Aquileia e l'oriente mediterraneo. Atti della 7. Settimana di studi aquileiesi 1976*, 165–83. Udine.

Rheidt, K., W. Radt, and S. Karagöz (1986) "Ein römischer Grabbau auf dem Niyazitepe bei Pergamon," *IstMitt* 36: 99–146.

Roos, P. (1972) *The Rock-cut Tombs of Caunos* (*SIMA* 34), Göteborg.

Saller, R.P. (1994) *Patriarchy, Property and Death in the Roman Family*, Cambridge.

Scheid, J. (1984) "Renversements et déplacements dans les rites funéraires," *AnnArchStorAnt* 6: 117–39.

Schmidt-Colinet, A. (1989) "L'architecture funéraire de Palmyre," in J.-M. Dentzer and W. Orthmann, eds., *Archéologie et Histoire de la Syrie* II, 447–456. Saarbrücken.

Strocka, V.M. (1978) "Zur Datierung der Celsusbibliothek," in E. Akurgal, ed., *Proceedings of the Xth International Congress of Classical Archaeology 1973*, 893–900. Ankara.

_____ (1988) "Wechselwirkungen der stadtrömischen und kleinasiatischen Architektur unter Trajan und Hadrian," *IstMitt* 38: 291–307.

Strong, D.E. (1978) "The Early Roman sarcophagi of Anatolia and the West," in E. Akurgal, ed., *Proceedings of the Xth International Congress of Classical Archaeology 1973*, 677–83. Ankara.

Strubbe, J.H.M. (1991) "Cursed be he that moves my bones", in C. Faraone and D. Obbink, eds., *Magika Hiera*, 33–59. Oxford.

Stupperich, R. (1991) "Das Grabmal eines Konsularen in Attaleia," *IstMitt* 41: 417–422.

Thomas, C.M. (1996) "The Ephesian ossuaries and the rise of the sarcophagus," *AJA* 100: 393 (abstract).

Toynbee, J.M.C. (1971) *Death and Burial in the Roman World*, Ithaca.

Von Hesberg, H. (1992) *Römische Grabbauten* , Darmstadt.

Von Hesberg, H. and P. Zanker, eds. (1987) *Römische Gräberstrassen. Selbstdarstellung - Status - Standard*, Munich.

Waelkens, M. (1982) "Hausähnliche Gräber in Anatolia vom 3. Jht. v. Chr. bis in die Römerzeit," in D. Papenfuss and V.M. Strocka, eds., *Palast und Hütte. Beiträge zum Bauen und Wohnen im Altertum von Archäologen, Vor- und Frühgeschichtlern*, 433–45. Mainz.

_____ (1986) *Die Kleinasiatischen Türsteine. Typologische und epigraphische Untersuchungen der kleinasiatischen Grabreliefs mit Scheintür*, Mainz.

Walker, S. (1990) *Catalogue of Roman Sarcophagi in the British Museum*, London.

Ward-Perkins, J.B. (1978) "The architecture of Roman Anatolia: the Roman contribution," in E. Akurgal, ed., *Proceedings of the Xth International Congress of Classical Archaeology 1973*, 881–91. Ankara.

Wiegartz, H. (1965) *Kleinasiatische Säulensarkophage (IstForsch 26)*, Berlin.

10. Aspects of 'Romanization':
The Tomb Architecture at Palmyra and its Decoration

Andreas Schmidt-Colinet

The Question

In Hellenistic times, the caravan city of Palmyra, situated in the Syrian desert, had almost no direct ·contact with the great centers in the west such as Pergamon in Asia Minor or Rome. During this early period, the politics, economy and culture of Palmyra were all oriented towards the east, to the recently founded Seleucid cities on the Euphrates and Tigris, such as Seleucia or Dura-Europos, and later to Parthian cities such as Hatra. It was only later, after the peace treaty between Rome and the Parthians (20 BC), that Palmyra developed closer relations to western centers – to Emesa and Antioch, to cities in Asia Minor and to Rome – in a period when, especially through the unifying power of normative Augustan politics, a Hellenistic-Roman 'koine', a common language also in the arts was established. At that very period, the first monumental buildings were also built at Palmyra, including sanctuaries, such as the temple of Bel dedicated in AD 32, and funerary monuments, such as the tower tomb of Atenatan built in 9 BC.

The temple of Bel (Fig. 1; Amy 1950: 98ff.; Seyrig *et al.* 1968/1975; Browning 1979: 114ff.; Starcky and Gawlikowski 1985: 116ff.; Will 1992: 134ff.) is considered, with good reason, as the best examplar of cultural exchange in the border area of Palmyra at the beginning of the first century AD. The temple demonstrates how closely the Greco-Roman architectural tradition, on the one hand, was connected with oriental Parthian forms on the other, and how by this fusion a completely new architectural language was created. The ground plan of the building is a copy of the Hellenistic temple of Artemis at Magnesia in Asia Minor, built by the Greek architect Hermogenes. (It may be of interest that a Palmyrene inscription refers to an architect with the Greek name Alexandros working at the temple of Bel). Yet something completely different was erected at Palmyra on this 'classical' groundplan. The short sides of the temple are crowned with pediments, suggesting from a side view the presence of a sacred building of Greco-Roman type. Seen from the long side, however – which, following oriental tradition, is the front of the temple – the pediments turn out to be false, with an oriental flat roof behind them crowned by a row of battlements, also drawn from oriental models.

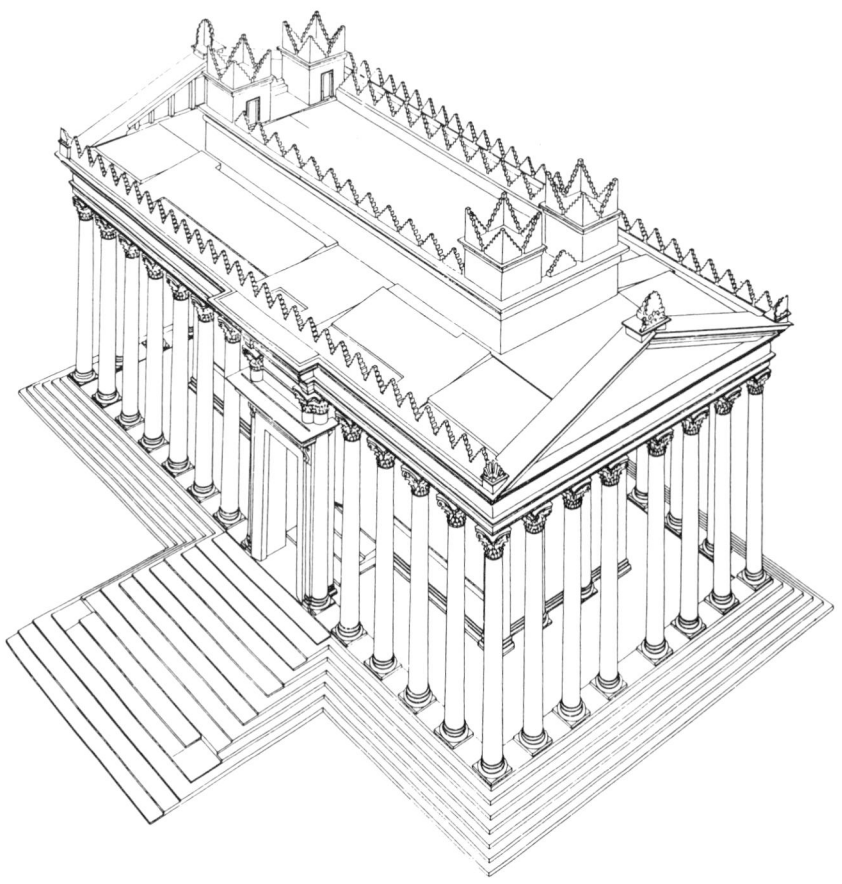

Fig. 1. Temple of Bel at Palmyra, dedicated AD 32 (after Amy 1950: 102, Fig. 17)

No later buildings of Palmyra show such a close fusion of western and eastern traditions. Instead, civic architecture of the second and third centuries AD seems to be quite similar to that of other towns in Roman Syria. For that later period, in terms of its architecture, Palmyra appears to have been very much a Greco-Roman town, and this material evidence is usually interpreted as reflecting also the historical development of the city. The history of Palmyra from the first to the third century (up to the conquest of the city by Aurelian in AD 273) has been understood as one of a continuing process of 'Romanization', as a gradual and progressive realignment of the city with the Greco-Roman world, a process taking place in parallel with the political and military expansion of Rome in the Middle East and in parallel with the steadily increasing interests of Rome in the area (Seyrig 1950; Schlumberger 1969; Gawlikowski 1973; Drijvers 1977; Starcky and Gawlikowski 1985; Bounni 1989; Will 1992).

Before accepting this picture too readily, however, it should be noted that, to date, only approximately 5% of the architecture of the second and third century city has been investigated. Moreover, this sample comprises just the better preserved monumental stone buildings – structures such as temples, theaters, nymphaea, baths, peristyles and so on. All of these structures, of course, clearly reflect standard types in Roman imperial architecture. Consequently, it is hardly surprising that such structures should find corresponding buildings in other parts of Syria, and even across the empire at large. Judging a general process of increasing 'Romanization' by the increasingly Roman appearance of this 'official' civic architecture emerges, therefore, as a dangerously circular argument. We shall see that this picture of 'Romanization' will change indeed when an analysis of private tomb architecture is introduced.

It should also be noted that the architectural decoration of the buildings at Palmyra bears an unique local character (e.g. Fig. 13), one distinctly different from that of other known parts of Roman Syria (Filarska 1967; Schmidt-Colinet 1992: 65ff.). This local character is manifest in the structure of the syntax of decorative patterns, as well as in a rich variety of individual motifs. The exceptional position held by Palmyra up to the third century must be understood as the expression of an historical reality, which can not be explained simply by a steadily increasing Roman influence, but as the result of a very complex process, of increasing interaction of eastern and western traditions (Rostovtzeff 1926: 248; Teixidor 1984: 92ff.; Schmidt-Colinet 1992: 1; 1995: 30). Recent research on private tomb architecture and its decoration, again, can help to draw here a more complex picture of 'Romanization' in Palmyra.

The Necropolis

More then 150 monumental tombs are still visible today at Palmyra, forming the largest necropolis complex of Greco-Roman times in the Middle East (Wiegand 1932: 45ff.; Gawlikowski 1970; Browning 1979: 192ff.; Parlasca 1989/90; Schmidt-Colinet 1989; 1995: 28–46). One third of these buildings are dated precisely to the years between 9 BC and AD 253 by inscriptions (Table 1), primarily foundation inscriptions written in Greek and Palmyrene on the tomb lintels. The tombs from Palmyra thus possess the best attested and surest chronological framework in the region's architectural history from the first to third century AD.

From the inscriptions we learn that all these funerary structures were family tombs or tombs of clans, some of them having more then 400 burial places, or *loculi*, within which the deceased were deposited. The *loculi* then were closed with terracotta or stone slabs bearing the portrait of the dead in high relief (Colledge 1976: 67ff., 245ff.; Parlasca 1985; Tanabe 1986: 279–373, figs. 194–208; Schmidt-Colinet 1992: 110ff., 139ff.; Dentzer-Feydy and Teixidor 1993; Sadurska and Bounni 1994; Sadurska 1994; Ploug 1995).

Three fundamental types of tombs can be distinguished: tower tombs, underground tombs (hypogea) and so-called temple-like (or house- or palace-like) tombs (Table 1). One very obvious change, from tower tombs to temple tombs during the first half of the second century, has been explained in general terms by an increasing western influence. But till now there has been no answer to other questions, such as why some Palmyrenes were buried in tower tombs, or later in temple tombs, while others chose underground tombs. Is it merely due to the present state of our archaeological and epigraphic evidence that no hypogea, but only temple tombs, appear to have

Table 1. *Chronological chart of different tomb types at Palmyra, dated by foundation inscriptions (years AD unless otherwise noted)*

Date	Tower tombs	Underground tombs	Temple tombs
	9 BC		
	9 AD		
10			
20			
30	33		
40	40		
50			
60			
70	73. 79		
80	80. 83. 83. 89	81. 87. 89	
90		94. 98. 98	
100	103	106. 108. 109	
110	118	113. 114. 115. 116. 118	
120	120. 128	123. 124	
130		133. 138. 138. 138	
140		142. 144	143. 149
150			150. 159
160			
170		179	171
180		186	
190		193	
200			
210			212
220			225
230		232. 239	236
240			
250		251	253

been constructed between AD 144 and 179, that in the following generation only underground tombs were built, and then, for the next thirty years, temple tombs predominate again? It would be very interesting to discover whether fluctuations in tomb type through time reflects economic and political conditions, as well as religious and social aspects of the history of Palmyra (Schmidt-Colinet 1995: 31ff.).

In contrast to the public buildings of the city, the tombs, which are sometimes of monumental size, represent much more directly the individual choices and private intentions of their commissioners. In general, the tombs from Palmyra, in their structure and form, reveal much more sign of local oriental traditions than the 'official' buildings of the town. Analysis and interpretation of the tomb architecture and its decoration promises an instructive re-examination of the question of 'Romanization.'

Tower Tombs

The origin and diffusion of tower-like tombs in the Hellenistic-Roman Near East can be accounted for within indigenous oriental traditions, in which the Palmyrene tower tombs represent a local variant (Wiegand 1932: 77ff.; Will 1949; Gawlikowski 1969; 1970: 9ff., 52ff.; Parlasca 1989). According to the building inscriptions, these tombs, reaching up to five stories in height, were erected from 9 BC to AD 128 (Table 1). During the first century AD a certain standardized type was developed, with winding staircases leading up to flat roofs. The outside decoration of the buildings remained simple, with an emphasis on the entrance façades. The interiors of the tomb chambers, especially those of the main chambers on the ground floor, were normally sumptuously equipped with architectural decoration, as well as with funerary reliefs.

For the architectural decoration of these tomb chambers, only pilasters with Corinthian capitals and entablatures with Ionic dentil-friezes and modillion-friezes were employed, never half-columns, Doric or Ionic capitals, or the Doric triglyph-frieze. Details of the decoration argue for a Hellenistic-Seleucid origin. These decorative forms had found their way to Palmyra at the beginning of the first century AD and were preserved there in the isolated 'hinterland' of the desert, preserved behind the conservative façades of the local tower tombs. These forms endured up to the second century AD, much longer than in other regions of Romanized Syria (Schmidt-Colinet 1991: 138ff.; 1995: 34ff., fig. 38; al-As'ad and Schmidt-Colinet forthcoming: pls. 11–16).

A reorientation of the Palmyrene upper class towards the west took place during the first half of the second century, in the Trajanic-Hadrianic period. This process was encouraged and supported by general imperial policies, notably the incorporation of the Nabatean kingdom (AD 106) and, consequently, the extension and improvement of the direct trade route connecting the Mediterranean Sea and the Euphrates River, and running through the Syrian desert. This reorientation of the Palmyrene upper class is documented through both epigraphical and archaeological evidence, but the trend is testified to especially clearly in funerary architecture. As already mentioned, after the visit of the emperor Hadrian to Palmyra (AD 129), tower tombs ceased to be erected. From that time onwards, that particular local type of tomb was replaced by another type, one oriented more towards western architectural forms (Table 1).

Already at the beginning of the second century, however, tower tombs had begun to demonstrate a stronger Roman influence. Details of their architectural decoration at that time can be traced back to forms drawn from the city of Rome itself. Furthermore, the pediments over the doors now become steeper in pitch (more than 20°). In this they follow Roman, rather than a Greco-Hellenistic tradition (Schmidt-Colinet 1991: 137ff.; 1995: 32ff., fig. 37, 40–43; al-As'ad and Schmidt-Colinet forthcoming: pls. 6–8). The area (now enlarged) of the pediment also received a new function; instead of scrolls or pictures of gods or goddesses adorning the center of pediments, they now bore the portraits of the founder or commissioner of the tomb!

The best example of this process is an extremely well preserved and recently discovered pediment (Fig. 2; now in the museum of Palmyra). It can be dated to the first half of the second century AD by its stylistic, as well as by its iconographic evidence. In the center of the pediment is the bust of a priest, wearing his official local dress and surrounded by scrolls of blossoms and pomegranates, symbols of eternal life in western iconology (Schmidt-Colinet 1995: 32ff., fig. 40–42). The organization and iconography of such pediments, with portrait representations, can be understood only by direct

*Fig. 2. Pediment from the entrance of a tower tomb representing the tomb's founder in the dress of a local priest.
Beginning of the second century AD (Palmyra Museum)*

*Fig. 3. Detail of the funerary relief from the Tomb of the Haterii, Vatican Museum, Rome.
Second half of first century AD (Photo courtesy German Archaeological Institute, Rome)*

reference to the development of Roman funerary portrait sculpture of the first century AD. A relief from the Tomb of the Haterii in Rome, dating about a generation before the pediment from Palmyra, provides one fine comparison (Fig. 3).

In this and other instances, the upper classes of Palmyra employed Roman forms to express and to assert their own religious and social claims. Such Roman influence operates in yet another, very fundamental way: the enlarged pediment leaves 'more space' for self-representation, complying with the desire for such depictions among the Palmyrene elite. In other words, the formal Roman structure provided more space, more room for the representation of indigenous contents. It invited and even provoked the representation of local social power more successfully than was possible through other, indigenous means.

This process can be related to an historical phenomenon to which our written sources rarely refer, in which the ancient social structures of the Middle East (upon which a veneer of 'Hellenization' had been superimposed) were articulated through the Roman institution of *clientela* (Rostovtzeff 1926: 248). The Roman system of *clientela* – in contrast to the Greek polis-structure – was organized hierarchically and focussed on a single individual personality (be it paterfamilias or imperator) at the top of the social pyramid or of a small leading group. Prior to the onset of 'Hellenization', such a social structure had long existed in the Near East. The establishment of relationships of *clientela*, which involved all aspects of social life, consequently led, like a chain reaction, to a revival and redevelopment of ancient local structures of power in the east. In other words, the process of 'Romanization' can at the same time be understood as 're-orientalization', a phenomenon recognizable already in the second century, and increasingly in the third (Schmidt-Colinet 1992: 40, 81 nn. 106–108, 203; 1995: 39). Viewed in this way, the political separation of Palmyra from the Roman empire in AD 273 no longer appears as a spectacularly ambitious act on the part of a notorious and elusive queen Zenobia. Instead, it can be explained as the final and consistent conclusion of a process which, in the last analysis, had its roots in the 'Romanization' of Palmyra itself (for the local historical background of Zenobia's 'revolt' see also Graf 1989).

Underground Tombs

At Palmyra, archaeological evidence attests to burials in underground tombs already in the Hellenistic period (Fellmann 1970). This then becomes the most common type of burial from the first to the third century AD (Ingholt 1935; 1936; 1938; Amy and Seyrig 1936; Gawlikowski 1970: 48ff. 107ff.; Sadurska 1977; Saliby 1992; Sadurska and Bounni 1994: plans I-XIV). Dated inscriptions refer to the construction of such hypogea between AD 81 and 232 (Table 1). These underground chambers often were decorated with rich architectural ornaments or with wall paintings. From the second century onwards an increasing number of representations utilizing Roman funerary symbolism can be observed, such as the famous paintings in the so-called 'Tomb of Three Brothers' with representations of Ganymede and the Eagle of Zeus, Victory figures, etc. Towards the end of the second and especially in the first half of the third century, in addition to such rich decoration, sarcophagi of monumental size were also installed, sometimes in an arrangement of triklinia (Colledge 1976: 77ff.; Parlasca 1984; Makowski 1985; Tanabe 1986: figs. 188–193, 209, 221–232, 237–246, 393–415; Schmidt-Colinet 1992: 105ff., 133ff., pls. 33–45, 69–75; Sadurska 1994; Sadurska and Bounni 1994: figs. 230–50).

With these sarcophagi two concurrent phenomena again emerge: a new wave of Roman influence on the one hand and – at the same time – an intensified recourse to indigenous oriental traditions (for the latter, see also Ploug 1988). This development may be exemplified by a recently discovered and extremely well preserved sarcophagus which can be dated, on iconographic and stylistic grounds, to the second quarter of the third century AD (Fig. 4; today in the museum of Palmyra; Schmidt-Colinet 1995: 36ff., figs. 48–51). The monument consists of two parts: the chest of the sarcophagus proper, carved in the shape of a bed (*kline*), and the lid, carved in the form of a man reclining on a mattress.

The front of the chest shows seven upright figures between the legs of the bed: three persons stand, carrying sacrificial utensils and offerings, on each side of the central figure. In the middle, that principal figure appears wearing the toga, official Roman dress, and making a bloodless sacrifice over the altar. The high rank of this person is demonstrated not only by the diadem on his head, but also by two other insignia that can be seen behind him in relief: an honorary wreath and a Palmyrene priest's hat (Schmidt-Colinet 1992: 112ff.).

Above this scene, on the sarcophagus lid, an over life-size reclining man appears wearing Sasanian dress: kaftan with sleeves, trousers and boots (for the dress, Seyrig 1937; Schmidt-Colinet 1992: 112). The figure also sports rich jewellery and weapons, which again demonstrate his high local status, as does the riding horse standing to his side (Schmidt-Colinet 1992: 109, n. 397).

Fig. 4. Palmyrene sarcophagus, second quarter of the third century AD. The lid represents the deceased as a local caravan leader; the chest as a Roman citizen. (Palmyra Museum)

There can be no doubt that this reclining figure represents the same individual as the sacrificing man below, thus presenting two different social personae of the deceased. At the sacrifice he appears as a Roman citizen (*cives Romanus*), equipped at the same time with the badges of rank suitable to a high priest of Palmyra. In the figure above, he appears as a local caravan leader of the highest social, economic and military rank (Will 1957). Only when reading the information of both chest and lid *together* are we able to recognize the ambivalence existing at this time in the self-perception and in the choice of representation of the Palmyrene upper classes: pride both in Roman citizenship and in local traditions. Yet far from being contradictory or conflicting impulses, these were complementary trends. The adoption of the image of a Roman citizen should not be understood as an alternative to an emphasis on local practices; instead, a growing revival, and more obvious demonstration of traditional roots, were rather the consistent consequences of increasing 'Romanization'.

Temple Tombs

About half of the tombs visible above ground at Palmyra in antiquity were so-called temple- or house-tombs (Gawlikowski 1970: 51, 129ff.; Schmidt-Colinet 1992: 42ff.). According to the inscriptions, these 'houses of eternity' were constructed between AD 143 and 253 (Table 1), which means they replaced the local type of tower tombs, in use only till the time of Hadrian's visit to Palmyra in AD 129. The new type of tomb shows much closer connections to western sacral, domestic or palatial architecture than do the tower or underground tombs. Because of this, these tombs would seem to be most relevant to the issue of 'Romanization'.

The type may be exemplified by Tomb No. 36, recently investigated, analysed and published in detail (Figs. 5, 6; see detailed refernces in al-As'ad and Schmidt-Colinet 1985; Schmidt-Colinet 1992; 1995: 39ff., figs. 54–57). This tomb is the largest of its type known to date at Palmyra. Its size corresponds approximately to that of the Library of Celsus at Ephesos, and thus surpasses all comparable buildings, even in Rome. The tomb was built ca. AD 210/20 by a man, probably of Parthian origin, but belonging to the highest social stratum of Palmyra.

Taken as a package, this building testifies to the obvious social, economic and cultural power of its commissioner, as well as his desire to demonstrate political and religious ambitions. The systematic use of formulae drawn from Roman sacral, palatial or triumphal architecture create clear associations with certain desirable concepts: prestige, privilege, claims to leadership, heroization. At the same time, and equally characteristic on all levels, is an eclectic mixing and fusion of western, Roman elements with oriental, Parthian ones. The architecture and architectural sculpture of the tomb, to be discussed in detail below, present the close relationship between its commissioner and the Roman west, and his claim to leadership on those grounds. On the other hand, this claim is also based on indigenous local tradition, as witnessed both by the use of local architectural elements and decorative forms, and the use of indigenous types of funerary sculpture.

Tomb No. 36, Roman architectural form and local prestige

The ground plan of Tomb No. 36 (Fig. 5) combines the indigenous local burial style (*loculi*) with a peristyle courtyard in the tomb's center. An element in the vocabulary of elite Hellenistic-Roman

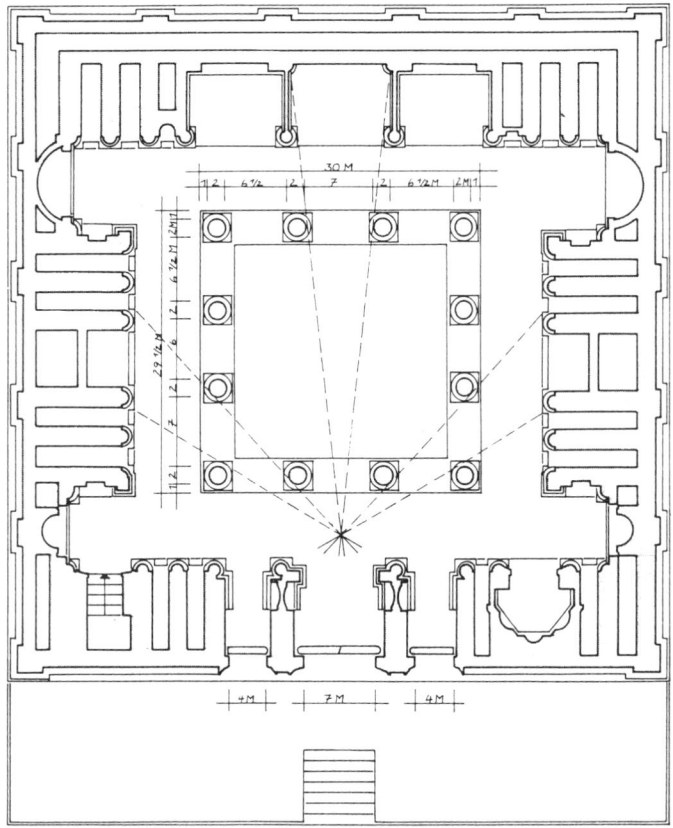

Fig. 5. Reconstructed ground plan of Tomb No. 36, Palmyra. Beginning of the third century AD

residential architecture is thereby used as a 'quotation', and as such is transferred to a private funerary world. At the same time, however, the tomb adhered to the local funerary system with *loculi*, and the design of its plan is based on the Persian ell.

One detail of the ground plan is especially instructive. The intercolumniations (distances between individual columns) of the peristyle are not identical, but are wider between certain columns. This slight differentiation would certainly not have been consciously realized by a visitor in ancient times, but this trick nevertheless aimed to create a very deliberate optical effect. Immediately on entering the peristyle, the viewer was forced to see – at the very same moment – the complete prospect of the tomb's three main niches (the great niche opposite the entrance and the two niches in the centers of the side wings), together with their programmatic funerary sculptures commemorating the family of the tomb's founder. To put it another way, the architect used a very sophisticated peculiarity of Roman perspectival architecture to display and to assert a bold programmatic statement of local prestige.

Fig. 6. Reconstructed entrance façade of Tomb No. 36, Palmyra

The entrance façade of the tomb also significantly combined local oriental elements with western Roman ones (Fig. 6). The external façades of tombs, of course, most immediately exhibit the desired self-representation of their founder to ancient visitors. Here flat roofing, and the arrangement of deep wall niches, with filigran framings, on several stories are clearly related to oriental constructions, for example to the façade of the Parthian palace at Assur (Fig. 7). On the other hand, individual architectural forms, such as columns and pediments, hearken back to western tradition. One detail in particular may be taken as especially instructive. The plan of the upper floor of the façade's niche architecture follows a design characteristic for Roman theater buildings in the west (Fig. 8). The architect here called on the vocabulary of official Roman civic architecture, transferring it to the private funerary realm to convey the desired self-representation of the tomb's founder. Public Roman forms are again employed in a private setting to assert local prestige.

The same phenomenon can be demonstrated at other temple tomb façades, twenty of which can be reconstructed in detail (Figs. 6, 9; Schmidt-Colinet 1992: 42ff., figs. 16–32; 1995: 38ff., fig. 52). Some of these façades are reminiscent of Nabatean rock-cut tombs, others of Hellenistic-Roman temples, others of Parthian palaces. Roman principles of composition, such as the high

Fig. 7. Detail of Parthian palace at Assur. Second century AD (after Andrae 1933: Pl. 14)

podium, the articulation of walls by pilasters, and the decorative accentuation of the upper line of orthostats, are combined with local oriental architectural elements, such as the quadratic proportion of the façades, flat roofing and the crown of battlements. These oriental forms are taken up more obviously and increasingly from the beginning of the third century onwards.

Of these oriental forms, the flat roof is maintained even if the structure boasted a portico with columns crowned by a pediment (Fig. 9; Schmidt-Colinet 1986; 1992: figs. 27, 28c; 1995: fig. 52; al-As'ad and Schmidt-Colinet forthcoming: figs. 4–7). Seen from the side, the pediments turn out to be 'false,' with, behind them, flat oriental roofs, sometimes with orientalizing battlements, abruptly joined. A similar construction, of course, was seen already at the temple of Bel some two hundred years before (Fig. 1).

The concept of 'portico with pediment,' originally developed within Greco-Roman sacral architecture, at Palmyra was displaced and transferred to private local funerary architecture, there to serve for claims of prestige and to afford a space for self-representation. The façade of the building on the one hand, and the actual structure behind it on the other, have no formal and logical relation to each other. Seen from the front the building pretends to be something completely different than what is seen from the side view. This is a characteristic of the architecture of the ancient Near East, particularly Parthian architecture. In Tomb No. 36, Roman and oriental architectural traditions meet abruptly in one and the same building at the beginning of the third

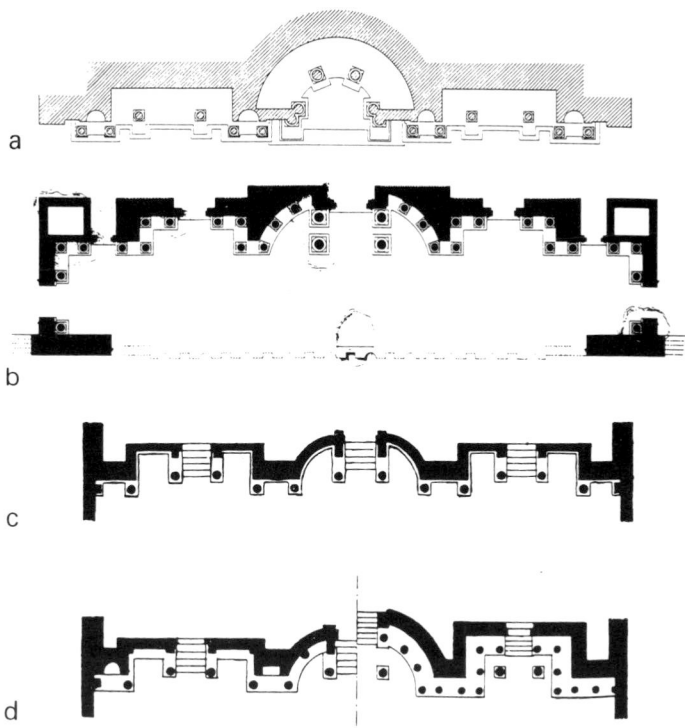

Fig. 8. Comparison of ground plan of the upper part of the façade of Tomb No. 36, Palmyra (a, top) with plans of Roman theater stages (b-d, below). (b: after Wiegand 1932: Pl.23 [Palmyra]; c-d: after Fiechter 1914: Fig. 109–110).

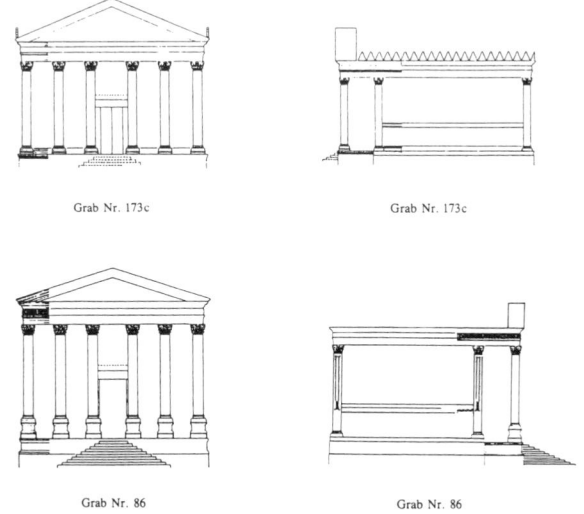

Fig. 9. Reconstructed front and side views of temple tombs nos. 173c and 86, Palmyra. Beginning of the third century AD

century, with the two traditions working upon each other. The Roman mentality of façade construction encounters the local mentality of flat-roof architecture, with their combination allowed through the use of projecting and fictitious façades. Once more the Roman structure connives, abets and supports the employment of local elements, as we have seen elsewhere.

The Transmission of Roman Patterns of Sculpture to Palmyra

The process of adopting Roman forms can be followed up and examined concretely and in detail when looking at the architectural sculpture of Tomb No. 36 (Schmidt-Colinet 1992: 89ff.; 1995: 48ff.; 1996: 417ff., figs. 1–6). One example may be adduced. A *putto*, which once decorated the niche over one of the main tomb entrances as the companion of a maritime *thiasos* (Fig. 10), rides on a dolphin and carries a parasol. Among the innumerable representations in Roman art of *putti* riding dolphins, only a single iconographic parallel exists for such a figure also carrying a parasol. This parallel comes from the side view of a sarcophagus made in the city of Rome during the Antonine period, dating about two generations before the relief at Palmyra (Fig. 11; today in the Villa Albani). This unique but strikingly close parallel clamors for an explanation. As the mason at Palmyra could hardly have seen the sarcophagus in Rome, we must envision the existence of some sample cartoon or copy of a pattern book which could have been used by sarcophagus workshops in Rome and then conveyed to Syria in later times, where its designs were transferred into monumental architectural sculpture.

A similar process is argued by other evidence from Tomb No. 36. It is even possible to reconstruct in part how such western patterns or cartoons found their way to Palmyra. On this point, the stylistic evidence of Tomb No. 36's architectural sculpture is instructive. The organic nature and plastic structure of twisted figures in a three-quarter view, shown by the *putto* for example, is completely inconsistent with the graphically linear and frontally hieratic structure of the local tradition of Palmyrene funerary sculpture. This pointedly suggests that the architectural sculpture of this tomb was not created by local Palmyrene workshops.

So where might the workmen have come from? In the great centers on the Syrian coast, such as Tyre and Sidon, permanent ateliers were established which evidently imported western sarcophagi in great quantities, sometimes even as half-finished products. Not only did they transport them further into the 'hinterland', they were also able to imitate such sarcophagi in an adequately 'westernized' manner, suggesting that pattern books of western sarcophagi must have been at their disposal. On occasion, these workshops also transformed their models into monumental architectural sculpture. In sum, it can be proven that a foreign workshop from the Syrian coast was employed in the creation of the sculptures of Tomb No. 36, a workshop which was able to realize such distinctly Greco-Roman themes as mermaids and *putti* riding on dolphins, maritime *thiasoi* with sea monsters, Bacchus-Dionysos in a vineyard, and other motifs.

Patterns of Architectural Decoration and Local Textile Ornaments

In contrast to the architectural sculpture of Tomb No. 36, its ornamental architectural decoration was definitely elaborated by local Palmyrene workshops (Schmidt-Colinet 1992: 65ff. 125ff.; 1995: 43ff.). This is attested by general stylistic and typological evidence, as well as by the use of Palmyrene

Fig. 10. Putto *from the architectural sculpture of Tomb No. 36, Palmyra. Beginning of the third century AD*

Fig. 11. Side view of a Roman sarcophagus, Villa Albani, Rome. Mid-second century AD (Photo courtesy German Archaeological Institute, Rome)

letters (the abbreviations of names of local masons) cut in several decorated blocks, especially those of the cornice. These local workshops also used pattern books or cartoons, but ones of a very different origin. By cataloguing and systematizing all the different individual motifs of Tomb No. 36's architectural decoration, it was possible to reconstruct the pattern books or pattern sheets used by these ancient masons. Utilizing the same method, the textile ornaments of the tombs' funerary sculpture were likewise drawn, catalogued and systematized. Comparing these pattern catalogues to each other, and broadening the research to other buildings and to other sculptures of Palmyra, one phenomenon becomes quite evident: the architectural workshops of Palmyra primarily employed exactly the same patterns as the local sculpture ateliers (Schmidt-Colinet 1996: figs. 7–8). This is true for simple, as well as for more complicated, patterns (cf. Figs. 12, 13).

The question is thus raised whether the 'arabesque' and other typical Palmyrene architectural decoration can be traced back to patterns drawn originally from local textiles, of which, luckily,

Fig. 12. Textile decoration of sleeve and trousers of the reclining man of the sarcophagus shown in Fig. 4 (Palmyra Museum)

Fig. 13. Pilaster from an arch, detail of architectural decoration, Palmyra. Beginning of the third century AD (Compare Fig. 12)

Fig. 14. Comparison of original Palmyrene textile decoration of the first century AD (above) with dated examples of Palmyrene architectural decoration of the second and third century (below)

significant amounts are well preserved (Pfister 1934; 1937; 1940; Stauffer 1995). Indeed, it can be proven that, at Palmyra, textile patterns were transferred to stone sculpture and to architecture. Of course, complex interrelationships with other media, such as mosaics and wall paintings, must also be taken into account. But many patterns appear first on local textiles, then later in sculpture or architecture, proving conclusively the general direction of this transfer from textile patterns to architectural decoration (Schmidt-Colinet 1995: 46ff., figs. 71–81; 1996: figs. 7–14).

To offer just one example: a woollen textile fragment found recently in the tower tomb of Kitot (built in AD 43) can be dated to the end of the first or the beginning of the second century AD. Its decoration comprises a system of vertical stripes with different patterns of rosettas and scrolls which reappear, identically, in Palmyrene sculpture, as well as in the architectural decoration of Palmyrene buildings dated to the second and third century AD (Fig. 14).

The architectural decoration of Palmyra, therefore, now appears in a new light, being traced back to the extremely rich, usually vertically striped patterning, of local textiles. How to explain this

Fig. 15. Local carpet decorating the balcony at the official opening of the Palmyra Folklore Museum, 1992.

process? The use of textiles within architectural contexts is well attested already for antiquity by written sources, as well as by archaeological evidence. One modern example may help explain this phenomenon. For the official opening of the Folklore Museum of Palmyra in 1992, the ceremonial balcony of the museum was decorated with a colourful local carpet (Fig. 15). To perpetuate the character of this celebration for posterity, one would merely have to paint the decoration of this carpet on the balustrade, or to carve it there in relief. Essentially the same effect was given in the architectural decoration of ancient Palmyra (Fig. 16).

Even here, however, it was the Roman concept of vertical pilaster decoration that enabled and encouraged the transformation of such vertical design elements into architecture. Again, the Roman structure appears as vehicle or medium to be 'filled' – literally – with local forms or contents. Here again, we may call this phenomenon the 're-orientalization' that accompanied 'Romanization' – a process much more complicated than a simple linear increase of Roman influence.

Bibliography

al-As'ad, Kh. and A. Schmidt-Colinet (1985) "Das Tempelgrab Nr. 36 in der Westnekropole von Palmyra," *DM* 2: 17–35.

_____forthcoming "Aspects of 'Hellenism' and 'Romanization' in Nabataean and Palmyrene Funerary Architecture," *Annales Archéologiques Syriennes.*

Fig. 16. Detail of architectural decoration of an arch, Palmyra. Beginning of the third century AD

Amy, R. (1950) "Temples à éscaliers," *Syria* 27: 82–136.

Amy, R. and H. Seyrig (1936) "Recherches dans la nécropole de Palmyre," *Syria* 17: 229–266.

Andrae, W. (1933) *Die Partherstadt Assur*, Berlin.

Bounni, A. (1989) "Palmyre et les Palmyréniens," in J.-M. Dentzer and W. Orthmann, eds., *Archéologie et histoire de la Syrie II: La Syrie de l'époque achéménide à l'avènement de l'Islam* (Schriften zur Vorderasiatischen Archäologie 1), 251–66. Saarbrücken.

Browning, I. (1979) *Palmyra*, London.

Colledge, M.A.R. (1976) *The Art of Palmyra*, London.

Dentzer-Feydy, J. and J. Teixidor (1993) *Les antiquités de Palmyre au Musée du Louvre*, Paris.

Drijvers, H.J.W. (1977) "Hatra, Palmyra und Edessa," *ANRW* II.8: 837–863; 899–902.

Fellmann, R. (1970) *Die Grabanlage (Le sanctuaire de Baalshamin à Palmyre 5)*, Rome.

Fiechter, E.R. (1914) *Die baugeschichtliche Entwicklung des antiken Theaters*, Berlin.

Filarska, B. (1967) *Études sur le décor architectural à Palmyre* (Etudes Palmyréniennes 3), Warsaw.

Gawlikowski, M. (1969) "Classement, chronologie et évolution de la Tour funéraire à Palmyre," *Etudes et Travaux* 3: 168–191.

_____(1970) *Monuments funéraires de Palmyre*, Warsaw.

_____(1973) *Le temple palmyrénien. Etude d'épigraphie et de topographie historique* (Palmyre 6), Warsaw.

Graf, D.F. (1989) "Zenobia and the Arabs," in D.H. French and C.S. Lightfoot, eds., *The Eastern Frontier of the Roman Empire* (*BAR-IS* 553.1), 143–167. London.

Ingholt, H. (1935) "Five Dated Tombs from Palmyra," *Berytus* 2: 57–120.

_____(1936) "Inscriptions and Sculptures from Palmyra I," *Berytus* 3: 83–125.

_____(1938) "Inscriptions and Sculptures from Palmyra II," *Berytus* 5: 93–140.

Makowski, C. (1985) "La sculpture funéraire Palmyrénienne et sa fonction dans l'architecture sépulcrale," *Études Palmyréniennes* 8: 69–117.

Parlasca, K. (1984) "Probleme der palmyrenischen Sarkophage," *MarbWPr* 1984: 283–296 and 309f.

_____(1985) "Das Verhältnis der palmyrenischen Grabplastik zur römischen Porträtkunst," *RM* 92: 343–356.

_____(1989) "Beobachtungen zur palmyrenischen Grabarchitektur," *DM* 4: 181–190.

_____(1989/90) "Die palmyrenische Grabkunst in ihrem Verhältnis zur römischen Gräbersymbolik," in E. Pochmarski *et al.*, eds., *Akten des 1. internationalen Kolloquiums über Probleme des Provinzialrömischen Kunstschaffens, Mitteilungen der Archäologischen Gesellschaft Steiermark* 3/4: 112–136.

Pfister, R. (1934) *Textiles de Palmyre*, Paris.

_____(1937) *Nouveaux textiles de Palmyre*, Paris.

_____(1940) *Textiles de Palmyre III*, Paris.

Ploug, G. (1988) "East Syrian art of 1st century BC- 2nd century AD," *Acta Hyperborea* 1: 129–139.

_____(1995) *Catalogue of the Palmyrene Sculptures. Ny Carlsberg Glyptotek*, Copenhagen.

Rostovtzeff, M. (1926) *The Social and Economic History of the Roman Empire*, Oxford.

_____(1932) *Caravan Cities*, London.

Sadurska, A. (1977) *Le tombeau de famille de 'Alainé* (Palmyre 7), Warsaw.

_____(1994) "L'art et la société. Recherches iconologique sur l'art funéraire de Palmyre," *Archeologia War* 45: 11–23.

Sadurska, A. and A. Bounni (1994) *Les sculptures funéraires de Palmyre* (*RdA* Supplement 13), Rome.

Saliby, N. (1992) "L'hypogée de Sassan fils de Malè à Palmyre," *DM* 6: 267–289.

Schlumberger, D. (1969) *Der hellenisierte Orient. Die griechische und nachgriechische Kunst ausserhalb des Mittelmeerraumes*, Baden-Baden.

Schmidt-Colinet, A. (1986) "Flachdach und Giebel," in G. Bucher *et al.*, eds., *Orient und Okzident im Spiegel der Kunst. Festschrift H.G. Franz*, 329–331; 621–624. Graz.

_____(1989) "L'architecture funéraire de Palmyre," in J.-M. Dentzer and W. Orthmann, eds., *Archéologie et histoire de la Syrie II: La Syrie de l'époque achéménide à l'avènement de l'Islam* (Schriften zur Vorderasiatischen Archäologie 1), 447–56. Saarbrücken.

_____(1991) "Aspects of 'Hellenism' in Nabataean and Palmyrene Funerary Architecture," in European Cultural Centre of Delphi, ed., *O ellinismos stin Anatoli. International Meeting of History and Archaeology, Delphi 1986*, 131–144. Athens.

_____(1992) *Das Templegrab Nr. 36 in Palmyra. Studien zur palmyrenischen Grabarchitektur und ihrer Ausstattung* (Damaszener Forschungen 4, two volumes). Mainz. (In collaboration with Kh. al-As'ad and C. Müting-Zimmer)

_____ed. (1995) *Palmyra. Kulturbegegnung im Grenzbereich*, Mainz.

_____ (1996) "East and West in Palmyrene Pattern Books," in *Palmyra and the Silk Road. International Colloquium Palmyra 1992, Annales Arquéologiques Syriennes* 42: 418–23.

Seyrig, H. (1937) "Armes et coutumes iraniens de Palmyre," *Syria* 18: 3–31.

_____(1950) "Palmyra and the East," *JRS* 40: 1–7.

Seyrig, H., R. Amy, and E. Will (1968/1975) *Le temple de Bèl à Palmyre* (Bibliothèque archéologique et historique 83, two volumes), Paris.

Starcky, J. and M. Gawlikowski (1985) *Palmyre*, Paris.

Stauffer, A. (1995) "Kleider, Kissen, bunte Tücher. Einheimische Textilproduktion und weltweiter Handel," in A. Schmidt-Colinet, ed., *Palmyra. Kulturbegegnung im Grenzbereich,* 57–71. Mainz.

Tanabe, K., ed. (1986) *Sculptures of Palmyra I* (Memoirs of the Ancient Orient Museum 1), Tokyo.

Teixidor, J. (1984) *Un port romain du désert, Palmyre et son commerce d'Auguste à Caracalla, Semitica* 34: 7–125.

Wiegand, T., ed. (1932) *Palmyra. Ergebnisse der Expeditionen von 1902 und 1917* (two volumes), Berlin.

Will, E. (1949) "La tour funéraire de Palmyre;" "La tour funéraire de la Syrie et les monuments apparentés," *Syria* 26: 87–116; 258–312.

_____(1957) "Marchands et chefs de caravanes à Palmyre," *Syria* 34: 262–277.

_____(1992) *Les Palmyréniens. La Venise des sables*, Paris.

11. The Origins of the Icon:
Pilgrimage, Religion and Visual Culture
in the Roman East as 'Resistance' to the Centre

Jas' Elsner

According to the *Historia Augusta*, when the emperor Aurelian (AD 270–275) had taken the rebellious town of Tyana in Cappadocia in the eastern part of Asia Minor and was considering the slaughter of its inhabitants, he was visited in his tent by a sacred vision (*HA, Divus Aurelianus* 24.2–9, with Homo 1904: 91–92). The deified first-century holy man, Apollonius of Tyana, recognizable because he manifested 'in the form in which he was usually portrayed', appeared to the emperor and persuaded him to spare the lives of his 'fellow citizens' of Tyana. As proof of his divine versatility, Apollonius addressed Aurelian in Latin rather than Greek, 'in order that he might be understood by a man from Pannonia'. Aurelian, we are told:

> recognized the countenance of the venerated philosopher, and, in fact, he had seen his portrait in many a temple. And so, at once stricken with terror, he promised him a portrait and statues and a temple, and returned to his better self.

This story – whether strictly 'true' or not (and the *Historia Augusta* is a distinctly unreliable source) – points to a remarkable continuity in the ancient imagination between the sacred arts of the pagan east and their Christian successors. The eastern empire, in its early Byzantine incarnation, has long been seen as the crucible in which were formed such particular Christian forms of visual representation as icons (see e.g. Cormack 1985; Brubaker 1995). The worship of icons, one of the more characteristic manifestations of medieval spirituality (Belting 1994), was to become a substantial arena for theological debate from the fourth century until the Iconoclastic controversy of the eighth and ninth centuries (e.g. Pelikan 1990; Barasch 1992) and beyond. One of the most characteristic uses of Christian icons was as a means for visualising the holy. Just like Apollonius, whom Aurelian recognized from his resemblance to his statue, visions of Christian saints were recognized by their worshippers from their likeness to their icons (Kazhdan and Maguire 1991: 4–6; Dagron 1991: 31–33). Like Apollonius, whom the emperor propitiated with 'a portrait and statues and a temple', the Christian saints were offered portraits in the form of icons and churches by their grateful or fearful worshippers.

Nothing appears now to survive of the temple erected at Tyana on the site of the sage's birth, a temple which was – according to Apollonius' third-century AD biographer, Philostratus – 'singled out and honoured with royal officers, for the emperors have not denied to him the honours of which they themselves were worthy' (Philostratus, *VA* 8.31, see also 1.5). But we know from later sources of a persistent tradition of magical talismans associated with Apollonius which circulated throughout the Christian east (Dzielska 1986: 99–127), of pilgrimage to his shrine at Tyana – which attracted among others the earliest known Christian pilgrim to the Holy Land (*Itinerarium Burdigalense* 578.1) – and of Apollonius' place in the hierarchy of late pagan sages as, for example, a figure portrayed in the fourth-century contorniate medallions issued as tokens of exchange by the Roman aristocracy (Fig. 1; Settis 1972: 244–47; Alföldi 1990: 53–55, 102–103). Apollonius of Tyana, once a man but now a divine being, had become by the third century a miracle-working and oracle-producing deity typical of imperial Roman polytheism: he attracted pilgrims, offered visions and blessed the social interrelationships of late antique Roman citizens. The world evoked by his images and their use is the world of religious visual culture in the Roman east.

Fig. 1. Apollonius of Tyana, bronze contorniate medallion from Rome (obverse), diameter 3.7 cm. Fourth century AD. The inscription reads APOLLONIUS TEANEUS. Bibliothèque Nationale, Cabinet des Médailles, Paris. (Photo: Museum). Scale 1:1

One feature of the interview in the *Historia Augusta* between Apollonius and Aurelian is of particular interest. It presents, in a Latin text designed to be read in the Latin-speaking west, a perhaps surprising instance of a Roman emperor – albeit still alive and not yet a *divus* – subordinate to an eastern sage. Like Philostratus' *Life of Apollonius*, in which the much travelled sage is cast as the Greek holy man who counsels, confronts and triumphs over various Roman emperors (from Nero via Vespasian and Titus to Domitian) and who inaugurates a religious revival in the Roman empire before ascending into divinity (Elsner forthcoming, a), Aurelian's interview at Tyana hints at a new east-centred cultural dynamic. In the second and third centuries AD, the eastern provinces subject to Rome began to assert their independence of the west – even their dominance within the empire – through religious proselytism rather than political control, through the promulgation of sacred cult as opposed to temporal power. Whether this process appears on the high imperial level of Elagabalus attempting to transfer his Syrian god Elagabal to Rome, or on the rather more populist dissemination of eastern cults throughout the empire, there is little doubt that the second and third centuries saw the east 'strike back' at its western conqueror through religion. This was not, so far as we can tell, a programme planned through the agency of any particular individuals; rather it was a cultural phenomenon – the so-called 'Second Sophistic' (Bowersock 1969; 1974; Bowie 1970; Anderson 1993; Müller 1994: 139–70) – in which the unity of the empire was re-asserted in Greek-speaking cultural terms through the revival of Greek rhetoric and philosophy, the promulgation of eastern mythology and *paideia*, the affirmation of eastern religions and iconographies. The highly symbolic icons produced by eastern religions were a prime means by which the propagation of such cults was achieved.

The aim of this chapter will be to follow some of the implications of Aurelian's vision of Apollonius, by tracing a double theme: the pagan pre-history of the icon in the eastern Roman world and the east's self-assertion against the centre through religion. For the worship, cultivation and visionary experience of Christian sacred images has its roots in the extraordinary and generally neglected culture of image-worship, pilgrimage and sacred art generated by the polytheism of the Roman east; and the eventual triumph of Christianity, in many ways (including in its eccentricities) a typical eastern cult, was prepared by the ascendance of the eastern cults in the later Roman world, propagated through images and rituals.

In fact these two apparently divergent implications of Aurelian's vision – the pre-history of the icon and the intimation of eastern resistance to the centre – are more closely connected than appears at first. I shall argue that the visual propaganda of iconographically idiosyncratic eastern 'icons' (from mystery cults like Mithraism and Christianity as well as more civic religions like the worship of Ephesian Artemis or the Syrian goddess) was disseminated throughout the Roman empire in part as a parade of the east's difference from and hence resistance to Rome. Here the excellent recent literature on the development of communal and cultural identity in the east (e.g. Millar 1987; 1993: 225–36; Alcock 1993) needs to be supplemented with an emphasis on visual culture as a prime signifier of identity. The importance for the history of Christian art of this empire-wide growth in the cult of pre-Christian icons is twofold. First, the origins of Christian art appear to have been motivated by visual competition with the symbolic arts of the other cults (Grabar 1968: 27–30; Mathews 1993: 3–10). Second, the visual impetus behind the process of Christianization after the fourth century (on which see Elsner 1995: 280–87) borrowed its methods from the cults which Christianity supplanted, in particular a reliance on the dissemination of sacredly 'loaded' imagery as a marker of cult identity.

In what follows, I shall explore the themes of the prehistory of the icon and the affirmation of eastern identity through imagery tied to the expansion of religious cults by looking at two loosely related areas. The first section examines the interrelationship of cult deity, city and empire using the example of Artemis of the Ephesians. The second section evokes something of the phenomenology of pilgrimage as a ritual practice in the polytheist east.

'Great is Artemis of the Ephesians' (Acts of the Apostles 19.28)

The God and her City

About a decade before Aurelian's vision of Apollonius at Tyana, another city in Ionian Asia Minor which revered Apollonius among its gods (Oster 1976: 26–27; Oster 1990: 1684–85) suffered a catastrophe. The Gauls, who had taken advantage of the military and political crisis in the Roman empire during the middle years of the third century AD, sacked the wealthy coastal city of Ephesos and destroyed its famous temple of Artemis in about 262. One of the fabled 'seven wonders of the world' (Clayton and Price 1988), the temple of Artemis Ephesia and its famous cult image (Figs. 2 and 3) had been an archetypal site of pagan religious activity since archaic times. It was a major pilgrimage centre, lauded in at least one Graeco-Roman epigram as the pinnacle of sights:

I have gazed on the walls of lofty Babylon with its chariot road,
and the statue of Zeus by the Alpheus,
the hanging gardens and the colossus of the Sun,
the huge labour of the high pyramids,
and the vast tomb of Mausolus; but when I saw
the house of Artemis which mounted to the clouds,
those other marvels lost their brilliancy and I said, 'behold,
except Olympus, the Sun never looked on anything so grand'
(Antipater of Sidon in the *Palatine Anthology* 9.58)

Fig. 2. Artemis of Ephesos, Roman marble copy with head, hands and feet of bronze. 1.15 m in height. Imperial, perhaps second century AD. Museo Conservatori, Rome. (Photo: DAI 80.3343)

Fig. 3. Artemis of Ephesos, Roman marble copy found in Lepcis Magna in 1912. 1.57 m in height. Second century AD, perhaps Hadrianic. Tripoli Museum, Libya. (Photo: DAI 61.1728)

The worship of the goddess had many manifestations and was utterly integral to the cultural and political life of the city of Ephesos. It was also perhaps the prime sanctuary in all Ionia as Pausanias, the second-century AD traveller, informs us:

> The land of the Ionians has the finest possible climate, and sanctuaries such as are to be found nowhere else. First of these, because of its size and wealth, is that of the Ephesian goddess (7.5.4).

Earlier in his *Description of Greece*, Pausanias writes:

> All cities worship Artemis of Ephesos, and individuals hold her in honour above all the gods. The reason, in my view, is the fame of the Amazons, who traditionally dedicated the image, also the extreme antiquity of the sanctuary. Three other points as well have contributed to her renown, the size of the temple, surpassing all buildings among men, the eminence of the city of the Ephesians, and the renown of the goddess who dwells there (4.31.8).

Here the pre-eminence of the Ephesian Artemis is presented in a sacred topography which leads from the actual image, with its famed mythic dedicators and sanctuary whose origins are lost in irrecoverable antiquity, to the house of the image – the temple which (as in Antipater's poem) 'surpasses all buildings among men' – and culminates in the city itself where the temple stands. This interrelationship of image, temple and city – that is, of deity, the house of the deity and the worshippers most closely identified with her – is of central significance to sacred images in pagan antiquity. It was expressed not only spatially (as in Pausanias' brief account), but also as a series of liturgical or processional rituals which actively linked the urban spaces of the city with the 'goddess who dwells there' (cf. Price 1984: 101–14).

An inscription of the early second century AD, carved in both the theatre and the Artemisium of Ephesos (perhaps the city's most public and most sacred spaces), records a bequest made to the boulê and dêmos of the Ephesians in AD 104 by a wealthy Roman *eques* called Caius Vibius Salutaris (Rogers 1991). The inscription dedicates to Artemis thirty-one statue-types made mainly of silver but some gilded and one of solid gold. These were to be carried in a procession – 'a conveyance before everyone, from the temple to the theatre and from the theatre into the temple of Artemis' (*I.Ephesos* 27.90–92: Rogers 1991: 156–57). This procession went through the heart of the city, beginning and ending at its most sacred temple; it appears to have been repeated roughly every two weeks on sacred and festal days (Rogers 1991: 80–115) and was linked with the distribution of public doles and lotteries (Rogers 1991: 39–72).

The images in the Salutaris bequest represented not only Artemis herself but also the emperor Trajan, his empress Plotina, the Roman Senate, the Equestrian order and the people of Rome, as well as some fifteen statues which personified the tribes, boulê and city of the Ephesians. In effect, the evidence of this one private (if very generous) bequest portrays a civic culture centred on the Ephesian goddess, where the city, its myths and its very place within the wider context of the Roman empire were remembered and re-enacted through the rite of the public procession of images. The sacred identity of Ephesos as myth, ritual and space was continually reaffirmed in this repetition. We cannot know how long the Salutaris processions continued after the donor's death (although the grand inscriptions announcing the dedication have survived to the present day) nor whether the statues carried through the city ever changed (for example, with the addition of images representing the emperors who succeeded Trajan and Plotina). Salutaris' foundation was only one of many such bequests and rituals (for analogous examples, see Rogers 1991: 186–90), and in some respects it may have been exceptional. But it vividly brings to life a culture of images – visual embodiments of the sacred and political world – which could be used symbolically to re-enact the myths which linked Ephesian Artemis with her city and to perpetuate ritually the harmonious existence of the city within the empire. The culture of urban liturgy anticipates very similar sacred practices in early Christian times (Baldovin 1987), including – in particular – the parading of icons and relics in cities like Constantinople and Rome (Belting 1994: 47–77; Limberis 1994: 45–97).

An evocation of the atmosphere of processions like that of Salutaris is given in the second-century AD description of a festival of Artemis Ephesia in a novel – the *Ephesian Tale of Anthia and Habrocomes* by Xenophon of Ephesos:

> The local festival of Artemis was in progress, with its procession from the city to the temple nearly a mile away. All the local girls had to march in the procession, richly dressed, as well as all the young men... There was a great crowd of Ephesians and visitors alike to see the festival, for it was the custom at this festival to find husbands for the young girls and wives for the young men. So the procession filed past – first, the sacred objects, the torches, the baskets and the incense; then horses, dogs and hunting equipment ... And when the procession was over, the whole crowd went into the temple for the sacrifice, and the files broke up; and men and women, girls and boys came together (1.2–3).

While the romantic emphasis is clearly related to the theme of Xenophon's love story, the carnivalesque enthusiasm in which the normal distinctions of age, society and sex were broken down in the fervour of ritual points to the function of such festivals in attempting to unify the diverse interests of the local community in a single identity. The whole of Xenophon's novel is ultimately a testament to Artemis' care for her devotees, even in adversity; and it ends with the lovers Anthia and Habrocomes, finally reunited, dedicating 'an inscription in honour of the goddess, commemorating all their sufferings and all their adventures' (5.15).

The central focus of these various forms of civic and sanctuary ritual was the famous cult image of Artemis. To understand the full range of meanings and social significances which a statue of this prestige came to embody and to symbolise, we have to look beyond it to some of the roles and implications of the Ephesos temple. First, the Artemisium was both ritually and spatially apart from the city; this very peripheral quality served to enhance its centrality as sacred guarantor for a whole range of highly civic activities. The rituals and taboos surrounding the temple served to demarcate and enhance the sanctity of the deity by emphasising the god's liminal position beyond ordinary space, in a location which needed a special (ritualised) means of approach, and beyond ordinary time, since the origins of the sanctuary lay in mythic tradition. At the same time, rituals like the Salutaris procession linked the goddess with the temporal world outside her temple by taking images of Artemis around the city, and by taking images of the city and the empire into the Artemisium.

A vivid account of some of the taboos surrounding Ephesian Artemis is to be found in Achilles Tatius' second-century AD novel *Leucippe and Clitophon*, whose climax is set in Ephesos:

> From ancient days the temple had been forbidden to free women who were not virgins. Only men and virgins were permitted here. If a non-virgin woman passed inside, the penalty was death, unless she was

a slave accusing her master, in which case she was allowed to beseech the goddess, and the magistrates would hear the case between her and her master. If the master had in fact done no wrong, he recovered his maid-servant, swearing he would not bear a grudge for her flight. If it was decided that the serving girl had a just case, she remained there as a slave to the goddess (7.13).

While one must exercise some circumspection in using the evidence of fiction in history (see Hopkins 1993; Bowersock 1994), there is little doubt that this passage – even if it does not tell the whole story – represents the kinds of religious regulations which would have come as little surprise to the novel's readers. Such precise rules about who might enter a temple and when, or about what sort of offerings might be made and to which images, are typical of Greek religious practice.[1]

What is of particular interest in Achilles Tatius' novel is the emphasis on Artemis' divine intervention in matters of law (Oster 1976: 35–36). The statue of Artemis, spatially peripheral but spiritually central to the city of Ephesos, came to stand for a final divine insurance for the social life of the city and its dealings with the wider world. Underlying the cultural interpenetration of god and city which image processions like that of Salutaris continually emphasised, was the shrine's economic and legal centrality. Both Leucippe and Clitophon (the novel's heroine and hero) seek asylum in the temple (7.13; 7.15; 8.2–3). The sacred nature of Artemis (rather like the name of Caesar in Apuleius' *Golden Ass* 3.29; cf. Price 1984: 192–93 for other examples of asylum) serves as a final court of appeal and a divine guarantee for justice, despite the shortcomings and machinations of human beings (see *Leucippe and Clitophon* 8.8–14).

Beside this function as ultimate legal arbiter, the sanctity of Artemis also served as a potent financial guarantee. Dio Chrysostom writes of the

> large sums of money... deposited in the temple of Artemis, not only money of the Ephesians but also of aliens and of persons from all parts of the world, and in some cases of commonwealths and kings, money which all deposit in order that it may be safe, since no one has ever dared to violate that place, although countless wars have occurred in the past and the city has often been captured (*Oratio* 31.54).

While Dio exaggerates the safety of the Artemisium (and demonstrates why it should have been so appealing to the Gauls), his comments give a clear sense of the security inspired by the goddess. As a financial centre, the sanctuary of Artemis not only held money, but made money through loans carrying interest, mortgages and other financial services (Oster 1990: 1717–19). In these financial and legal dealings, the image of the goddess stood as a talisman for divine sanction and security. Apart from her particular iconographic form and religious meanings, one aspect of the statue's significations was as the ultimate arbiter of all these civic activities.

The God and the Roman World

While the great statue of Artemis which was the ultimate cult focus for these varied activities – religious, financial and legal – has not survived, it is striking that she was repeatedly copied throughout Graeco-Roman antiquity (Fleischer 1973; 1978; 1984). These copies (ranging from large-scale marble replicas via small bronze or terracotta statuettes to gems and coins) allow us to make some sense of the appearance of the original cult image (e.g. Fleischer 1984: 762–63). The statue was a *xoanon* made of wood, with only face, hands and feet visible to the viewer, peeping beyond robes whose designs offered a highly symbolic iconography. In some copies (e.g. Fig. 2), the blackened colour of the original's wooden head and extremities (constantly treated with oil) is apparent. The most famous feature of the iconography are the 'breasts' – so called in Christian polemical attacks on the idol – whose pagan significance and even correct identification have never been sufficiently explained. But it is clear that the goddess' robes included references to the natural world (in the images of a large number of animals including horses, lions and bulls as well as mythical beasts such as griffins) and to the cosmological or astrological order (in the zodiac on the breast of Figure 3, for instance). In a number of versions, the Ephesian Artemis wears a lofty *polos* crown or *kalathos* (Figs. 3, 4, 5, 7, 9 and 10), and fillets hang from her wrists (Figs. 4, 5, 7 and 8).

Large replicas of the Ephesian goddess appeared in temples throughout the Roman Empire from the Near East and Greece to Africa, Italy and Gaul. The stereotypical replication of what was visually and iconographically a highly idiosyncratic statue was part of a deliberate missionary expansion of the cult of the Ephesian Artemis (Oster 1990: 1703–1706), whereby sanctuaries were established throughout the Graeco-Roman world (Wernicke 1895: 1385–86). Of the examples illustrated here, Figure 2 is probably from Rome (Stuart Jones 1926: 51–54; Thiersch 1935: 24–26), while Figure 3 comes from Lepcis Magna in North Africa (Thiersch 1935: 38–51); both are likely to have been made in the second century AD. They indicate that while some aspects of the iconography (the pose, the 'breasts', the animals depicted on the goddess's body) were standardised, others (such as the colour of the face) could vary from replica to replica. In the more schematic versions (e.g. Figs. 4–10), the pose, 'breasts', fillets and crown appear to be the most significant identifying features. In every case, from the very schematic to the most elaborately finished, what is striking is the image's particularity in the pantheon of Graeco-Roman deities – its visual difference from the more naturalistic norms of representing ancient deities.

In addition to this network of Ephesian sanctuaries and statues spread throughout the empire, the cult centre at Ephesos produced a plethora of small images to be distributed outside the city. The range of items includes coins struck in the imperial mints of Ephesos, whose celebration of the goddess was a tribute to the financial clout of her sanctuary as well as to the sacred significance of her shrine, and tokens made for the pilgrims who visited Artemis' shrine to take home with them. The coins, struck in the names of a variety of emperors from Claudius in the first century

Fig. 4. Silver coin (cistophoric tetradrachm) with Claudius on the obverse (bearing the legend TI CLAUD CAES AUG) and the temple of Artemis at Ephesos on the reverse (bearing the legend DIAN EPHE). The cult statue of Artemis (Diana) is shown in characteristic form, with fillets hanging from her wrists and polos crown on her head, standing in the centre of her temple which is represented as a tetrastyle building on a four-stepped podium with a decorated pediment. Mint of Ephesos, probably AD 41–42. British Museum, London (BMC Claudius 229). (Photo: Museum)

186   *Jas' Elsner*

Fig. 5. Silver coin (cistophoric tetradrachm) with Hadrian on the obverse (bearing the legend HADRIANUS AUGUSTUS PP) and the cult statue of Artemis on the reverse (bearing the legend DIANA [EPHESI]A COS). The cult statue, wearing veil and polos crown, stands between two stags, with fillets hanging from her wrists. Mint of Ephesos, 130s AD. British Museum, London (BMC Hadrian 1085). (Photo: Museum)

to Valerian and Maximus in the third, testify to the continued importance of the temple until the Gallic sack. They show the cult image of Artemis Ephesia, the goddess in her temple or the goddess and temple flanked by other temples – for instance belonging to the imperial cult (Figs. 4–6; Thiersch 1935: 78–85; Price and Trell 1977: 127–32).

The earlier coins imply both an imperial acknowledgment of the importance of a provincial eastern cult, and a civic alignment on the part of the Ephesians with the charisma of the imperial centre, where the image of Artemis (standing for the city of Ephesos) proudly decorates the reverse of coins with the imperial portrait (Figs. 4–5). These coins of the first and early second centuries AD, inscribed in the Latin language of the conquering foreigner (just as Augustus' *Res Gestae* was inscribed in Latin into the cities of Asia Minor, see Elsner 1996) place the balance of emphasis on the east's dependence on – or alignment with – the western emperor. But the pattern of priority is interestingly reversed in later coins (such as Fig. 6) where temples to the imperial cult nestle around the temple of Artemis – as if drawing their sacred charisma from hers. Such later imperial coins, inscribed not in Latin but in Greek, and often supporting the claims of emperors with eastern connections (like Septimius Severus or Elagabalus) attest a transformation in the weight of charismatic authority from the imperial centre towards the peripheral cult.

Fig. 6. Bronze coin with bust of Septimius Severus on the obverse (bearing the legend ΑΥΚΑΙΛΣΕΠ ΣΕΟΥΗΡΟΣΠΕΡ) and, on the reverse, the tetrastyle temple of Ephesian Artemis containing her statue flanked on either side by a distyle temple in each of which is a nude male statue (probably) of the emperor resting on a sceptre (bearing the legend ΕΦΕΣΙΩΝ ΠΡΩΤΩΝ ΑΣΙΑΣ). Late second or early third century AD. British Museum, London (BMC Ionia, Ephesos 261). (Photo: Museum)

Fig. 7. Artemis of Ephesos, centre, with a deer on either side of her, between busts of Helios and Selene (facing her) and a Nemesis of Smyrna on each side. Sard gem. 19 × 15 mm. Second century AD. British Museum, London. (Photo: Museum)

Fig. 8. Artemis of Ephesos, bronze statuette. 0.11 m in height. Imperial period. Museo Civico, Bologna. (Photo: DAI 34.1152)

While the coins emphasise the continuing public significance and imperial appropriation of the Artemis cult at Ephesos in the visual politics of state propaganda, the many surviving small-scale statuettes and gems depicting Artemis Ephesia give vivid material evidence for the personal impact of the goddess on her numerous pilgrims and worshippers. Such objects – gems (e.g. Fig. 7; Thiersch 1935: 70–77) and statuettes which survive in bronze (e.g. Fig. 8; Thiersch 1935: 56–57; Fleischer 1973: 25–27; Flesicher 1984: 762) and in terracotta (e.g. Figs. 9 and 10; Thiersch 1935: 58–62; Fleischer 1973: 27–34; Fleischer 1984: 761–62) – are testimony to the kinds of pilgrimage souvenirs generated by important pagan cults and taken home by pilgrims. In the case of the Ephesian goddess, these sacred mementos appear to have been purchased mainly by relatively local pilgrims from Asia Minor (if we are to accept the pattern of archaeological finds as evidence for the ancient distribution of such objects, see Fleischer 1973: 27–34). It is possible that the gems were used as protective amulets and in magic (cf. Bonner 1950; Philipp, 1986). The statuettes (e.g. Figs. 8–10) are, of course, considerably less grand than the fine large-scale replicas of the cult statue – not only in size but in the relative cheapness of their material, the

Fig. 9. Artemis of Ephesos, terracotta statuette
from Ephesos. 0.25 m in height. Imperial
period. British Museum, London. (Photo:
Museum)

Fig. 10. Artemis of Ephesos, terracotta statuette.
0.17 m in height. The back of the image is inscribed
MAXIMOU. The findspot is unknown. Imperial
period. British Museum, London. (Photo: Museum)

rough quality of their workmanship and the fact that they were made by a process of mass production. They are highly schematic (certainly not exquisite miniatures), purchased as an act of devotion – like so many *linga* (the phallic cult form of the Hindu god Shiva) in modern Indian Shiva temples, or Virgin statuettes in the great pilgrimage centres of Catholic Europe or Latin America. They speak of the depth and range of the goddess' constituency in a class of worshippers not usually evoked by the evidence of our literary texts.

What all the images and coins have in common, despite the differences in expense, grandeur and execution, is their iconographical particularity. They make stereotypical reference to one original and authentic statue of Artemis Ephesia, housed in the great temple at Ephesos. The wider their distribution, the more strongly the visual argument worked to focus the mind of the viewer, coin-handler or devotee onto that sacred statue whose correct cultivation at Ephesos, and in her shrines around the empire, helped to establish the continued prosperity of the city where she dwelt, the success of its relations with the outside world, and the general well-being of the empire as a whole.

The spread of the Ephesian cult, like that of so many other eastern and mystery religions in the periods of the Second Sophistic and late antiquity, was one way – perhaps a major way – in which the Roman east claimed its priority, even its superiority, over the empire which governed it. By the second century AD, it would be possible for worshippers of Artemis Ephesia (wherever they lived) to see the heart of the Roman world as focused not around the political centre (in Rome) but around the sacred centre where their goddess dwelt. The same shift towards a sacred (and usually eastern) deity was, of course, open to devotees of other cults (such as Lucius in Apuleius' *Golden Ass* or Kalasiris in Heliodorus' *Aethiopica* 7.8, both of whom are worshippers of Isis) – and, not least, the Christians. Indeed, it is one of the marked features of the spirituality of the polytheistic east in the second century and after, that cultural resistance to Rome could be expressed as devotion to deities from the periphery whose spread throughout the whole empire, whose offers of salvation and whose iconography often carried cosmic allusions which gave them a claim to universal sovereignty in the spiritual if not the temporal realm. Such universal implications are present, for example, in the mastery of the astrological world implied by the zodiac above the 'breasts' of Figure 3 (a motif frequently repeated on the larger replicas of the Ephesia) and by the zodiacs which often encircle or arch over Mithraic images (for instance, the bull-slaying scene from the London Mithraeum).

While the eastern religious cults, including that of Ephesian Artemis, were not backed by the kind of unifying religious organisation apparent in the case of the state-propagated imperial cult (Price 1984: 130–31), their spread through the empire and their collective impact does have certain resemblances to the promulgation of emperor-worship. Through religious expansion, the Roman east struck back at the imperial appropriation of its sacred and civic spaces. This was not a process of overt resistance; indeed, on the contrary, the eastern provinces incorporated the charisma of the centre through upholding the imperial cult (Price 1984: 205–206). Rather, the religions of the east mastered a policy parallel to that of the imperial cult, and modelled on it, whereby the local religions of the periphery (like that of Ephesian Artemis) or mystery cults (like those of Isis, Serapis, Cybele and Attis, Mithras or Jesus) were promulgated on an empire-wide basis (on these cults see Ferguson 1970; Turcan 1989). 'Resistance' in this sense represents not an active manning of barricades or fomenting of rebellion (as in the earlier case of, say, the Jewish wars); but rather it lies in the provision of religious identities – on an empire-wide basis, but with their centre or origin provocatively located on the empire's eastern periphery. Such religious identities provided a space of more intense or exclusive subjectivity, to those who subscribed to them, than the normal rituals of Roman citizenship. Ultimately, one such form of eastern initiate identity – Christianity – would (like the proverbial poacher turned gamekeeper) cease to represent a culture of silent resistance and take over the establishment... It is ironic that the model for the universal spread of these cults was the earlier spread of the imperial cult.[2]

All these religions, through their highly symbolic and non-Roman iconographies, their mythologies and their cosmological systems rooted in often iconographic allusions to eastern and even non-

Graeco-Roman sacred myths, foregrounded their origins and identities as *eastern* cults (cf. Liebeschuetz 1994: 195).[3] For example, Mithras invariably and Attis frequently, as well as a number of recurring characters in Christian iconography from the Hebrews in the fiery furnace to the Magi, appear in Roman art wearing the Phrygian cap (Figs. 11–13). Thus, iconographically they signalled their eastern genesis – at least to anyone who wished to notice such signals (for example, initiates). Specific visual allusions to non-normative forms of religious action (for instance, Mithras' sacrifice of the bull, see Fig. 11, with Gordon 1988: 49; Turcan 1981: 352) or to non-Roman mysteries (from the Incarnation to the 'breasts' of the Ephesia) only added to the potential effect of otherness. Despite considerable syncretism, adaptation and reinterpretation in a Roman context, Isis and Serapis always maintained a link with their Egyptian origins, Mithras in his Phrygian clothing appeared and claimed to be Persian, and Jesus – so often represented in connection with Old Testament typologies – was Palestinian-Jewish. Even Ephesian Artemis, who occupied a much more civic and less mystic point in the spectrum of eastern religions within the empire, insistently proclaimed her non- (or perhaps pre-) Graeco-Roman identity through the imagery and iconography of her cult statue. Given their much more defined ethnic roots, more complex initiatory systems and insistence on a stronger degree of personal faith than the imperial cult, such religions, in particular the mystery cults, clearly

Fig. 11. White marble relief of the Tauroctone from a mithraeum in Rome, excavated in 1932. Mithras, in Persian dress, slays the bull, with the scorpion at the bull's genitals, and the dog and serpent licking the blood. To the left and right respectively are the torchbearers, Cautes and Cautopates, also in Persian dress. To the left is a grotto with Mithras (again in Persian dress) carrying the bull in front of its entrance and the raven perched above. The busts to left and right represent Sol and Luna. 0.87 × 1.64 m. Second half of the third century AD (Photo: DAI 34.227)

Fig. 12. Marble altar from the Via Appia, Rome, with Cybele in a biga *drawn by two lions and Attis in a Phrygian cap leaning against a pine tree. The altar, whose inscription records L. Cornelius Scipio Orfitus as the donor, is dated to 26 February AD 295. Villa Albani, Rome. (Photo: DAI 35.100)*

had the potential for generating much more powerful systems of symbolic meaning, belief and commitment – founded on complex salvific iconographies of the Other World – than the loosely inclusive participation in state religion, which was much more rooted in broadly accepted social norms. For these reasons, it is perhaps not entirely surprising that one of these cults – Christianity – would eventually replace the imperial cult as the official religion of the empire.

Pilgrimage at Home and Elsewhere: Pausanias and Lucian

The double case for the importance of the arts in the religions of the eastern empire and for the use of such sacred art in a discourse of the east's self-affirmation can be made by looking at pilgrimage texts. We possess two remarkable writings in this genre from the polytheism of the eastern empire, both dating to the second century AD. The first, and most famous, is Pausanias' *Description of Greece* which – for all its aesthetic, historical and antiquarian interests (Habicht 1985; Arafat 1992; Meadows 1995) – is also an account of the great sacred and religious centres of Greece from the point of

Fig. 13. The marble sarcophagus of Adelphia, detail of the Magi in Phrygian dress before the Virgin and Child. From the catacomb of San Giovanni, Syracuse. Fourth century AD. Museo Archeologico, Syracuse. (Photo: DAI 71.865)

view of an initiate and believing participant in ancient Greek religion (Elsner 1995: 125–55). The second pilgrimage account I will use is the *De Dea Syria*, a text which has often been denied to, but is now largely accepted as being by, Lucian of Samosata (Oden 1977: 4–46; Jones 1986: 41–43). Like Pausanias, the narrator of the *De Dea Syria* – who says he writes 'as an Assyrian' (1), whether as Lucian himself or his persona – tours a series of important sanctuaries in Syria (including Tyre, Sidon and Byblos, 1–9) before coming to the sacred site of his prime interest, the temple of the Syrian Goddess at Hirê (Millar 1993: 245–46). Like Pausanias, the narrator of the *De Dea Syria* is a believer and participant in the religious activities he describes; his entire account ends with an affirmation of this in the following sentence:

> When I was still a youth I, too, performed this ceremony [of offering one's beard] and even now my locks and name are in the sanctuary (60).

Among several shared features, both these texts emphasise the processes of temple visiting as a key feature of religious experience, presenting their narratives as first-person accounts whose validity is guaranteed by authorial autopsy. Both have a marked interest in matters of ritual (Elsner forthcoming, b), in art – not only in its stylistic or iconographic particularities but also in its cultic functions, and in myths (on Pausanias, see Veyne 1988: 92–102), as well as in wonders (whether natural, man-made or supernatural). Both texts show a certain religious reticence or taboo in describing the most sacred parts of holy buildings or the most profound myths told about sacred places or images (on Pausanias, see Elsner 1995: 144–52).

In the case of both these texts, it is worth emphasising their insistent parochialism. Other kinds of temple visiting in the Second Sophistic took the form of empire-wide travel, such as Artemidorus' search for dreams 'in the different cities of Greece and at great religious gatherings in that country, in Asia and in the largest and most populous of the islands' (*Oneirocritica* 1.proem, c.f. 5.proem; generally on such travel see Hunt 1984). By marked contrast, Pausanias focuses single-mindedly on Greece and Lucian on Syria.[4] In each case, there is an assertion of a kind of sacred primacy about the locale which is described in the text. Pausanias' Greece – an idealising version of the lost pre-Roman Greece, an amalgam of history, myth and art which serves to create a canon – exists as a permanent metonymic link to a religious and mythical reality of archaic times, peopled by long-dead heroes, to which access is still available through ritual and through art. Lucian's Syria is a place of sanctuaries and temples, less ancient than those of Egypt but explicitly more venerable than those of Greece and Rome (2–3). For example:

> ...the sanctuary of Heracles at Tyre. This is not the Heracles whom the Greeks celebrate in story. The one I mean is much older and is a Tyrian hero (3).

In this rhetoric of parochial sanctity, shared by Pausanias and Lucian, there is a distinctive quality of local self-assertion, presented in terms of what has been called 'a landscape of memory' (Alcock 1996). A province on the periphery of empire is presented as the central focus for a sacred world of ancient and animated images, of ritual traditions, of myths reaching back to the beginnings of time. Whether this is to be read as a directly anti-Roman propagation of peripheral (i.e. non-Roman, whether Syrian or Greek) spirituality, is hard to determine. But it certainly fits with the visual rhetoric of 'otherness' espoused with such success by the eastern cults in their spread through the Roman world.

Let us examine the self-assertion of the east in Pausanias and Lucian's *De Dea Syria*, by looking at their detailed descriptions of some privileged cult statues. For these images, the principal sacred focus of the main sites visited in these texts, not only epitomise the most visual aspects of pilgrimage but also provide a focus for the key myths and rituals evoked at a sacred centre. In Pausanias, the great set-piece descriptions of chryselephantine cult statues also happen to be among his major *ekphraseis* of the 'masterpieces' of Classical sculpture – the Athena Parthenos and Olympian Zeus of Phidias (1.24.5–7; 5.10.2 and 5.11.1–9), the Hera by Polyclitus at Argos (2.17.4) – as well as the Asclepius at Epidaurus (2.27.2) and Apollo at Amyclae (3.18.9–19.3).

What is striking about Pausanias' cult statues is his concentration on iconography as a means for representing Greek mythology. The Athena Parthenos becomes the occasion for learned digressions on sphinxes and griffins – creatures from the imaginary world of archaic myth, for brief references to Medusa and the Athenian Erichthonius, and to the mythical first woman Pandora. The Epidauran Asclepius evokes 'the exploits of Argive heroes', Bellerophon and Perseus (2.27.2). The throne of

Apollo Amyclaeus is an excuse for a resumé, virtually a catalogue, of major Greek myths (3.18.10–16), and the visual surroundings of Zeus at Olympia likewise refer to numerous myths from the death of Niobe's children to the labours of Heracles (5.11.2–8). While the images connected with each statue have a particular local resonance (the significance of Erichthonius for Attica, Bellerophon and Perseus for Argos and Heracles for Olympia), the overall effect is of a deeply Greek mythological system surrounding and grounding these Greek artistic and sacred masterworks in an ethos of Hellenic localism. The iconography of Polyclitus' Argive Hera points both to mythology (the tales of Zeus and Hera, which Pausanias claims to disbelieve at 2.17.4, though he later comes round to viewing such stories allegorically as 'one kind of Greek wisdom', 8.8.3) and to mysteries which cannot be written about or spoken of.

It may be that these moves from imagery to mythology were obvious – the natural and immediate reflex of any observer looking at the art in a temple. But it may also be that Pausanias deliberately chooses to set these special and significant objects within his discourse in the light of a mythological master-narrative. His insistence on apparently parochial (that is, specifically local Greek) myths has the effect of deliberately affirming the sacred Greece of pre-Roman times. Implicitly – but inevitably – this Greek mythological *paideia* or antiquarianism by which Pausanias interprets the objects he describes (and not just the cult images) and through which his whole travelogue is presented, largely excludes thought of Rome or of the present day. In this sense Pausanias' cult images become arguments in a narrative of Hellenism's monumental sacred and mythological self-affirmation (on Pausanias and the Romans, see Elsner 1995: 140–44; Alcock 1996; Bowie 1996: 216–29).

Lucian's statues, by contrast, are presented not by means of a mythological narrative but in comparison with other (more familiar) iconographic types:

> In this chamber are set statues of the gods. One is Hera and the other is Zeus, whom, however, they call by another name. Both are of gold and both are seated, but lions support Hera, while the god sits on bulls. The statue of Zeus certainly looks like Zeus in every respect: his head, clothes, throne. Nor will you, even if you want to, liken him to anyone else. As one looks at Hera, however, she presents many different forms. On the whole she is certainly Hera, but she has something of Athena, Aphrodite, Selene, Rhea, Artemis, Nemesis and the Fates... (31–32).

Here we have, in a Syrian context presented by a Syrian author writing in Greek, a Zeus who is not Zeus (since he is called something else) but who looks just like (the Greek) Zeus, and a Hera who 'is certainly Hera' but who clearly has as much in common with nearly every other female deity in the Greek pantheon. The attempt to present non-Greek gods to a Greek readership in Greek terms leads to a discourse of visual identification through iconography (the Zeus is Zeus because, despite his name, he looks like Zeus) and of syncretism whereby peculiarities are explained by Hera having 'something of' a whole catalogue of other Greek deities. What all this succeeds in affirming (despite, even perhaps because of, the attempt to assimilate the gods of Hirê to those of Greece) is the radical difference, the cultural otherness, of Lucian's Syrian religion. It is distinct not only from Greek cult (and the language which describes Greek cult), but implicitly also from the religion of the Roman masters of the east.

The superiority of these non- (or are they anti-?) Graeco-Roman attitudes becomes explicit as Lucian proceeds to discussing other increasingly non-Greek gods in the sanctuary. There is a golden

'Sêmeion': 'not at all like the other statues. It does not have its own particular character, but it bears the qualities of the other gods' (33). This may be a *xoanon*, but its nature as a divine epitome for all the gods in the temple is certainly not typical in Greek terms. There is a throne but no statue for Helios – 'they say it is right to make images for the other gods, for their forms are not visible to everyone, but Helios and Selene (the Sun and the Moon) are completely visible and all see them. So, what reason is there to make statues of those gods who appear in the open air?' (34). The target of this criticism (as much a self-affirmation of the unusual visual tradition at Hirê) is not made explicit, but Greek and Roman religious practice is surely implied. And finally there is a miraculous image of 'Apollo' represented (in direct contrast with Greek tradition) as bearded and clothed:

> All others think of Apollo as young and show him in the prime of youth. Only these people display a statue of a bearded Apollo. In acting in this way they commend themselves and accuse the Greeks and anyone else who worships Apollo as a youth. They reason like this. They think it utter stupidity to make the forms of the gods imperfect and they consider youth an imperfect state (35).

Here finally is a self-assertive assault on the Graeco-Roman culture of the conqueror. In matters of deep religious knowledge and representational practice, not only are the Syrians different from the Greeks and 'anyone else' but they are proclaimed as wiser. Despite centuries of conquest, hellenization and romanization, Lucian's sacred Syria – his aptly named city of Hirê – affirms its superiority through the continuance of its most holy traditions of knowledge manifested in images. In focusing his entire text on the sacred world of Syria, Lucian makes the marginal, the self-confessedly eccentric (by Greek standards) into something not only central and significant in a religious sense, but also important beyond the peripheral confines of the Levant because it is presented in terms accessible to Greek speakers from a Greek cultural context.

As pilgrimage texts, rare narrative survivals of a thriving ancient culture of temple visiting and worship, the works of Pausanias and Lucian present a literary discourse of eastern self-assertion. This supports the visual arguments for eastern self-affirmation made by the art and iconography of cults like that of Ephesian Artemis, Mithras or Attis. The great icons are a principal locus for the pilgrims' discussions, and they argue a rhetoric – both iconographic and mythological – of localism. The sacred centre is located, in this discourse, not in Rome – the far away political centre – but in the east, wherever stands the main shrine of whichever deity one has taken as one's prime object of worship. As we saw in the case of the Artemisium, the sacred centre, even if spatially peripheral, was symbolically the fundamental guarantor of a whole range of non-sacred or ritual activity; it was the insurance underlying social life. So the positing of sacred centres in the eastern periphery of the empire was not merely an act of ideological and sacred resistance to Rome. It was implicitly a marginalisation of Rome, the conqueror; it suggested that fundamentally Roman dominion was an irrelevance.

Of course the modes of resistance varied in the range of eastern cultures: Pausanias affirms Greece (implicitly against Rome), while Lucian denies both Greece and Rome in his Greek apologia for the sanctity of Syria. The bulk of eastern mystery cults did not reject the imperial cult but implicitly their promise of salvation suggested that individual salvation was not a commodity available from state religion. Judaism and Christianity – affirming a monotheist intolerance for religious pluralism – tended to an exclusivity which was to deny all the polytheist religions of the Roman empire, east and west. Moreover, in the period before Constantine, we should not expect that all manifestations of cults which were scattered over the breadth of the empire (least of all Christianity) professed the same beliefs or practices even if they assumed more or less stereotypical iconographies. Yet despite all these nuances and variations, one feature shared by the religions of the east from the highly traditional (as in Pausanias) and the civic-local (as in Lucian or the cult of Artemis Ephesia) to the mystical and initiate fringe (as in Mithraism or Christianity) was a profession of eastern identity which proved simultaneously iconographic and ideological. This served as a means of self-definition by the affirmation of difference from the visual norms and cult practices of the centre. In looking non-Roman, the eastern cults implied that their kind of religion was not Roman and – implicitly – was better than Roman religion, at least for their devotees.

Conclusion

In tracing the origins of the icon as a principal expression of spirituality in the Christian east, we have uncovered a culture in which pagan cult images served as the centre of a sacred nexus for defining identity, mythology and locality. The icons of pagan polytheism in the east were used during and after the second century AD – in rituals like that of Salutaris, in texts like that of Pausanias and in the visual propagation of the cults through the empire – as a prime means for ethnic and religious self-assertion. That visual self-assertion was by definition articulated by difference from Rome, in the use of non-naturalistic styles and of iconographies evoking the east. The particular feature of this use of sacred art for eastern self-affirmation was that it never denied the logic of empire: it never argued for nationalism or separatism. Instead, the east appropriated the universalist and centralizing religious techniques created by the imperial cult to spread a variety of polytheisms originating in the periphery but with universal claims. Such universalism manifested in numerous ways – from the emphasis on a ritual space and time whose value lay beyond the present (in Pausanias, for instance, but also in early Christianity), to specifically missionary expansion (as in the case of sanctuaries of the Ephesia and other deities like Isis or Mithras), to the claims of access to particular and exclusive forms of salvation (in many of the mystery cults including Christianity). Iconography, often stereotypical and frequently overdetermined with mystic or astrological or typological symbols, proclaimed both the peripheral origins and the universal claims of a cult.

By the third and fourth centuries, the universalizing aspirations of a plurality of cults led to increasing syncretism (one thinks for instance of the sanctuary of Severus Alexander who is said to have combined statues of the deified emperors with images of Apollonius of Tyana, Christ, Abraham and Orpheus, as well as Vergil, Cicero, Achilles and Alexander the Great; *HA, Severus Alexander* 29.2–3, 31.4–5). The growing strength of the eastern religions motivated several attempts by the weakening centre to appropriate their success and appeal to itself. In AD 218, Elagabalus brought the cult of Elagabal and other Syrian rites to Rome (*HA, Antoninus Elagabalus* 3.4, 6.9, 7.1–5) and explicitly attempted to establish Elagabal as the supreme god (Cassius Dio, *Historia Romana* 80.11.1), in the 270s Aurelian emphasised the cult of Sol Invictus as the supreme deity (Homo 1904: 184–88) and ultimately in the early fourth century Constantine would convert to the religion of Christ. The appropriation of Christianity by the centre was nothing new: it was an already typical instance of using the energy and drive of an eastern cult as a means to inject new life into the old religion. But Christianity, by being monotheist and exclusive, was unlike anything generated within the broad and pluralist aegis of Graeco-Roman polytheism. Although it brilliantly adapted the successful dynamics of the eastern cults (their liking for the visual, for public ritual, for great official temples), it was to supplant the others and to invigorate the Roman state in ways of which Constantine could never have dreamt. In the light of my argument here about the importance of cult images as a visual means for the propagation of the polytheistic cults, there is a small irony in Christianity's development of the icon as its most characteristic visual form.

Acknowledgments

This article was commissioned by Sue Alcock for this volume – and I thank her especially for her very detailed critique and helpful comments. A version was delivered to the London University Seminar on Classical Art held at the Institute of Archaeology in Spring 1996, and I am most grateful to all those who discussed various points with me on that occasion.

Notes

1. Pausanias, for example, is full of similar quite specific injunctions about temple-entry (Elsner 1995: 144–50) and of equally systematic attention to the details of ritual (Elsner, forthcoming b). In such careful ritual regulation – as in Achilles Tatius' careful distinction of free women into virgins and non-virgins by contrast with slave-women (who either have just cause or not, but need not be virgin) – the correct cultivation of the deity lies in the detail.

2. Recent scholarship on Roman Greece has begun to recognise the resistance of Greece to many aspects of romanization (Woolf 1994), in particular in areas of traditional cult (Alcock 1993: 213–14). Such resistance in matters of religion was clearly offered by other conquered peoples in the empire, not least Jews (de Lange 1978) and Druids (King 1990). What I suggest here is a more sophisticated kind of spiritual subversion of the centre in which the state's universalist strategy of supporting an imperial cult was emulated by the religions of the periphery in spreading their non-Roman cults with universalist claims throughout the empire. While implicit non-Romanness was clearly far from being the only or main reason for following such religions, it may well have offered an added attraction for adherents. The effects of the tendency to universalism in the late empire (both from the centre and from the periphery) were to encourage increasing syncretism and ultimately to prepare the ground for the monotheist universalism of Christianity (see Fowden 1993: 37–60).

3. In the case of Mithraism, we need slightly to refine the new orthodoxy that there was nothing Persian about Roman Mithraism. This was established in the wake of the theories of Franz Cumont and his followers, who argued that Roman Mithraism was an Iranian cult for which the texts of Iranian Mazdaism could be used in order to elucidate its beliefs and practices (see especially the refutation of Gordon 1975 and Ulansey 1988: 3–14). There may well have been nothing Iranian about the internal workings of Roman Mithraism, but its iconography continually affirmed its claims to eastern (above all non-Roman) origins and values.

4. This kind of parochialism has often been equated with antiquarianism. Which is correct, but elides the politics that may lie behind the choice of subject matter. For example, in a very different context, the Brothers Grimm's selection of *German* folktale as a subject for antiquarian scholarship had a crucial contemporary political context. It is here that Paul Veyne's excellent account of Pausanias as 'the equal of any of the great German philologists or philosophers' (Veyne 1988: 3 and 95–102) does not quite do full justice to some aspects of the impetus behind his author's scholarship.

Bibliography

Alcock, S.E. (1993) *Graecia Capta: The Landscapes of Roman Greece*, Cambridge.

_____ (1996) "Landscapes of memory and the authority of Pausanias," in J. Bingen, ed., *Pausanias historien* (Entretiens Fondation Hardt 41), 241–67. Geneva.

Alföldi, A. and E. Alföldi (1990) *Die Kontorniat-Medaillons: II, Text*, Berlin and New York.

Anderson, G. (1993) *The Second Sophistic: A Cultural Phenomenon in the Roman Empire*, London.

Arafat, K. (1992) "Pausanias' attitude to antiquities," *BSA* 87: 387–409.

Baldovin, J. (1987) *The Urban Character of Christian Worship*, Rome.

Barasch, M. (1992) *The Icon: Studies in the History of an Idea*, New York.

Belting, H. (1994) *Likeness and Presence: A History of the Image before the Era of Art*, Chicago.

Bonner, C. (1950) *Studies in Magical Amulets*, Ann Arbor.

Bowersock, G.W. (1969) *Greek Sophists and the Roman Empire*, Oxford.

_____ ed. (1974) *Approaches to the Second Sophistic*, University Park.

_____ (1994) *Fiction as History: Nero to Julian*, Berkeley and Los Angeles.

Bowie, E.L. (1970) "Greeks and their past in the Second Sophistic," *PastPres* 46: 3–41.

_____ (1996) "Past and present in Pausanias", in J. Bingen, ed., *Pausanias historien* (Entretiens Fondation Hardt 41), 207–30. Geneva.

Brubaker, L. (1995) "The sacred image," in R. Ousterhout and L. Brubaker, eds., *The Sacred Image East and West*, Urbana and Chicago.

Clayton, P., and M.J. Price (1988) *The Seven Wonders of the Ancient World*, London.

Cormack, R. (1985) *Writing in Gold: Byzantine Society and Its Icons*, London.

Dagron, G. (1991) "Holy images and likeness," *DOP* 45: 23–33.

Dzielska, M. (1986) *Apollonius of Tyana in Legend and History*, Rome.

Elsner, J. (1995) *Art and the Roman Viewer: The Transformation of Art from the Pagan World to Christianity*, Cambridge.

_____ (1996) "Inventing Imperium: texts and the propaganda of monuments in Augustan Rome," in J. Elsner, ed., *Art and Text in Roman Culture*, 32–53. Cambridge.

_____ (forthcoming, a) "Hagiographic geography: travel and allegory in the *Life of Apollonius of Tyana*," *JHS* 117 (1997).

_____ (forthcoming, b) "Image and ritual: reflections on the religious appreciation of classical art," *CQ* 47 (1997).

Ferguson, J. (1970) *The Religions of the Roman Empire*, London.

Fleischer, R. (1973) *Artemis von Ephesos und verwandte kultstatuen aus Anatolien und Syrien*, Leiden.

_____ (1978) "Artemis von Ephesos und verwandte kultstatuen aus Anatolien und Syrien. Supplement," in S. Sahin, E. Schwertheim and J. Wagner, eds., *Studien zur Religion und Kultur Kleinasiens: Festschrift für F.K.Dörner*, 324–58. Leiden.

_____ (1984) "Artemis Ephesia," *LIMC* II.1, 755–63.

Fowden, G. (1993) *Empire to Commonwealth: Consequences of Monotheism in Late Antiquity*, Princeton.

Gordon, R.L. (1975) "Franz Cumont and the doctrines of Mithraism," in J.R.Hinnells, ed., *Mithraic Studies*, Vol.1, 215–48. Manchester.

_____ (1988) "Authority, salvation and mystery in the Mysteries of Mithras," in J. Huskinson, M. Beard and J. Reynolds, eds., *Image and Mystery in the Roman World*, 45–80. Gloucester.

Grabar, A. (1968) *Christian Iconography: A Study of Its Origins*, Princeton.

Habicht, C. (1985) *Pausanias' Guide to Ancient Greece*, Berkeley and Los Angeles.

Homo, L. (1904) *Essai sur la règne de l'empereur Aurélien*, Paris.

Hopkins, K. (1993) "Novel evidence for Roman slavery," *PastPres* 138: 3–27.

Hunt, E.D. (1984) "Travel, tourism and piety in the Roman Empire," *EchCl* 28: 391–417.

Jones, C.P. (1986) *Culture and Society in Lucian*, Cambridge, Mass.

Kazhdan, A., and H. Maguire (1991) "Byzantine hagiographical texts as sources on art," *DOP* 45: 1–22.

King, A. (1990) "The emergence of Romano-Celtic religion," in T.F.C. Blagg and M. Millett, eds., *The Early Roman Empire in the West*, 220–41. Oxford.

de Lange, N.R.M. (1978) "Jewish attitudes to the Roman empire," in P.D.A. Garnsey and C.R.Whittaker, eds., *Imperialism in the Ancient World*, 255–81. Cambridge.

Liebeschuetz, W. (1994) "The expansion of Mithraism among the religious cults of the second century," in J.R. Hinnells, ed., *Studies in Mithraism*, 195–216. Rome.

Limberis, V. (1994) *Divine Heiress: The Virgin Mary and the Creation of Christian Constantinople*, London.

Mathews, T.F. (1993) *The Clash of Gods: A Reinterpretation of Christian Art*, Princeton.

Meadows, A.R. (1995) "Pausanias and Classical Sparta," *CQ* 45: 92–113.

Millar, F. (1987) "Empire, community and culture in the Roman Near East: Greeks, Syrians, Jews and Arabs," *Journal of Jewish Studies* 38: 143–64.

——————— (1993) *The Roman Near East: 31 BC – AD 337*, Cambridge, Mass.

Müller, F.G.J.M. (1994) *The So-Called Peleus and Thetis Sarcophagus in the Villa Albani: Iconological Studies in Roman Art I,* Amsterdam.

Oden, R.A. (1977) *Studies in the* De Syria Dea, Missoula.

Oster, R.E. (1976) "The Ephesian Artemis as an opponent of Early Christianity," *JbAC* 19: 24–44.

——————— (1990) "Ephesus as a religious centre under the Principate," *ANRW* II.18.3: 1662–1728.

Pelikan, J. (1990) *Imago Dei: The Byzantine Apologia for Icons*, New Haven and London.

Philipp, H. (1986) *Mira et Magica*, Mainz am Rhein.

Price, M.J. and B. Trell (1977) *Coins and their Cities*, London.

Price, S.R.F. (1984) *Rituals and Power: The Roman Imperial Cult in Asia Minor*, Cambridge.

Rogers, G.M. (1991) *The Sacred Identity of Ephesus: Foundation Myths of a Roman City*, London.

Settis, S. (1972) "Severo Alessandro e i suoi lari (*S.H.A., S.A.* 29.2–3)," *Athenaeum* 60: 237–51.

Stuart Jones, H. (1926) *A Catalogue of the Ancient Sculptures Preserved in the Municipal Collections of Rome: The Sculptures of the Palazzo dei Conservatori*, Oxford.

Thiersch, H. (1935) *Artemis Ephesia: Eine Archäologische Untersuchung*, Berlin.

Turcan, R. (1981) "Le sacrifice mithriaque: innovations de sens et de modalités," in J. Rudhardt and O. Reverdin, eds., *Le sacrifice dans l'antiquité* (Entretiens Fondation Hardt 27), 341–80. Geneva.

——————— (1989) *Les cultes orientaux dans le monde Romain*, Paris.

Ulansey, D. (1988) *The Origins of the Mithraic Mysteries*, Oxford.

Veyne, P. (1988) *Did the Greeks Believe in Their Myths?*, Chicago.

Wernicke, K. (1895) "Artemis," *RE* ii.1: 1335–1440.

Woolf, G. (1994) "Becoming Roman, staying Greek: culture, identity and the civilizing process in the Roman East," *Proceedings of the Cambridge Philological Society* 40: 116–43.

12. A View from the West

Martin Millett

When I was invited by the editor of this volume to offer a contribution to this collection of essays which I understand is designed to complement the one I once helped to edit on the western empire (Blagg and Millett 1990), my thoughts (and hers!) turned to Rudyard Kipling's 'Ballad of East and West' with its notorious line:

> Oh, East is East, and West is West, and
> never the twain shall meet...

Such a view, after all, has a very long tradition in Roman archaeology: those who work on the eastern empire too rarely read or write about the west and vice versa. However, if you read further in Kipling's ballad you will find:

> But there is neither East nor West, Border,
>   nor Breed, nor Birth,
> When two strong men stand face to face,
>   though they come from the ends of the earth!

I would like to suggest that this second quotation (*pace* the 'strong men') holds a lesson for those working on the archaeology of the Roman world.

At this point, I wish to offer no more than a few reflections on the 'East-West' divide in Roman archaeology. On first reading the papers published here, it did seem true that the contributions differed in approach and subject matter from those which might have been expected from archaeologists working on the western empire (cf. Metzler *et al.* 1995). This reflects the current academic situation and perpetuates a disciplinary division which I would argue is false and is impeding the proper development of an empire-wide Roman archaeology. When looked at more closely, however, several of the papers do seek to cut across this division. I particularly noted the western parallels appropriate for Rizakis' study of urban foundations in Greece and Cormack's emphasis on east-west links in the development of the art of the sarcophagus. The latter certainly underlines the role of the Mediterranean as an integrating force. Despite such tentative bridges, I believe it is still important to be aware of the nature of the underlying East-West divide in archaeological analysis and interpretation.

The reason for its existence are complex, but undoubtedly relate to at least two factors. First are distinctions in the character of the evidence; second are the different traditions of study: not least those which are the product of modern geopolitical contexts. Certainly differences exist in the nature of the evidence available, contrasting sources which result from the varying regional histories of East and West. Beyond the obvious importance of the Greek language (which has often had the result of deterring the less linguistically able and of encouraging the interests of those with 'a proper classical education'), some very real archaeological distinctions emerge as well. Areas with a long pre-Roman history of centralized and urbanized communities produced different patterns of settlement and society under Roman rule from those zones where urbanism was essentially a Roman phenomenon (cf. Woolf, this volume). Equally, the balance in the eastern evidence towards high quality, much admired monumental art and architecture has resulted in a stronger tradition of art historical analysis in that part of the empire.

It is equally clear that the early modern and modern histories of these regions have been an influential factor. In the West, nationalism has had a major impact on the study of the Roman past, and great emphasis has been placed on linking the present with its Roman heritage in order to legitimate individual national regimes (for example, that of Napoleon). In the East, however, other trends may be noted. On the one hand, one dominant tradition has been to deny the importance of Rome in the Hellenistic world, thus privileging the ancient Greek contribution – which in turn plays its own especial role in legitimating nationalism. On the other hand, colonial interests have identified with Roman military control over areas like the eastern frontier, or with the Roman civil government in places like Libya under Italian control (cf. Napoleon's interest in Rome itself: Ridley 1992). In both cases, the role of outside influences in developing the East was stressed, and both initiated archaeological activities deeply connected and implicated in modern imperial interests. Those with imperial designs seem to have needed to distinguish Rome's importance in their own countries (in the West) from its influence in their own colonies (in the East). To this extent, the very distinction between East and West in European studies of the Roman empire may be an aspect of our colonial history (cf. Said 1978).

I would argue that perceived distinctions between East and West have obscured other characteristics of the empire and have distracted us from looking at the Roman world as a whole. At one level, the importance of reading the essays in this volume has been to increase my own knowledge; more significantly, it has provided an increasing appreciation of the potential complementarities of approach which could aid the study of the entire Roman empire.

Once we appreciate that the whole of the empire was heterogeneous, and that differences between adjacent areas were often great, it becomes obvious that we should dispose of any simple binary distinction between East and West. The character of each province and region was a result of a complex historical interplay between the evolving imperial system and a patchwork of different indigenous societies. The social and political organizations of the indigenous inhabitants themselves influenced Rome's evolving approach to her provinces and resulted in a varied mix of immensely different Romanized societies. A study of the papers here will demonstrate that there are as many distinctions between regions in the 'East' as there are between areas in East and West (compare for instance the different character of rural settlement outlined in the chapters by Gawlikowski, Tate and Hirschfeld). An understanding of this enables us to look at each region afresh and to attempt to understand more clearly the processes of cultural change which were taking place. It allows for a cross-fertilization of ideas that should stimulate us to think more closely about which particular elements were characteristic of Rome at particular stages of her development (Woolf 1994). Equally, by realizing and accepting variability across the empire, we may become more aware of possible connections between different zones: in particular the links created by the Mediterranean, with the result that its shores often shared more in common with each other than with 'closer' areas further inland.

By becoming more aware of the richly varied nature of the empire, and by disposing of any notion that it was made up of two distinct and homogenous halves, we can begin to draw closer comparisons between regions (preferably within the same temporal horizon). Such comparative studies surely offer important prospects for new research. I would, for example, see great value in comparing the patterns of urban development in the former Hellenistic kingdoms of Asia Minor with the much less well known, but equally impressive sites from southern Spain. These two regions seem likely to have shared more in common with each other than each did with adjacent peoples. Similarities and differences in their development under Roman influence would potentially provide important insights into the character of Roman imperialism itself. Equally, by drawing on the rich literary and epigraphic evidence from across the empire at large we might be able to gain better insights into the developing processes of Roman administration. I note, for instance, the potential of using evidence relating to Pompey's organization of urbanism in Bithynia for understanding the later organization of Roman Gaul. Finally, I would observe how studies such as that by Rose on imperial imagery can use high quality evidence available from one region to shed new light on broader processes elsewhere, processes which will never be understood as clearly if studied in splendid isolation.

These few thoughts should suggest that there are exciting prospects for developing more broadly-based approaches to the archaeology of the Roman empire. Military archaeologists realized this long ago with the foundation of the Limeskongress in 1949. This volume goes a long way towards making aspects of the East more accessible to a wider audience; I trust that it will also help break down the largely artificial barrier between East and West.

Bibliography
Blagg, T.F.C. and M.J. Millett, eds. (1990) *The Early Roman Empire in the West*, Oxford.
Metzler, J., M.J. Millett, N. Roymans, and J. Slofstra, eds. (1995) *Integration in the Early Roman West: The Role of Culture and Ideology* (Dossiers d'Archéologie du Musée National d'Histoire et d'Art 4), Luxembourg.
Ridley, R.T. (1992) *The Eagle and the Spade: The Archaeology of Rome during the Napoleonic Era 1809–1814*, Cambridge.
Said, E.W. (1978) *Orientalism: Western Concepts of the Orient*, London.
Woolf, G. (1994) "Becoming Roman, staying Greek: culture, identity and the civilizing process in the Roman East," *Proceedings of the Cambridge Philological Society* 40: 116–43.

Index of Names